Nayef R.F. Al-Rodhan

Sustainable History and the Dignity of Man

Sustainable History and the Dignity of Man
A Philosophy of History and Civilisational Triumph

Nayef R.F. Al-Rodhan

Earth Cover Picture:
Credits: NASA Goddard Space Flight Center Image by Reto Stöckli (land surface, shallow water, clouds).
http://earthobservatory.nasa.gov/Features/BlueMarble/BlueMarble_2002.php

Bibliographic information published by the Deutsche Nationalbibliothek
The Deutsche Nationalbibliothek lists this publication in the Deutsche Nationalbibliografie; detailed bibliographic data are available in the Internet at http://dnb.d-nb.de.

ISBN 978-3-643-80005-3

A catalogue record for this book is available from the British Library

©LIT VERLAG GmbH & Co. KG Wien,
Zweigniederlassung Zürich 2009
Dufourstr. 31
CH-8008 Zürich
Tel. +41 (0) 44-251 75 05
Fax +41 (0) 44-251 75 06
e-Mail: zuerich@lit-verlag.ch
http://www.lit-verlag.ch

LIT VERLAG Dr. W. Hopf
Berlin 2009
Fresnostr. 2
D-48159 Münster
Tel. +49 (0) 2 51-620 32 22
Fax +49 (0) 2 51-922 60 99
e-Mail: lit@lit-verlag.de
http://www.lit-verlag.de

Distribution:
In Germany: LIT Verlag Fresnostr. 2, D-48159 Münster
Tel. +49 (0) 2 51-620 32 22, Fax +49 (0) 2 51-922 60 99, e-Mail: vertrieb@lit-verlag.de

In Austria: Medienlogistik Pichler-ÖBZ GmbH & Co KG
IZ-NÖ, Süd, Straße 1, Objekt 34, A-2355 Wiener Neudorf
Tel. +43 (0) 22 36-63 53 52 90, Fax +43 (0) 22 36-63 53 52 43, e-Mail: mlo@medien-logistik.at

In Switzerland: B + M Buch- und Medienvertriebs AG
Hochstr. 357, CH-8200 Schaffhausen
Tel. +41 (0) 52-643 54 85, Fax +41 (0) 52-643 54 35, e-Mail: order@buch-medien.ch

Distributed in the UK by: Global Book Marketing, 99B Wallis Rd, London, E9 5LN
Phone: +44 (0) 20 8533 5800 – Fax: +44 (0) 1600 775 663
http://www.centralbooks.co.uk/html

Distributed in North America by:

Transaction Publishers
New Brunswick (U.S.A.) and London (U.K.)

Transaction Publishers
Rutgers University
35 Berrue Circle
Piscataway, NJ 08854

Phone: +1 (732) 445 - 2280
Fax: + 1 (732) 445 - 3138
for orders (U. S. only):
toll free (888) 999 - 6778
e-mail: orders@transactionpub.con

CONTENTS

	Acknowledgements	11
1	**Introduction**	13
	1. A Sustainable Approach to History	16
	2. The Ocean Model of One Human Civilisation	29
	3. The Purpose and Structure of the Book	39

PART 1: The Foundations of Life   43

2	*Where Are We?* **Cosmology and the Big Universal Picture**	45
	1. The Universe	46
	2. Life on Earth	56
	3. Conclusion	63
3	*Who Are We?* **Neurochemical Man and Emotional Amoral Egoism**	65
	1. Approaches to Human Nature	66
	2. Emotional Amoral Egoism	74
	3. Conclusion	83
4	*Why Are We Here?* **A Proposed Theory of the Meaning of Existence: "Sustainable Neurochemical Gratification" (SNG)**	85
	1. Approaches to the Meaning of Life	86
	2. The Meaningfulness of the Question	93

  3. A Proposed Theory of the Meaning of Existence:
    "Sustainable Neurochemical Gratification"   96
  4. Conclusion   99

5   ***What Do We Know for Certain?***
  A Proposed Theory of Knowledge:
  "Neuro-rational Physicalism" (NRP)   **101**

  1. The Nature of Knowledge   102
  2. Sources of Knowledge   103
  3. A Proposed Theory of Knowledge:
    "Neuro-rational Physicalism"   125
  4. Conclusion   134

PART 2: Civilisational Triumph and Sustainable History   **135**

6   ***How Can We Collectively Succeed?***
  Triumphs of Individual Geo-cultural Domains   **137**

  1. Triumphs of Individual Geo-cultural Domains:
    The Example of the Arab-Islamic World   139
  2. Cultural Borrowing   142
  3. Innovation   146
  4. More Reason, Less Dogma   162
  5. Mutual Respect and Tolerance of Diversity   164
  6. Commonalities in the Rise, Decline and Fall of
    Geo-cultural Domains   168
  7. The Challenges   172
  8. The Way Forward   173
  9. Conclusion   178

7   ***How Can Dignity Be Attained?***
  Minimum Criteria of Human Needs and Dignity   **179**

  1. The Concept of Human Dignity   180
  2. Minimum Criteria of Human Dignity at the National Level   187
  3. Minimum Criteria of Human Dignity at the Global Level   191
  4. The Challenges   195
  5. The Way Forward   200
  6. Conclusion   211

8	*How Can We Achieve Justice?* **Minimum Criteria of Global Justice**	**213**
	1. Civilisational Triumph	214
	2. Global Justice	219
	3. Global Security	231
	4. The Challenges	234
	5. The Way Forward	237
	6. Conclusion	242
9	*What Is Needed for Good* **National** *Governance?* **Minimum Criteria of Inclusive, Effective and Good** *National* **Governance**	**243**
	1. The Concept of Good Governance	244
	2. Universal Standards of Good Governance?	247
	3. Minimum Criteria of Good Governance	252
	4. The Challenges	257
	5. The Way Forward	262
	6. Conclusion	269
10	*What Is Needed for Good* **Global** *Governance?* **Minimum Criteria of Inclusive, Effective and Good** *Global* **Governance**	**271**
	1. The Existing Global Governance Framework	272
	2. Problems of Global Governance	279
	3. Adapting to New Circumstances	290
	4. Conclusion	295
11	*How Can We Achieve Sustainable Security?* **The Multi-sum Security Principle and Sustainable Security**	**297**
	1. The Multidimensional Nature of Security	298
	2. The Interrelated Nature of Security Threats	313
	3. The Challenges	324
	4. The Way Forward	328
	5. Conclusion	331

12 *How Should We Approach International Relations?*
  Symbiotic Realism   333

    1. The Problems of Realism   334
    2. Symbiotic Realism   336
    3. The Dynamics of the Global System   341
    4. Foreign Policy Challenges   345
    5. The Way Forward   349
    6. Conclusion   353

13 *How Should Statecraft Be Conducted?*
  Neo-statecraft **and** ***Meta-geopolitics***   355

    1. Traditional Concepts of Statecraft and Geopolitics   356
    2. *Meta*-geopolitics   362
    3. Sustainable National Security   367
    4. Just Power   368
    5. Reconciliation Statecraft   369
    6. The Future of Geopolitics in a Transnational World   379
    7. Conclusion   383

14 *How Should Cultures Interrelate?*
  Transcultural Synergy and Universal Axiology   385

    1. Culture and Geo-cultural Domains   386
    2. Essentialism and Hegemony   390
    3. The West and the East: Never the Twain Shall Meet?   394
    4. Asian and Islamic Values   397
    5. Transcultural Synergy   400
    6. Universal Axiology and Values   406
    7. Conclusion   413

**PART 3: History and the Future of Human and Trans-human
  Civilisation**   415

15 *Where Are We Going?*
  The Future of Human Civilisation and History   417

    1. The Future of Human Civilisation   418
    2. A Post-human Destiny?   424
    3. Ethical Issues   431
    4. Conclusion   433

16	**Conclusion: Sustainable History and the Dignity of Man**	**435**
	Glossary	445
	Index	451

ACKNOWLEDGEMENTS

The author would like to thank the following people for their help with this manuscript:

> For coordination and production of the manuscript:
> **Bethany Reichenmiller**
> For research and drafting assistance: **Lisa Watanabe**
> For editing assistance: **Andrew Mash**
> For critique and commentary:
>
> **Professor Michael Freeden**
> Professor of Politics,
> Director of the Centre for Political Ideologies,
> Professorial Fellow, Mansfield College,
> University of Oxford,
> United Kingdom
> **Professor George Joffé**
> Lecturer, Centre of International Studies,
> University of Cambridge,
> Former Deputy Director of the Royal Institute of International Affairs (Chatham House), London,
> Cambridge, United Kingdom
> **Ambassador Alyson J.K. Bailes**
> Visiting Professor, Department of Political Science,
> University of Iceland,
> Reykjavik, Iceland
> **Dr. Graeme Herd**
> Faculty Member, Geneva Centre for Security Policy,
> Geneva, Switzerland
> **Ambassador Dr. Fred Tanner**
> Director, Geneva Centre for Security Policy,
> Geneva, Switzerland

The author is also grateful for the general support of the management, faculty and staff of the Geneva Centre for Security Policy.

The views expressed in this book are entirely those of the author and do not necessarily reflect those of the Geneva Centre for Security Policy (GCSP).

CHAPTER 1

INTRODUCTION

What drives history has been explored from a number of different angles, some of which inspire optimism, while others instil fear about the current and future eras. Discussions of transcultural relations, which are often framed in terms of relations between "civilisations", are underpinned by assumptions about the progression of history, although these assumptions are not always made explicit. Depending on which approach to history is subscribed to, the present age may be classified as the ultimate phase of human freedom or a time of decay or conflict over fundamental values. Yet, none of these views of history provides the means with which to ensure a *sustainable history*. *I define sustainable history as a durable progressive trajectory in which the quality of life on this planet or other planets is premised on the guarantee of human dignity for* all *at* all *times and under* all *circumstances*. Nevertheless, these various views of history inform prominent ways of thinking about the problems and challenges faced today. It is therefore critical that we explore the various ways in which history has been conceived, and the possibilities and limitations these place on the present and future. What drives history? How can a sustained improvement in the human condition be achieved? *The sustainable history approach set out in this study views history as propelled by good governance paradigms that balance the tension between* **human nature attributes** *(emotionality, amorality and egoisms)*, on the one hand, and **human dignity needs** *(reason, security, human rights, accountability, transparency, justice, opportunity, innovation and inclusiveness)*, on the other (see Diagram 1).

This approach suggests that with the right governance structure, the progression of human dignity and civilisational triumph are possible without this necessarily implying a *uniform* journey towards Western liberal democracy. While the latter has proven to be very successful, there are some aspects of liberal democracies, such as economic inequalities, that are not ideal. Good governance should include a number of minimum criteria, though such criteria may take different forms in different localities as a result of the ways in which local cultures and histories shape them. While we might expect subsequent variations to share some similarities with liberal democracies, it is unlikely that they will be exact replicas of them. *What is important is that a minimum criteria of governance is met rather than the exact form of governance that a particular political system adopts. Yet, they must be appropriate, acceptable and affordable to each system and cultural domain. These criteria should also meet a certain common global standard to ensure maximum political and moral cooperation.*

A sustainable progressive trajectory also depends on our collective triumph. For this to occur, *transcultural synergy* is essential. This is because the success of any one *geo-cultural domain* is likely to be dependent on that of another: a geo-cultural domain cannot excel in isolation from others. Many of the great achievements in history that are commonly attributed to one geo-cultural domain often owe a great debt to those of others. In this sense, some of the greatest achievements of human civilisation have been collective efforts and are part of the same human story. Moreover, the fate of many geo-cultural domains partly depends on that of others in an increasingly interconnected world. Cultures and wider geo-cultural domains are always in a process of evolving, as is collective human civilisation.[1] If people are left feeling in a state of disarray as a result of rapid changes within a broader environment, the response may manifest itself in the construction of defensive identities, which may be made even more rigid if perceived or real injustices are shaping relations. In such instances, difference risks being equated with danger and a clash of cultures may become all the more likely.

---

[1] N.R.F. Al-Rodhan and L. Watanabe, *A Proposal for* Inclusive *Peace and Security* (Genève: Éditions Slatkine, 2007), p. 91.

Diagram 1: Sustainable History

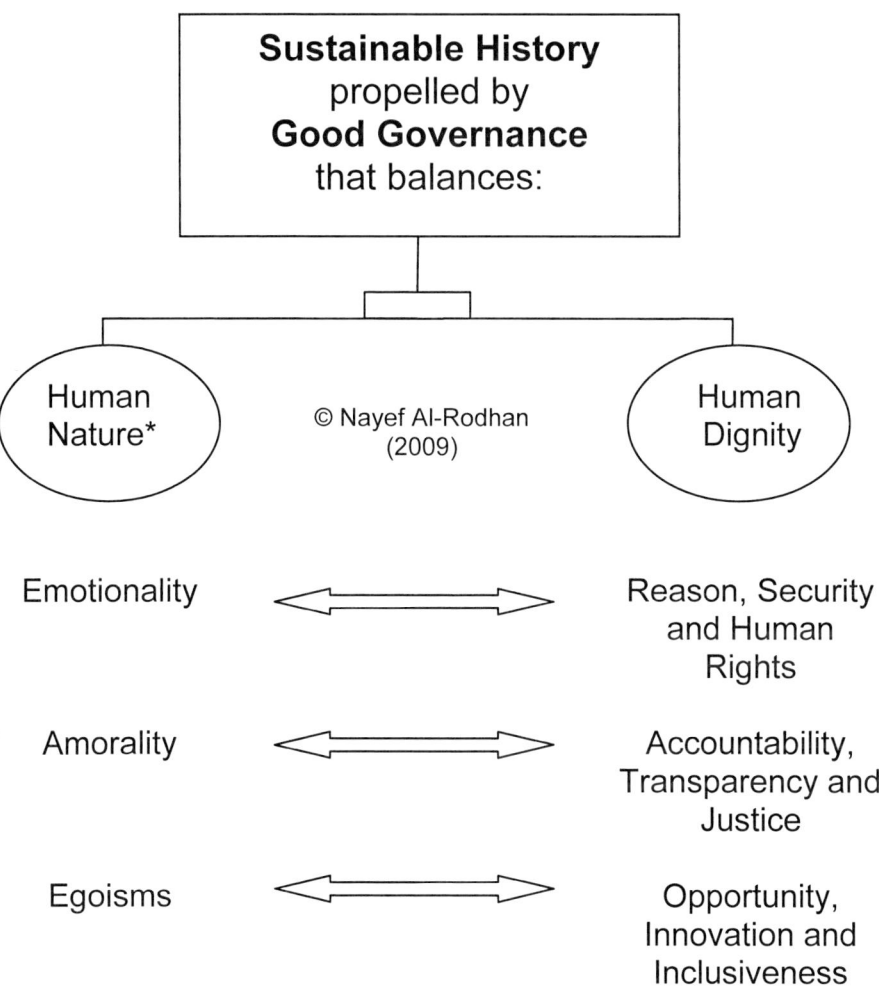

* See N.R.F. Al-Rodhan, *"emotional amoral egoism": A Neurophilosophical Theory of Human Nature and its Universal Security Implications* (Berlin: LIT, 2008).

1. A Sustainable Approach to History

The driving forces of history that tend to inform discussions of global politics have been conceived in a number of ways in relation to "civilisations" or geo-cultural domains. It is useful to recall that the term civilisation arose within a specific context. It emerged in 18th century France as a derivative of "civilised" and "to civilise", which had already been in use for several centuries. The term was used to specify the opposite of barbarism, which was at that time associated with "primitive peoples". Against the backdrop of a linear notion of history and progress thought to culminate in Europe, civilisations in the plural began to enter into popular discourse.[2] Enlightenment thinkers tended to view history as progressive. Humanity was believed to be moving towards an ideal level of civilisation.[3] The plural use of the term was therefore bound up with imperialism and Europe's civilising mission around the globe. While Europeans were obliged to acknowledge the existence of "the Other", the expectation was that those Others would eventually come to resemble them as their societies advanced.[4] Thus, reference to civilisations in the plural is intertwined with a particular context, marked by Europe's economic and technological strength.[5] Material domination went hand-in-hand with modes of thought that reflected the relationship between the dominant and the dominated.[6] Edward Said's notion of "orientalism" refers precisely to the relationship between knowledge and power in structuring relations between the "West" and the "Orient".[7]

A similar notion of history is reflected in key contributions to the philosophy of history. Linearity also informs Immanuel Kant's (1724-1804) and Georg Wilhelm Friedrich Hegel's (1770-1831) conception of history as the unfolding of human freedom. Kant's attempt

---

[2] F. Braudel, *A History of Civilizations*, Translated by R. Mayne (New York: Penguin Books, 1995), pp. 3-7.
[3] D. Little, "Philosophy of History," *Stanford Encylopedia of Philosophy*, First Published 18 February 2007, http://www.science.uva.nl/~seop/entries/history/.
[4] R.W. Cox with M.G. Schecter, *The Political Economy of a Plural World: Critical Reflections on Power, Morals and Civilization* (London: Routledge, 2002), pp. 176-177.
[5] *Ibid.*, p. 179.
[6] *Ibid.*
[7] E.W. Said, *Orientalism*, 25th Anniversary Edition, With a New Preface by the Author (New York: Vintage Books, 1979).

to put forward a universal history in the latter half of the 18th century marked all others thereafter. He argued that history would effectively come to an end when humankind attained freedom guaranteed through liberal institutions.[8] Humankind would reach this objective through the development of human enterprise resulting from the application of reason rather than instinct.[9]

Like Kant, Hegel believed that history would end when human beings attained freedom.[10] The philosophy of history was at the heart of Hegel's philosophy.[11] History was conceived as being propelled by a dialectic in which internal contradictions eventually bring about the fall of systems and the rise of new ones.[12] The evolution of freedom in history was believed to be determined by the "logic" of this dialectic. This dialectic suggests that when the exploration of an idea (thesis) reaches its limits a counter idea (antithesis) becomes apparent. The conflict between the thesis and the antithesis produces a new idea (synthesis).[13] Hegel had argued that the Battle of Jena in 1806, in which the forces of Napoleon I of France defeated those of Frederick William III of Prussia, marked the end of history because the principles of liberty and equality had permeated advanced countries.[14] Ancient China, India and Persia, however, he identified as "stationary civilisations", which lay outside world history because their development, he believed, had come to an end. The factor that these oriental societies had in common was thought to be the absence of individually generated law and morality.[15]

---

[8] F. Fukuyama, *The End of History and the Last Man* (New York: The Free Press, a Division of Simon & Schuster, Inc., 1992), pp. 57-58; I. Kant, "Idea for a Universal History with a Cosmopolitan Purpose," in H.S. Reiss, *Kant: Political Writings* (Cambridge: Cambridge University Press, 2006), pp. 45-46.
[9] Kant, *ibid.*, p. 43.
[10] G.W.F. Hegel, *Lectures on the Philosophy of World History, Introduction: Reason in History*, edited by J. Hoffmeister, Translated by H.B. Nisbet, With an Introduction by Duncan Forbes (Cambridge University Press, 1981), pp. 50-51; Fukuyama, *op. cit.*, note 8, p. 60.
[11] Fukuyama, *ibid.*
[12] *Ibid.*
[13] M. Hughes-Warrington, *Fifty Key Thinkers on History*, Second Edition (Milton Park, Oxon: Routledge, 2008), p. 152.
[14] F. Fukuyama, "The End of History," in G.O. Tuathail, S. Dalby, P. Routledge (eds.) *The Geopolitics Reader*, Second Edition (New York: Routledge, 2006), p. 108.
[15] G.W.F. Hegel, *The Philosophy of History* (Mineola, New York: Dover Publications, Inc., 2004), pp. 111-112; Hughes-Warrington, *op. cit.*, note 13, p. 149.

Karl Marx (1818-1880) was strongly influenced by Hegel's philosophy. In the *Phenomenology of Spirit* (1807), Hegel wrote that people who are not conscious that they comprise part of Mind or "Geist" see themselves in competition with one another. In the struggle, some enslave others. The relationship between master and slave is therefore a result of a false belief that others represent a threat to them.[16] Following Hegel's death, the "Young Hegelians" believed that Mind could be interpreted as collective human minds, making the purpose of history the freeing of humanity. In Marx's view, people were alienated from themselves because of capitalist social relations, but Marx's conception of history was different from that of Hegel.[17] He believed that it was not ideas but the material conditions of life that were the driving force. Material forces of production give rise to social relations of production which shape the political and legal institutions of society. Material conditions, therefore, determine social consciousness and not the other way around.[18]

According to John Hobson, Marx privileged the capitalist West as an active subject and denigrated the East as a passive one. Marx is believed to have assumed that the capitalist West was unique in its capacity to develop capitalist relations of production, something which was assumed to be absent in the social history of the East. Private property and class struggle were thought to be missing from the East due to the existence of a despotic state. This was thought to explain the unchanging nature of this part of the world as compared to the progressive West.[19] According to Hobson, in the *German Ideology* (1845), Marx and Engels identify the source of Western modernity as Ancient Greece.[20]

In France, Hegelianism influenced thinkers such as Jean-Paul Sartre (1901-1980), Jacques Lacan (1901-1981) and Alexandre Kojève (1902-1968); and in Germany, Theodor Adorno (1903-1969), Jürgen Habermas (b. 1929) and H.G. Gadamer (1900-2002).[21] In *In-*

---

[16] G.W.F. Hegel, *Phenomenology of the Spirit*, Translated by A.V. Miller, Analysis of the Text and Forward by J.N. Findlay, (Delhi: Motilal Banarsidass, 1998), pp. 541-542.
[17] Hughes-Warrington, *op. cit.*, note 13, p. 243.
[18] *Ibid.*, pp. 244-245.
[19] J.M. Hobson, *The Eastern Origins of Western Civilisation* (Cambridge: Cambridge University Press, 2004), pp. 12-13.
[20] *Ibid.*, p. 13.
[21] Hughes-Warrington, *op. cit.*, note 13, p. 152.

troduction to the Reading of Hegel: Lectures on the Phenomenology of Spirit, Kojève, for example, elucidates Hegel's philosophy. He explains that the evolution of the individual is perceived as a voluntary progression made by a free individual. He also points out that all human desire – conceived as distinct from animal desire or instinct – is the desire for recognition. Self-consciousness is, therefore, the struggle for recognition of one's value.[22]

Francis Fukuyama's "End of History" thesis, which still holds sway among some in the contemporary period, is similarly linear. Fukuyama put forward an alternative paradigm in the wake of the Cold War and the collapse of the majority of communist regimes. He claimed that the future would be characterised by the spread of liberal democracy as the ultimate and last form of political system best suited to humankind's needs. His thesis was captured in the title of his book *The End of History and the Last Man* (1992),[23] which is based on the notion that history is moving in one direction and is therefore universal. According to Fukuyama, a pattern is developing that indicates the triumph of one form of economic and political organisation: liberal democracy. This is based on more than simply Western triumphalism. It rests on an assumption about human social evolution.[24] The end of history relies on an assumed universal history determined by the search for recognition and resulting in the pursuit of liberty and equality.

Fukuyama's intellectual heritage owes much to both Kant and Hegel, as he himself points out.[25] Contrary to what some observers claim with regard to Fukuyama's idea about the end of history, he does, in fact, recognise the follies of idealising Western liberal democracy, which he considers an imperfect form of governance since it is based on the acceptance of economic inequalities. Indeed, he suggests that this is perhaps the most fundamental contradiction and limitation of this particular political form in terms of the politics of recognition. To some extent, this seems to reflect an unspoken longing for the continuation of history marked by continued challenges to existing orders.

---

[22] A. Kojève, *Introduction to the Reading of Hegel: Lectures on the Phenomenology of Spirit*, Assembled by R. Queneau, Edited by A. Bloom, Translated by J.H. Nichols, Jr. (Ithaca: Cornell University, 1980), pp. 7-8.
[23] Fukuyama, *op. cit.*, note 8.
[24] *Ibid.*, p. 45.
[25] *Ibid.*, p. xii.

However, this understanding of universal history is not sustainable. Apart from the problems related to assuming that liberal democracy fulfils human beings' perceived desire for liberty and equality, it cannot be said with any degree of confidence that the human need for recognition is manifested in the same form in different cultural and historical contexts. The path that Europe or the West took was contingent.[26] The *Magna Carta* of 1215, on which liberal individual rights are said to be based, was a response to a particular conjuncture. It was the result of an effort to defend the feudal rights of English barons against the power of the sovereign and it took several centuries for this to be translated into liberal individual rights.[27]

Might recognition equally be sought within the group or the tribe rather than in terms of liberal individual rights? Instead of identifying a *universal history*, what is needed is to discern a *sustainable history*, which allows for the possibility of human needs being sought within different political systems. Global security will depend on a more sustainable understanding of history, which allows for greater inclusion of cultural and historical specificities.

History has also been thought about in non-linear, non-progressive terms. Some approaches to history, for example, have attempted to identify stages of history. Arab-Islamic scholar Abū Zayd 'Abdu r-Rahman bin Muhammad bin Khaldūn (1332-1406) or Ibn Khaldūn adopted a cyclical view of history.[28] He stressed the social, political, economic, cultural and physical conditions that gave shape to *'umran* or civilisations. He examined civilisations in general and in the particular context of the Maghreb in the 11th to the 14th centuries. His focus was on the transition from primitive to more advanced societies and on how the latter decline. Looking at the specific case of the Maghreb, he distinguished between the *'umran badawi* (nomadic, Bedouin life) and *'umran hadari* (urban sedentary life). The former represents the first phase in the development of a civilisation, which develops into the latter. Among the nomadic group, Ibn Khaldūn identifies camel nomads of the desert, semi-nomadic people and sedentary

---

[26] D. Senghaas, *The Clash within Civilizations: Coming to Terms with Cultural Conflicts* (London: Routledge, 2002), p. 18.
[27] *Ibid.*, p. 107.
[28] See *An Arab Philosophy of History: Selections from the Prolegomena of Ibn Khaldun of Tunis (1332-1406)*, Translated and Arranged by C. Issawi (Princeton, N.J.: The Darwin Press, Inc., 1987).

farmers. Within *'umran hadari*, he identifies those who live close to towns and those who live in them. Each of these groups represents a different level of development. Town dwellers aspire to luxury and culture, but also mark civilisation's decay. *'Umran hadari* is destroyed by *'umran badawi*, which sows the seeds of a new state with many of the old characteristics and develops into *'umran hadari*.[29]

This cyclical view of history is driven by what Ibn Khaldūn refers to as *'asabiya*, which is thought to represent something like a vital force derived from the group solidarity that exists in *'umran badawi*. This cycle is associated with the waging of war. *'Asabiya* is present in times of war, when group feeling is high, but the raising of taxes and the spoils of war introduce hierarchy and lead to the disappearance of *'asabiya*. This has caused some to declare that his thinking is a precursor to Marx's dialectic.[30]

Several centuries later, Giambatttista Vico (1668-1744) maintained that there is an identifiable universal pattern of growth and decline that all nations share in common. This pattern was thought to be caused by "Providence". In a later publication *The New Science of Giambattista Vico* (1725), he attempted to elaborate on the notion of growth and decline. Vico held that most periods of history can be classified as either an "age of poetry", an "age of heroes" or an "age of humans".[31]

In the age of poetry, people are believed to be brutal and irrational, but endowed with a rich imagination that nourishes the myths that underpin language, institutions, laws and values, and elevates those who claim to communicate with God to a privileged position in society. In the age of heroes, these individuals begin to lose their privileged position as people lose their faith in them. This, Vico argues, signals the need for institutions based on justice and humanity. In the age of heroes and the age of humans, people grow out of non-rational, mythic consciousness and develop a more rational consciousness. This transition is not in fact viewed as progressive, since doubt in God is believed to result in moral corruption and a lack of creative power. World history is thus conceived as generally cyclical. However, specificities, such as disease, climate, conflict, and so on, cause variations

---

[29] Hughes-Warrington, *op. cit.*, note 13, pp. 191-192.
[30] *Ibid.*, pp. 192-193.
[31] *Ibid.*, p. 376.

in this general pattern.[32] Through the study of history, Vico believed that we can better understand the factors that shape our own times.[33]

In *The Decline of the West* (1918), Oswald Spengler (1880-1936) also identified historical stages. In this publication, he undertook a comparative study of the birth, growth, decline and eventual demise of eight cultural domains: Babylonian, Indian, Chinese, Egyptian, Mayan-Aztec (Mexican), Classical (Greco-Roman), Magian (Arabian, Syrian, Jewish, Byzantine and Islamic) and the so-called Faustian (Western Europe). He suggested that cultures pass through similar phases. They experience their spring when society is agricultural and feudal; their summer when urbanisation takes place; their autumn when cities and commerce are established, monarchies become centralised and religion and tradition are questioned; and their winter when materialism, scepticism and imperialism form and with the emergence of world cities. A culture may also cease to exist as the result of an external attack or be prevented from developing due to the continuing influence of a dominant older culture. According to Spengler, employing a common comparative framework in which there is a birth, growth, decline and death of cultures helps make possible predictions about the future of any given culture.[34]

In Arnold J. Toynbee's (1889-1975) view, civilisations generally go through four stages of development: (1) an age of growth; (2) a time of troubles; (3) a universal state; and (4) an interregnum or disintegration.[35] If a "primitive" society is to develop into a sophisticated civilisation, it must surmount challenges, which typically are posed by external factors such as climate at this stage. If the time of troubles prompts the breakdown of civilisation, this is likely to be due to internal factors, such as excessive nationalism; the idolisation of an individual, institutions or processes; and a general erosion of creativity. The disintegration of a civilisation is thus thought of in terms of suicide. As the result of the outbreak of war in this phase, a universal state is established by a dominant minority. Although less pessimistic than Spengler regarding the fate of the West, he did maintain that the West demonstrated suicidal characteristics. The disintegration of a

---

[32] *Ibid.*, p. 377.
[33] *Ibid.*
[34] *Ibid.*, pp. 325-327.
[35] See A. Toynbee, *A Study of History: Abridgement of Volumes VII-X* (Boston, MA: Oxford University Press, 1987).

civilisation is thought to take place in three phases involving three social groups: a dominant minority; an internal proletariat; and an external proletariat. Toynbee does not conceive of the proletariat in the same way as Marx. According to Toynbee, proletariat refers to those who did not gain dominance in an age of growth. In a time of troubles, the dominant minority attempt to maintain their position. During this period some members of the dominant minority leave it to become the internal proletariat. At the same time, pressure is placed on the stability of the civilisation by an external proletariat. Finally, the internal proletariat leads the uncreative majority to exploit the opening for change.[36]

Cyclical notions of history, however, tend to suffer from the weakness of monocausality. Spengler, Toynbee and Ibn Khaldūn all discern similar challenges responsible for different historical phases. Ibn Khaldūn's generalisation may have been made easier due to the fact that he was using historical knowledge of only the Persians, Arabs, Berbers and, to some degree, Spaniards, in all of which he encountered the same basic forms of state (tribal states, despotic kingdoms and empires).[37] Cyclical approaches, nevertheless, do have the benefit of demonstrating that geo-cultural domains contain internal struggles and, therefore, highlight the need to avoid conceiving of them as monolithic entities.

Non-essentialistic conceptions of "civilisations", such as that provided by Fernand Braudel (1902-1985), for example, understand the histories of different "civilisations" as intertwined, with the achievements of one often owing a debt to those of another: "The history of civilizations, in fact, is the history of continual mutual borrowings over many centuries, despite which each civilization has kept its own original character."[38] Time and geography play an important role in Braudel's conception of the evolution of "civilisations".[39] He set out the threefold view of time: (1) individual time; (2) social time; and (3) geographical time. Individual and social time are classified as l'histoire événementielle and geographical time as la longue durée (long time span). He believed that in order to gain a better understanding of the world, we must examine la longue durée. The deeds of indi-

---

[36] Ibid., pp. 362-364.
[37] C. Issawi, "Introduction," in Issawi, op. cit., note 28.
[38] Braudel, op. cit., note 2, p. 8.
[39] Ibid., p. 14.

viduals are believed to be of relevance only insofar as they reveal underlying structures.[40]

While there are those who believe that it is possible to have a general theory of history, the notion that there is a "total" history is not shared by all. Some maintain that there is no such coherence to history and that there are a number of specific histories.[41] This does not mean that objectivity about historical events is impossible. We know that specific events occurred. However, how the meaning of those events is portrayed is a question of interpretation. This raises an additional question about who gets to write history. Do the victors always write the dominant version of history?

Another approach to history is hermeneutic and, thus, based on a theory of interpretation. At the heart of Paul Ricoeur's (1913-2005) approach, for instance, is hermeneutics. Ideas and actions are believed to be informed by particular historical contexts. Ricoeur is interested in the interpretation of texts, which are defined in a broad sense. Dreams, ideologies and narratives as well as human actions are thought to be open to interpretation.[42] In *Memory, History and Forgetting* (2004),[43] Ricoeur sets out a "historiographical epistemology" which emphasises the selective nature of representations of the past. Despite his recognition of the narrative of history, he nevertheless may be distinguished from others who approach hermeneutics from a post-structuralist position, such as Jean Baudrillard (1929-2007), Jacques Derrida (1930-2004), Jean-François Lyotard (1924-1998) and Richard Rorty (1931-2007). Ricoeur holds that the past exists in a similar way as unperceived objects exist.[44]

French philosopher and historian Michel Foucault (1926-1984) argued that for the most part people's thoughts are shaped by rules and regularities that they are not conscious of. These rules and regularities – the "archive" – place limits on what can be thought and said. The archive is itself historically determined and, thus, subject to change. Because the archive can place limits on the possible, it is be-

---

[40] Hughes-Warrington, *op. cit.*, note 13, pp. 21-22, 24.
[41] Little, *op. cit.*, note 3.
[42] Hughes-Warrington, *op. cit.*, note 13, pp. 304-306.
[43] P. Ricoeur, *Memory, History and Forgetting,* Translated by K. Blamey and D. Pellauer (Chicago: Chicago University Press, 2004).
[44] Hughes-Warrington, *op. cit.*, note 13, pp. 302-306.

lieved to be connected to questions of power. It is generally linked to the power relations in society at any given historical conjuncture.⁴⁵

Table 1: A Comparative View of Philosophies of History*

Approach	Key Figures & Year	Short Description
Pre-modern Cyclical History *propelled by 'asabiya or "group solidarity"*	Ibn Khaldūn (1332-1406) *An Arab Philosophy of History* (1377)	1. Cyclical conception of history 2. Emphasised the social, economic, political, cultural and physical conditions that produced "civilisations" 3. Focused on the transition from more primitive to advanced "civilisations" and their subsequent decline
Cyclical History *propelled by religious spirituality*	Giambattista Vico (1668-1744) *New Science* (1725)	1. Generally cyclical pattern to history 2. A universal pattern of growth and decline that nations share 3. Periods of history are identified as the (1) "age of poetry"; (2) "age of heroes" and (3) "age of humans"
Linear History *propelled by a dialectical "logic" of thesis, antithesis, synthesis*	Georg Wilhelm Hegel (1770-1831) *The Philosophy of History* (1837)	1. Idealistic in the sense that the realm of ideas determines the material realm 2. Linear conception of history 3. History would end when human beings attained freedom through liberal institutions
Cyclical History *propelled by moral creativity*	Oswald Spengler (1880-1936) *The Decline of the West* (1918)	1. Cyclical view of history 2. Cultures are believed to pass through similar phases: (1) Spring (agricultural-feudal); (2) Summer (urbanisation); (3) Autumn (cities and commerce, centralised monarchies, decline in faith and tradition); and Winter (materialism, scepticism, imperialism and formation of world cities)

---

⁴⁵ *Ibid.*, pp. 110-111.

Approach	Key Figures & Year	Short Description
Cyclical History *propelled by the presence or lack of creativity*	Arnold J. Toynbee (1889-1975) *A Study of History* (1934-1961)	"Civilisations" are believed to go through 4 stages: (1) an age of growth; (2) a time of troubles; (3) universal state; and (4) an interregnum or disintegration
Longue Durée History *propelled by geographic time*	Fernand Braudel (1902-1985) *A History of Civilizations* (1962)	1. The history of "civilisations" is believed to be a history of mutual borrowings 2. Time and geography play an important role in history 3. A three-fold conception of time is proposed: (1) individual time; (2) social time; (3) geographical time. Individual and social time are classified as "histoire événementielle" and geographical time as the "longue durée"
Linear History *propelled by the human need for recognition*	Francis Fukuyama (present) *The End of History and the Last Man* (1992)	1. Inspired by Hegel's philosophy of history 2. Idealistic in the sense that the realm of ideas drives history 3. Linear conception of history 4. Universal conception of history 5. The ultimate and last form of political system that fulfils the human need for recognition is thought to have been reached in liberal democracy

Approach	Key Figures & Year	Short Description
"Sustainable History" *propelled by the presence of good governance which balances the attributes of human nature ("Emotional Amoral Egoism") with human dignity needs* (reason, security, human rights, accountability, transparency, justice, opportunity, innovation and inclusiveness)	Nayef Al-Rodhan (present) *The present volume (Sustainable History and the Dignity of Man)*	1. Sustainable history is defined as a durable progressive trajectory in which the quality of life on this planet or other planets is premised on the guarantee of human dignity *for all* at *all times* and under *all circumstances* 2. Sustainable history is propelled by the presence of good governance *which balances the attributes of human nature* ("Emotional Amoral Egoism") with *human dignity needs* (reason, security, human rights, accountability, transparency, justice, opportunity, innovation and inclusiveness) 3. A good governance paradigm that limits excesses of human nature and ensures an atmosphere of happiness and productivity by promoting reason and dignity is required 4. A minimum criteria of governance should be met rather than the exact form of governance that a particular political system adopts. Yet, they must be appropriate, acceptable and affordable to each system and cultural domain. These criteria should also meet a certain common global standard to ensure maximum political and moral cooperation 5. Humankind is an insignificant part of existence 6. Human beings are "emotional amoral egoists", driven above all by emotional self-interest. All of our thoughts, beliefs and motivations are neurochemically mediated, some pre-determined for survival, others alterable

Approach	Key Figures & Year	Short Description
"Sustainable History" *continued*	Nayef Al-Rodhan	7. What makes our existence meaningful is highly subjective and ultimately determined by sustainable neurochemical gratification. 8. All knowledge is acquired through the application of reason and has a physical basis 9. There is only one collective human civilisation comprised of geo-cultural domains and cultures 10. The history of human civilisation is a history of mutual borrowings 11. Contemporary events can be comprehended through an understanding of human time 12. Dignity is central to the sustainability of history 13. A life governed by reason is more likely to be useful and dignified 14. Security, stability and prosperity will depend on the application of the multi-sum security principle that captures the multi-dimensional aspects of security and insists on the centrality of global justice for lasting security 15. Harmonious interstate relations will be guided by the paradigm of symbiotic realism that stresses the importance of absolute rather than relative gains 16. Effective statecraft is characterised by the successful reconciliation of all interests 17. The concept of just power ought to guide the use of power in an interdependent and interconnected world

Approach	Key Figures & Year	Short Description
"Sustainable History" *continued*	Nayef Al-Rodhan	18. The interaction of geo-cultural domains should be synergistic to maintain global harmony 19. A set of global values in keeping with human nature and dignity need to be identified and developed 20. Strict ethical guidelines need to be developed in anticipation of significant technological and biotechnological advances in order to guarantee human dignity

* The approaches to history depicted here have been chosen because of their pertinence to the study of geo-cultural domains. The table does not reflect the totality of the ideas of the thinkers, but is meant as a brief synopsis.

2. The Ocean Model of One Human Civilisation

The notion of civilisation is increasingly employed in efforts to discern the factors shaping global dynamics. A prominent contemporary account of the relevance of "civilisations" to world order is provided by Samuel Huntington. In *The Clash of Civilizations and the Remaking of World Order* (1996),[46] Huntington puts forward what he claims to be a new paradigm with which to capture the general tendencies in motion at the dawn of the 21st century. Huntington's general argument is that we are now in a period of history in which major ideological conflicts are over, and conflicts between civilisations are believed to be replacing the ideological battles of the bifurcated bipolar world of the Cold War. A civilisation-based order is believed to be emerging.[47]

Whether Huntington really does offer a new paradigm with which to understand the world is doubtful. His argument rests on a number of assumptions that for the most part do not represent a rupture with the dominant realist framework in international relations. At first sight, his analysis may appear to focus on civilisations as the major actors within international relations rather than states, which constitute the principal actors within the international system as far as

---

[46] S.P. Huntington, *The Clash of Civilizations and the Remaking of World Order* (London: Simon & Schuster, 1996).
[47] *Ibid.*, pp. 19-20.

realists are concerned. However, Huntington does not in fact imply that states are being replaced by civilisations as the main actors in global politics. Instead, he seems to suggest that while states are likely to retain their centrality, their interests and practices will be increasingly defined by their membership of a particular civilisation.[48] Thus, while states remain the principal actors as they do in realism, culture is recognised as an important factor shaping global politics.

Despite this recognition, the realist assumption of international anarchy and its consequences in terms of self-help is not fundamentally challenged by Huntington. This is because the national interests of states are still considered to be defined by power, albeit increasingly by cultural factors as well.[49] China and Muslim countries are assumed to be the major sources of threat to the West. Although he stresses the importance of a resurgence of religious identities within "Islamic civilisation", it is not extremism that is thought to pose a threat to the West but "Islamic civilisation" itself. His argument runs as follows: Muslims are convinced of the superiority of their religion, culture and values, and, at the same time, are obsessed by their lack of power in the global realm. The West is equally perceived to be a problem for the Islamic world, due to its belief in the universality of its values and the applicability of liberal democracy, as well as its declining relative power.[50] Given demographic trends, growth in Muslim populations will, he claimed, continue to fuel opposition to the West and affirmation of resistant Islamic identities.[51] China is thought to pose a threat to the West because continued Asian economic growth will, in Huntington's view, shift the balance of global power. Asian civilisations are thought to be the potential winners in this slow modification of the status quo, with China emerging as a challenger to the West.[52]

Huntington's predictions about potential instability caused by population growth in the Islamic world and economic growth in East Asia are clearly informed by realism's theory of the balance of power, which holds that states will form alliances in order to prevent a rising

---

[48] L. Rajendram, "Does the Clash of Civilisations Paradigm Provide a Persuasive Explanation of International Politics after September 11?" *Cambridge Review of International Affairs*, Vol. 15, No. 2, 2002, p. 219.
[49] *Ibid.*, p. 220.
[50] Huntington, *op. cit.*, note 46, pp. 217-218.
[51] *Ibid.*, p. 121.
[52] *Ibid.*, pp. 82-83.

power from destabilising established power relations in the international system. East Asia's economic growth is believed to be the cause of increased future instability as China rises and other states in the region attempt to balance it in order to prevent a change in the balance of Asian civilisations. Against this backdrop, greater economic resources will contribute to a military build-up, making the situation even more dangerous.[53]

Lacking a "core" state, such as China in Asia, that is capable of enforcing order, the Arab-Islamic world is thought to portend even greater instability. Huntington argued that civilisations that lack core states are more unstable and will pose a greater threat to other civilisations. The Arab-Islamic world is thought to be volatile for this reason. A core state is thought to be lacking because of the continued prominence of religious and tribal loyalties, which militate against the emergence of strong states. Latin America and Africa are also believed to lack core states, but they are weak economically and militarily and, as a result, perceived to be less of a threat.[54] According to Huntington's criteria, however, the Kingdom of Saudi Arabia would qualify as an emergent core state.

At the global level, civilisations are expected to try to balance each other, forming alliances only when it is in their interest to do so. Huntington does not anticipate a general anti-Western coalition forming as a result of an alliance between Sinic and Islamic civilisations,[55] although he does identify some emerging civilisational alignments. The Soviet-Afghan war of 1979–1989 is cited as a first instance of a civilisational war. In the West, this war was viewed as an ideological war in the struggle between communism and capitalism. Yet, according to Huntington, it was widely perceived by Muslims as a victory for Islam. What Huntington seems to want to say but stops short of saying is that power is at stake, but culture is being securitised, that is, identified as a security issue, both by those intent on fuelling tension and by those who unwittingly reinforce the belief that there is a coming clash of civilisations. This in fact highlights the need to contextualise tensions and conflicts and to remain alert to the instrumental use of cultural diversity.[56]

---

[53] *Ibid.*, p. 218.
[54] *Ibid.*, pp. 156, 176, 240.
[55] *Ibid.*, pp. 128, 185-186.
[56] Senghaas, *op. cit.*, note 26, pp. 83, 85.

Interpreting all conflicts as civilisational in character is highly misleading. Greater cultural identification may lead to increases in tribal, ethnic and national loyalties as much as identity formation along civilisational lines. A more visible trend in international politics seems to be for communities to fragment into ethnic or national units and to try to obtain statehood. Huntington identifies a number of "fault line conflicts", including Chechnya and Bosnia,[57] but for many people in the communities involved, these conflicts principally involved national liberation. Nationalism therefore remains an important factor which drives conflict. Nevertheless, Huntington does highlight that some states are torn or cleft along cultural/"civilisational" lines.[58]

Huntington acknowledges that the arrogance of the West may also be adding to the formation of cultural affiliations. In addition to intensified contact, the West's belief in the universality of its values and applicability of liberal democracy is thought to be aggravating relations with other civilisations.[59] Having acknowledged this, he then goes on to state that a major challenge facing the West is its promotion of the universal appeal of its culture and values and its diminishing capacity to be successful in this endeavour.[60] Huntington concludes that the West should recognise that its culture and values are not universal but *unique*. This acknowledges that Western liberal democracy and values such as individualism may be specific to the particular historical and cultural context of the West, and that it cannot simply be assumed that they may be transposed elsewhere, at least not in the same form. The United States (US) – presumed to be synonymous with the West – is thus encouraged to concentrate on defending the uniqueness of the West.[61] Yet, this uniqueness, according to Huntington, comes from the fact that the West has been able to disproportionately affect the world system for the past 500 years.[62] Again, the analysis seems plainly to come back to a question of power. Since Huntington defines power as the capacity to alter the behaviour of others, the West is unique because of its power – and its uniqueness or power ought to be preserved from challengers.

---

[57] Huntington, *op. cit.*, note 46, pp. 268-269.
[58] M. Bassin, "Civilisations and Their Discontents: Political Geography and Geopolitics in the Huntington Thesis," *Geopolitics*, Vol. 12, 2007, p. 361.
[59] Huntington, *op. cit.*, note 46, pp. 21, 29.
[60] *Ibid.*, p. 183.
[61] *Ibid.*, p. 21.
[62] *Ibid.*, p. 302.

The future resilience of the West, if we are to believe Huntington, will depend in part on how it responds to the "moral decay" that members of Asian and Islamic civilisations often charge it with. While this may seem reasonable enough, he goes on to argue that "[o]ne such challenge comes from immigrants from other civilisations who reject assimilation and continue to adhere to and propagate the values, customs, and cultures of their home societies."[63] Yet, to imagine that assimilationist policies will help to reduce tensions seems foolhardy at best. Simply because minorities are "visible" in terms of dress and customs does not mean that they represent a threat to societal stability. Conflict perhaps seems inevitable in Huntington's clash of civilisations paradigm because he adopts a view of human nature that assumes that the need for identity is synonymous with a tendency towards enmity.[64]

Moreover, civilisational vitality, it would seem, does not depend on reducing borrowing and exchanges across cultures. In fact, cultures have risen in part because of an openness to cultural borrowing and exchanges. It is simply inaccurate and misleading to say, as Huntington does, that "[d]uring most of human existence, contacts between civilizations were intermittent or non-existent."[65] Arab-Islamic and Western/European histories, for example, cannot be understood in isolation from one another. There has in fact been a great deal of cross fertilisation between different geo-cultural forms. The technologies that enabled the European agricultural revolution, for example, largely came from the East. The watermill, the windmill, the heavy mouldboard plough, particular types of animal harnesses and the iron horseshoe all appear to have entered Europe from the East.[66] Muslim communities drew on Greek heritage. East of Egypt, the territories that came under Muslim rule in the 7th century once formed part of Alexander the Great's realm and were influenced by Greek philosophy. To Egypt's West, the Arab-Islamic caliphate included parts of North Africa, Iberia and southern France, which were once under Roman rule and equally influenced by Greek culture.[67] In the Middle

---

[63] *Ibid.*, pp. 304-305.
[64] Rajendram, *op. cit.*, note 48, pp. 223, 227-228.
[65] Huntington, *op. cit.*, note 46, p. 29.
[66] Hobson, *op. cit.*, note 19, pp. 100-102.
[67] R.W. Bulliet, *The Case for Islamo-Christian Civilization* (New York: Columbia University Press, 2004), p. 16.

Ages, stimuli from Muslim lands influenced philosophy, theology, mathematics, chemistry, medicine, music, literature, manufacturing and cuisine across Europe. Many of these borrowings helped to lay the foundations for Europe's later scientific and intellectual advances,[68] but are often missing from the West's own historical account.

Rather than thinking in terms of *multiple civilisations*, we need to think in terms of *one fluid human story* with internal characteristics linked to the time and place in which it manifests itself. Thinking in terms of the totality of human civilisation requires an approach to history that allows one to conceive of a period of time that extends beyond that of the longue durée outlined by Braudel. A philosophy of history needs to encompass a span of human time that captures human nature and its mastery of its environment.

Rather than thinking of competing and separate civilisations, we should think in terms of only one human civilisation (one human story), comprised of multiple geo-cultural domains that contain sub-cultures, as is shown in Diagram 2.

---

[68] *Ibid.*, p. 31.

Diagram 2: Human Civilisation

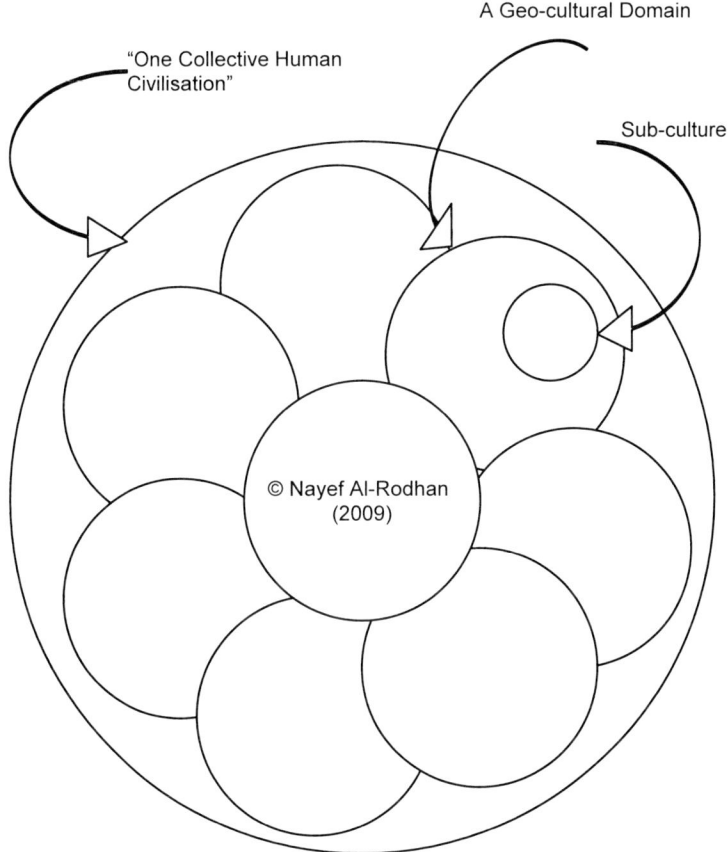

Thus, into collective human civilisation flow rivers, representing different geo-cultural domains, into which flow tributaries, representing sub-cultures, as is shown in Diagram 3. At the points where rivers (geo-cultural domains) enter the ocean of human civilisation, there is likely to be a concentration or dominance of that culture. Over time, all rivers become one. Thus, in the middle of the ocean an equal mix of all cultures exists, although it may be weighted towards the dominant culture of the day. A fluidity at the centre of the ocean exists, nevertheless, which means that the weighting will alter depending on whichever culture happens to be globally more dominant, or on the particular balance that is found between cultures. Borrowing between cultures occurs, particularly between geographically adjacent geo-cultural domains, represented in the diagram as rivers G and H. However, proximity can also generate friction between members of different cultures as shown by G and F. The size and influence of the dominant culture of the day is subject to change and may decline as the influence of another rises, or as other cultures are better accommodated.

Efforts to help facilitate a better understanding of such specificities have taken a number of forms in recent years and are based on the notion that common ground exists with regard to fundamental values on which to base dialogue. From the point of view of this study, such efforts are positive because they help to avoid assuming a hierarchy among cultural achievements. Diverse cultures are viewed as different expressions of a broader human experience.[69]

In 2005, for example, the Alliance of Civilizations (AoC), a project aimed at facilitating greater understanding and reconciliation between people of different cultures and communities in order to marginalise polarising discourses and extremist tendencies, was established as a result of a joint Turkish and Spanish initiative under the auspices of the United Nations (UN). While the focus is on the promotion of increased understanding between cultures in general, that between "Muslim" and "Western" societies is given special emphasis. The AoC aims to facilitate platforms of dialogue between political and religious media and civil society personalities.

---

[69] M.H. Mitias, "Universalism as a Path to Dialogue between Civilizations," *Dialogue and Universalism*, No. 5, 2003, pp. 50-51.

SUSTAINABLE HISTORY AND THE DIGNITY OF MAN 37

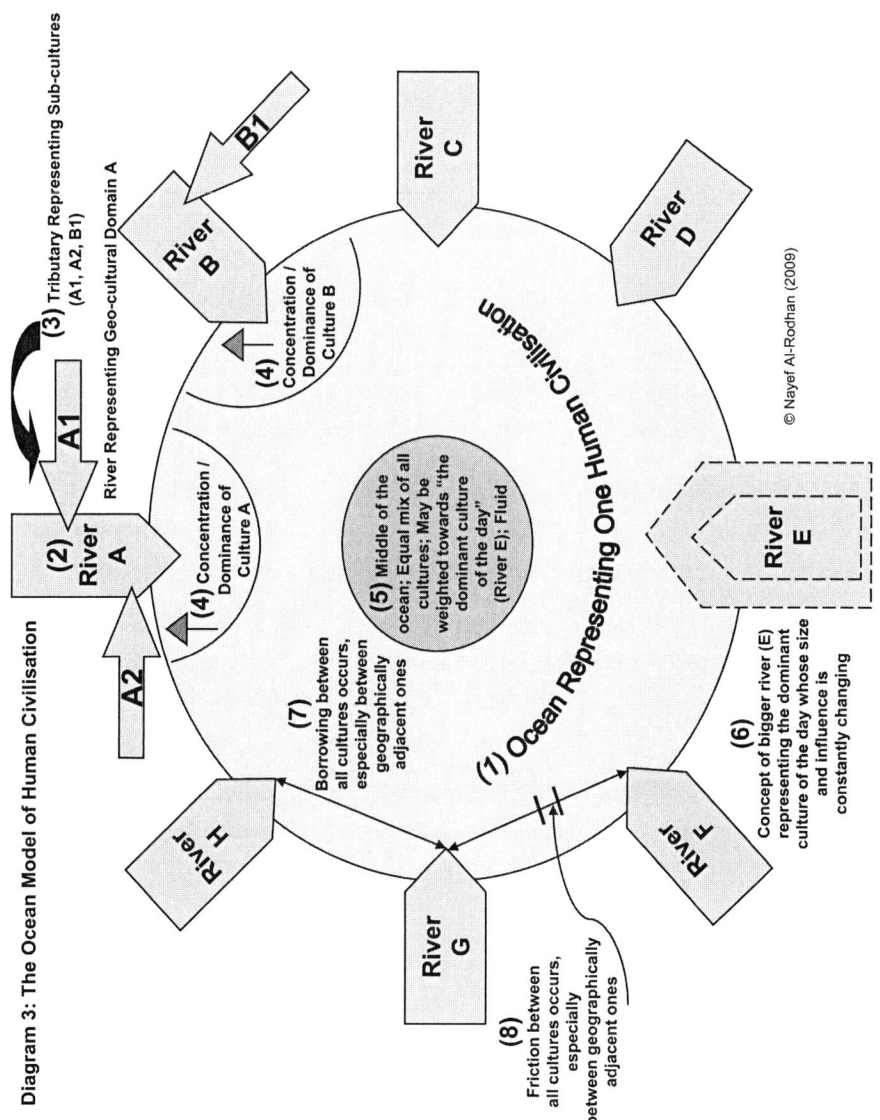

Diagram 3: The Ocean Model of Human Civilisation

It also aims to facilitate educational initiatives, student exchanges and media initiatives, among other things.[70] The need for a dialogue among civilisations has also been emphasised. In 2008 in Madrid, for instance, Saudi Arabia and Spain held an interfaith dialogue among Christians, Muslims and Jews.[71] Some have suggested that dialogue should take place as a rational conversation focused on comprehending a subject or concept. In order for one culture to understand another culture, Michael Mitias, for example, suggests first that participants in a dialogue need to occupy some common ground, which he believes already exists by virtue of our shared humanity. In other words, the universality of human needs is what we share in common no matter what cultural background we possess. Moral values, such as courage, justice and compassion are, for instance, considered universal because of our common human nature. Dialogue takes the form of a search for truth, which should not only take place between high-level representatives from diverse cultures, but also take the form of continual cultural communication based on experiencing other cultures and working together on common projects to deal with shared concerns or aspirations.[72]

The usefulness of dialogue based on the rational search for truth has, however, been challenged by some commentators. Ken Tsutsumibayashi, for example, argues that this approach is unlikely to result in more than minimalist principles, which would not amount to a global ethic.[73] Instead of dialogue based on rational discourse, Tsusumibayashi suggests an intercivilisational dialogue leading to a "fusion of horizons" – "a term that signifies a dialogic process by which the interlocutors gradually come to achieve mutual understanding through the transformation or extension of their value criteria."[74] In order for intercultural dialogue to lead to mutual understanding, he contends that the importance of the issue of identity has to be taken into account because it is central to people's sense of due recognition

---

[70] See the Alliance of Civilization's Website: http://unaoc.org/content/view/29/83/lang,english/.
[71] "Inter-faith Meet to be Held in Spain," *Saudi Gazette*, 22 June 2008, http://www.saudigazette.com.sa/index.cfm?method=home.regcon&contentID=200806 229871.
[72] Mitias, *op. cit.*, note 69, pp. 56-59.
[73] K. Tsutsumibayashi, "Fusion of Horizons or Confusion of Horizons? Intercultural Dialogue and Its Risks," *Global Governance*, Vol. 11, 2005, p. 105.
[74] *Ibid.*

and, thus, mutual respect, which is a prerequisite for fruitful intercultural dialogue.[75]

The idea of a fusion of horizons implies an interaction during which different participants come together to create a shared ethos. He makes reference to the tension between Asian values and Western conceptions of human rights. In many Asian countries, resentment has been generated in response to the West's promotion of human rights. According to Tsutsumibayashi, this reaction occurs not because Asians tend to disagree with the content of human rights but because people feel that the moral idioms embedded in their own cultures, traditions and religions are not recognised or understood, and they become offended by what they view as the patronising attitude of people in the West.[76]

Several themes relate to this issue: the value-laden nature of social actions and the value-laden interpretations of the historian. This raises the question of whether there is an objective historical reality or if such a reality is dependent on the specific meanings that people attribute to it. We can say that historical objectivity is possible insofar as historians can undertake "good-faith" investigations. This, however, does not mean that there is an objective historical "truth". A new philosophy of history would take into account the various representations of history.[77]

3. The Purpose and Structure of the Book

The purpose of this book is to set out a new philosophy of sustainable history, understood as a durable progressive trajectory, which is achievable through the preservation and promotion of *human dignity*. It sets out a concept of human civilisation made up of different, but intertwined, geo-cultural domains in what I call the **Ocean Model of Human Civilisation**. If we view civilisation as a single collective civilisation, comprised of a number of different geo-cultural domains, we need to develop a philosophy of history that considers human time as a means of understanding human nature and associated needs. At the individual level, ***the exercise of reason, as opposed to the acceptance of dogma, is more likely to lead to a dignified life***. From

---

[75] *Ibid.*, p. 106.
[76] *Ibid.*, p. 107.
[77] Little, *op. cit.*, note 3.

this we can discern the kinds of institutions and arrangements that are required to ensure a sustainable history, to which there is no end but instead a coexistence of different geo-cultural domains which share a minimum set of fundamental values but retain their distinctiveness.

However, for human civilisation to flourish transcultural synergy is needed – synergy meaning a situation where two or more agents or influences together produce an effect that is greater than the net effect of each individual entity or force.[78] We need to discern the practical bases on which such synergy may occur. Transcultural synergy implies and depends on the development of a universal axiology, axiology meaning the study of values and of the criteria for making value judgements.[79] A universal axiology would seek to identify points of overlap between value systems as a means of facilitating dialogue and eventual synergy. One of the major tasks in the early 21st century is to identify more clearly what unites the members of different cultures and the extent to which the achievements of certain geo-cultural domains have frequently been dependent on those of others, making large parts of history a common human history.

The book has three parts. The first part provides the means with which to take a longer view of human time, focusing on cosmology and human evolution, human nature, the meaning of existence and the acquisition of knowledge. In relation to the latter, a new philosophy of knowledge is advanced: the *neuro-rational physicalism* (**NRP**) paradigm. Together, these factors provide the bases with which to understand what drives human beings and how they understand the world around them. I then consider an instance of individual geo-cultural triumph as a simultaneous moment of synergy. This demonstrates the sense in which human civilisation is built on the collective achievements of all geo-cultural domains. The chapters that follow present a diagnosis of what is required for sustainable history and the dignity of Man. I consider: (1) human dignity needs, (2) minimum criteria for global justice; (3) minimum criteria for good and effective national governance; (4) minimum criteria for good global governance; (5) a *multi-sum security principle* that is adequate for a complex and interconnected global environment; (6) *symbiotic realism* as a

---

[78] N.R.F. Al-Rodhan, *Symbiotic Realism: A Theory of International Relations in an Instant and an Interdependent World* (Berlin: LIT, 2007), p. 124.
[79] *Encyclopaedia Britannica Online*, http://www.britannica.com/dictionary?book= Dictionary&va=axiology&query=axiology, s.v. "axiology"

framework for international relations; (7) ***neo-statecraft, meta-geopolitics*** for the 21st century and ***reconciliation statecraft***; and (8) transcultural synergy and the need for a ***universal axiology*** and the identification of fundamental human values and their articulation in different cultures. Finally, I identify tendencies and possible scenarios for planetary civilisation given the global interconnectedness resulting from globalisation; and Kardashev's scale, which envisages the emergence of civilisations that are far more technologically advanced than those that currently exist and may be capable of colonising the solar system or the universe. I also consider the implications of technological developments for the future of humankind and for human nature itself.

Part 1

The Foundations of Life

CHAPTER 2

WHERE ARE WE?
COSMOLOGY AND THE BIG UNIVERSAL PICTURE

As explained in the previous chapter, understanding history requires that we consider a time frame that is long enough to capture the factors that make human nature what it is. I suggested that this time frame may be understood as human time. However, if we are to understand human time, which is necessary in order to achieve a sustainable history, we need to ask the question: Where are we? This question has been answered in a number of ways and it has two dimensions. The first relates to space: where is the planet Earth situated in the universe? The second pertains to time: how old is the universe and our planet, and when did modern humans emerge? Answers to these questions have, of course, been sought for thousands of years. Some of the earliest known efforts to try to understand the universe were based on mythological accounts.[80] Ancient Greeks, notably Plato (472-347 BCE) and Aristotle (384-322 BCE), pondered the nature of the universe. The universe imagined by these Greek philosopher-scientists was, however, little more than our solar system. Arab-Islamic astronomers and mathematicians built on the knowledge of the ancients, paving the way for modern scientific cosmology, culminating in the Big Bang theory that is commonly accepted today. Fundamental to this theory is a notion of how creation began, which itself leads to particular beliefs about humankind's presence on Earth and how we have evolved, often in direct opposition to religious beliefs about the Creation. Religious and spiritual cosmologies have also sought to provide meaning to patterns in nature and the universe, although not all contain explanations of creation and the origin of humankind.

---

[80] L. Butler Feffer, "Cosmology in the Ancient World," in N. Schlager and J. Lauer (eds.) *Science and Its Times*, Vol. 1 (Detroit: Gale Group, 2001), http://galenet.galegroup.com.library3.webster.edu/servlet/SciRC?ste=1&docNum=CV2643450023.

This chapter discusses the variety of ways in which people have attempted to answer the question of where we are, either in space or time, or in both, and the controversies that have existed and persist to this day, based on what we know or what we can assume to be the case on the basis of logic. The purpose of this chapter is thus to provide a history of the universe and where humankind is situated in it that goes well beyond what we can learn from written historical records[81] and highlights the different interpretations that inform competing views about human nature and our place in the world.

1. The Universe

Early written records show that attempts to understand the universe took the form of mythological accounts. Later, the Greek philosophers in the 6th century BCE attempted to construct naturalistic explanations. These gave way to increasingly more complex models. In the 2nd century, for example, Claudius Ptolemy proposed a mathematically complex, geocentric (Earth-centric) model of the universe.[82] Arab-Islamic mathematicians and astronomers later corrected Ptolemy's model, offering insight into aspects of a heliocentric (sun-centric) conception of the universe, which were later taken up by Nicolaus Copernicus (1473-1543) in the 16th century, laying the foundation stones of modern scientific cosmology that led to the Big Bang theory which dominates today. Religious and spiritual cosmologies seek not only to explain the universe, but also to provide a guide to how humankind ought to relate to it.

The Cosmology of the Ancients
Babylonians acquired quite accurate knowledge of the Sun, the Moon and the planets, based not simply on observations, but also on mathematical theory. Their desire to understand the universe was driven by the search for explanations for periodic events such as eclipses for religious and astrological reasons, as well as for their lunar calendar and for agricultural purposes. Yet, they seem to have turned to mythology to try to explain the causes of movements of these celestial

---

[81] See C. Stokes Brown, *Big History: From the Big Bang to the Present* (New York: The New Press, 2007) for an account of "big history".
[82] Butler Feffer, *op. cit.*, note 80.

bodies as well as their creation. Ancient Egyptians similarly sought to explain these phenomena through mythological accounts.[83]

Western notions of nature and time were greatly influenced by the Greek philosopher-scientists, who attempted to understand the universe. Plato envisaged two dimensional spheres. His pupil, Aristotle, imagined eternal, three dimensional spheres.[84] Aristotle believed that the Moon, the planets and the Sun orbited the Earth, which was thought to be stationary. Greek philosopher-scientists set themselves the task of measuring the distance to the Moon as well as the size of the universe. Yet, the cosmos envisaged by Aristotle amounted to little more than our solar system and was, thus, very limited. One of the reasons for his belief in a geocentric universe was his observation that matter close to the Earth is pulled towards it. Among the four elements that he identified – water, earth, fire and air – he believed that water and earth were drawn towards the centre of the Earth, whereas air and fire rose up away from it. Based on this, he conjectured that the centre of the Earth must be at the centre of the cosmos.

While Ancient Greeks were aware that it was possible that the Earth might orbit the Sun over the course of one year, they generally dismissed this proposition on the grounds that if this were the case, the Earth would have to be moving at a tremendous speed. This was deemed impossible since objects that were dropped did not fall some distance away but instead fell straight down. When an object is dropped from a rapidly moving horse, for instance, it falls some distance away from the point at which it is dropped, not directly beneath it. Since objects were observed to fall straight down, it was concluded that the Earth could not be moving at any such speed. Thus, it was believed that the Earth could not be moving around the Sun.[85]

Ptolemy continued the work of Platonic and Aristotelian cosmology through his systematisation of Ancient Greek geometrical cosmology. A rotating sphere was believed to carry the Sun, Moon and planets in its orbit around the Earth.[86] This geocentric model was

---

[83] *Ibid.*
[84] *Ibid.*
[85] D. Lehoux, "Astronomy and Cosmology: Pre-Eighteenth Century," in B.S. Baigrie (ed.) *History of Modern Science and Mathematics* (New York: Charles Scribner's Sons, 2008), http://galenet.galegroup.com.library3.webster.edu/ servlet/SciRC?ste=1&docNum=CV2640700009.
[86] "The Greek Worldview," *Cosmic Journey, A History of Scientific Cosmology*, http://www.aip.org/history/cosmology/ideas/greekworldview.htm.

predominant in Ancient Greece. Similar ideas are thought to have been dominant in Ancient China.[87]

Much of early Greek scientific knowledge was lost when the Roman Empire collapsed, along with its school system. The monastic schools that followed no longer required knowledge of Greek and much information about the natural sciences tended to derive from secondary sources rather than the original works. As a result, much of Greek astrology was lost to the Latin-speaking West during the Middle Ages and would not be known of again until the 12th century, when the scientific treatises of the Ancient Greeks were translated into Latin from Arabic – the Arab-Islamic world having maintained scholarly use of Greek and, thus, access to Ancient Greek cosmology.

Arab-Islamic astronomers and mathematicians rescued and improved on Ptolemy's cosmology. His *The Great Treatise*, also known as the *Almagest*, was translated into Latin by Catholic and Jewish translators in 12th century Muslim Spain. In Baghdad in the early 11th century, Ibn Al-Haytham (965-1039) suggested that the Ptolemic geocentric model needed to be modified.[88] Nasir Al-Din Al-Tusi (1201-1274) carried out work on the solar system and Ibn Al-Shatir (1305-1375) on the motion of the Moon.[89] In 1271, Al-Tusi produced a table of planetary movements. His best known work is a description of a geometric construction, called an Al-Tusi couple, which describes a rectilinear movement from a point on one circle rolling inside another. His observations enabled corrections to Ptolemy's planetary theory in which all planetary movements were based on uniform circular motion. This technique later informed the work of Ibn Al-Shatir and Copernicus.[90] Thus, "Copernicus may have formalized the heliocentric model of the solar system in the early 1500s, for example, but the Pole only did so with the help of vast tables of astronomical measurements taken 200 years earlier in Iran."[91]

---

[87] C. Ronan, "Astronomy in China, Korea and Japan," in C.B.F. Walker (ed.) *Astronomy before the Telescope* (New York: St. Martin's Press, 1996), pp. 264-265.
[88] M.H. Morgan, *Lost History: The Enduring Legacy of Muslim Scientists, Thinkers, and Artists* (Washington, DC: National Geographic, 2007), p. 103.
[89] "The Greek Worldview," *op. cit.*, note 86.
[90] "Al-Tusi, Khwajah Nasir (1201-1274)," *Islamic Philosophy Online*, http://www.muslimphilosophy.com/ip/rep/H036.htm.
[91] J. Cartwright, "Synchrotron Proves Europeans Were Not the First Painters to Use Oils," Physicsworld.com, 25 April 2008, http://physicsworld.com/cws/article/news/33918.

In the early 14th century, Ibn Al-Shatir served as head muwaqqit at the Umayyad Mosque in Damascus, where he was charged with astrologically regulating prayer times. Based on his observations at Damascus, he put forward a planetary theory. His models bore striking similarity to those later proposed by Copernicus. His most significant contribution was a correction to Ptolemy's calculation of the motion of the Moon.[92]

Scholars in the Latin West became increasingly aware of and interested in the work being done by their Arabic-speaking neighbours. European scholars and translators travelled to Muslim Spain and gradually Arabic and Greek scientific texts were translated into Latin. One scholar who was influenced, although rarely acknowledged as so, was Copernicus. Copernicus overcame some of the limitations of Ptolemy's contribution at least in part by drawing on the work if Ibn Al-Haytham, through Al-Tusi and Ibn Al-Shatir.[93]

In the time of Copernicus, the seasons were thought to be in line with the movements of the Sun. He realised that more accurate calculations about planetary positions could be achieved if the assumption were made that the Earth moved around the Sun and not the other way round. He hypothesised that the Earth orbited the Sun and that the Earth occupied a relatively unimportant place in a vast universe. This represented a further departure from the Ancient Greek conception of the Earth.[94] He also hypothesised that the Earth rotated on its own axis. The notion that the Earth orbited the Sun went against accepted wisdom. Martin Luther (1483-1546), for example, was adamantly against the heliocentric model of the universe proposed by Copernicus. His book, *On the Revolution of the Heavenly Spheres* (1543) was on the list of books banned by the Roman Catholic Church until 1835.[95] Nevertheless, Copernicus' heliocentric theory was demonstrated in the early 17th century by Johannes Kepler (1571-

---

[92] FSTC Limited, "The Scholars of Damascus," *MuslimHeritage.Com*, 12 April 2005. http://www.muslimheritage.com/topics/default.cfm?articleI D=501.
[93] Lehoux, *op. cit.*, note 85.
[94] "Nicolas Copernicus," in K.L. Lerner and B. Wilmoth Lerner (eds.) *World of Earth Science* (Detroit: Thomson Gale, 2006), Science Resource Center, http://gale net.galegroup.com.library3.webster.edu/servlet/SciRC?ste=1&docNum=K264191002 4>.
[95] *Ibid.*

1630), who also showed that not only the Earth but all other planets move around the sun[96], as depicted in Figure 1.

A satisfactory explanation of why the planets orbit the sun, continually retracing their path, was not provided until Sir Isaac Newton's (1643-1727) theory that objects move under the force of gravity.[97] Before this, a divine presence was believed to move objects through the force of gravity.

In the late 18th century, William Herschel (1738-1822) was able to see further into space than ever before with the aid of his sophisticated telescopes, which enabled him to outline the structure of our galaxy. In Herschel's vision of the universe, our solar system was located within a larger stellar system.[98] Thus, our understanding of the universe went from being a small universe with the Earth at its centre to a big universe with the Earth far from its centre.[99]

Albert Einstein (1879-1955) published his theory of relativity in 1915. It is the closest thing we have to a general theory of the universe. In 1917, Einstein attempted to find a cosmological solution for his theory. The models that he proposed suggested that the universe was neither expanding nor contracting, but static. According to David Berlinski, cosmologists tend to overlook this.[100] A few months after Einstein discovered possible solutions to his field equation, Willem de Sitter discovered another. In de Sitter's universe, there was no matter, just radiation filling space.[101]

In 1922, Alexander Friedmann, a Russian meteorologist and mathematician, produced possible solutions to Einstein's field equations that suggested a non-static universe. The Belgian astrophysicist George Lemaître (1894-1966) published a model in 1927 that indicated an expanding universe.

---

[96] "The Start of Scientific Cosmology," *Cosmic Journey: A History of Scientific Cosmology*, http://www.aip.org/history/cosmology/ideas/start-of-scientific-cosmology.htm.
[97] *Ibid.*
[98] "The Mechanical Universe," *Cosmic Journey: A History of Scientific Cosmology*, http://www.aip.org/history/cosmology/ideas/mechuniverse.htm.
[99] "From Our Galaxy to Island Universes," *Cosmic Journey: A History of Scientific Cosmology*, http://www.aip.org/ history/cosmology/ideas/island.htm.
[100] D. Berlinski, "Was There a Big Bang?" *Commentary*, 1998, Vol. 105, No. 2, p. 35.
[101] *Ibid.*

Figure 1: Sun and Orbiting Planets

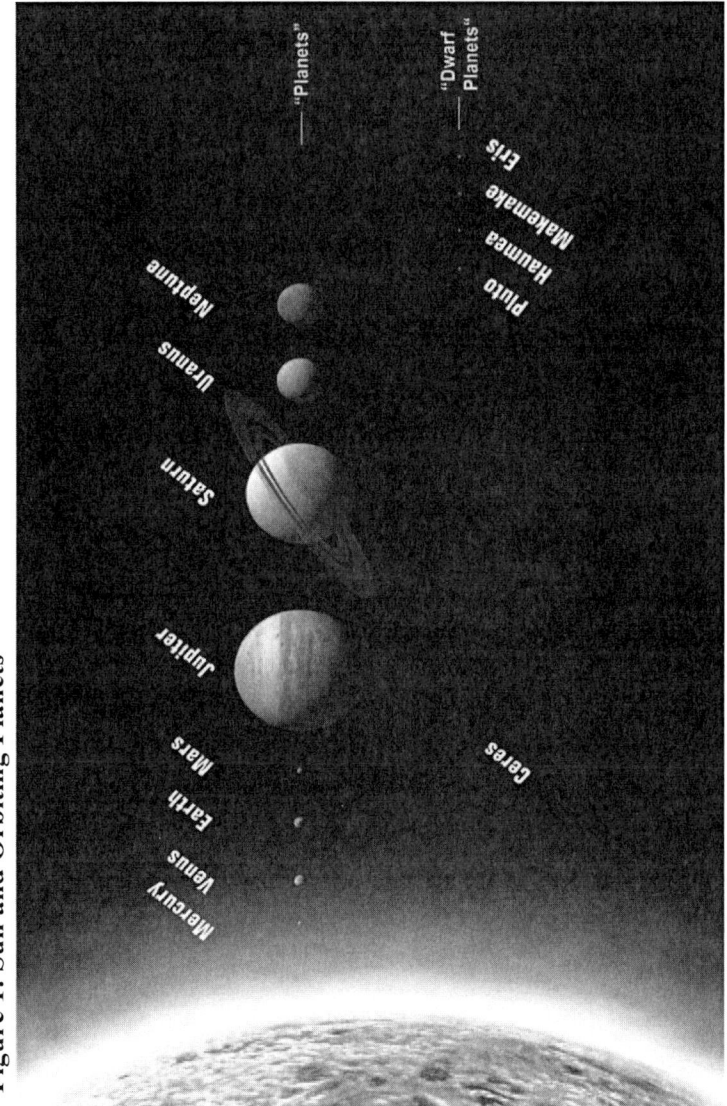

Source: Image by NASA, appears with modifications http://en.wikipedia.org/wiki/File:Planets2008.jpg

Figure 2: Spiral Galaxy (NGC 4414)

Source: Magnificent Details in a Dusty Spiral Galaxy: NASA Headquarters - Greatest Images of NASA (NASA-HQ-GRIN) http://nix.larc.nasa.gov/info;jsessionid=1sl2so6lc9mab?id=GPN-2000-000933&orgid=12

Note: The spiral galaxy in Figure 2 (named NGC 4414) was imaged by the Hubble Space Telescope in 1995. Its estimated distance from us is approximately 60 million light-years away – the equivalent of 600 million trillion kilometres – and there are still other galaxies that are further away. This is suggestive of the enormity of the known universe.

In 1931, when the value of his work was beginning to be recognised, Lemaître proposed what may be considered as the first version of the Big Bang theory of the origins of the universe. The universe, Lemaître argued, is the ashes and smoke of bright fireworks. The observation that the universe was expanding implied that other galaxies were all moving away from each other.[102]

Advances in nuclear physics helped to enable quantitative calculations to be made concerning the nature of the universe. Following on from Lemaître's 1930s "firework" theory, George Gamow (1904-1968) argued a decade later that the universe is a process of expansion and cooling that originated from a single point of infinite density and temperature. Electrons, protons and neutrons were believed to have collided in a sea of high energy radiation.

It was soon realised that elements heavier than helium and hydrogen could have been formed later inside stars. The notion that such elements were created in stellar interiors was viewed as supporting a rival theory to that of the Big Bang. This rival theory proposed that there was never a big bang and that the universe has always been as it is now. The theory of a steady state universe was supported by Fred Hoyle (1915-2001), Thomas Gold (1920-2004) and Hermann Bondi (1919-2004).[103]

The Big Bang theory, nevertheless, continued to dominate for the rest of the 20th century. It is thought to have all started with the so-called big bang, approximately 10-20 billion years ago.[104] Compressed space exploded, hurtling matter and energy in all directions. The smallest components of matter, quarks, began to group together in threes, forming both protons and neutrons, which then began to clump together to form the nuclei of hydrogen and helium, two of the lightest elements. As the temperature of the universe dropped, each cloud of hydrogen and helium became an individual galaxy of stars, formed by the collision of these elements, held together by gravity.[105]

---

[102] "The Expanding Universe;" *Cosmic Journey: A History of Scientific Cosmology*, http://www.aip.org/history/cosmology/ideas/expanding.htm.
[103] "Big Bang or Steady State?" *Cosmic Journey; A History of Scientific Cosmology*, http://www.aip.org/history/cosmology/ideas/bigbang.htm.
[104] *Ibid.*
[105] Stokes Brown, *op. cit.*, note 81, pp. 4-5, 8.

The nearest star and the one we know best is the Sun, which is composed of burning hydrogen. Cynthia Stokes Brown provides us with a sobering thought:

> When its hydrogen is used up, in about 5 billion years, our sun will switch to burning helium, called helium fusion. Since helium fusion is a hotter process with greater energy output, the pressure from the extra energy will expand the sun until it becomes what is called a red giant. When the helium fuel is used up, the red giant will collapse to a white dwarf. Then it will slowly cool until it becomes a cinder called a black dwarf.[106]

Heavier large-scale structures were created inside stars and dispersed by supernova explosions.[107]

The Big Bang theory is supported by several pieces of evidence. In 1929, Edwin Powell Hubble's (1889-1953) observations of the expanding universe suggested a large amount of light elements, such as hydrogen and helium. Furthermore, in 1965 Arno Penzias (b. 1933) and Robert Wilson (b. 1936), from Bell Laboratories in New Jersey, observed that 2.7K microwave background radiation was consistent with the Big Bang theory.[108] Their discovery was made by accident while they were carrying out work on satellite communications. They detected a constant low-noise signal that had no identifiable source. At the same time, astronomers at Princeton University, working in a team directed by Robert Dicke (1916-1997), were undertaking work on the early universe. Dicke realised that the noise picked up by Penzias and Wilson was in line with radiation that would have been present just after the Big Bang. This radiation was believed to be a remnant of the initial explosion that created the universe.[109] More recent satellite data supports this observation. The Big Bang theory, however, fails to explain the cause of the Big Bang itself.[110]

---

[106] Ibid., p. 9.
[107] "Big Bang," in K.A. McGrath (ed.) *World of Physics* (Detroit: Thomson Gale, 2008), Science Resource Center, http://galenet.galegroup.com.library3.webster.edu/servlet/SciRC?ste=1&docNum=CV2434500037>.
[108] Ibid.
[109] C. Fraser, "Astronomy and Cosmology: Twentieth Century," in B.S. Baigrie (ed.) *History of Modern Science and Mathematics* (New York: Charles Scribner's Sons, 2008), Science Resource Center, http://galenet.galegroup.com.library3.webster.edu/servlet/SciRC?ste=1&docNum=CV2640700010.
[110] McGrath, *op. cit.*, note 107.

David Christian suggests a compressed timeline of the universe that helps to situate humankind in the broader history of the universe (see Table 2).

Table 2: A Compressed Timeline of the History of the Universe

If the universe had been created 13 years ago . . .

The Earth would be five years old

Large organisms with many cells would have existed for seven months

The asteroids that brought about the extinction of the dinosaurs would have hit Earth three weeks ago

Hominids would have existed for 3 days

Homo sapiens would have existed for only 53 minutes

Agricultural societies would have emerged 5 minutes ago

The recorded history of civilisation would have begun 3 minutes ago

Industrial societies would have existed for 6 seconds

Source: D. Christian, "World History in Context," in C. Stokes Brown, *Big History: From the Big Bang to the Present* (New York: The New Press, 2007), p. 39.

The desire to understand the connection between the patterning of human life and the universe has motivated scientists and astronomers, and has also inspired religions and spiritual systems, for example, through myths and symbolism. As Mary Evelyn Tucker points out, these deep patterns go by different names in different religions and belief systems: in Buddhism and Hinduism it is called Dharma, meaning law; in Confucianism it is li, understood as principle; in Daoism it is called Dao (Tao) or "the way"; in Judaism it is known as seder bereishit, or order of creation; in Islam it is shari'a or law; in Christianity it appears as logos or "the word"; and in aboriginal belief systems it is known differently. For example, Native American Algonguins call it Manitou or "spirit presence". These may all be understood as efforts to link inner meaning with the forces of nature and the universe.

In contrast to science, religious and belief systems employ an understanding of the universe not simply to explain how things are, but to express how things *ought* to be. Religious or spiritual cosmologies are embedded in metaphysics and ethics so that they may help to give moral direction to life.[111] Buddhist cosmology, for example, envisages planes of spiritual existence and an infinite number of universes.

2. Life on Earth

Plato put forward the idea that what is not perceivable by our senses is not real, but rather an imperfect replica of an immutable form in a transcendent world. Religious scholars similarly believe that the world was created according to God's plan and what we are able to perceive are variants of this ideal. Aristotle believed that nature was driven by a purpose or function. In this view, form is dictated by function. This perspective was compatible with the religious view of Special Creationism, which contends that an omnipresent Creator that stands outside of nature created the universe at one point in time. God is also believed to have created the stars, the planets and the galaxies.[112] However, biological evolution and modern science have posed a challenge to this understanding of Creation and life on Earth. Indeed, the debate between evolution and creationism goes back several centuries. The central controversy is related to what happened in terms of creation.

Evolutionary Theory

Although Charles Darwin (1809-1882) is the principal figure associated with evolutionary theory, he was not in fact the first to recognise the possibility of species change. The notion of a dynamic universe was present in Ancient Greek thought, albeit in rudimentary form. However, the notion of a static universe espoused by Aristotle and his

---

[111] M.E. Tucker, "Worldviews and Ecology," in H. Selin (ed.) *Nature Across Cultures: Views of Nature and the Environment in Western Culture* (Boston, MA: Kluwer Academic Publishers, 2003), pp. 118-119.

[112] E.C. Scott, *Evolution vs. Creationism: An Introduction*, Foreword by Niles Eldredge (Wesport, CT: Greenwood Press, 2004), pp. 73-74.

medieval and Renaissance followers became predominant. The static view of the universe held that a number of different organisms were created at some point and remained unaltered. Species were conceptually organised in a "scala naturae" or "ladder of creation", with less complex organisms at the bottom and more complex ones closer to the top. The metaphor of the ladder of creation became displaced by the idea of a "great chain of being".[113]

However, early theories of evolution were put forward in the Middle Ages by a number of Arab-Islamic scholars, namely Al-Jahiz (781-868/9), the Ikhwăn Al-Safă' or "Brethren of Purity" and Al-Khazini (900-971).[114] In Europe, during the Enlightenment era, the notion of species change began to gain ground. This shift in paradigm was accompanied by the establishment of the scientific discipline of geology, which suggested that fossils were once living organisms. Comte de Buffon (1707-1788) questioned the notion of a static universe. He suggested a theory of species change or transmutation that resembled the one that Darwin would later propose, but his ideas were rejected. Another Frenchman, Jean-Baptiste Lamarck (1744-1829), put forward a theory of species transmutation that was prompted by his interest in how species adapted morphologically and physiologically to their environment. Nevertheless, he failed to provide a way of explaining how physical transformation took place. He attempted to explain structural transformation by drawing on contemporary theories that suggested that species modification occurred due to rises in temperature produced by physical exertion, which could not explain hereditability. Subsequently, Robert Chambers (1802-1871) set out a theory of species change that generated such fierce criticism that it persuaded Darwin to wait to publish his own thoughts for some 15 years.[115]

Darwin's theory was, thus, some time in the making.[116] While the captain's companion on *HMS Beagle*, Darwin became the ship's naturalist, collecting and shipping home birds, plants and fossils. The variations within species that he found prompted him to think about

---

[113] V.B. Smocovitis, "History of Evolutionary Thought," in R. Robinson (ed.) *Biology* (New York: Macmillan Reference USA, 2002), http://galenet.galegroup.com.library3.webster.edu/servlet/SciRC?ste=1&docNum =CV2642150187.
[114] "History of Evolutionary Thought," AbsoluteAstronomy.com, http://www.absoluteastronomy.com/topics/History_of_evolutionary_thought.
[115] Smocovitis, *op. cit.*, note 113.
[116] *Ibid.*

evolution. In 1838, he posited that the mechanism that explained variation within evolution was the process of natural selection driven by the need to survive and reproduce. Darwin did, however, accept the notion of an omnipresent designer that worked through the process of natural selection. Darwin was only prompted to publish his theory of evolution by natural selection when a Welsh-born naturalist, Alfred Russel Wallace, sent him an essay in 1858 detailing almost the exact same process of evolution.[117]

In *On the Origin of Species* (1859), Darwin made two central claims: that living things had evolved from a common ancestor with variations; and that this evolutionary process occurred through natural selection.[118] Natural selection is based on the idea that all species exhibit variation in both behavioural and psychological characteristics. Natural selection is premised on this very idea of variation. Part of this variation is transmitted. Those genetic differences that make an organism more successful in its environment are those that give it an edge over others.[119] In 1871, Darwin published *The Descent of Man* in which he applied his evolutionary theory to human evolution.[120]

However, Darwin's Theory of Natural Selection was based on differences in phenotype. There was, thus, no description of a mechanism of inheritance. Moreover, an additional problem was presented by the supposed age of the Earth. At the time, the Earth was believed to be just 400 million years old, which did not allow for enough time for the gradual process of variation that Darwin described to take place. This would not be resolved until radioactivity was discovered in the late 19th century, which suggested that the age of the Earth was closer to 5 billion years old. This new estimation would have left enough time for Darwin's notion of evolution to occur.[121]

In addition to the mystery surrounding the heredity mechanism and the age of the Earth, Darwinian evolutionary theory also provoked considerable criticism at the time of publication due to its implications for theological and philosophical beliefs about the origins

---

[117] M. Ruse, *The Evolution-Creation Struggle* (Cambridge, Mass.: Harvard University Press, 2005), pp. 67, 69-70, 72.
[118] Scott, *op. cit.*, note 112, p. xxii.
[119] N.R.F. Al-Rodhan, *"emotional amoral egoism": A Neurophilosophical Theory of Human Nature and Its Universal Security Implications* (Berlin: LIT, 2008), pp. 93, 95, 97.
[120] C. Darwin, *The Descent of Man* (1871).
[121] Smocovitis, *op. cit.*, note 113.

of species. Natural selection put forward an explanation of species change that did not involve divine intervention. It therefore called into question one of the foundational arguments for the existence of God.[122]

The problem of heredity would only be solved with the emergence of modern science. We now know that modifications of phenotype are produced by genetic traits and the environment. Alterations in phenotype are the result of genetic mutations caused by a change in DNA or the genetic code.[123] Mutations occur as a result of changes in the set of genes, which alters the instructions given for the creation of a particular organism. Those organisms that are able to replicate themselves the most are likely to have some advantage due to the mutation behind their composition. This is essentially Darwin's notion of natural selection through random mutation. Evolution may, however, also take place by replication of a simple strand of DNA and dividing, with a strand of DNA contained in every new cell. Finally, it may occur through symbiogenesis, which takes place when a symbiotic relationship between two organisms becomes permanent.[124]

Modern science suggests that life on Earth began in the seas and oceans. According to scientists, it is likely that the genetic molecules formed in the Earth's oceans three to four thousand million years ago at some time formed a replicator molecule – a molecule that possessed the peculiar capacity of replicating itself. However, mistakes in the copying process occurred. These mistakes created variations among replicas, some of which were more stable than others. Varieties of replicator molecules would have been in competition for building block molecules. Those better able to compete were able to build a protective wall of protein around them, thereby becoming the first cells.[125]

Where and when did *Homo sapiens* first appear? According to scientific theory, the apes that evolved into humans appeared in Africa 25 million years ago. Approximately 18 million years ago they also appeared in Asia and Europe but encountered difficulties in there regions and only thrived in eastern Africa, where the Rift Valley system

---

[122] *Ibid.*
[123] Al-Rodhan, *"emotional amoral egoism,"* *op. cit.*, note 119, p. 98.
[124] Stokes Brown, *op. cit.*, note 81, p. 20.
[125] *Ibid.*, p. 94.

provided a varied climate, tropical forests, woodlands and open savannah grasslands.[126]

The climate in this area is thought to have played an important role in the evolutionary transition from apes to humans. Great fluctuations in climate occurred. During the glacial era, the savannah entered into a dryer and cooler period. As a result, there would have been more grassland. Interglacial periods would have been characterised by a warmer and wetter climate. Coolness and dryness in the tropics in particular is thought to have been critical to the emergence of our species. Over the course of the past one million years the Earth has experienced approximately 10 ice ages caused by tiny modifications to the tilt of the Earth's axis, its orbit around the sun and its wobble on its axis.[127]

According to scientific theory, it is not known exactly when human beings emerged, but somewhere between five and seven million years ago a mutation in apes is believed to have occurred that eventually led to the appearance of hominids, leading later to *Homo sapiens*.[128] This evolution was, however, slow and unpredictable. Up to 20 species of bipedal apes existed at one point. The oldest type of bipedal apes are known as *Australopithicus*. Based on the remains of one of the most famous *Australopithicus*, "Lucy", a North African bipedal ape, great apes are believed to have come down from the trees and developed the capacity to stand upright *before* their brains increased in size. They are believed to have descended from the trees as food became scarcer as forests transformed into savannas. An upright position would have offered the advantage of seeing further into the distance when looking for food and freeing up hands and arms to carry infants and food. As their legs became stronger, their centre of gravity would have shifted allowing them greater balance when standing.[129]

Until half-a-million years ago several *Australopithici* existed simultaneously. At the same time, other species emerged. Approximately 2.5 million years ago, the Homo line began to develop. It first appeared as a small-boned ape with a larger brain. Some 2 million years ago, *Homo habilus* emerged, with a larger brain and greater

---

[126] *Ibid.*, pp. 33-34.
[127] *Ibid.*, pp. 41-42.
[128] *Ibid.*, p. 40.
[129] *Ibid.*, pp. 43-44.

height. Among the advantages of bigger brains were tool-making capacities and increased cooperation.

Homo erectus appeared about 1.8 million years ago. These were taller than *Homo habilus* and had a larger brain. *Homo erectus* made weapons, such as spears and axes, hunted large game and possessed the capacity for primitive speech. Hunting would have required a greater degree of social cooperation. Conjugal bonds between men and women are also thought to have developed at this stage. The knowledge of how to use fire enabled them to eat a greater variety of foods and would eventually enable *Homo erectus* to move out of the warm planes of Africa.[130]

This evolution from bipedal apes to Hominids took place only in eastern Africa. Between 1 and 1.8 million years ago, *Homo erectus* started to leave Africa, spreading out over the globe. Approximately 100,000 to 200,000 years later, another group, which had evolved into *Homo sapiens* also left eastern Africa and started to inhabit other areas of the Earth. *Homo erectus*, however, became extinct.[131]

One theory claims that *Homo sapiens* evolved independently at the same time in different parts of the world. This is referred to as the Candelabra Theory – each branch of the candelabra is like a branch of human development. A second theory, which Stokes Brown adheres to, affirms that modern human beings spread out from Africa. This hypothesis is called The Noah's Ark, Out of Africa or Garden of Eden Theory. The Candelabra Theory enjoyed popularity when fossil specimens were found in Europe, the Near East and Asia. However, when fossils began to be discovered in Africa in the 1970s, the Out of Africa theory became dominant.[132]

The latter theory is supported by evidence from molecular genetics, which suggests that all human beings have common ancestors who lived in Africa some 100,000 to 200,000 years ago. This group populated the whole of sub-Saharan Africa. Then one population crossed the Levant approximately 70,000 years ago and, over the next 30,000 years, crossed Eurasia and travelled to Australia, finally reaching the Bering Straits and spreading into the Americas some 15,000 years ago.

---

[130] *Ibid.*
[131] *Ibid.*, p. 40.
[132] *Ibid.*, p. 54.

There are several implications of the Out of Africa hypothesis. First, it means that human beings are not direct descendants of the Neanderthals of Europe and western Asia. Second, it implies that all human beings have the same ancestors and could not have evolved out of different populations of *Homo erectus*. Third, the rapidity with which early humans spread across the globe suggests a tremendous adaptability, considering the environmental and geographic challenges they must have faced when crossing and settling new lands so different from those which their evolutionary heritage in Africa would have prepared them for.[133]

Creationism

Scientific findings have posed a challenge to religious explanations of the Creation. Creationism has a broad definition. In general, creationism holds that a supernatural force is responsible for the Creation. Within the three Abrahamic religions, this force is believed to be God, whereas in other religions it is thought to be other deities.[134] These religions reject the Big Bang theory of the creation of the universe. They also reject one of Darwin's two central hypotheses: that all living things evolved from one common ancestry. While evolution on the basis of some modification may have occurred within similar "kinds" (something higher than species),[135] the notion of common descent is also rejected by biblical "special creationism".[136] Old Earth Creationists see God as the supernatural force behind creation. While they accept most of the scientific arguments about creation, they nevertheless reject the biological foundations of evolution.

Intelligent Design Creationism (IDC) is the newest form of creationism, which posits that the order and design found in the world is proof of a larger design. IDC follows on from William Paley's *Argument from Design* (1803), in which he used the analogy of the watch. If one were to find a watch and to examine it one would discover that it was produced by a watchmaker and was conceived with a

---

[133] L. Barret, R. Dunbar and J. Lycett, *Human Evolutionary Psychology* (Basingstoke: Palgrave, 2002), pp. 16-17, Box. 1.
[134] Scott, *op. cit.*, note 112, p. 51
[135] *Ibid.*, p. 60.
[136] *Ibid.*, p. 81.

specific purpose in mind. This view is in opposition to Darwin's mechanism of natural selection.[137]

Hinduism and Buddhism
Hinduism supports the notion of evolution, although not in the same way as science. Moreover, given that these spiritual systems do not believe in a creator God, they do not contain notions of creation. Rather than focusing on the physical evolution of life on Earth, Hinduism emphasises the mental and spiritual evolution of life on Earth. It is based on a transition from an initial stage of ignorance to a stage of illumination. This evolution is believed to progress in three stages. In the initial phase of ignorance bodies are believed to be driven by the unconscious – driven purely by impulse and instinct. In the second phase, individual egos are thought to gain greater concretization, largely driven by desires and survival instincts, experiencing repeated deaths and births. In the third and final stage, ego dissolves into truth, consciousness and serenity. Thus, in Hinduism, evolution is a result of individual effort and will. Within a broader universe, there are different planes of consciousness. Nature determines the evolution of human beings only in so far as they let it, which is quite distinct from evolutionary theory.[138] Buddhism envisages a spiritual evolution through three initial phases of "desire", "form" and "formlessness", and then beyond these three stages Nirvana or enlightenment. Movement from one plane to the next is driven by the search for perfection and transcendence.[139]

3. Conclusion

In an effort to comprehend human time, which is essential to understanding what drives history and therefore how to achieve a sustainable approach to history, this chapter outlined the major responses to the question of where we are. Early written records show that the people of ancient civilisations sought to understand the universe through mythology. Later, mathematicians and astronomers developed models

---

[137] *Ibid.*, pp. 61-63.
[138] J. V., "Hinduism and Evolution of Life and Consciousness," Hinduwebsite.com, last Updated 27 February 2009, http://www.hinduwebsite. com/evolution.asp.
[139] Y. Zhuo, "Buddhist Cosmology," *Newsfinder*, 26 September 2008, http://www. newsfinder.org/site/more/buddhist_ cosmology/.

of the universe that culminated in modern scientific cosmology. Religious and spiritual cosmologies have sought not only to comprehend the universe, but also to understand our place in it and to give guidance on how humankind is related to it. Different ways of "seeing" where we are have an impact on views of our origins. This, in turn, affects how we understand human nature, as is demonstrated in Chapter 3.

CHAPTER 3

WHO ARE WE?
NEUROCHEMICAL MAN AND
EMOTIONAL AMORAL EGOISM

Having examined the issue of where we are, let us now consider the question of who we are, i.e. human nature. Looking at the question of human nature is important, because it is a central driver of human thought and behaviour and therefore of history. There is no shortage of answers to this question, all of which depend on some notion of human nature. Debates about human nature centre on whether we, as human beings, are "good" or "bad", rationally or emotionally driven, egoistic or altruistic and endowed with free will or predisposed to behave in a certain way. How we answer these questions also shapes our view of morality. This chapter explores the various perspectives on human nature: religious, spiritual, philosophical, psychological and evolutionary. It then outlines my own theory of human nature, *emotional amoral egoism*, which is set out in more detail in "*emotional amoral egoism": A Neurophilosophical Theory of Human Nature and its Universal Security Implications* (2008). In the view of human nature offered in that volume, the human mind is not conceived as a tabula rasa or clean slate. We are influenced not simply by our environment but also by our genetic make-up, which primes us for survival. This does not mean that we ought to succumb to determinism. This code for survival is emotionally based and mediated through neurochemistry. We essentially do what is gratifying. Since neurochemistry is alterable, so too is human nature to a large extent, which makes the environment a significant factor shaping psyche and behaviour. Reason, reflection and conscious moral behaviour are relatively rare, despite what we might like to think. This does not mean that humankind is immoral, however, but that the direction in which its moral compass points will depend on circumstances.[140]

---

[140] Al-Rodhan, *"emotional amoral egoism," op. cit.*, note 119.

1. Approaches to Human Nature[141]

Ancient Greek philosophy and Hebrew-Christian views of the Bible, and particularly the Old Testament, have heavily influenced Western views of human nature. In both instances, human beings are understood as rational beings possessing free will. Philosophical views of human nature vary. However, it is possible to categorise different views into a number of debates: perfection through reason versus constraint by emotions, nature versus nurture and innate morality versus radical freedom to choose one's own personal truth. Psychology tends to emphasise the extent to which people are emotional rather than rational beings, particularly those strands which draw on evolutionary theory. This is, of course, even more pronounced in sociobiology, which explicitly attributes human psyche and behaviour to selection pressure and subsequent evolution. Approaches to human nature based on increased knowledge of the evolutionary and genetic factors that are believed to help shape who we are raise profound questions for some religious belief systems, given that they touch on notions of the Creation.[142]

Religious and Spiritual Belief Systems
In Abrahamic religions – Islam, Christianity and Judaism – human beings are believed to be endowed with reason and free will. In Christianity, humankind is believed to be inherently good, free and responsible. Being created in God's image, humans occupy a special and privileged place in relation to other species. To this end, human beings are not simply one part of an interconnected universe as Hinduism, for example, suggests. That said, all of humanity is believed to be in a state of sin, alienated from God. Adam's sin is thought to have become that of the whole of humankind.[143] Some Christians hold to the doctrine of original sin, in which human beings are believed to be

---

[141] For an overview of the approaches discussed in this chapter and their relation to one another, see Al-Rodhan, *"emotional amoral egoism,"* op. cit., note 119, especially Table 1, pp. 141-145.
[142] R.J. Berry and M. Jeeves, "The Nature of Human Nature," *Science and Christian Belief*, Vol. 20, No. 1, 2008, p. 3.
[143] L. Stevenson and D.L. Haberman, *Ten Theories of Human Nature* (New York: Oxford University Press, 2004), p. 63.

born sinful and to lack the free will with which to redeem themselves.[144]

Like Christians, Jews believe that human beings are made in God's image and, as such, have the capacity for reason. Humankind is thought to be motivated by both moral conscience and the desire to satisfy inner needs and desires. However, the doctrine of original sin is rejected.[145] As in Christianity and Judaism, in Islam human beings are believed to have the free will with which to choose to submit to Allah,[146] but there is also no notion of original sin in Islam.

In polytheistic and animistic belief systems, human beings are not thought to be a species set apart from other spiritual and mythical beings. Rather than being saved from sin, people are believed in two major polytheistic religions – Buddhism and Hinduism – to be in need of liberation from suffering caused by desires that can never be satisfied. As is discussed in Chapter 2, in Hinduism, as in Buddhism evolution is conceived as the movement towards enlightenment through the will to overcome suffering and ignorance.[147] Animism, which is still practiced by some native and aboriginal communities, sees no separation between body and soul. Some sort of purpose is believed to be achievable through harmony with all other living things.[148]

Philosophical Belief Systems
There are those who believe that there is a particular teleology or logical end point to human development. In this view, human beings are perfectible. Within this approach to human nature, a person can perfect his or her nature by employing reason. Aristotle, for instance, believed that human existence has a purpose and that is to put the human capacity for reason to use in the pursuit of a virtuous life. Aris-

---

[144] Religion Facts, www.religionfacts.com, s.v. "Christian Beliefs about Human Nature."
[145] Religion Facts, www.religionfacts.com, s.v. "Jewish Beliefs about Human Nature."
[146] Religion Facts, www.religionfacts.com, s.v. "Islamic Beliefs about Human Nature."
[147] L.P. Pojman, *Who Are We: Theories of Human Nature* (New York: Oxford University Press, 2006), pp. 88, 90-91, 94-98; R.P. Hayes, "Buddhist Philosophy, Indian," in E. Craig (ed.) *Routledge Encyclopedia of Philosophy* (London: Routledge, 1998), http://www.rep.routledge.com.library3.webster.edu/article/F001SECT.
[148] S. Wenner, "Basic Beliefs of Animism," MSU EMuseum, Minnesota State University, Mankato, 2007, http://www.mnsu.edu/emuseum/cultural/religion/animism/beliefs.html.

totle, however, was hardly a believer in equality. Not everyone was deemed equally capable of fulfilling this function and, therefore, people were not believed to have the same worth. A virtuous life is believed to be achieved through moderation by self-perfection using reason to overcome desire.[149]

By contrast, there are views which hold that human beings are constrained by emotions and that reason is not in the full possession of humankind – there are limits to our capacity to reach a higher state of being. Jeremy Bentham (1748-1832), for instance, argued that human beings are motivated by pleasure and pain. Whether something is judged good or bad is believed to depend on the amount of pleasure or pain it causes. The greatest happiness for the greatest number is thought to be attainable if the correct framework is put in place to guide people's behaviour.[150]

Thomas Hobbes (1588-1679) subscribed to the nature side of the nature-nurture debate. In a Hobbesian worldview, human beings are driven by the fear of death and the desire for self-preservation. Human beings are believed to be egoistic. Selfish desires are thought to be rooted in insecurity – in a state of nature, with no overarching authority structure to guarantee their security, people of similar physical and mental capacities can pose an equal threat to each other's survival. Free will, in this perspective, does not have any great significance. As a result, human nature is not malleable, but unchanging.[151] To the extent that it exists, moral behaviour is believed to stem from self-interest. Seemingly altruistic acts are therefore ***pseudo-altruistic*** rather than truly selfless.[152]

In contrast, on the nurture side of the debate there are those who believe that human nature can be modified. John Locke (1632-1704), for example, argued that the human mind was a tabula rasa or clean slate. In his view, human beings are born with no innate ideas.[153] He was a critic of dogmatism. Our ideas, he argued, are formed by

---

[149] Pojman, *op. cit.*, note 147, pp. xiv, 68-69.
[150] T. Fuller, "Jeremy Bentham and James Mill," in L. Strauss and J. Cropsey (eds.) *History of Political Philosophy*, Third Edition (Chicago: The University of Chicago Press, 1987), p. 714.
[151] T. Hobbes, *Leviathan* (1651); Pojman, *op. cit.*, note 147, pp. 105-107, 111-117.
[152] Al-Rodhan, *"emotional amoral egoism,"* *op. cit.*, note 119, p. 40.
[153] J. Locke, *An Essay Concerning Human Understanding*, with the Notes and Illustrations of the Author and An Analysis of His Doctrine of Ideas, Thirtieth Edition (London: William Tegg & Co., 1849), p. 10

two phenomena: sensation and perception. All ideas are therefore derived from experience, which implies that knowledge cannot exist prior to experience. Locke was one of the founding figures of empiricism.[154] Thus, in this perspective, experience and a person's environment are attributed great importance in explaining human psyche and behaviour. Culture and education are believed to play a central role in shaping the individual.[155]

Locke acknowledged that desire for one's own happiness or pleasure motivated people, although he believed that reason could prevail. On the basis of rational calculation, humankind is thought to engage in behaviour that is likely to secure the maximum degree of pleasure. In terms of morality, Locke nevertheless believed that the prudent pleasure-seeking individual would choose virtuous behaviour. This, however, depends on the individual acting on the basis of long-term interests.[156]

The emotions–reason dualism informs various views on moral behaviour. Plato held a dualist conception of human nature. In his view, the soul or mind was thought to be separate from the material body.[157] He contended that the soul was composed of an intellectual, a rational and an appetitive part. Human beings are thus driven by a combination of rationality and desires. Justice is believed to prevail when rationality is able to check desire. Plato was unclear about whether people have a sufficient degree of free will with which to modify their nature without the help of an institutional framework. He did, however, attribute a role to the environment in shaping the human mind and behaviour, and education was thought particularly important.[158]

Some go beyond this dualism, arguing that human beings have an innate morality that precedes both emotions and reason. John Rawls (1921-2002) argued that people have an innate moral awareness. Morality is thought to be derived from this pre-existing sense of fairness and good, rather than as the result of emotions or rational

---

[154] B. Russell, *History of Western Philosophy* (London: Routledge, 2006), p. 556.
[155] Al-Rodhan, *"emotional amoral egoism," op. cit.*, note 119, p. 41.
[156] J. Seigel, *The Idea of the Self: Thought and Experience in Western Europe since the Seventeenth Century* (Cambridge: Cambridge University Press, 2005), pp. 90-92; Russell, *op. cit.*, note 154, pp. 559-560.
[157] Plato, *The Republic*, Book 10, Edited by T. Griffith and Translated by G.R.F. Ferrari (Cambridge: Cambridge University Press, 2000).
[158] Stevenson and Haberman, *op. cit.*, note 143, pp. 77-79, 82-83.

calculation. In 1999, he published *A Theory of Justice as Fairness* in which he suggested that people possess an innate morality. In his discussion of justice as fairness, he employs a hypothetical situation to demonstrate people's unconscious principles. He asks us to imagine what kind of society we would like to live in if we had no prior knowledge of our status in that society – this he terms the "veil of ignorance". Individuals are most likely to opt to live in a just – understood as fair – society. To this end, even self-interested individuals have a natural sense of fairness.[159]

In existentialist thinking, human beings are radically free to choose who they are. Through self-examination people are believed capable of constructing their own life philosophies. There is no "true" or transcendental self awaiting discovery.[160] We have to decide for ourselves who we are and how we wish to live. In the religious strand of existentialism, God is thought to be there to guide people in their search for personal truth.[161] Thus, in general, three major concerns are identifiable in existentialist writing. First, universal laws governing claims about human nature are rejected and, instead, the uniqueness of the individual is stressed. Second, subjective "truth" is privileged over objective truth. Finally, the idea that we must find our own meaning in life is paramount, although in religious versions of existentialism God is thought to act as a beacon.[162]

Psychological Approaches to Human Nature
Psychological approaches to human nature tend to challenge the notion that we are primarily rational beings. Some psychologists have focused on human needs and desires. Sigmund Freud's (1856-1939) approach to human motivation was considered revolutionary within the discipline of psychology. His pan-sexuality and psychoanalysis were premised on the assumption that the human psyche and human behaviour are largely shaped by sexual desires. His psychology was thus highly materialist.[163] In his structural theory of the mind, the so-called id is the part of the mind that is associated with basic survival

---

[159] See J. Rawls, *A Theory of Justice*, Revised Edition (Oxford: Oxford University Press, 1999).
[160] G. Marino, "Introduction," in G. Marino (ed.) *Basic Writings of Existentialism* (New York: The Modern Library, 2004), p. xiv.
[161] Pojman, *op. cit.*, note 147, pp. 157, 160.
[162] Al-Rodhan, *"emotional amoral egoism,"* *op. cit.*, note 119, p. 46.
[163] Stevenson and Haberman, *op. cit.*, note 143, pp. 157, 161.

needs that require immediate satisfaction. The ego is connected to conscious mental states that inform our behaviour. To the id and the ego is added the superego, which determines the part of the mind that makes moral judgements.[164]

In contrast to Freud, B.F. Skinner (1904-1990), a behavioural psychologist, was concerned with observable behaviour, which he believed was shaped by the environment. He developed a radical behaviourism in which social context was given a paramount role in explaining human behaviour. Although he did leave a role for genetic heritage,[165] human behaviour was thought to be malleable enough to be influenced by the environment.[166]

In an effort to take account of the whole range of human existence, Maslow's humanistic psychology aimed to explain behaviour as a result of different hierarchically organised human needs. At the lower end of the scale are basic physiological needs, such as food shelter and sleep. When these basic survival needs have been met, security concerns are thought to preoccupy human beings. As basic needs and security are satisfied, higher functions, such a love, reputation and belonging, also start to motivate human beings. When all of these aspects of life are taken care of, people can focus on self-actualisation.[167]

Evolutionary thought in psychology attempts to understand the human psyche and behaviour according to the group selection approach, which has now lost favour to gene-centric approaches to natural selection. Konrad Lorenz (1903-1989) put forward the particularly controversial idea that human beings have inherited an "aggressive gene". In other words, evolutionary adaptation has resulted in the creation of a gene that predisposes human beings to aggressive behaviour. It is selected probably because it helps to eliminate rivals to sex-

---

[164] S. Freud, *The Ego and the Id* (London: Blackwell Publishing, 2003), p. xvii.
[165] R.H. Blank, "Neuroscience, Free Will, and Individual Responsibility: Implications for Addictive Behaviour," in A. Somit and S. Peterson (eds.) *Human Nature and Public Policy: An Evolutionary Approach* (New York: Palgrave Macmillan, 2003), p. 59; B.F. Skinner, "The Behaviour of Organisms At Fifty," in J.T. Todd and E.K. Morris (eds.), Forward by E.R. Hilgard, *Modern Perspectives on B.F. Skinner and Contemporary Behaviourism*, Contributions to Psychology, No. 28 (Wesport, Connecticut: Greenwood Press, 1995), p. 159.
[166] N. Sheehy, *Fifty Key Thinkers in Psychology* (London: Routledge, 2003), p. 206.
[167] R.J. Zalenski and R. Raspa, "Maslow's Hierarchy of Human Needs: A Framework for Achieving Human Potential in Hospice," *Journal of Palliative Medicine*, Vol. 9, No. 5, 2006, p. 1121.

ual partners and encourages individuals to disperse over wider areas of terrain, thereby reducing the pressure on scarce resources.[168]

Evolutionary Approaches to Human Nature
Sociobiologists and evolutionary psychologists present more explicitly evolutionary approaches to human nature. Sociobiologists start from the assumption that all social behaviour has biological origins. A central idea in sociobiology is that we have inherited particular traits because they increased our ancestors' chances of survival and reproductive success. The most prominent proponent and pioneer of sociobiology is E.O. Wilson. He argued that natural selection drives human behaviour, and that radical free will is an illusion.[169] From the standpoint of sociobiology, morality is something that we have developed from common core moral sensitivities that have ultimately helped human beings to be successful in their environment.

Evolutionary psychology seeks to explain universal psychological characteristics, such as emotions, seemingly moral behaviour and communication. Marc Hauser argues that we have a "common moral grammar" that we are born with. Morality, he argues, is not a function of culture; it is prior to culture. From this baseline, specific moral systems may be built. However, in Hauser's view, this common moral grammar originates neither from emotions nor from reason. This is not to say that emotions and reason play no role in shaping moral behaviour; they are simply not causal. Instead, an innate moral sense is at the source of moral behaviour. This supports a Rawlsian conception of morality.[170]

Frans de Waal similarly examines the biological roots of morality and concludes that moral values are the result of selection pressure. To make his argument, he draws on his observations of primates. He claims that living in groups has favoured cooperative tendencies.[171]

---

[168] J.D. Singer, "Genetic and Cultural Evolution: Implications for International Security Policies," in A. Somit and S. Peterson (eds.) *Human Nature and Public Policy: An Evolutionary Approach* (New York: Palgrave Macmillan, 2003), pp. 244-245; Stevenson and Haberman, *op. cit.*, note 143, p. 227.

[169] E.O. Wilson, *Sociobiology: The New Synthesis* (Cambridge, Mass.: Harvard University Press, 1975).

[170] M.D. Hauser, *Moral Minds: How Nature Designed Our Universal Sense of Right and Wrong* (New York: HarperCollins, 2006), p. 222.

[171] F. de Waal, *Primates and Philosophers: How Morality Evolved* (Princeton: Princeton University Press, 2006), p. 4.

In contrast to Hauser, however, he argues that morality is likely to be emotionally driven.[172] Even though evolution may have favoured self-interested behaviour, this does not have to mean that altruistic behaviour is impossible. Indeed, kin selection and reciprocal altruism are believed to make altruism possible.[173] In-group solidarity may have been needed to coordinate responses to danger and to find food, for example, which, in turn, is likely to have provided the building blocks on which more elaborate forms of morality could be constructed. Thus, while human beings may have a considerable capacity for egoistic behaviour, they are also capable of cooperation.[174]

In sum, the question of who we are has been answered in a number of ways. Religious and spiritual approaches to human nature vary greatly. The monotheistic Abrahamic religions conceive of humankind as made in God's image. Human beings are therefore necessarily good, although often inclined to sin. Individual salvation is thought to be achieved through union with God. Philosophical perspectives on human nature have tended to fall on either side of the nature-nurture debate, with some going beyond it. Thus, some philosophical figures emphasise the power that emotions have on human psyche and behaviour, while others stress the capacity that human beings have for reason and that they are malleable. In the extreme, freedom to shape human nature reaches its apex in existentialism. Rationality, by contrast, is rejected by key figures in psychology. Here, unconscious and innate needs take on greater importance in determining human thought and action. Finally, evolutionary perspectives on human nature view our genetic heritage as a paramount factor in explaining what drives human beings.

---

[172] *Ibid.*, p. 57.
[173] *Ibid.*, pp. 14, 16.
[174] *Ibid.*, pp. 23, 25.

2. Emotional Amoral Egoism

In *"emotional amoral egoism"*, I put forward a synthetic view of human nature, which is depicted in Diagram 4. Human beings are largely emotionally driven. At the most fundamental level, our motivations are rooted in our biological heritage, evolved over thousands of years, which reflect the conditions under which our ancestors had to survive.[175] These emotions have been inherited through the process of natural selection. Fear, for example, is likely to have helped early humans to be alert to danger, to live longer lives and to go on to reproduce. Love may have helped us to form the bonds required during a relatively long childrearing period, and to form family and group solidarity, which are also vital for survival in a harsh environment. In general, the strongest drivers of human nature – fear, pain, grief, pleasure, ego needs and greed – are connected to self-interest. Only occasionally are we motivated by conscious reason and moral judgements.[176] The gamut of human motivations and their consequences are shown in greater detail in Diagram 5.

Expressions of emotion are the same across cultures. Rather than being learned, they are part of our genetic make-up. Darwin put forward a theory of emotions. At the heart of his theory was the idea that emotions are innate and universal, and that the way in which we express what we are feeling is therefore due to our genetic heritage. Quite remarkably, Darwin's theory would not have been radically altered by the findings of neuroscience. He hypothesised that emotions are generated by a functional process, act to satisfy a desire and become habitual due to repetition. They were thought to come from the nervous system. Since Darwin's time, neuroscience has furthered our knowledge of emotions.[177] We now know that emotions are mediated through combinations of chemicals in our brains. Indeed, the findings of neuroscience emphasise that we are a "psychophysical unity",[178] that is, our emotions are both psychological and physiological states, and, given that they derive from chemicals in the brain, they are material.

---

[175] Al-Rodhan, *"emotional amoral egoism,"* op. cit., note 119, p. 65.
[176] *Ibid.*, p. 73.
[177] C. Darwin, *The Expression of Emotions in Man and Animals* (New York: BiblioBazaar, 2007).
[178] Berry and Jeeves, op. cit., note 142, p. 5.

Diagram 4: A General Theory of Human Nature: "Emotional Amoral Egoism"

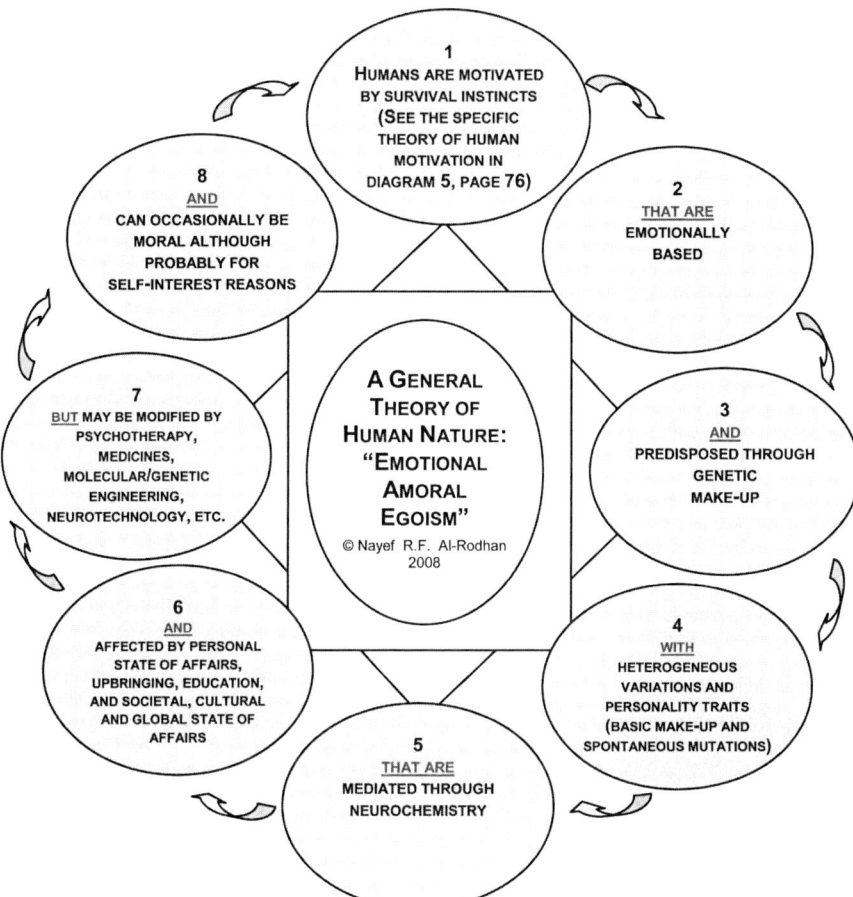

Source: N.R.F. Al-Rodhan, *"emotional amoral egoism": A Neurophilosphical Theory of Human Nature and its Universal Security Implications* (Berlin: LIT, 2008), p. 67, reprinted with permission from LIT, appears with modifications.

Diagram 5: A Specific Theory of Human Motivation and Its Consequences

	MEASURED EXPRESSION	EXCESSIVE EXPRESSION
	SUCCESS	CONFLICT
	EXCELLENCE	CRIMINALITY
	HARD WORK	DECEPTION
	SUCCESS	HARM
	CAUTION	DEBILITATION
	LAW-ABIDING	INTIMIDATION
		LACK OF INITIATIVE
		RISK-AVERSE
	SELF-ESTEEM	DOMINANCE
	COMPETITION	CULTURAL ARROGANCE
		EXCEPTIONALISM
	REPRODUCTION	RACISM
	COMPANIONSHIP	ALIENATION
		ADDICTION
	HAPPINESS/ SERENITY	PROMISCUITY
		CRIMINALITY

1. GENERAL SELF-INTEREST (REWARD)

2. FEAR, PAIN AND GRIEF (DESPAIR, DETACHMENT, LONELINESS, ANGER, TERROR, SHOCK, AWE, BETRAYAL, ANXIETY, INSECURITY)

3. EGO, PRIDE AND REPUTATION (ANGER, JEALOUSY, ENVY, LOVE, DISLIKE, ATTRACTION, SHAME, EMBARRASSMENT, BELONGING, SECURITY)

4. PLEASURE (SURPRISE, LOVE, PASSION, LIKE, TRUST, ATTRACTION, SYMPATHY, EMPATHY, GRATITUDE, BELONGING)

A SPECIFIC THEORY OF HUMAN MOTIVATION AND ITS CONSEQUENCES
© Nayef R.F. Al-Rodhan 2008

5. GREED (PLEASURE, HOPE, REWARD, GRATITUDE)

8. INFREQUENT REFLECTION AND MORALITY (SYMPATHY, EMPATHY, RESENTMENT, INDIGNATION, DISGUST, CONTEMPT, TRUST, BETRAYAL, GUILT, REGRET, ALIENATION)

7. OCCASIONAL REASON (DETACHMENT, INSECURITY, ANXIETY, BETRAYAL)

6. SPECIFIC INDIVIDUAL INCLINATIONS (LIKE, LOVE, PASSION, BELONGING, ANGER, FETISHISM, INFATUATION)

EXCESSIVE EXPRESSION	MEASURED EXPRESSION
PSYCHOPATHIC TENDENCIES	SYMPATHY
RADICALISM	EMPATHY
DEMONISATION OF OTHERS	
RACISM	
PSYCHOPATHIC TENDENCIES	DISTINCTION
SUSPICION	EXCELLENCE
PARANOIA	
PATHOLOGIES	HOBBIES
ADDICTION	INTERESTS
CRIMINALITY	
VIOLENCE	EXCELLENCE
CRIMINALITY	HARD WORK
DECEPTION	STATUS
FRAUD	

Source: N.R.F. Al-Rodhan, "*emotional amoral egoism*": *A Neurophilosphical Theory of Human Nature and its Universal Security Implications* (Berlin: LIT, 2008), p. 74, reprinted with permission from LIT.

Indeed, a great deal of neuroscientific research is being undertaken on emotions. Functional magnetic resonance imaging (FMRI) has increased our knowledge of brain activity. For example, fear is produced in the part of the brain known as the Amygdala. The amygdala is connected to the autonomic nervous system, which controls physiological reflexes, including heart rate. When an external occurrence is perceived as dangerous, the amygdala prompts a response through a huge biochemical release that prepares the body for either "flight or fight". Consciousness is not involved in this reaction.[179]

While emotions are mediated by neurochemistry, they are not necessarily caused by neurochemistry, even though they are unconscious. Mental processes may also provoke neurochemical changes that initiate emotions,[180] as is indicated in Diagram 6. Improved brain-scanning technology indicates that mental processes may provoke changes in the brain, suggesting that there is "neuroplasticity" (i.e., changes that occur in the brain's organisation in response to experience).[181]

Research into the impact of experience on inherited neurochemistry is also under way. It seems possible, for instance, that the way in which we are brought up may generate physiological modifications that, in turn, help to alter a child's temperament.[182]

Given that we are overwhelmingly emotionally driven, conscious reasoning and reflection motivate a comparatively small dimension of our behaviour. Therefore, a great deal of who we are comes from our genes. We are largely motivated by ***emotional self-interest***.[183] To this end, we are not radically free to shape our nature as existentialists suggest. However, this does not mean that we are determined entirely by our emotions, as those who argue that we are overwhelming driven by "the passions" claim. The environment also plays an important role in shaping our psyche and behaviour. Environment means our total environment, which includes our personal life situation, our upbringing and broader education, society, culture and the global state of affairs.

---

[179] R. Winston, *Human Instinct: How Our Primeval Impluses Shape Our Modern Lives* (London: Bantam Books, 2003), p. 49.
[180] Al-Rodhan, *"emotional amoral egoism,"* op. cit., note 119, pp. 69-70.
[181] Berry and Jeeves, op. cit., note 142, p. 21.
[182] W. Gallagher, "How We Become What We Are," *Atlantic Monthly*, Vol. 274, No. 3, September 1994, p. 38.
[183] Al-Rodhan, *"emotional amoral egoism,"* op. cit., note 119, p. 16.

Diagram 6: A View of Neurochemistry and Mental Processes

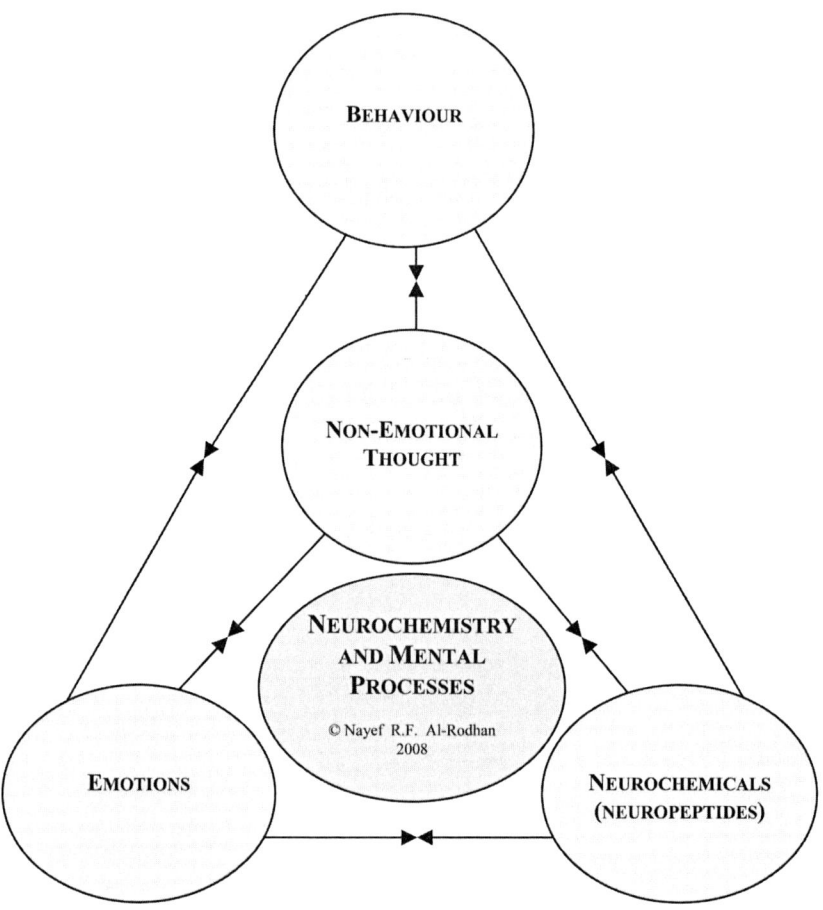

Source: N.R.F. Al-Rodhan, *"emotional amoral egoism": A Neurophilosphical Theory of Human Nature and its Universal Security Implications* (Berlin: LIT, 2008), p. 69, reprinted with permission from LIT.

Our personal experiences and relations with others are vital in shaping who we are. The most important set of relations to affect our psyche is likely to be the family. Children who receive sufficient love and support are likely to grow into more confident adults than those who lack love, encouragement and praise. The family also plays a critical role in a child's moral education, which is particularly important given the lack of innate morality possessed by humankind. Family context may also influence our worldview and awareness of other places and peoples. In addition to this more informal type of broad education, formal education can also be a critical factor in shaping our psyche and behaviour. It is also a means of diffusing moral norms.

Societal influences also shape human nature. If society fails to provide for the basic needs of members of its population, it will reduce the likelihood of ethical behaviour. Basic needs, it should be remembered, concern not only shelter, food, safe drinking water and physical safety; psychological and identity needs are also central to human well-being. Society therefore needs not only to ensure welfare and health provision, but also an environment in which every member feels he or she belongs. An inclusive national identity that allows enough room for people to hold multiple identities forms an essential part of meeting society's needs. The cultures to which we belong are important media through which we make sense of the world, and are vital building blocks of our collective identities.[184] Recognising, and respecting, cultural group rights insofar as they do not violate individual human rights is equally part of ensuring that people's basic needs are satisfied.[185] Cultural and ethnic plurality should be viewed as adding to *cultural vigour*, just as molecular/genetic diversity gives rise to "hybrid vigour" manifested in resilience and strength.[186] Religious and spiritual belief systems also help to inform how we think and act in the world.

The global state of affairs forms part of the environmental totality that shapes who we are. In some instances, global social forces and events may have a negative impact on the human condition. For those societies that are not reaping the benefits of globalisation, the contemporary character of the global political economy may contrib-

---

[184] *Ibid.*, pp. 15-16, 18.
[185] N.R.F. Al-Rodhan, Neo-*statecraft and* Meta-*geopolitics: Reconciliation of Power, Interests and Justice in the 21st Century* (Berlin: LIT, 2009), p. 205.
[186] Al-Rodhan, *"emotional amoral egoism," op. cit.*, note 119, p. 139.

ute to the failure to meet basic needs, anxiety about the present and future, as well as health and educational deterioration. In addition, rapid change associated with globalisation may dislodge familiar cultural, religious and societal reference points, thereby helping to generate issues related to identity.[187] The human mind is thus a *predisposed tabula rasa*, as illustrated in Diagram 7, stemming from both our genetic heritage and the totality of our environment. Emotional amoral egoism supports a dualistic conception of human nature. Neither side of the nature/nurture debate provides an adequate view of who we are.

While we are largely motivated by an emotional repertoire that we have developed as a result of selection pressure, we are, nevertheless, capable of morality and reflection. However, these capacities only come into play when basic survival needs have been satisfied. While emotions may be needed for moral behaviour, this does not mean that morality is innate as Hauser suggests. We may possess some moral sensitivities, but these are based on emotions and they should not be equated with a moral system. We are neither inherently moral nor immoral, but *amoral*. Our neuronal structural design is preprogrammed for gratification, regardless of the reason for this "feel good" factor. ***Circumstances are likely to determine the survival value of humankind's moral compass.***[188]

In most cases, morality is contingent on the extent to which basic human needs are met. There are, of course, exceptions. Clearly, some people are capable of truly altruistic acts rather than simply ***pseudo altruism***, and some are able to live moral lives despite their own hardship and deprivation – but these individuals represent a minority of the world's population. In general, insecurity and existential anxiety are not conducive to consciously altruistic acts. Reflection, which is required for *conscious* moral judgements, only occurs when people are no longer preoccupied with satisfying basic survival needs. This has serious implications in situations where the rule of law has broken down, for instance. Such circumstances can generate ***fear(survival)-induced pre-emptive aggression.***[189]

---

[187] Al-Rodhan, *"emotional amoral egoism,"* op. cit., note 119, p. 118.
[188] *Ibid.*, pp. 70-71.
[189] *Ibid.*, pp. 135-140.

Diagram 7: Predisposed Tabula Rasa

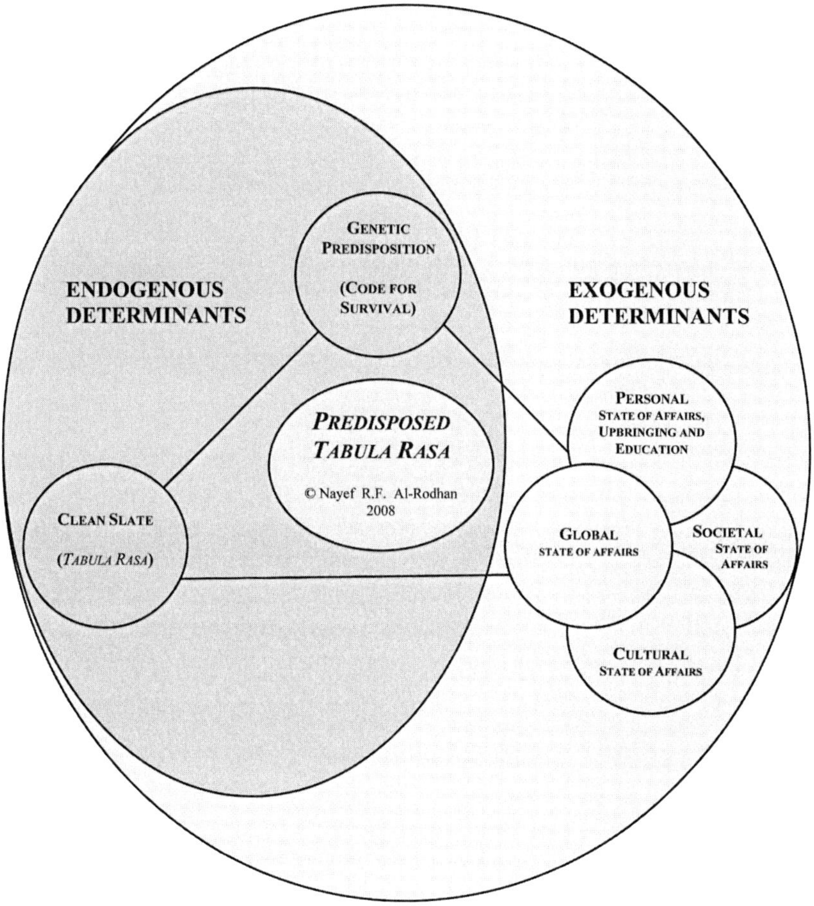

Source: N.R.F. Al-Rodhan, *"emotional amoral egoism": A Neurophilosphical Theory of Human Nature and its Universal Security Implications* (Berlin: LIT, 2008), p. 66, reprinted with permission from LIT.

Thus, like Malsow's "hierarchy of human needs", emotional amoral egoism takes into account human needs in their entirety; that is, both physiological and psychological needs. It also shares Maslow's approach in that it organises human needs hierarchically, with basic survival needs requiring satisfaction before conscious ethical behaviour and reflectivity can occur. In addition, it is a multidisciplinary approach to human nature that incorporates insights from a number of disciplines, ranging from philosophy to neuroscience. It is also cross-cultural. Our genetic heritage is largely the same. What tiny variations there are reflected in highly individualistic personality traits. Plato also emphasised the role of our genetic heritage in shaping who we are, although he did not use the term itself. He did so to demonstrate that intellectual capacities determined whether individual's would discover a transcendental self, but intellect plays merely a small role in shaping humankind.

Emotional amoral egoism also prioritises the role of emotions over reason. To this end, it differs from conceptions of human nature that emphasise the role of reason in determining who we are, such as those of Aristotle or Kant. Accordingly, it shares more similarities with those approaches that view emotions as the primary drivers of humankind, such as Hobbes, Hume, Bentham, Darwin, Kierkegaard, Freud, Skinner and Maslow. Most moral judgements result from chemically mediated emotions. Yet, even though the role of the nature dimension of the nature-nurture debate is deemed central to human nature, the totality of a person's environment also plays a role in shaping them. However, emotional amoral egoism does not conceive of individuals as completely free to define who they are. There is a dimension of ourselves that is simply given.[190]

Recognising that human nature is largely influenced by neurochemically mediated emotional self-interest does not mean that all hope is lost. The fact that a great deal of our behaviour depends on combinations of chemicals in our brains means that all attitudes are transformable and explainable, and if we feel gratification from something we will not give up what is creating that "feel good" factor, unless it is replaced by some other gratifying stimulus at the neurochemical level. We will do many things, but only repeat what gratifies us. Ultimately, we can live a "good life" if our actions are not detrimental to our own existence and the existence of others. Under such

---

[190] *Ibid.*, pp. 138-140.

conditions, there would be sustainable neurochemical gratification or, in other words, neurochemically mediated gratification that is connected to behaviour that can be sustained over the long term.

From a political and policy point of view it is essential that the conditions are created to encourage and support the kind of behaviour and policy objectives that we wish to achieve. Recognition of the emotionality, amorality and egoism of human nature should be built into policies and institutional frameworks. Avoiding the detrimental side of emotional self-interest requires that we do our utmost to prevent and, where it exists, reduce alienation, inequality, deprivation, fear, injustice and the loss of the rule of law.[191] Given that humankind has no innate morality that goes beyond our immediate family and close relations, the environment is an essential factor that will determine whether our moral commitments are expanded to a broader context.

3. Conclusion

The way in which we understand human nature is central to achieving a sustainable history, given that its attributes – emotionality, amorality and various types of egoisms – help to propel history. This chapter therefore outlined the central ways in which people from different disciplines have sought to answer the question: "Who are we?" The debate revolves around whether we are driven primarily by emotions or by reason; whether we are free to choose who we are or are determined by our genes; and whether we are innately moral or overwhelmingly self-interested. My own theory of human nature – emotional amoral egoism – seeks to go beyond these dichotomies and argues that human beings are largely motivated by neurochemically mediated emotional self-interest, employing reason and engaging in reflection and conscious moral behaviour only when basic survival needs have been satisfied. Survival needs, however, should be understood as going beyond the need for shelter, food and water. They include factors related to ego, such as belonging and a positive sense of self, making the totality of the environment paramount to how people behave. Our neurochemical architecture has pre-programmed us to do whatever makes us feel good. Yet, since much of our psyche and be-

---

[191] *Ibid.*, pp. 16-17.

haviour is neurochemically mediated, it is alterable with the help of normative and institutional frameworks. Indeed, our neurochemical make-up helps to determine how we answer the question of why we are here, since the factors that drive human nature directly affect how meaning is given to existence. I turn to this question in the next chapter.

CHAPTER 4

WHY ARE WE HERE?
A PROPOSED THEORY OF THE MEANING OF EXISTENCE: "SUSTAINABLE NEUROCHEMICAL GRATIFICATION" (SNG)

Why are we here? This is a question about the meaning of life. It helps to explain certain forms of human behaviour and is therefore relevant to sustainable history. The question itself comes in a variety of forms, such as "What is the meaning of life?"; "Does the universe have a purpose?"; "Do humans exist for some purpose?"; "What is the purpose of life?"; "If not, how can life have any meaning?", and so on. Given that the question comes in a number of forms, we might expect the answer to take a number of shapes. Several approaches to the riddle of the meaning of life may be identified: (1) the theistic answer; (2) the non-theistic answer; and (3) the approach that questions the meaningfulness of the question of existence. According to the first of these approaches, the meaning of existence is derived from a belief in a God or deities. The second attempts to answer the same question without relying on the existence of a God. With no omnipotent being to endow life with meaning, there is believed to be no objective meaning to life outside the natural world.[192] The third approach to the problem comprises those who argue that the question itself is meaningless as well as those who believe that the problem can be interpreted in a way that has some meaningfulness.

      This chapter attempts to decipher which questions inform the various types of answers, and to explore the different ways in which people seek to answer them. It examines theistic approaches to the question of existence, as well as the non-theistic perspectives, and finally considers the approaches that examine the validity of the question of the meaning of life. ***Ultimately, I conclude that however we***

---

[192] E.D. Klemke, *The Meaning of Life* (New York: Oxford University Press, 1981), pp. 4-5.

understand existence, what gives meaning to our lives are those things that serve our neurochemically based emotional self-interest in a sustainable way.

1. Approaches to the Meaning of Life

Theistic approaches to the meaning of life emphasise the human need to find ways of living with the certain knowledge of our finitude. Religious and spiritual belief systems provide a means of doing so through the promise of infinitude. Non-theistic answers to the meaning of life reject the idea of an absolute "truth" behind our existence. There is, nevertheless, a similar recognition that it is the certainty of our death that prompts us to ask about the meaning of existence. Yet, in non-theistic approaches to the question, there is no universal and ultimate meaning to life; existence can only be given meaning in a highly personal or subjective way.

Theistic Answers
The first set of answers is theistic, that is, based on belief in the existence of God or gods. In the Abrahamic religions, the purpose of life is something that God knows. One has therefore to have faith in God's intended purpose.[193]

In *My Confession* (1887), Leo Tolstoy asks himself why people hang on to life. For him, life is captured by an old Eastern story in which a traveller from the Steppe is confronted by an angry beast. In an effort to save himself, the traveller jumps into an empty well. However, to his horror, he sees a hungry dragon at the bottom of the well ready to devour him. So, he clings onto the twig of a wild bush growing in a crevice of the well. However, he notices that there are two mice nibbling at the trunk of the bush to which he is clinging.[194] The traveller understands that he will die, but he still finds the strength to lick the honey on the leaves of the bush. In a similar way, Tolstoy describes himself clinging to the branch of life, knowing that he will perish but still wanting to taste the drops of honey that used to bring him pleasure. The will to continue remains, even when the dragon is

---

[193] R. Niebuhr, "The Self and Its Search for Ultimate Meaning," in *ibid.*, p. 43.
[194] L. Tolstoy, "My Confession," Translated by L. Wiener. London: J.M. Dent and Sons, 1905. Reprinted in *ibid*, p. 11.

in sight and will devour him eventually, and even though the honey no longer tastes as sweet as it used to.[195]

Tolstoy believed that it is not possible to explain why people cling to life by resorting to rational knowledge. Rational knowledge simply leads to the conclusion that there is no meaning. This answer does not provide an answer that allows people to live. If the meaning of life cannot be answered by rational knowledge, it is because it requires an irrational knowledge to be able to relate the finite to the infinite. Only faith makes it possible to live. Even though faith remained irrational to Tolstoy, he recognised that it was the only thing that gave meaning to life and enabled people to live. In this interpretation, faith provides the reason why humankind does not destroy itself and finds the means to continue living.[196] Here, people must believe in something in order to go on living.

David Swenson also highlights the inability of finite "this-worldliness" to sustain itself without some kind of absolute "other-worldliness": "Take away from life every relation to the absolute, and the relativities of life lose their adequate ordering principle." [197] In his view, the belief in immortality gives humankind a goal in life in which he or she can participate.[198] Similarly, Reinhold Niehbuhr argues that the self has a dimension that does not fit into historical time. His justification for this is that human beings are not satisfied by their achievements and the satisfaction of being part of a community. Fulfilment of this part of the self can, he argues, only be realised through faith.[199]

Søren Kierkegaard (1813-1855) is known as the "father" of existentialism. In *The Sickness unto Death* (1849), Kierkegaard conceived of human beings as a "synthesis of the infinite and the finite, of the temporal and eternal, of freedom and necessity."[200] One must appropriate the certainty of one's own death as a means of developing an

---

[195] *Ibid.*, p. 12.
[196] *Ibid.*, pp. 15-17.
[197] D.F. Swenson, "The Transforming Power of Otherworldliness," in Klemke, *op. cit.*, note 192, p. 32.
[198] *Ibid.*, p. 36.
[199] Niebuhr, *op. cit.*, note 193, p. 51
[200] Excerpt from S. Kierkegaard, *The Sickness Unto Death*, Translated by H.V. and E.H. Hong, Princeton University Press, 1980, in G. Marino (ed.) *Basic Writings of Existentialism* (New York: The Modern Library, 2004), p. 41.

understanding of our own mortality that is highly subjective.[201] Giving meaning to one's own life can, according to Kierkegaard, be achieved through a relationship with God. Failing to reconcile finitude and infinitude may, for example, result in despair. When a human wishes to be infinite, he or she is in a state of despair. The Self, according to Kierkegaard, can only escape despair through God. Just as finitude and infinitude are considered paramount to the process of "becoming", so too are possibility and necessity. While finitude is the restraining aspect of infinitude, necessity is a constraining element of possibility. With God all is rendered possible. Salvation can only come when a beleaguered person gains possibility. A lack of possibility means that either everything is necessary or that it is trivial. When in despair over all that is earthly, the Self may find itself through the eternal.[202]

Within other religions and belief systems, such as Hinduism, Islam, Daoism and Buddhism, striving to be a type of being endows life with meaning.[203] In Daoism, the individual's life is shaped by the aim of increasing both spiritual and physical health by becoming at one with the Dao or natural cosmos, which can lead to transcendence.[204] Within Hinduism, the material world is thought to be simply an illusion. In this empirical world, human nature is characterised by ignorance. It is driven by desires, the satisfaction of which is ephemeral because the satisfaction of one desire is simply replaced by another. The real world can only be grasped through meditation, devotion, philosophy and forms of yoga. Human beings are believed to be not mortal, but immortal. The soul is thought to transmigrate from body to body – it is the body that is mortal, not the soul. Whether one's fate in the next life will be better than in the present one depends on the moral law of Karma. The vices or virtues of this life determine the form of reincarnation in the next life. Life is given meaning by trying to sow virtuous seeds in order to be reincarnated as a high-level being until finally one reaches nirvana and duly escapes the cycle of reincarnation.[205]

Beginning as a reform movement within Hinduism, Buddhism retains the fundamentals of Karma: the basic moral laws, reincarnation

---

[201] Marino, *op. cit.*, note 160, p. xii.
[202] Kierkegaard, *op. cit.*, note 200, pp. 59-60, 65, 68, 70, 98.
[203] Niebuhr, *op. cit.*, note 193, p. 43.
[204] J.A. Adler, *Chinese Religions* (London: Routledge, 2002), p. 69.
[205] Pojman, *op. cit.*, note 147, pp. 86-87.

and nirvana. However, the moral law of Karma is slightly different than that of Hinduism. The law of Karma is one of cause and effect. Life is therefore given meaning by striving to do good and to follow the teachings of Buddha.[206] What we become in the next life is determined by unresolved Karma. However, endless rebirth also implies endless death. Liberation from the cycle of rebirth, or samsara, through reaching nirvana is therefore sought as it is in Hinduism.[207] Thus, the purpose of life in Buddhism is to escape suffering.[208]

Non-theistic Answers
Another set of answers is provided by non-theistic approaches to the meaning of life. Existentialism is a philosophical movement that is concerned not simply with the question of existence, but with the need to find new categories with which to think about human existence.[209] Although he rejected the label of existentialist, Martin Heidegger (1889-1976) is seen as a precursor to existentialist thought and a key figure in conscious efforts to think about existence. His conceptual thought was influenced by Edmund Husserl's (1859-1938) phenomenological method, which is concerned with structures of consciousness.[210] Husserl conceived of consciousness as relevant to the transcendental field of intentionality rather than psychology. Consciousness is understood not as a property of the individual mind, but rather as a framework through which life is rendered intelligible through an understanding of the constitution of meaning.

Heidegger applied phenomenology to the meaning of being.[211] According to Heidegger, therefore, there is no fixed or unchanging basis on which to make judgements about how one should live. With no objective or universal standards underpinning human existence, people are thought to succumb to one of two consequences: they may

---

[206] *Ibid.*, pp. 95, 97.
[207] Adler, *op. cit.*, note 204, pp. 74-75.
[208] Religion Facts, www.religionfacts.com, s.v. "The Purpose of Life According to Buddhism."
[209] S. Crowell, "Existentialism," *Stanford Encyclopedia of Philosophy*, First Published 23 August 2004; Substantive Revision 26 November 2008, www.http://plato.stanford.edu/entries/existentialism/.
[210] D. Woodruff Smith, "Phenomenology," *Stanford Encyclopedia of Philosophy*, First Published 23 August 2004; Substantive Revision 28 July 2008, www.http://plato.stanford.edu/entries/ phenomenology/.
[211] Crowell, *op. cit.*, note 209.

lose all sense of purpose or they may choose to destroy all existing standards.[212] The latter, for Heidegger, is the ultimate consequence of a misunderstanding of what is fundamental to existence. This misconception prevents humankind from authentic ethical and political existence. The result is believed to be nihilism.

Misconception of existence is thought to be the result of the influence of Ancient Greek philosophy, particularly that of Plato's definition of Being as eternal presence. In Heidegger's view, this conception of existence was not only flawed, but also led to a complacency about the question of Being itself and an inability to even recognise the inadequate nature of Plato's answer.

Nihilism, as Heidegger conceives it, is not only negative. It may lead to an obliteration of all standards, prompting unchecked brutality to come to the fore, but this destruction may create an opening for a renewed sense of mystery and wonder. In this sense, nihilism may sow the seeds of its own destruction and pave the way for salvation. It is the knowledge of the certainty of our death that reveals the finite nature of our existence. The question of our existence derives from the recognition of our death at some future point.[213]

Heidegger was also inspired by Kierkegaard and Friedrich Nietzsche (1844-1990). Kierkegaard had argued that life becomes meaningful when the individual submits to moral laws. The truths that make life meaningful are, thus, not obtained from an objective science; they are subjective.[214] In contrast to Kierkegaard's religious existentialism, for Nietzsche the true meaning of existence becomes apparent when it is realised that there are no theistic foundations for morality. However, nihilism, when strong and creative and individual, can be a liberating force. Thus, like Kierkegaard, Nietzsche's focus is on the meaning of the individual's existence devoid of any transcendental basis.[215]

Jean-Paul Sartre (1905-1980) similarly argued that without God humankind has no identifiable nature or purpose. Consequently,

---

[212] M. Gillespie, "Martin Heidegger," in L. Strauss and J. Cropsey (eds.) *History of Political Philosophy*, Third Edition (Chicago: The University of Chicago Press, 1987), pp. 888-889.
[213] *Ibid.*, pp. 891-894.
[214] Crowell, *op. cit.*, note 209.
[215] *Ibid.*

human beings are free to define the purpose of their lives.[216] The significance of existence is not subject to a general account. Rather, the meaning of existence is given in the process of existing itself. For example, a person is what she is because of what she makes of herself. What her existence means is not subject to a general formula.[217]

Existentialism, according to Sartre, is a doctrine that makes existence possible through every truth and action being attributed to a highly individual subjectivity. In the absence of God, the only being whose existence precedes essence is Man. The notion that existence precedes essence is intended to mean that only once a person exists does he or she define him or herself. This equally implies that human nature is not given, it is only what Man consciously chooses to be. Existentialism therefore aims to make people aware of this and to make them responsible for their own existence. The latter is, nevertheless, a greater responsibility than may at first be appreciated. Sartre argues that in the act of choosing what we wish to be, we are choosing to favour a particular image of humankind. The extent of this responsibility places humankind in a condition of anguish.[218]

Among the non-religious existentialists, Albert Camus (1913-1960) argued that there is only one real philosophical problem: suicide. Discerning whether to go on living or to choose to end life is the biggest philosophical problem there is. The meaning of life is, therefore, a paramount question.[219] He writes, "Living is never easy. You can continue making the gestures commanded by existence for many reasons, the first of which is habit. Dying voluntarily implies that you have recognised, even instinctively, the ridiculous character of that habit, the absence of any profound reason for living, the insane character of that daily agitation, and the uselessness of suffering."[220] When humankind recognises the absurdity of life, it is robbed of what is required for life. Weariness of the monotony of life is, for Camus, the beginning of consciousness. Either this weariness subsides and we

---

[216] J.-P. Sartre, "Existentialism is a Humanism," in W. Kaufman (ed.) *Existentialism from Dostoyevsky to Sartre* (New York: Plume Books, 1988).
[217] Crowell, *op. cit.*, note 209.
[218] Excerpt from J.-P. Sartre, *Existentialism and Human Emotions*, in G. Marino (ed.) *Basic Writings of Existentialism* (New York: The Modern Library, 2004), pp. 342, 345-347.
[219] A. Camus, "The Absurdity of Human Existence," in Klemke, *op. cit.*, note 192, p. 70.
[220] *Ibid.*, p. 71.

recover or we choose suicide.[221] While this may appear utterly pessimistic, Camus actually thought that one should confront the absurdity of existence with acceptance and courage.[222]

Thomas Nagel (b. 1937) addresses the issue from a slightly different angle. He asks "Why isn't it all right for your life to be pointless?"[223] For Nagel, life is absurd. When there is a great discrepancy between aspirations and reality, there has to be something absurd about this situation. While we take our lives and the things we care about seriously, at the same time we recognise that there is a possibility that our lives and our actions may be meaningless. The problem is that we, as human beings, reflect on our lives. Some may attempt to find purpose in something bigger than themselves in the belief that it is absurd to be serious about something small and important only to an individual. It is the self-consciousness and the self-transcendence that enable human beings to recognise the potential for doubt that renders them absurd. The only way to escape this absurdity is suicide. Nagel argues that absurdity is one of the things that makes us human. Absurdity is testimony to our degree of insight.[224] Yet, even though life is absurd, there is still the possibility of living a meaningful life: "If there's any point at all to what we do, we have to find it within our own lives."[225]

Human freedom comes from consciousness and the questioning that follows from this. While the natural world is one to which we must ultimately submit, we are free in our aspirations. We can, Bertrand Russell (1872-1970) argues, learn from faith and the capacity of the faithful to live according to what is deemed good. However, he impels us to do so in the world of fact. Russell too identifies the gap between our aspirations and reality. Submission to the limits of our existence is equivalent to wisdom. Meaning may be given to life by the things that we value. But, before we realise this our lives will be imprinted with abandoned hopes and despair. Only when we realise

---

[221] *Ibid.*, pp. 71, 76.
[222] J. Baggini, *What's It All About? Philosophy and the Meaning of Life* (London: Granta Books, 2004), p. 158.
[223] T. Nagel, *What Does It All Mean? A Very Short Introduction to Philosophy* (Oxford: Oxford University Press, 1987), p. 98.
[224] T. Nagel, "The Absurd," in Klemke, *op. cit.*, note 192, pp. 153, 155, 160-161.
[225] Nagel, *op. cit.*, note 223, p. 96.

that the non-human world is not worth adulation can we gain wisdom and engrave meaning into our lives.[226]

In both the theistic and the non-theistic answers to the question "What is the meaning of life?" there is the common sense that the very fact that human beings pose this question is part of what it may mean to be human. We are, as Terry Eagleton notes, the only animal that is conscious of the fact that we live in the shadow of death, and are capable of objectifying our own existence.[227] In this sense, knowledge of our death has a great deal to do with the meaning of life.

2. The Meaningfulness of the Question

A third approach to the meaning of life stresses the importance of asking the right questions. The question "what is the meaning of life?" does not in fact have a clear and consistent use. It is often employed in a quest for the objectives worth seeking in life.[228] For example, when Camus asks about the meaning of existence he is asking about the existence of God. If there is a God, the purpose of life is already determined. However, if there is no God, then the meaning of life is for each human being to decipher for his or herself, becoming a question of our individual choices.[229] As Kai Nielsen points out, this does not tell us about the meaning of life. A question about the meaning of life is a question about how man should live and die. When people ask about the meaning of life they want to know how they should live their lives.[230]

This highlights the way in which questions about the meaning of life are often conceptually unclear. Life cannot have a meaning as a phrase does. However, an action or a gesture can have meaning in the sense of having a purpose. According to this logic, life is meaningful when it is purposeful. Yet, according to Ronald Hepburn, employing this kind of reasoning already alters the commonplace way of talking about the meaning of life. Meaning is not something to be discovered but something to be given by the individual. If a person seeks meaning

---

[226] B. Russell, "A Free Man's Worship," in Klemke, *op. cit.*, note 192, pp. 58-59.
[227] T. Eagleton, *The Meaning of Life: A Very Short Introduction* (Oxford: Oxford University Press, 2007), pp. 12-13.
[228] K. Nielsen, "Linguistic Philosophy and the 'Meaning of Life'" in Klemke, *op. cit.*, note 192, p. 182.
[229] *Ibid.*, p. 184.
[230] *Ibid.*, pp. 185-186.

outside of his or herself, frustration will necessarily follow. If we believe that a meaningful life is determined by pursuing worthwhile ends then it necessarily involves making value judgements. If we focus on the question "What is the purpose of life?", we are asking about the ends that we should choose.[231]

Julian Baggini shares the view that the question "What's it all about?" is unclear. In his view, it is not so much a question as a series of questions. He advocates taking a rational approach to the question. By this, he means that we should not start from supposed truths, religious doctrines or sacred texts when trying to answer this question. This is because a diverse array of historical contexts have shaped various religions and sacred texts. They therefore lose credibility as definitive truths.[232] Moreover, the meaning of life is not a form of esoteric knowledge that only a select few can discover. Baggini shares the view that the meaning of life is deeply personal.[233] However, he suggests several means by which we might attempt to answer the question for ourselves. Can we find out more by looking at our origins? This is the question "From whence did I come?" According to Baggini, this will not necessarily help us to determine the meaning of life understood as the purpose of life. He identifies several prominent approaches to the purpose derived from two different viewpoints about our origins: naturalism and creationism.

The naturalist version of the story of life on Earth is agreed on by the majority of scientists. It is touched on in Chapter 2. It begins with the Big Bang and the later emergence of our single cell organisms in the seas and oceans from which all species, including *Homo sapiens*, emerged approximately 200,000 years ago. In the naturalist account presented by Richard Dawkins in the *Selfish Gene* (1989), for example, our genes define our purpose. Genes wish to increase their chances of survival and, therefore, our purpose is to increase the chances of the survival of our genes either through reproduction or increasing the likelihood that people with the same genes pass on those genes.[234] If we accept this view, evolution is an accident, based

---

[231] R.W. Hepburn, "Questions about the Meaning of Life" in Klemke, *op. cit.*, note 192, pp. 210-211.
[232] Baggini, *op. cit.*, note 222, p. 2.
[233] *Ibid.*, p. 4.
[234] See R. Dawkins, *The Selfish Gene* (Oxford: Oxford University Press, 1989).

on purely random mutations.[235] The Big Bang theory generates a crisis for theistic accounts of human purpose.

Those who accept that there is no purpose outside ourselves might simply accept that life is meaningless or might believe that there still exists the possibility of determining one's own purpose. In the latter case, life is not without meaning; rather it has no a priori meaning. This may not be tragic news. What matters is that we have a purpose in the present. Sartre, for example, believed his brand of existentialism was optimistic precisely because human beings possess the freedom with which to determine that purpose.[236]

Creationists are committed to the belief that humankind was created by God and that the purpose of our lives is predetermined by God. Yet, Baggini makes an interesting point in relation to creationism. He argues that even if man were created by God this does not necessarily endow life with meaning. If we accept that God created humankind, this only tells us that we were created by Him with a specific purpose. Whether His purpose renders our lives meaningful or whether we should welcome that purpose is not obvious. Moreover, he argues that looking into our past does not necessarily give us clues to the present and the future. Even if we were created by God for a specific purpose, this does not mean that that purpose has not changed or will not change.[237]

The majority of religions posit some form of transcendental reality. Baggini notes that while belief in God does not provide us with a definitive answer to the question "What is the meaning of life?", it does allow one to cease worrying about that question. A faith in a transcendental reality in the form of the existence of God allows one to give up the quest for the meaning of life. It requires faith, as Tolstoy pointed out. It requires that one remove rationality from the loop.[238]

Some argue that if there is no afterlife, then life on Earth lacks meaning. Is this correct? Baggini notes that this prompts two questions. The first is whether there is such a thing as life after death and the second is whether life can be meaningful in the absence of an afterlife. Belief in life after death requires faith. If we accept that there is

---

[235] Baggini, *op. cit.*, note 222, p. 9.
[236] *Ibid.*, pp. 10-13.
[237] *Ibid.*, pp. 17, 22.
[238] *Ibid.*, pp. 43, 48.

no transcendental realm, life can still be meaningful, according to Baggini. In fact, the finite quality of our existence may be in part what gives it meaning. After all, much in life is shaped by knowledge that we will die. Therefore, life can have meaning even if there is no afterlife.[239]

Helping others may help to give meaning to our lives. But is it the purpose of life? Why might helping others make us feel good? Presumably, it is because we consider all life to have equal worth and, therefore, we feel better if we can help reduce the hardship or upset of someone. Baggini argues that there is something in our inherently social character that makes helping others seem worthwhile and helps to give meaning to life.[240]

Baggini himself offers a rational humanist answer to the meaning of life. It is rational because it is based on reasoned argument rather than intuition, dogma or revelation. It is humanist because it is based on the assumption that an individual's life has its own worth. One need not accept something that does not seem to be convincing based on reason, but reason is not enough on which to base philosophy. We might be able to rationally justify doing something that most of us would find abhorrent. We may engage in acts that are good because we love in a variety of ways. There is still room for some degree of mystery because it is not based on dogma. If a convincing argument can be made for a transcendental realm, then one assumes that Baggini would accept it. Therefore, understanding the meaning of life is not dependent on esoteric wisdom.[241] It is something that is open to us all and likely to be based on what gives our lives value and meaning, such as love, friendship and a broader sense of community: "each of us has the power and responsibility to discover and in part determine meaning for ourselves."[242]

3. A Proposed Theory of the Meaning of Existence: "Sustainable Neurochemical Gratification"

Regardless of existing approaches to the problem of existence, human beings function based on neurochemical events, as is explained in

---

[239] Ibid., pp. 51, 54-55.
[240] Ibid., pp. 64, 69.
[241] Ibid., pp. 174, 179, 182, 185.
[242] Ibid., p. 186.

Chapter 3. This insight suggests a different answer to the question of the meaning of existence to those discussed thus far. As a species, we are coded for survival through our genetic make-up. A significant part of this coding is manifested in the range of emotions with which we are endowed. Fear, attachment, hate, jealousy, pity and so on all assisted early human beings in their struggle for survival. While the environment in which humans exist today has significantly changed, human nature has not. Human beings are therefore highly emotional and predominantly driven by emotions rather than reason. This does not mean that individuals who live their lives based on reason do not exist, simply that emotions drive a greater part of the human psyche than reason.

As a result, emotions are, for the most part, behind what motivates human beings, such as the need for a positive sense of self, which may be manifested in pride, reputation concerns, greed, the desire to dominate, the need for belonging, etc. Given that emotions are neurochemical in origin and serve particular egoisms, we may say that human beings are motivated by neurochemically mediated self-interest. Of course, the particular form that this emotional self-interest takes will depend on the psychological make-up of the individual and the conditions of his or her existence. Upbringing, education and family situation are among the most fundamental exogenous aspects of an individual's life that are likely to shape personality. The cultural, societal and global state of affairs that form the backdrop of a person's life are also extremely important factors that all help to shape an individual's psychodynamics.

Thus, neurochemically mediated gratification is highly individualistic and behaviour that serves that end will take a variety of forms, some more benign than others. This has potentially dangerous implications. It helps to explain why an individual may be able to rationalise harmful or abhorrent behaviour and, moreover, why that behaviour may make that person's life meaningful. For instance, addiction uses our existing neuronal networks. Addictive drugs misuse the brain's existing pre-programming, activating reward mechanisms and extreme feelings of pleasure. When stimulated, the brain's pleasure centres emit signals to repeat the behaviour. In this sense, *the brain is pre-programmed to "feel good"*.

However, a number of positive consequences may result from this pre-programming. This is, for example, demonstrated by neurochemical gratification linked to libido, attraction and attachment. The neuronal circuits associated with these facets have developed in order to regulate the reproductive cycle through neurochemical rewards and therefore have a positive function. The desire for sexual gratification, manifested in libido, is stimulated by oestrogens and androgens. Attraction, understood as the increased focus on a preferred sexual partner, is, in turn, connected to dopamine, norepinephrine and serotonin. Attachment or the desire to stay with a partner is related to oxytocin and vasopressin.[243]

Indeed, most human behaviour is a form of psychological addiction that has a neurochemical foundation. In this sense, we are all addicts of one sort or another. Whether "addictions" have positive or negative implications will in part depend on a person's psychological profile as well as external factors. Parenting, education and society can positively influence neuronal architecture and physiology by associating gratification with behaviour that is constructive for the individual and society as a whole.

The meaningfulness of existence is therefore highly individualistic and connected to whatever behaviour brings the most neurochemically mediated gratification. Human beings will do many things, but they will only repeat what gratifies them in some way, whether related behaviour is instinctive or pre-conditioned by social or cultural norms. This perhaps explains why some philosophical approaches to the meaning of existence conclude that what makes life meaningful is a matter for the individual to discover. For some people engagement in family life may bring the most gratification, for others faith may provide the ultimate meaning in life, for others still practicing a sport or being a member of a charitable organisation may be what gives life meaning. In this sense, Baggini is correct in claiming that there is no esoteric wisdom behind the meaning of life. Meaning is inherently personal and therefore this does not mean that it cannot be found in the spiritual or transcendental.

Yet, true meaning is likely to be shaped by neurochemically gratifying behaviour that is durable. A person may engage in a particular form of behaviour, which, while gratifying, harms him or herself as well as others. The individual in question will most likely suffer as a cause of that behaviour. Sustainable gratification and a more meaningful life is therefore likely to be associated with behaviour that

---

[243] Al-Rodhan, *"emotional amoral egoism," op. cit.*, note 119, pp. 108-111.

is not harmful to the individual or to other people. It is possible that the avoidance of excesses may provide the foundation for sustained neurochemical gratification and, as a consequence, a more fulfilling life. Yet, avoiding excesses may prove very difficult for the majority of people, given that human beings are emotionally and therefore neurochemically driven. It would depend in part on the exercise of reason and morality, which may be encouraged by cultural, societal as well as global institutions. Good governance needs to ensure that adequate mechanisms are in place to check harmful excesses related to human nature and to promote human dignity through encouraging more reason, security, human rights, accountability, transparency, justice, opportunity, innovation and inclusiveness.

We may conclude therefore that ***whatever makes existence meaningful serves our neurochemically mediated emotional self-interest.***[244] Love, the search for knowledge and transcendental standards are believed to support the meaning of being – insofar as they lend meaning to our lives, they do so because they gratify us as individuals in some way. Those facets of our lives, whether family, friends, religion, scholarship or community, that bring sustained neurochemical gratification are likely to lend enduring meaning to life.

4. Conclusion

This chapter examined some of the principal ways in which the quest for the meaning of life has been approached and outlined the theistic and non-theistic ways in which the question "why are we here?" has been answered. It also highlighted the different meanings given to the question, sometimes referring to a quest for the purpose of life rather than the meaning of life. For approaches that accept the existence of God, the purpose of life is predetermined. For those that believe in deities, such as Buddhism or Hinduism, the purpose of life is also given and meaning is found by striving to be a particular kind of being. In non-theistic accounts, there is no appeal to the transcendental. Meaning is generally thought to be subjective and grounded in worldly things, such as loving relationships of various kinds. I also proposed a theory of the meaning of existence termed ***Sustainable Neurochemical Gratification*** that argues that whatever meaning we

---

[244] See *ibid.*

may attribute to existence, life is rendered meaningful by those things, whether activities, beliefs or relationships, that provide sustained neurochemically mediated gratification. Humankind has, of course, sought to understand the meaning not only of its existence, but also of the world around it. The search for knowledge is the focus of Chapter 5, in which we explore the nature of knowledge and the methods by which it may be acquired.

CHAPTER 5

WHAT DO WE KNOW FOR CERTAIN?
A PROPOSED THEORY OF KNOWLEDGE:
"NEURO-RATIONAL PHYSICALISM" (NRP)

What do we know for certain? A great deal of what we think we know may simply be a point of view held without sufficient grounds – in other words, dogma. Understanding the nature of knowledge is therefore an important means of discerning how we know what we know and with what degree of certainty we can make claims to "truth". Since our knowledge claims affect how we behave, it is important to understand how they are constituted since they have a profound impact on the sustainability of history. In order to answer this question we need to turn to epistemology or the theory of knowledge. However, the question of what knowledge is and how it may be acquired is subject to debate. In this chapter, we first examine several ways in which we may discern what the nature of knowledge is and how it may be acquired. One of the major debates about how knowledge can be acquired has historically taken place between empiricists and rationalists. Empiricists hold that all knowledge is based on experience or sensory perception, whereas rationalists maintain that reason is pre-eminent in how we gain knowledge. Both empiricism and logic are deemed the most important means of acquiring knowledge. In some instances, rationalists argue that knowledge may be derived from innate ideas and concepts. Logical positivists have attempted to update empiricism. They reject metaphysical knowledge on the basis that it is deemed not to stand up to the proofs of logic. Yet, to some extent, all knowledge, even sense-data, is inferred or involves some degree of interpretation. Constructivist epistemology highlights this social dimension of knowledge. I review all these approaches. I then outline an approach to the sources of knowledge, which I term *"neuro-rational physicalism"*. This approach to knowledge and its acquisition suggests that what we know, we only know with a reasonable amount of certainty. Yet, the best explanations available are, nevertheless, the source of sustainable progress in the natural sciences. In the nonnatural sciences a considerably greater degree of interpretation is implied in "knowing".

1. The Nature of Knowledge

Knowledge is generally understood as justified true belief. Justification can come before or after an event. However, the standard account of knowledge, first outlined by Plato,[245] which is known as the tripartite account, states that:

1. p,
2. a believes p,
3. a believes that p is justified.[246]

In this account, belief is central to knowledge. Even if something is true, it is not knowledge unless the individual believes it. Yet, belief is not the only condition for knowledge. A belief may be true or false, but knowledge must be true. For a belief to qualify as knowledge it must also be true.[247] A person may be justified in believing p, but p may be false. Such a situation is called a Gettier counter-example. Thus, in order to know something there must not exist further truths that would defeat the belief that p is justified.[248]

A true belief cannot be considered knowledge when it is based on a false belief. However, does this mean that nothing can be considered knowledge unless it is validly deduced from true premises? The answer to this question, according to Russell, is no, because the premises not only need to be true, they also need to be known.[249] However, this takes for granted that we know what is intended by "known prem-

---

[245] Plato, *Meno*, available on Project Gutenberg, www.gutenberg.org.
[246] J. Dancy, *Introduction to Contemporary Epistemology* (Oxford: Blackwell Publishers, 1985), p. 23.
[247] M. Toll, "Justified True Belief and Critical Rationalism," *Symposia: the Online Philosophy Journal,* http://journal.ilovephilosophy.com/Article/Justified-True-Belief-and-Critical-Rationalism/220.
[248] Dancy, *op. cit.*, note 246, pp. 23, 25, 29.
[249] B. Russell, *The Problems of Philosophy* (Indianapolis: Hackett Publishing Company, Reprint of the 1912 Edition in the Home University), p. 132.

ises". In some cases, they may be thought of as relating to derivative knowledge, which is derived from premises that are intuitively known.

An objection to derivative knowledge may be that it is arrived at by a process of reasoning that is wrong. Thus, derivative knowledge is the end product of intuitive knowledge. But, what about the intuitive knowledge? If we rely on derivative knowledge, then we are depending on the validity of intuitive knowledge. If a belief is supported by a fact, we may consider the belief to constitute knowledge of the fact. However, knowledge can also be the result of perception.[250]

Even true beliefs based on true beliefs and good reasoning may not constitute knowledge.[251] For example, I may assume that my neighbour is at home, because I can hear her music playing. I think that I know that she is at home, because whenever she is at home she plays music. However, it may be that a friend of my neighbour is staying in her flat and it is this friend who turned on the music. In this case, I do not know that my neighbour is home.

With regard to derivative knowledge, the final premises and the conclusion drawn from them must have some degree of self-evidence. Thus, for both derivative knowledge and the intuitive knowledge on which it is based, we assume that there is a degree of trustworthiness in terms of their self-evidence.[252] This prompts one to ask what counts as justification.

2. Sources of Knowledge

The principal debate about how philosophical knowledge may be acquired has, as is mentioned above, traditionally taken place between those who favour empiricism and those who argue in favour of rationalism. The central point of contention between proponents of each approach is the extent to which our sense experience can be relied on as a source of knowledge. Rationalists contend that knowledge and concepts can be derived without relying on immediate sense experi-

---

[250] *Ibid.*, pp. 133-134, 136.
[251] P.D. Klein, "Knowledge, Concept of," in Craig, *op. cit.*, note 147.
[252] Russell, *op. cit.*, note 249, p. 139.

ence, whereas empiricists insist that the only reliable source of knowledge is sense experience.[253]

Empiricism

Empiricism emphasises the fundamental role of experience in acquiring knowledge. This means that all knowledge stems from direct experience. David Hume (1711-1776), for example, argued that all concepts and propositions that are not derived from sense-data, and are therefore purely metaphysical, should be discarded from thinking.[254] Another figure among the British empiricists is Locke, who firmly believed that human beings possess no innate ideas or knowledge. The human mind, in his view, was a tabula rasa (a blank slate). Instead, he maintained that ideas derive either from sensation or from perception of the functioning of our own mind. However, since what we think is derived from our sense experiences, all knowledge comes from experience.[255] The notion of the mind as a blank slate was outlined first by Aristotle, elaborated by Ibn Sina (Avicenna) (980-1037) and later illustrated by the Ibn Tufayl (1110-1185).[256]

This position is based on foundationalism, which assumes that some beliefs are basic beliefs that do not require other beliefs to support them.[257] Within classical foundationalism, beliefs are separated into two types: those that need support from others and those that can stand alone. The first type are thought to form an epistemological superstructure, which sits on foundations constituted by the second types of belief. Beliefs that are not derived from our own sensory experiences need to be supported by beliefs that stem from our own sensory experience. Through this distinction, classical foundationalism provides the basic premise of empiricism: that all knowledge originates from experience. Yet, how is it that beliefs that are derived from

---

[253] P. Markie, "Rationalism vs. Empiricism," *Stanford Encyclopedia of Philosophy*, First Published 19 August 2004; Substantive Revision 6 August 2008, http://www.science.uva.nl/~seop/ entries/rationalism-empiricism/.
[254] A. Einstein, "Remarks on Bertrand Russell's Theory of Knowledge," in P.A. Schlipp (ed.) *The Philosophy of Bertrand Russell*, The Library of Living Philosophers, Vol. 5, Fourth Edition (La Salle, Illinois, 1971), pp. 287-288.
[255] Russell, *op. cit.*, note 154, p. 556.
[256] See S. Attar, *The Vital Roots of European Enlightenment: Ibn Tufayl's Influence on Modern Western Thought* (Lanham: Lexington Books, 2007); G. A. Russell, *The 'Arabick' Interest of the Natural Philosophers in Seventeenth-Century England*, (Leiden: E. J. Brill, 1994), pp. 224-262.
[257] Klein, *op. cit.*, note 251.

our sensory states can stand alone without the support of other beliefs? According to classical foundationalism, beliefs derived from sensory states are infallible and therefore do not require any further support.

Table 3: Approaches to Knowledge*

Approach	Key Figures & Year	Short Description
Empiricism	Ibn Sina (980-1037) John Locke (1632-1704) David Hume (1711-1776)	1. All knowledge is derived from direct experience (sense-data) 2. All metaphysical concepts and propositions (i.e. those not derived from sense-data) should be discarded 3. No innate ideas or knowledge
Logical Positivism of the "Vienna Circle"	Moritz Schlick (1882-1936) Otto Neurath (1882-1945) Rudolf Carnap (1891-1970) A.J. Ayer (1910-1989)	1. Conceived as a reformulation of empiricism using advances in scientific knowledge 2. No particular kind of knowledge acquisition that is specific to philosophy 3. Combines empiricism and logic in a comprehensive approach 4. Seeks to clarify meanings of propositions and discards meaningless propositions qualified as metaphysical 5. Belief that metaphysical knowledge cannot be proved through the application of logic

Approach	Key Figures & Year	Short Description
Rationalism	Aristotle (384-322 BCE) Parmenides (c. 450 BCE) Al-Farabi (c. 870-950) René Descartes (1596-1650) Spinoza (1632-1677) Georg Wilhelm Friedrich Hegel (1770-1831)	1. Reason plays a paramount role in the acquisition of knowledge 2. Two principle means of gaining knowledge of things beyond our immediate environment: deduction and induction 3. Deduction occurs when an inferential belief is assumed to be justified, because the initial premises are correct; induction when a belief is thought to be justified because it is more probable than alternatives 4. Assumes that there are propositions that are innate or a priori 5. Logic is essential to analysis 6. Some approaches (i.e. Parmenides, Spinoza, Hegel) adopted a monist approach in which only the whole, which in some instances is conceived as God, has a reality
Innate Knowledge	Plato (472-347 BCE) René Descartes (1596-1650) Immanuel Kant (1724-1804) Steven Pinker (b.1954) Marc Hauser (b. 1928)	1. Assumes that human beings are endowed with innate knowledge as part of their rational nature 2. Innate concepts and ideas are not the result of experience 3. This innate knowledge is conceived of in a number of different ways, i.e. the soul's recollection (Plato), innate ideas of God (Descartes), a sense of time, space, causality and comparison (Kant), innate grammar (Pinker and Chomsky) and innate moral grammar (Hauser) 4. The source of innate moral knowledge is believed to be selection pressure

Approach	Key Figures & Year	Short Description
Atomism	Leucippus (c.440 BCE) Democritus (460-370 BCE) Arab-Islamic Ash'arites (founded in the 9th century)	1. An approach to knowledge close to modern scientific method 2. No unified purpose to the universe 3. Materialist: everything is composed of atoms governed by mechanical laws 4. Medieval Arab-Islamic scholars posited that there are atoms and accidents; atoms being those things that occupy space and accidents those that exist, but do not occupy space
Logical Atomism	Bertrand Russell (1872-1970) Ludwig Wittgenstein – early career (1889-1951)	1. An approach that sought to clarify philosophical issues through the use of logic 2. Evolved as a rejection of neo-Hegelian idealism 3. Atomistic logic as opposed to monist logic of neo-Hegelians Thus, the world is composed of separate entities or "atoms" However, these atoms are logical and not physical 4. It has a metaphysical dimension – the notion that the world is comprised of separate entities that have specific qualities – and a methodology for philosophy – the reduction of notions to their simplest form 5. No innate knowledge resulting from humankind's rational nature

Approach	Key Figures & Year	Short Description
Constructivism	Thomas Khun (scientific knowledge) (1922-1996)	1. Knowledge is thought to be acquired passively 2. Knowledge is expressed in symbolic form and is socially constructed 3. Emphasis is placed on the process of constructing scientific knowledge. Scientific "facts" do not gain authority due to certainty, but because they correspond to a dominant paradigm 4. Knowledge cannot be separated from power 5. No true way of knowing the external world exists
Neuro-rational Physicalism (The present volume)	Nayef Al-Rodhan (present)	1. Knowledge derived from sense-data is not certain. Thus, pure empiricism is rejected 2. Knowledge is also inferred from what is accepted as established knowledge, with new knowledge being based on the best explanation. This includes "possible truths subject to proof" 3. Knowledge about things beyond our immediate environment may be acquired through deduction, if the initial premises are believed to be correct 4. The notion of innate knowledge (including moral knowledge) is rejected, but that of moral sensitivities is accepted 5. Knowledge is based on sense-data and reason 6. It has a high probability of being subject to error or incomplete understanding 7. All knowledge is to some extent interpreted 8. Interpretation is the prism through which we order sense-data

Approach	Key Figures & Year	Short Description
Neuro-rational Physicalism continued	Nayef Al-Rodhan	9. All knowledge is ultimately indeterminate, and may also be temporally, spatially and culturally constrained 10. All the universe and its energies are physical, and some matter and energy may be unobservable with our current technologies, making them "possible truths subject to proof" 11. There is a physical neuro-biological substrate to all human knowledge, including thoughts, memories, perceptions and emotions. To this end, mental states and thought processes are physical

* This table is intended to provide only a brief synopsis of the approaches to knowledge deemed relevant to neuro-rational physicalism.

Thus, according to classical foundationalism, if we can show that beliefs are basic beliefs, there are no further epistemological requirements.[258]

In the absence of infallibility, classical foundationalism cannot be maintained. However, there are weaker types of foundationalism that do not require infallibility. One version states that basic beliefs cannot be justified, even in part, by non-basic beliefs. However, non-basic beliefs may increase the likelihood of a basic belief being true at least by not disconfirming it. There are also foundationalists who argue that our beliefs about our sensory states are always, to some extent, justified because they are non-inferential, whereas all other beliefs are only justifiable inferentially – if they can be justified at all. Other foundationalists hold that basic beliefs could be infallible because they are either incorrigible or indubitable.[259] In the former case, a basic belief would be a belief that could never be corrected; in the latter, an indubitable belief would be one which there is no reason to doubt. However, as Jonathan Dancy argues, once we admit that basic

---

[258] Dancy, *op. cit.*, note 246, pp. 53-54.
[259] *Ibid.*, pp. 58, 62-63.

beliefs are not infallible, foundationalism cannot be maintained. Therefore, if we accept this conclusion, we would have to reject foundationalism.[260]

The Logical Positivism of the "Vienna Circle"
Efforts were made to reinvigorate empiricism in the 20th century. Logical positivism refers to a method associated with a group of philosophers belonging to the Vienna Circle that sought to reformulate empiricism by drawing on advances in physical and formal science in the early 20th century. The group was especially active during the inter-war years. While there was a great deal of variety among the members of the Vienna Circle, they had in common the desire to update empiricism through scientific knowledge. The key figures associated with the Circle were Moritz Schlick (1882-1936), Rudolf Carnap (1891-1970) and Otto Neurath (1882-1945).

A logical positivist believes that there is no distinct way of knowing that which is specific to philosophy. Facts can only be derived by scientific method. Questions that can be answered without resort to experience are mathematical or linguistic. What distinguishes logical positivists from empiricists is their attention to mathematics and logic.[261] Logical positivism, nevertheless, retains the major principle of empiricism. In this sense, it aims to combine both empiricism and logic in a unified approach. As a philosophical approach, logical positivism seeks to clarify the meaning of propositions and to discard meaningless propositions. These meaningless propositions were classified as metaphysical.[262] In general, logical positivists believe that metaphysical knowledge of the universe cannot be proved by logic.[263] They therefore rejected knowledge claims derived from metaphysics.

A.J. Ayer (1910-1989) is considered to be the Circle's English protagonist. He studied with Schlick in Vienna in 1933. In *Language, Truth and Logic* (1936), he set out the main tenets of Logical Positivism and, by so doing, became the foremost English member of the movement. He saw himself as following in the footsteps of earlier

---

[260] *Ibid.*, p. 64.
[261] B. Russell, "Logical Positivism," in R.C. Marsh (ed.) *Logical and Knowledge, Essays, 1901-1950*, (London: George Allen & Unwin Ltd., 1971), p. 367.
[262] F. Stadler, "Vienna Circle," in Craig, *op. cit.*, note 147, http://www.rep.routledge.com.library3.webster.edu/article/DD076SECT2.
[263] Russell, *op. cit.*, note 249, p. 141.

British empiricists, such as Hume, in his belief that our knowledge of physical objects is derived from sensory experience. Moreover, he defended the claim that someone could be said to have knowledge if they had sufficient grounds to believe themselves to be right.[264]

In line with logical positivism's anti-metaphysical persuasion is its scientific conception of the world.[265] Logical positivists challenged the notion that there is a distinct difference between natural and human sciences. While the subject matters were recognised as being different, they maintained that the appropriate methodology for both domains was the same. Their explicit rejection of rational intuition represented a considerable challenge to philosophy.[266]

Rationalism
In contrast to empiricism, rationalism holds that reason plays a preeminent role in acquiring knowledge. Rationalism contains two central theses about how we can go beyond knowledge of our immediate environment by constructing new knowledge on the basis of old through the process of reasoning; that is, what we know can provide the basis for other beliefs. There are two types of reasoning: deductive and inductive. Deductive reasoning occurs when we assume that an inferential belief is justified. According to this type of reasoning, if our initial belief is justified, others originating from it must also be correct. By contrast, inductive reasoning takes place when we assume that our initial beliefs are justified enough without being conclusive, as in the case of deductive reasoning. An inductive belief is one that is more probable than the alternatives.[267] Thus, reason alone can provide us with knowledge, either through intuition of self-evident premises or deduction based on these initial premises. In either case, we assume that there are propositions that are innate or a priori. As such, they are thought to be independent of experience. In relation to deduction, it assumes that if the initial premises are correct the knowledge derived from them must also be true. Moreover, the notion of a priori knowledge privileges the observer over the observed. As long as the ob-

---

[264] G. MacDonald, "Alfred Jules Ayer," *Stanford Enyclopedia of Philosophy*, First Published 7 May 2005, http://www.science.uva.nl/~seop/entries/ayer/.
[265] Stadler, *op. cit.*, note 262.
[266] T. Uebel, "Vienna Circle," *Stanford Enyclopedia of Philosophy*, First Published 28 June 2006; Substantive Revisions 18 September 2006, http://www.science.uva.nl/~seop/entries/vienna-circle/.
[267] Dancy, *op. cit.*, note 246, p. 197.

server's mind remains the same, the same deductive and inductive methods may be used across various different subject areas.[268]

Parmenides (c. 450 BCE) proposed a type of metaphysical argument that was still found in metaphysics up to Hegel. He argued that our senses may lead to illusions rather than knowledge. In his view, the only true entity was God. This whole is present in everything and everywhere. As such, God is indivisible and infinite. In addition, he maintained that since we cannot know the past, the past cannot really exist; it must be part of a continual present. Thus, change cannot exist.[269]

According to Aristotle's theory of universals, the universal may be predicated by many subjects whereas an individual thing has no such predication. The universal, thus, cannot exist on its own, but only as part of particular things. In the area of logic, Aristotle's most significant work was on the doctrine of syllogism. A syllogism is an argument that has three elements: a principle premise, a minor premise and a conclusion; for example, all men are mortal, Socrates is a man, therefore Socrates is mortal. The point is that inferences can be made from one premise. Aristotle believed that all deductive inference is syllogistic. Identifying all valid syllogisms and establishing an argument in syllogistic form was thought to avoid fallacies. This system was, in effect, the beginning of formal logic.[270]

In the Arab-Islamic world, Abu Nasr Muhammed Ibn Muhammed Ibn Tarkhan Al-Farabi (c. 870-950) – known in the West as Al-Farabi – was a major contributor to Aristotelian logic in Arabic. He argued that logic was essential to analysis in law and theology. He was especially interested in the relationship between logic and language.[271] Like Aristotle, he held a monist notion of a unified reality. The world was thought to emanate from God. In this sense, his thinking was also imbued with neo-Platonism and was an effort to reconcile the requirements of monotheism with those of rationally explaining the universe.[272]

---

[268] Markie, *op. cit.*, note 253.
[269] Russell, *op. cit.*, note 154, pp. 55, 58.
[270] *Ibid.*, pp. 160, 163, 188-189.
[271] T. Street, "Arabic and Islamic Philosophy of Language and Logic, *Stanford Encyclopedia of Philosophy,* First Published 23 July 2008, http://www.science.uva.nl/~seop/entries/arabic-islamic-language/.
[272] D. Collinson and R. Wilkinson, *Thirty-Five Oriental Philosophers* (Abingdon, Oxon: Routledge, 1994), pp. 19-20.

René Descartes (1596-1650) developed a method of philosophical inquiry. His work was influenced by the new sciences of physics and astronomy. During the winter of 1619-1620, he developed his *Discours de la Méthode* (1637) (*Discourse on Method*). He was enlisted in the Bavarian army at the time of the Thirty Year's War. It is said that he climbed into a stove to escape the cold, and when he came out his philosophy was half complete. In order to establish a sound basis for philosophic enquiry, he attempted to doubt as much as possible. Mind was believed more certain than matter. Moreover, what is in an individual's mind was believed to be more certain for the individual than that which is in someone else's mind. This suggests subjectivism. Matter is thought to be known only by inference from what is in the mind. In this sense, the "I" that exists is inferred because it thinks. All things that we perceive very clearly must be true.[273]

The metaphysical system of Spinoza (1632-1677) is similar to that of Parmenides. For Spinoza, soul and matter are not entities but simply aspects of God. There is only one "substance" – that of God. No other substance is believed to be self-sufficient. The mind and, thus, thought is believed to be an attribute of God. Spinoza's metaphysical system is, thus, pantheistic. Within this system, everything is believed to be governed by logical necessity. Free will and chance are not believed to exist.[274]

Hegel's philosophy was the culmination of the strand of German philosophical thought that began with Kant. Hegel rejected the idea of plurality. The world was not, in his view, made up of separate units or atoms. Only the whole had a real quality to it. His position, therefore, differs from that of Parmenides and Spinoza in that he conceives of the whole as a complex system. Moreover, the real is thought to be rational. The real, here, is not intended to mean the same thing as the empirical. The whole is referred to as the "Absolute", which is conceived as spiritual. The nature of Reality is believed to be deduced through logic. Another distinct aspect of his metaphysical position is the "dialectic", which comprises the thesis, antithesis and synthesis, as mentioned earlier. The whole is the only thing that is real.[275]

---

[273] Russell, *op. cit.*, note 154, pp. 511-512, 515-517.
[274] *Ibid.*, pp. 522-523.
[275] *Ibid.*, pp. 661-663.

Innate Knowledge and Concepts

The innate knowledge thesis contends that we have knowledge that is derived from our rational nature, but not from deduction or induction. Plato believed that reason is the heart of what it means to be human.[276] In his view, human beings have knowledge through the "soul's" recollection. The notion of innate knowledge suggests that we are certain of some things even when there is no way of explaining how we arrived at the idea.[277]

Similar arguments have been made in relation to our capacity for language as well as our moral knowledge. Within the field of evolutionary psychology, for example, Steven Pinker (b. 1954) has argued that human beings are universally equipped with a common grammar.[278] This feature is innate in human beings and forms the foundation on which languages may be constructed. Pinker's position is informed by Noam Chomsky's (b. 1928) argument that we possess an unconscious knowledge of a universal grammar.[279] This language faculty is conceived as an innate aspect of the human mind.[280]

In relation to morality, Marc Hauser argued that human beings are similarly endowed with an innate moral grammar that forms the basis of morality. In his book, *Moral Minds: How Nature Designed Our Universal Sense of Right and Wrong* (2006), Hauser claims that selection pressure in the process of human evolution has created a universal moral instinct.[281]

In addition to the notion that there is such a thing as innate knowledge, the innate concept thesis holds that we possess some concepts that do not depend on experience. They too are believed to be arrived at by virtue of the rational nature of humankind. Descartes, for example, recognised the existence of innate ideas, such as ideas about God.[282]

---

[276] Al-Rodhan, *"emotional amoral egoism,"* op. cit., note 119, p. 60.
[277] Markie, op. cit., note 253.
[278] S. Pinker, *The Language Instinct* (New York: HarperCollins, 1994).
[279] See, for example, N. Chomsky, *Aspects of the Theory of Syntax* (Cambridge, Mass.: MIT Press, 1965).
[280] N. Chomsky, *Knowledge and Language: Its Nature, Origin and Use* (Westport, CT: Praeger, 1986), pp. 3-4.
[281] Hauser, op. cit., note 170.
[282] Markie, op. cit., note 253.

Atomism

Atomism was established by Leucippus (first half of the 5th century BCE) and Democritus (c. 460-370 BCE), whose works are closely associated. Leucippus' scholarship is dated to about 440 BCE. He belonged to the scientific rationalist tradition and was influenced by Parmenides and Zeno. Leucippus is, however, an elusive figure and little is known of him. He appears to have been drawn to atomism in an effort to find a middle ground between monism and pluralism. Democritus is better known and seems to have lived during the same period. Yet, both shared an approach to knowledge that was closer to modern scientific knowledge than the speculative approach of Ancient Greek philosophers. They held that everything is made up of atoms. In this sense, their approach was distinctly materialist. Democritus even conceived of the soul as composed of atoms. Thought too was conceived of as a physical phenomenon. In addition, no purpose was attributed to the universe; there were thought to be merely atoms governed by mechanical laws.[283]

Epicurus (341-270 BCE), like Democritus, conceived of the universe as comprised of atoms and a void. He was therefore a materialist, believing that the soul was composed of particles such as breath and heat. Sensation was conceived of as films from bodies that travel until they meet soul-atoms. Interestingly, these films were believed to exist even when the bodies from which they came from no longer existed.[284]

Atomism was also present within medieval Arab-Islamic natural philosophy and natural science. Of the two intellectual currents within natural philosophy that were prevalent – kalam and falsafa – kalam employed an atomistic framework in relation to physics. The atomism of kalam was based on the idea that there are atoms and accidents. Atoms were conceived of as those things that occupy space. Those things that do not occupy space were considered accidents. Those things occupying space, such as atoms, could be perceived by the senses and therefore could not be refuted. We know such substances as a result of direct knowledge. Moreover, the ultimate substances by which the world can be understood were believed to be

---

[283] Russell, *op. cit.*, note 154, pp. 71-73, 78.
[284] *Ibid.*, pp. 235-236.

discrete rather than continuous. Accidents were, for example, taste, force, power and will – things that exist, but do not occupy space.[285]

Logical Atomism
Russell proposed a philosophy of Logical Atomism. He sought to clarify philosophical issues through the use of logic. This philosophical approach was shaped by his work on the philosophy of mathematics. In *The Principles of Mathematics* (1903) he attempted to prove that analysis of mathematics always brings us back to logic.[286] Russell's Logical Atomism was developed in response to neo-Hegelian Idealism, which was prominent in Britain in the late 19th century.[287]

His work is also marked by a desire to explore whether knowledge is possible at all. The conviction that science and philosophy must be underpinned by scientific method is also central to his thought. In the discipline of philosophy, this expresses itself in his emphasis on logical analysis based on testing hypotheses by examining evidence. Philosophy was believed to differ from science only in its generality and in the prior nature of statements.[288]

The logic that he conceives is "atomistic" in the sense that it is opposed to the monistic logic supported by followers of Hegel. Atomistic implies simply that the world is made up of separate entities. The doctrine's "logical" dimension derives from the notion that the atoms that Russell wished to obtain were logical rather than physical atoms. His aim was to lend precision to philosophy, which he viewed as premised on vague and ambiguous things. This vagueness is seldom realised until we attempt to be more precise about the things we are referring to. Moreover, precise entities seem to be abstract from our commonplace way of thinking.

---

[285] J. McGinnis, "Arabic and Islamic Natural Philosophy and Natural Science," *Stanford Enyclopedia of Philosophy*, First Published 19 December 2006, http://www.science.uva.nl/~seop/entries/arabic-islamic-natural/.
[286] B. Russell, "The Philosophy of Logical Atomism," in R.C. Marsh (ed.) *Logical and Knowledge. Essays, 1901-1950* (London: George Allen & Unwin Ltd., 1971), p. 178.
[287] K. Klement, "Russell's Logical Atomism," *Stanford Encyclopedia of Philosophy*, First Published 24 October 2005, http://plato.stanford.edu/entries/logical-atomism/.
[288] A.D. Irvine, "Bertrand Russell," *Stanford Encyclopedia of Philosophy*, First Published 7 December 1995; Substantive Revision 1 May 2003, http://www.science.uva.nl/~seop/entries/russell/.

He agreed with Descartes that one should doubt things, and that only when doubt is impossible because of the clarity and distinctness of something should one believe it. Thus, Descartes' method is deemed a good starting point. The first truism Russell draws our attention to is that the world contains facts that we cannot deny and that there are also beliefs that make reference to facts that are either true or false. "Fact" does not refer to any particular existing entity. Fact is expressed as a full sentence, such as "Socrates is dead" and not a sentence such as "Socrates". Facts are conceived of as part of an objective world. The point he wished to make is that the objective world is comprised not only of physical objects, but also of facts. We should not confuse propositions with facts. There is a truth and a falsehood to each proposition. For example, "It is raining" and "It is not raining". This is not the case for facts.[289]

The simplest types of facts, Russell argued, are those that have a particular quality, such as being the colour blue. The next least complicated fact is a fact about a relation, that is, that something is next to something else. Relational facts get more complicated as the number of relations increases. These facts he calls "atomic" facts. Propositions about atomic facts are referred to as "atomic propositions". Russell also conceives of "molecular propositions", which are propositions that contain other propositions and comprise words such as "or", "if" and "and", for example. Russell also refers to "general propositions" that come in one of two forms: those that are about "all" and those that are about "some".[290]

Russell used the term logical atomism to refer to his approach throughout the 1910s and 1920s. Logical atomism comprised a metaphysical view and a methodology for philosophy. The metaphysical dimension of logical atomism proposes that a number of individual entities exist that have particular qualities and relations, and together form facts. All truths are believed to be dependent on atomic facts about particular entities or entities standing in relation to each other. The method involves reducing notions to their simplest forms. The truth of an atomic hypothesis is dependent on an atomic fact.

Underlying his approach is the belief that the fact that a is related to b makes neither a nor b complex entities, and that entities may

---

[289] Russell, *op. cit.*, note 286, pp. 178-183, 187.
[290] *Ibid.*, pp. 198-199, 207, 228.

form parts of many different complexes – hence the notion that the world is made up of distinct entities.[291]

Russell stressed the importance of an observational basis for science. To this end, he maintained the empiricist tradition. Russell's wish to reduce immediate observations to sense-data comes from a desire to find a foundation for knowledge that is certain.[292] In an essay on the development of his thought, Russell states that "Whatever is not experienced, must be known by inference."[293] Since knowledge that is derived from inference is considered doubtful, sense-data are favoured as being closer to absolute truth. Russell's epistemology, in this sense, follows the empiricist tradition.

However, according to Russell, many empiricists, including many logical positivists, confuse the relationship between knowledge and experience. This, he argues, stems from two errors: an inadequate understanding of the concept of "experience" and an error in terms of what is implied in the belief that some quality belongs to an undetermined subject. Two problems occur regarding significance and propositions about properties. Generally, it would be argued that something is not significant unless there is a way of verifying it, and that we cannot know that something has a particular property unless we know of a subject that has that property. Russell rejects these ideas. We can have significant opinions that cannot be verified. For example, we may believe that, if unchecked, nuclear warfare may lead to the destruction of life on Earth. This opinion is significant, but it cannot be verified. In relation to the second problem, can we really claim that Antarctica did not exist until it was discovered?[294]

Russell's logic is deductive. Its value lies in the fact that it represents an analysis of the analytic aspects of thought. Yet, he also recognises that there are other parts of thought that include inductive method.[295] For induction to be valid, it must be possible to know the existence of something without ever knowing any particular case of their truth, which is contrary to what empiricists would claim.[296] Russell points out that if we are to infer from data, such as about the past

---

[291] Klement, *op. cit.*, note 287.
[292] H. Reichenbach, "Bertrand Russell's Logic," in Schlipp, *op. cit.*, note 254, pp. 50-51.
[293] B. Russell, "My Mental Development," in Schlipp, *ibid.*, p. 16.
[294] Russell, *op. cit.*, note 261, pp. 373-374.
[295] Reichenbach, *op. cit.*, note 292, p. 47.
[296] Russell, *op. cit.*, note 261, pp. 379, 381.

that stretches further back than our individual memory, we require some sort of principles by which we can draw inferences. This means that we have to discern whether there is uniformity in nature. The uniformity of nature thesis is that everything that has occurred or will occur is part of a general law to which no exceptions exist. Science aims to discover laws or uniformities, such as the law of gravity. However, Russell asks if there is any reason to suppose that just because something has happened in the past, it will continue to occur in the future. What he has in mind is whether the association of a with b necessarily means that if a occurs so too will b. This, as he points out, is the principle of induction. There are two elements of this: (1) when a and b have been found to be associated and b has never occurred without a, there is a higher probability that a and b will always be found together; and (2) when the association of a and b happen in a sufficient number of cases, the probability of them occurring together is almost a certainty. The probability of this demonstrating a general law is increased by repetitions of the association. Probability supporting the near certainty of a general law is nevertheless based on the data that we have available. Either we accept the possibility of knowledge based on induction or we reject the possibility of justifying beliefs about the future altogether. Scientific knowledge as well as commonplace beliefs about our daily lives are dependent on acceptance of the principle of induction. Inductive knowledge cannot be proved by experience.[297]

In relation to the idea of innate knowledge, Russell finds the rationalists to be on safer ground than the empiricists, but he notes that although we may logically derive knowledge independent of experience, it is nevertheless drawn from experience. We become aware of the possibility of general laws due to experience. This does not, however, mean that we are born with notions of general laws. Instead of "innate", Russell suggests that we employ the term a priori knowledge. Yet, Russell argues that the empiricists were correct to affirm that nothing can be known except through the assistance of experience. Even if we wish to prove the existence of something of which we have no direct experience, we need to appeal to something of which we do have direct experience.[298]

---

[297] Russell, *op. cit.*, note 249, pp. 62-70.
[298] *Ibid.*, pp. 73-74.

Hume argued that a priori knowledge about the relation between cause and effect could not be established. Kant, a rationalist by training, was troubled by Hume's conclusion. Kant argued that we do know some things a priori. For example, we do not know who will be the inhabitants of London in 100 years, but we know that any two of them and any other two of them will make four of them. Here, we seem to have an ability to know something of which we have no experience. Kant argued that this is so because all of our experience is based on two elements: the object and our experience of the object (i.e. sense-data). Normally, it is assumed that knowledge of the object includes a part of ourselves in that it comprises our experience, through sense-data of the object. Kant argued that the sense-data is given by the object and we supply the arrangement of time and space. This is based on the belief that we appear to have a priori knowledge of time and space and causality and comparison, but not sense-data, such as colour. The former are a result of our own nature, not the object. In this sense, we have some a priori knowledge.[299]

Russell highlights a major problem with Kant's account of a priori knowledge. What Kant's method of arriving at the assertion of a priori knowledge depends on is the certainty that facts must always fit arithmetic or logic. If both arithmetic and logic are part of our nature, how can we be sure that our nature will not change. Our nature could change and make two plus two equal five.[300] According to Russell, "a priori knowledge, if it is not erroneous, is not merely knowledge about the constitution of our minds, but is applicable to whatever the world may contain, both what is mental and non-mental."[301] Our a priori knowledge is of entities like relations or qualities. Relations exist in a world that is neither mental nor physical. This world is important to the notion of a priori knowledge. What kind of thing is a relation? It is not sense-data, it is different from mind and it is not an object. Plato addressed this question in his "theory of ideas": "idea" or "form" is something that is not particular. Russell employs the word "universals" to replace Plato's use of the word "ideas", given that "idea" has taken on a different meaning to that of Plato's time.[302]

---

[299] *Ibid.*, pp. 83, 85-86.
[300] *Ibid.*, p. 87.
[301] *Ibid.*, p. 89.
[302] *Ibid.*, pp. 90-93.

Yet, as Ernest Nagel points out, it is actually rather difficult to arrive at non-inferred data. Experiments and observations always involve some sort of interpretation. Russell himself agrees on this point, but believes that it is possible to minimise this dimension of "primitive" knowledge. Nagel, however, insists that the distinction between "primitive" data and the "inferred" cannot be maintained in epistemological terms.[303] Sensory perception is given meaning through interpretation. The role of a socially constructed dimension of knowledge is taken up by constructivist epistemology.

A foremost figure in logical philosophical analysis is the renowned 20th century philosopher Ludwig Wittgenstein (1889-1951). Like Russell, with whom he was associated, Wittgenstein was also in his early career a logical atomist. In *Tractatus Logico-Philosophicus* (1922),[304] he contended that the world is comprised of atomic facts out of which larger facts are built. Similarly, language was thought to be made up of atomic sentences, which form larger propositions. Those propositions that are meaningful can be analysed to demonstrate their logical nature. Those that cannot be analysed in this way are not considered to be meaningful propositions. He argued that the grammar we employ can result in mistaking one proposition for another. Seemingly legitimate philosophical conundrums, in his view, were in fact the result of a misuse of language. The statement "I have a hat" is similar to that of "I have a pain", yet we do not have hats and pains in the same way. Grammar can therefore be deceptive.[305]

There are, of course, also those who depart from both rationalist and empiricist approaches to knowledge acquisition. For example, in *Against Method* (1975),[306] Paul Feyerabend (1924-1994) argued in favour of "epistemological anarchism". He argued that there exists no one epistemological method that guarantees the acquisition of "true" knowledge.[307]

---

[303] E. Nagel, "Russell's Philosophical Science," in Schlipp, *op. cit.*, note 254, p. 335.
[304] L. Wittgenstein, *Tractatus Logico-Philosophicus* (London: Routledge, 1922).
[305] Eagleton, *op. cit.*, note 227, pp. 3-4.
[306] P. Feyerabend, *Against Method* (London: New Left Books, 1975).
[307] J. Preston, "Paul Feyerabend," *Stanford Encylopedia of Philosophy*, First Published 26 August 1997; Substantive Revision 15 February 2007, http://www.scie nce.uva.nl/~seop/entries/ feyerabend/.

Constructivist Epistemology

The term constructivism appears to have been first employed in the 1920s by a group of Soviet artists and architects seeking to define a new artistic movement. Today, it is more commonly employed to refer to an epistemological position. In constructivism, knowledge is thought to be acquired passively. Epistemological constructivism, therefore, rejects the separation between the observer and the observed. It is premised on the notion that knowledge is expressed in symbolic form (language, symbols, images, etc.). Social constructivism puts a slightly different spin on this. It maintains that what we know is socially constructed. In this view, the social world is the product of social practices or endeavours. There are thus weaker and stronger varieties of knowledge.[308]

In relation to scientific knowledge, constructivists emphasise the significance of what goes into the formation of scientific knowledge. They stress that scientific "facts" do not gain their authority by satisfying a criterion for certainty or rationality.[309] Thomas Kuhn (1922-1996), for example, contended in *The Structure of Scientific Revolutions* (1962) that scientific progress is not linear. It has not progressed as a result of paradigm shifts. Periods of scientific progress, according to Kuhn, were thought to take place during adherence to a particular paradigm until confidence in it was lost as a result of the appearance of anomalies. This loss of confidence generates the emergence and dominance of a new paradigm, and so on. Kuhn's thinking marked a departure from positivistic science, given its suggestion that science is not neutral. The paradigms chosen by scientists depend on their disciplinary mindset.[310] In this sense, the legitimacy of ideas depends on the established "rules of the game" or conceptual systems.[311] This, in many respects, marked a departure from the strict separation of object and subject characteristic of conventional approaches to knowledge acquisition.

---

[308] R. Palan, "The Constructivist Underpinnings of the New International Political Economy," in R. Palan (ed.) *Global Political Economy: Contemporary Theories* (London: Routledge, 2000), p. 216.
[309] S.M. Downes, "Constructivism," in E. Craig (ed.) *Routledge Encyclopedia of Philosophy* (London: Routledge, 1998). Retrieved 16 July 2008, from http://www.rep.routledge.com.library3.webster.edu/article/Q017SECT4.
[310] A. Bird, "Thomas Kuhn," *Stanford Encyclopedia of Philosophy*, First Published 13 August 2004, http://plato.stanford.edu/entries/thomas-kuhn/.
[311] Hughes-Warrington, *op. cit.*, note 13, p. 213.

Constructivists emphasise the instrumental and functional roles that claims to knowledge seem to have. Knowledge, in their view, cannot be separated from power. This means that questions of knowledge are political in nature. The idea that one cannot fully separate the observer from the observed implies that there is no true way of knowing the external or observed world. In stronger versions of constructivism, there is no objective world. Discourse is constitutive of our knowledge of the world. What is normally understood as the ordinary nature of things is for constructivists a dominant discourse that naturalises what is in fact constructed. The dominant discourse is never entirely dominant and we can expect to find subordinate discourses as well. The domain of discourses is, however, not simply the battlefield of ideas. Discourses are embedded in different institutional structures that privilege certain discourses over others.[312]

The media and popular culture are important areas of investigation for national or global security. For example, some scholars have sought to show how both fictional and fact-based threats to US and global security have helped to shape a culture of fear that has wide-ranging implications. Doug Davis examines the use of narrative fictions from the past by national security analysts to bolster contemporary strategies and policies. He examines how fictions about nuclear terrorism help to construct its seeming political reality. These tales of catastrophic future scenarios come to occupy a space in the minds and imaginations of ordinary people as well as national security analysts. This ought to be a central concern because of the way in which "knowledge" – in this case about future world scenarios – is constitutive of reality. In this sense, "The catastrophic near-future worlds these imaginary narratives build are, in a dramatic way, the future of our world. The threats they represent are a licence to act, to arm, and to war."[313]

Since many of the symbols and signifiers of meaning are embedded in popular culture, references to popular culture infuse many of our practices and discourses and find their way, for instance, into journalism and security analyses. According to Andrew Martin, constructs of both national and global security find some of their most

---

[312] Palan, *op. cit.*, note 308, pp. 219, 223, 227.
[313] D. Davis, "Future-War Storytelling: National Security and Popular Film," in A. Martin and P. Petro (eds.), *ReThinking Global Security: Media, Popular Culture, and the "War on Terror"* (New Brunswick, NJ: Rutgers University Press, 2006), p. 16.

potent modes of representation by drawing on popular culture. These modes of representation have an important impact on the way in which we represent and see things. This is why popular culture should be taken seriously. National and global security discourses do not only draw on popular culture, they are also multilayered. For example, Martin notes that in the spring of 2003, as the war in Iraq got under way, references to the Vietnam War were frequently evoked in journalism and popular accounts of the war. However, the Vietnam War that was invoked was often the war as it had been reconstructed within popular culture, for example, in a number of films such as *Apocalypse Now* (1979), *Coming Home* (1978) and *The Deer Hunter* (1978).[314] References to popular culture are a means of working out our insecurities and anxieties to the extent that they provide fictive answers to real problems. Narratives that draw on popular culture are ideological in the sense that they both dupe us and help to construct social and political realities.[315]

The similarities between the framing of the so-called War on Terror and the Cold War are pointed out by Robert Ricigliano and Mike Allen. As with the Cold War, the War on Terror is premised on the construction of a world in which there is one overwhelming threat. In the latter case, this pre-eminent threat has three elements: terrorists, rogue states and weapons of mass destruction. Terrorism is the enemy that needs to be defeated, the moral cause is the defence of democracy and freedom and the end goal is to eradicate terrorism by capturing or killing all terrorists. Yet, as Ricigliano and Allen argue, this is based on flawed logic. Terrorism is not an entity that can be defeated. It is impossible to capture all terrorists.[316]

In Section 3, I propose a new theory of knowledge: neurorational physicalism, which shares some similarities with a number of the approaches to knowledge discussed thus far.

---

[314] A. Martin, "Popular Culture and Narratives of Insecurity," in Martin and Petro, *ibid.*, pp. 107-108.
[315] *Ibid.*, p. 110.
[316] R. Ricigliano and M. Allen, "Cold War Redux," in Martin and Petro, *op. cit.*, note 313, pp. 86-88.

3. A Proposed Theory of Knowledge: "Neuro-rational Physicalism"

The new theory of knowledge that I propose – neuro-rational physicalism – recognises that sense experience is a source of knowledge, as empiricists suggest. Yet, it claims that knowledge derived from sense-data involves a dimension of interpretation, which occurs when what is perceived is translated into something that is taken to be meaningful. In this sense it shares some similarities with constructivism. Scientific knowledge, for instance, is not acquired by observation alone. Questions are first raised. These questions are then formulated as hypotheses, which may be rejected or confirmed on the basis of evidence.[317] Yet, the questions that an investigator raises are informed by already established and accepted frameworks of understanding. There is therefore always some sense in which interpretation is the prism through which we acquire knowledge. We always impose our own interpretation on the facts. In relation to the truth in the human sciences, Gadamer, for example, spoke of the "horizon" or scope of vision of an interpreter that delimits what they can understand.[318] Gadamer argued that human thought and knowledge were influenced by tradition and prejudices to a greater extent than the Cartesian belief in the certainty of knowledge allows.[319] As human beings, we are thought to develop particular 'dispositions' formed from culture and education. Truth within the human sciences is a truth derived from this kind of 'formation' within human culture.[320] This may vary according to the geographical and temporal framework within which people exist. Knowledge may therefore be both temporally and spatially constrained as well as indeterminate to some degree, although knowledge that is to some extent indeterminate can be capable of transcending a particular place and/or time.

This is in many respects as true for natural science as it is for the human sciences, as Kuhn implied in his observation that scientific

---

[317] R. Audi, *Belief, Justification, and Knowledge* (Belmont, CA: Wadsworth Publishing Company), p. 121.
[318] See H-G. Gadamer, *Truth and Method*, Second, Revised Edition, Translation Revised by J. Wiensheimer and D.G. Marshall (London and New York: Continuum, 2004).
[319] J. Grondin, *The Philosophy of Gadamer*, Translated by K. Plant (Chesham: Acumen Publishing Ltd, 2003), p. 2.
[320] *Ibid.*, pp. 24-25.

progress appears to take place when a dominant paradigm is adhered to until events occur that cause it to be replaced by another, making scientific knowledge non-linear and somewhat approximate. Thus, within the natural sciences, knowledge is derived from the best available explanation.

Whether hypotheses can be justified using the method of induction and the knowledge derived from this considered scientific knowledge has been questioned. Karl Popper (1902-1994) rejected induction as a means of producing scientific knowledge. He substitutes it with the method of falsification. He argued that it is possible to find evidence to support almost any theory. Only evidence that justifies a highly improbable prediction was believed to be scientific. A theory may only be scientific if it can be proved wrong in a particular event. Scientific knowledge, therefore, has to be falsifiable in Popper's opinion.

Yet, Popper did not view unfalsifiable theories as having no value. An unfalsifiable theory may at some point become falisifiable due to advances in technology or in the theory itself. Indeed, a theory that has a high degree of corroboration through available evidence may be retained until it is rejected by an event that it prohibits. When rejected, it is likely to be replaced by a better theory. This occurred, for example, when Newton's theory of universal gravitation was replaced by Einstein's theory of relativity. There is therefore always some sense in which knowledge is based on the best available explanation. The best explanation is that which is supported by the greatest empirical evidence and, as a result, has the greatest predictive power. There is, thus, some element of empiricism in Popper's approach. Yet, in contrast to empiricists, he did not claim that empirical evidence in favour of a theory can verify it. In this account, all knowledge is provisional, given that all hypotheses may at some future point be falsified and rejected.[321]

If the best possible theories may be accepted as scientific knowledge until falsified, metaphysics can be a source of knowledge about reality. Metaphysics may, for example, tell us that a particular state of affairs may hold, it does not have to tell us that the state of

---

[321] S. Thornton, "Karl Popper," *Stanford Encyclopedia of Philosophy*, First Published 13 November 1997; Substantive Revision 9 February 2009, http://www.science.uva.nl/~seop/entries/popper/.

affairs actually exists.[322] Metaphysics is, indeed, beyond the realm of experience. This includes ideas that we believe to be logically true even if today we do not have the scientific methodologies to prove them. This kind of knowledge may be referred to as *"possible truths subject to proof"*.

Like rationalism, NRP holds that knowledge about things beyond our immediate environment may be acquired through deduction, if we can assume that our initial premises from which knowledge is derived are correct. In this instance, the conclusion is accepted because the initial premises are believed to be correct. Indeed, a great deal of the knowledge we gain is acquired in this way[323] and, as such, is based on what is considered reasonable within particular times and places, given that what is inferred relies on accepted knowledge, which itself depends to some degree on interpretation within a particular cultural and temporal setting. To this end, **knowledge is indeterminate as well as temporally, spatially and perhaps culturally constrained.**

NRP is thus distinct from empiricism, which assumes that all knowledge is derived from sense-data, and closer to rationalism, which recognises that all knowledge is to some extent based on prior assumptions. This does not mean that knowledge derived on the basis of reason does not rely at all on sense experience. Let us consider the statement that all vixens are female foxes. We know this to be true not simply because analytically it cannot be otherwise. Knowing this statement to be true involves bridging the gap between knowledge of conventions and knowledge of vixen. Reason, along with experience, is therefore a source of knowledge.[324] Knowledge is thus acquired through employing both sense experience and reason, both of which involve interpretation.

However, unlike some rationalists, such as Plato, Descartes and Kant, NRP rejects the notion that human beings possess innate knowledge. There is no knowledge that can be gained without experience of the external world, defined as the world outside the individual's mind. The human mind does not contain a priori concepts, although it is a predisposed tabula rasa in so far as it contains a code for

---

[322] E.J. Lowe, *The Possibility of Metaphysics: Substance, Identity, and Time* (Oxford: Clarendon Press, 1998), p. 22.
[323] Audi, *op. cit.*, note 317, pp. 68-69.
[324] *Ibid.*, pp. 61, 64.

survival as a result of evolution. NRP is also distinct from those who argue that humankind is endowed with innate moral knowledge, such as Hauser. The problem with the latter approach is that it confuses emotions relevant to moral values with moral knowledge. People are certainly equipped with emotions, such as sympathy and empathy, as a result of selection pressures that are essential to the capacity to develop moral codes. Yet, they are not born with innate moral concepts or ideas. *Morally relevant emotions are essential for living in social groups and they provide the basis on which we may construct conceptual frameworks that help guide our actions, but human beings should more accurately be thought of as being endowed with morally relevant capacities rather than innate moral knowledge.*

Another reason for departing from the notion that knowledge is acquired through sense experiences alone is that there may be non-visible matter, such as power and energy, that cannot be perceived, which means that we cannot simply rely on sense-data as the only true sources of knowledge. By observing a galaxy cluster three billion light years away, the "dark matter" that comprises a quarter of the universe has been observed. Dark matter is distinct from normal matter in that it cannot be seen using regular telescopes, since it emits no light or heat, and seems to relate to other matter only gravitationally. Such observations show that the universe is not only made up of visible matter, but also invisible matter.[325]

Scientists are also making progress on "cloaking", that is, making objects invisible. At Berkeley University, scientists have developed artificial matter capable of bending wavelengths of light differently, suggesting that it may be possible to gain greater control over the way in which light moves and, thereby, cloak objects.[326]

Therefore, pure empiricism, which holds that knowledge can only be acquired through empirical means, is too limiting. Scientific Realism, for instance, argues that knowledge is possible even when the subject of knowledge is unobservable. It assumes that given the fallibility of scientific method and the approximate nature of scientific

---

[325] K. Tuttle, "Dark Matter Observed," *SLAC Today*, 22 August 2006, http://today.slac.stanford.edu/feature/darkmatter.asp.
[326] "The Possibility of an Invisible Cloak," *National Public Radio, Talk of the Nation*, 15 August 2008, http://www.npr.org/templates/storystory.php?storyId=93636636&sc=emaf.

knowledge, we are warranted in accepting findings that appear secure.[327]

Yet, it is important to note that even unobservable subjects of knowledge have a physical base. Indeed, everything is physical, even if invisible. Even thoughts, for example, are physical in the sense that they are mediated through neurochemistry, as is explained in Chapter 3. Emotions and thoughts are therefore physical processes. While mental processes are the product of neurochemistry, mental processes may themselves prompt changes in brain chemistry that, in turn, modify initial neurochemistry and thus emotions or thoughts.[328] In a similar sense, what may be thought of as the soul is also physical, although unobservable. In this sense, reality is physical or "material".

This runs counter to idealism, which conceives of reality as the totality of minds and ideas. Idealism posits that objects are merely ideas in that it is ideas that we perceive and not objects themselves. In this sense, it is ideas that enable objects to be represented and therefore perceived. George Berkeley (1685-1753), for example, argued that everything that we directly perceive is ideas. He argued that sense experience could, in fact, be traced back to ideas.[329] This was an extreme form of empiricism. As is mentioned above, Hegel, in a more nuanced way, conceived of ideas as governing the material world. Spinoza took a slightly different position, conceiving of mind and matter as part of the same whole. The Cartesian dualist conception of the mind and body expounded by Descartes represents yet another approach to the relationship of the body to the mind.[330] Yet, even if this were to be the case, ideas themselves have a particular kind of physicality, making the source of everything physical, even if unobservable.

While the idea that mental processes are physical processes has been put forward by neuroscientists, it is less common within philosophical investigations. The association of mental states and processes with physical ones has nevertheless been made in the context of the philosophy of the mind by D.M. Armstrong, who explored

---

[327] R. Boyd, "Scientific Realism," *Stanford Encyclopedia of Philosophy*, First Published 12 June 2002, http://www.science.uva.nl/~seop/entries/ scientific-realism/.
[328] Al-Rodhan, *"emotional amoral egoism,"* *op. cit.*, note 119, pp. 69-70.
[329] L. Downing, "George Berkeley," *Stanford Encyclopedia of Philosophy*, First Published 10 September 2004, http://www. science.uva.nl/~seop/entries/ berkeley/.
[330] D.M. Armstrong, *The Materialist Theory of the Mind,* Second Edition (London and New York: Routledge, 1993), pp. 5-6.

whether humankind can be conceived in purely physical terms. Armstrong contended that there is no good philosophical argument on which to reject the notion that mental processes are not material. Colour, sound, taste, perception, and so on, are all conceived of as physical phenomena.[331]

To this end, NRP shares some similarities with atomism, although Ancient Greek and the Arab-Islamic conceptions of "atoms" were distinct from contemporary understandings of atoms, as well as Logical Atomism in its rejection of idealism.

Knowledge therefore relies on not only sense experience, but also reason, both of which are filtered by interpretation. Yet, decisions based on accepted knowledge must be guided by ethics, not in terms of how to acquire knowledge but in terms of its application. While we should seek certain knowledge, ethics have a role in applying it to everyday life in order to safeguard human dignity. This "ethical right of passage" is likely to become all the more important. As is discussed in greater detail in Chapter 15, what awaits us as a species in terms of biological and technological advances will require ethics as well as reason to ensure that the application of knowledge serves human dignity and sustainable history.

In summary, NRP, which is compared and contrasted with other philosophies of knowledge in Table 4, recognises the interpretive dimension of knowledge and its acquisition and, thus, shares something with constructivist epistemology. Yet, even though NRP accepts that the observer cannot be entirely separated from the observed, like empiricism, it recognises that sense-data are an important source of knowledge. However, it stresses that sense-data are subject to interpretation and cannot be relied on alone to contribute to knowledge. Even if we only know objects through sense experience, all thought processes are physical and, thus, material. NRP argues that reason too has a role to play in the acquisition of knowledge. This remains the case even if new knowledge derived from what is inferred on the basis of accepted knowledge is always itself the product of indeterminate knowledge. In this sense, it is the best available explanation. NRP departs from those strands of rationalism that adhere to the notion of innate knowledge and, instead, holds that only human beings possess an innate survival code or predisposed tabula rasa and innate moral sensitivities (see Diagram 8).

---

[331] *Ibid.*

Diagram 8: A Proposed Theory of Knowledge: "Neuro-rational Physicalism"

Neuro
All human knowledge has a physical neuro-biological foundation, including thoughts, memories, perceptions and emotions. Thus, mental states and thought processes are physical.

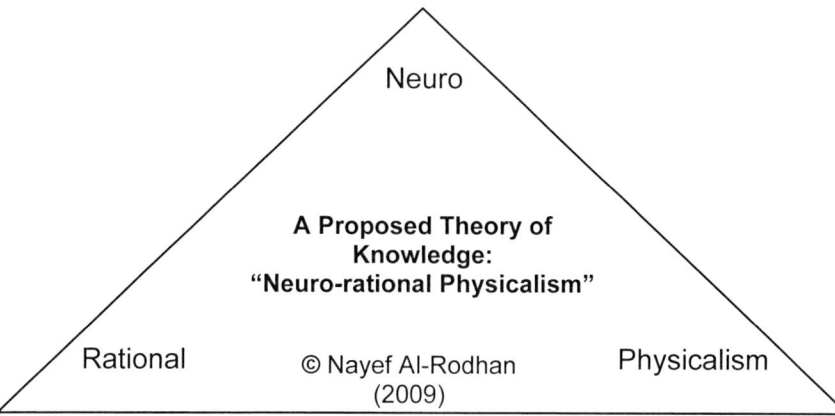

Rational
Knowledge derived from sense-data is not certain. Interpretation is the prism through which we order sense-data. Pure empiricism is therefore an inadequate means of acquiring knowledge. Knowledge is also inferred from what is accepted as established knowledge, with new knowledge being based on the best explanation. Knowledge about things beyond our immediate environment may be acquired through deduction, if the initial premises are believed to be correct. The notion of innate knowledge (including moral knowledge) is rejected. Thus, knowledge is based on both sense-data and reason, and has a high probability of being subject to error or incomplete understanding. While facts exist, all knowledge is to some extent interpreted and ultimately indeterminate, being perhaps also temporally, spatially and culturally constrained.

Physicalism
All the universe and its energies are physical, although some matter and energy may be unobservable with our current technologies.

Table 4: A Comparative View of Philosophies of Knowledge*

	Empiricism	Logical Positivism	Rationalism	Innate Knowledge
Sense data	√√	√√	√	
Reason			√√	√√
Logic		√√	√	√
Innate Ideas/ Concepts	Ibn Sina, Ibn Tufayl, Locke: tabula rasa		√ some argue yes	√√
Innate Morality				√ some argue yes
Innate Moral Sensitivities				
Monism			√ sometimes	
Atomism				
Materialism				
Idealism	√ in extreme cases			
Induction	√		√	
Deduction			√	
Falsification				
Interpretation				
Reproducibility	√		√	
Best Explanation Available	√		√	
Spatial and Temporal Constraints				
Cultural Constraints				
Non-neutrality of Science				
Uncertainty of Social Knowledge				
Existence of Some Invisible Matter				
Possibility of Metaphysical Knowledge			√	
Physical Nature of the Mind				

√ IMPORTANT √√ VERY IMPORTANT

*The elements of philosophies of knowledge shown in the table do not necessarily represent the totality of the concepts as originally proposed by some of the thinkers.

	Atomism	Logical Atomism	Constructivism	"Neuro-rational Physicalism"
Sense-data			√	√
Reason		√	√	√
Logic		√√		√
Innate Ideas/ Concepts				pre-disposed tabula rasa
Innate Morality				
Innate Moral Sensitivities				√
Monism				
Atomism	√√ physical	√√ logical		
Materialism	√			√
Idealism			√	
Induction				√
Deduction				√
Falsification				√
Interpretation			√√	√
Reproducibility				√ natural sciences
Best Explanation Available				√
Spatial and Temporal Constraints			√	√ sometimes
Cultural Constraints			√	√ sometimes
Non-neutrality of Science			√	√
Uncertainty of Social Knowledge			√	√ sometimes
Existence of Some Invisible Matter				√
Possibility of Metaphysical Knowledge				√ sometimes
Physical Nature of the Mind				√

√ IMPORTANT √√ VERY IMPORTANT

4. Conclusion

Due to the importance of knowledge claims to the sustainability of history, this chapter sought to examine what we know and how we arrive at that knowledge. As explained, there is a difference between our knowledge of things and knowledge of truths. In each case, there are two kinds of knowledge: one immediate and one derivative. Immediate knowledge of things we gain through "acquaintance". We may be acquainted with something through sense-data or through universals. In relation to our knowledge of truths, it may be immediate in the sense that it is "intuitive" or self-evident, such as statements about sense-data or arithmetical and abstract logical principles. We can derive knowledge from intuitive knowledge through the process of deduction.[332]

However, it is important to recognise that inference is part of knowledge acquisition, which implies the application of reason. Thus, pure empiricism is not tenable, since the observer and the observed are not entirely separable. Even sensory perceptions are to some degree inferred. Once we accept that all knowledge is to some extent inferred, employing reason through both deductive and inductive means is acceptable. Yet, knowledge gained through these means is always subject to some degree of interpretation. In addition, some matter and energy sources are not observable, which also calls into question the merits of pure empiricism. Yet, even non-observable subjects of knowledge are physical phenomena. In this respect, everything is material – even thought.

Given that scientific knowledge is premised on the best available explanation and is therefore somewhat approximate, and knowledge of the social world greatly infused with contingent meanings, it is very difficult to be dogmatic about what we think we know for certain. Yet, this does not mean that we are condemned to inaction. Knowledge based on a reasonable degree of certainty is still central to the progress that will make life sustainable in terms of scientific and technological advances. However, decisions that stem from reasonable certainty must always be looked at through ethical lenses.

---

[332] Russell, *op. cit.*, note 249, pp. 108-110.

Part 2

Civilisational Triumph and Sustainable History

CHAPTER 6

HOW CAN WE COLLECTIVELY SUCCEED?
TRIUMPHS OF INDIVIDUAL GEO-CULTURAL DOMAINS

The collective success of geo-cultural domains is a prerequisite for sustainable history, given the interconnectivity of our successes and difficulties. In the West, the Enlightenment, a period in history marked by faith in reason, is commonly thought of as referring to the political changes and their intellectual foundations in Europe and the Americas from approximately 1688 until the French Revolution. This story is one of the victory of reason and individualism over tradition. It is often perceived as a purely Western story that contrasts starkly with the "darkness" that is assumed to have fallen elsewhere.[333] In many respects, the West has been so successful in promoting itself as the source of the forces of light and progress that many associate Western culture with the Enlightenment, which is perceived in contradistinction to tradition and faith. Yet, what is referred to as the "Dark Ages" was a period of "light" for the Arab-Islamic world. Great thinkers, such as Ibn Sina (Avicenna), Ibn Tufayl, Ibn Rushd (Averroes) (1126-1198) and Ibn Khaldūn (1332-1406), flourished during this period. East and West met, and they formed a bridge across which ideas, innovations, products and elements of language were transferred. The notion that East and West have met only in conflict overlooks the peaceful and indeed crucial exchanges that took place over many centuries,[334] and that advanced the collective knowledge that we take for granted today. Yet, the contribution of Arab-Islamic thinkers to the European Renaissance and European Enlightenment has largely been written out of European history, except for occasional references

---

[333] S. Fleischacker, "Enlightenment and Tradition: The Clash within Civilizations," *Journal of Ecumenical Studies*, Vol. 42, No. 3, 2007.
[334] B. Bowden, "The River of Inter-civilisational Relations: The Ebb and Flow of Peoples, Ideas and Innovations," *Third World Quarterly*, Vol. 28, No. 7, 2007, p. 1359.

to the "keepers" of Greek heritage. The reasons for this were undoubtedly many and varied. However, competition and religious animosity, fear and cultural arrogance certainly played a role in the process of identity formation under way in Europe. That the rise of the West has some Eastern origins should not come as a surprise. *Each high point in the history of human civilisation has taken place where the conditions were ripe and has borrowed and built on the achievements of other cultures whose "golden age" may have passed.* In previous times, the decline and fall of a once magnificent geo-cultural domain would not have concerned another on the rise or at its peak, at least not to the same extent as today. However, in the current era of interdependence and increased interconnectedness the decline of other geo-cultural domains is a pressing concern for those that are at a high point. The triumph of one geo-cultural domain depends on the success of others.

This chapter takes a closer look at the conditions that underpinned the numerous golden ages of the Arab-Islamic world in order to demonstrate how advances in human civilisation are cumulative and appear where permissive conditions prevail, shifting geographically. *It is important to point out that this case constitutes but one of many possible examples. While it would be possible to look at a number of other geo-cultural domains to illustrate the importance of cultural borrowing and exchange, there are several reasons for choosing this example.* **First**, it is possible to easily identify the influences of other earlier geo-cultural domains, and to identify the way in which the Arab-Islamic world has influenced the current dominant culture. **Second**, highlighting the intertwined nature of the West and the Arab-Islamic world helps to break down essentialist conceptions of geo-cultural domains and to demonstrate that a "clash of civilisations" is by no means inevitable. **Third**, the Arab-Islamic world is geographically at the crossroads of other geo-cultural domains. This example reveals the extent to which many of the greatest achievements of Arab-Islamic culture drew on earlier contributions to human civilisation, such as those of the Ancient Greeks, China and India. **Fourth**, we can also see how some of the foundations of the Renaissance in Europe built on some of the contributions to various forms of knowledge advanced during the Arab-Islamic golden ages, which disrupts the notion of the West as a hermetically sealed entity that has developed along a particular trajectory that began with Ancient Greece and the Roman Empire, went through a dark period and miraculously took off again with the Renaissance. I then identify commonalities in the conditions enabling golden ages to occur in other geo-cultural domains. **Finally**, I consider whether there are commonalities in the fall and decline of successful geo-cultural domains that may be helpful to learn from in the present era.

1. Triumphs of Individual Geo-cultural Domains: The Example of the Arab-Islamic World

Individual triumphs of geo-cultural domains may be thought of as contributions to the advancement of human civilisation as a whole. Such advances appear to have occurred when certain conditions prevailed, such as good governance, cultural borrowing and innovation. This may be demonstrated by looking at the golden ages of the Arab-Islamic world.

The establishment of the Arab-Islamic geo-cultural domain took place at an incredible pace. The followers of the Prophet Mohammed started out from Western Arabia in 634. In the space of a decade, they had occupied Persia, Palestine, Iraq, Syria and Egypt. They went on to conquer Tunisia, Morocco and Algeria. In the early 700s, they made their way across the Mediterranean, advancing as far as the south of Paris. Following a defeat at Poitier in 732, they retreated back to the Iberian Peninsula, which was then known as Al-Andalus. If we were to sum up the factors that contributed to the golden eras in Baghdad, Al-Andalus, Central Asia, Ottoman Turkey and Mughal India, up to the 18th century,[335] we might include good governance, a lack of dogma and an emphasis on reason. These helped to create the conditions that enabled scientific and technological innovation, tolerance and open-mindedness, which certainly contributed to the capacity to absorb other cultures and build on the contributions of others. Another factor that was important to the rise of the Arab-Islamic world was the encouragement of theological innovation (Ijtihad) in order to allow religion to evolve according to changing historical circumstances and needs. Each of these factors is discussed in turn below.

---

[335] Morgan, *op. cit.*, note 88, p. xvii.

Good Governance

Good governance, albeit evaluated with reference to the historical periods to which it relates, meant that Islam acted as a unifying force that encouraged social solidarity and justice for all.[336] Ethnic belonging gave way to religious solidarity. In contrast to the societies that existed at the time of its inception, such as Persian feudalism, the Indian caste system, and the Byzantine and Latin European aristocracies, Islam carried a message of equality, although it did recognise some existing inequalities.[337] Under Islamic law there is no distinction between religious and state-related issues. Individuals are recognised as equal in their relationship to God. Moreover, the Prophet set out the moral responsibilities of the state as specified in the Koran and this might be considered a specific blueprint for "good governance".[338]

The position of women, while not equal to that of men, was improved in relation to pre-Islamic times. Their position was strengthened by the property rights they enjoyed. The property that they owned could not be appropriated by their husbands. The courts protected these rights, especially in relation to inheritance.[339]

People were not forced to convert to Islam. Contrary to what is often believed, conversion to Islam was not the primary goal of war. In fact, compared with conditions and practice at the time, rulers demonstrated remarkable tolerance. As is discussed below, other "Peoples of the Book", namely Christians and Jews, were granted protected status and were able to practice their religions, albeit within certain parameters.[340]

In most cases, conquered peoples were able to retain their landed property. Muslims were not allowed to buy land from the original inhabitants of the territories they conquered. This avoided a situation developing in which they would become the feudal lords of local farmers. Instead, the principle of sharing output between the state and farmers was introduced. The farmers paid the state's share in the form of a tax, which represented a relatively small proportion of

---

[336] M.U. Chapra, *Muslim Civilization: The Causes of Decline and the Need for Reform* (Markfield: The Islamic Foundation, 2008), p. 36.
[337] B. Lewis, *What Went Wrong: Western Impact and Middle Eastern Response* (New York: Oxford University Press, 2002), pp. 82-83.
[338] Chapra, *op. cit.*, note 336, pp. 8, 35.
[339] *Ibid.*, p. 145.
[340] B. Lewis, *The Middle East: A Brief History of the Last 2000 Years* (New York: Scribner, 1995), p. 58.

total output. Muslim jurisprudence also made it a moral obligation of the state to construct and maintain irrigation systems in order to improve agricultural productivity. Maintenance of irrigation systems was fairly constant in periods of stability from the Umayyads – the second Arab caliphate after the death of the Prophet Mohammed – to the Ottomans. Both of these measures contributed to agricultural and rural prosperity, which facilitated the economic development of other economic sectors.[341]

The conquering forces were relatively small and lacked experience of government. The Umayyads recognised that in order to govern large populations effectively they would have to retain the administrative systems of the Sassanid and Byzantine Empires.[342] Local governance structures were kept in place through a series of treaties and agreements. This gave the Arab-Islamic forces a solid bureaucratic foundation on which to build. Even local elites that had occupied positions within local bureaucracies were reintegrated into the administrative structure.[343] Thus, the social structure that existed in newly conquered lands went largely unchanged, providing a degree of continuity. This also helped to limit the power of the occupiers over the original inhabitants of these lands, which may have contributed to stability. While local governance structures were gradually modified as the Arabs became more established and sought to increase their power within the conquered lands, existing systems of taxation were retained.[344]

Moreover, the Abassids, who followed the Umayyads, retained the governance structures in place under the Umayyads. They also continued to advance the bureaucratic centralisation started by their predecessors. Yet, the central administration stayed in close touch with local community leaders and land owners. These local elites acted as intermediaries between local populations and the central administration, collecting taxes.[345]

---

[341] Chapra, *op. cit.*, note 336, pp. 39-40.
[342] P. Mansfield, *The Arabs*, Third Edition (Penguin Books, 1992), p. 42.
[343] I. Lapidus, *A History of Islamic Societies* (Cambridge: Cambridge University Press, 1988), p. 43.
[344] *Ibid.*, p. 44.
[345] *Ibid.*, p. 76.

2. Cultural Borrowing

The importance of cultural borrowing to the triumph of individual geo-cultural domains, and thereby to human civilisation as a whole, is evident in the case of the Arab-Islamic world. The Arab-Islamic world borrowed and built on the contributions of ancient civilisations and also helped to lay the foundations that would enable Europe to excel.

The Arab-Islamic World and the West
The so-called dark ages in Europe refer to the period between the Greco-Roman period and the Renaissance that is credited with leading to the Enlightenment and the scientific revolution in Europe. The usual historical narrative that European school children learn and later largely take for granted is the story of Ancient Greece, which later influenced Ancient Rome and was by some miracle rediscovered, after centuries of "darkness", during the Renaissance years. Yet, Greek heritage was not lost to history until these years of "re-birth". Within this narrative the West's rise occurred without the help of non-Western civilisations.[346] What is lost to history according to this narrative, as Michael Hamilton Morgan points out in his book *Lost History: The Enduring Legacy of Muslim Scientists, Thinkers, and Artists* (2007),[347] is that the so-called dark ages coincided with a period of remarkable discovery, intellectual development and artistry in the Arab-Islamic world. Many of the eminent figures that bring this period into sharp relief were themselves aware of and sometimes engaged in intellectual dialogue with Greek philosophy. Indeed, much of the history that was lost to Europe was rediscovered thanks to the work of Arab-Islamic scholars and those who translated Greek and Arabic texts into Latin, and later built on them.

I do not have space to list the myriad of figures who drew on and commented on the contributions of Ancient Greece. However, among them was Al-Mamun (786-833), an Abbasid caliph, who in the 9th century built a centre of rationalist learning in Baghdad modelled

---

[346] J.M. Hobson, "Deconstructing the Eurocentric Clash of Civilizations: De-Westernizing the West by Acknowledging the Dialogue of Civilizations," in M. Hall and P.T. Jackson (eds.) *Civilizational Identity: The Production and Reproduction of "Civilizations" in International Relations* (New York: Palgrave Macmillan, 2007), p. 152.
[347] Morgan, *op. cit.*, note 88.

on the Persian Academy of Gundeshapur, where exiled Nestorian Christians engaged in learning and Syriac scholars and translators from Byzantium worked. In order to build its successor in Baghdad, Al-Mamun sent emissaries to find the best books on all the disciplines of the time, including mathematics, science, astronomy and philosophy, and the best translators in order to translate earlier forms of learning into Arabic. The "House of Wisdom", as it was known, was home to scholars such as Mohamed Al-Khwarizmi, who would later be considered the father of algebra and the algorithm. Indeed, this house of learning in Abbasid Baghdad represented a summit of intellectual achievement of the period. [348]

In the far west of the Arab-Islamic world, in Muslim Spain, the coexistence of the three Abrahamic religions of Islam, Christianity and Judaism created a climate in which Iberian Christians, known as Mozarabs, similar to the Nestorians in Baghdad, put their linguistic skills to use and translated Latin, Greek and Hebrew classics into Arabic, contributing to the blossoming of knowledge and paralleling that in Baghdad. However, much of this history of coexistence was lost as Jews and Muslims fled or were forced to convert during the Spanish reconquest and history was rewritten and libraries burned by extremists.[349]

Ibn Rushd, who is known in the West as Averroes, was a philosopher and interpreter of Aristotelian and Platonic philosophy.[350] He discussed issues that would later be relevant to the Enlightenment as well as being prescient within his own historical and cultural context. Ibn Rushd was the only Arab-Islamic philosopher to write a whole treatise, *Fasl Al-Maqal*, on the relationship between religion and philosophy, in which he aims to demonstrate that there is no contradiction between philosophy or science and the shari'a. The study of philosophy, according to Ibn Rushd, is required by the shari'a in that it calls on people to reflect, and that reflection is carried out through reasoning.[351]

---

[348] *Ibid.*, pp. 56-57.
[349] *Ibid.*, pp. 70-71.
[350] F.M. Najjar, "Ibn Rushd (Averroes) and the Egyptian Enlightenment Movement," *British Journal of Middle Eastern Studies*, Vol. 31, No. 2, 2004, p. 203; D.H. Frank, "Political Philosophy in Classical Islam," *Islamic Philosophy Online*, 1998, http://www.muslimphilosophy.com/ip/rep/H012.htm.
[351] Najjar, *ibid.*, p. 206.

Platonic themes can be found in the philosophy of other prominent Muslim philosophers, particularly the notion of the philosopher king. In Al-Farabi's (872-950/51) philosophy, the role of the prophet is thought to be analogous to that of the philosopher king in Platonic thought. The Prophet is understood as a divine legislator, who puts forward a model of perfect governance capable of enabling human communities to thrive. For Ibn Bajja (1095-1138) and Ibn Tufayl, philosophy and politics are not compatible. Intellectual elitism can be found in Ibn Bajja's work, which is concerned with the state of a philosopher (and philosophy) in an imperfect society, which is believed to be achieved by isolation from the hopes and fears of the masses. Similarly, in Ibn Tyufal's *Hayy Ibn Yaqzan,* published in either 1160 or 1170, there is a similar pessimism about the capacity to alter the beliefs of people, resulting in the isolation of the philosopher.[352]

Arab-Islamic scholars also questioned established traditions in a number of areas, heralding a new scientific mode of thought that helped to lay the foundations of the European scientific revolution. Moreover, Ibn Sina critiqued Aristotelian induction. In contrast to Aristotle, Ibn Sina argued that knowledge derived through induction does not result in absolute certainty, favouring instead experimentation as a means of producing conditional principles. Many breakthrough discoveries, which are discussed in greater detail in Section 3, were enabled through the scientific method of induction.[353]

The Arab-Islamic World and the Far East
Mutual borrowings were not confined to the rich exchanges between Islam and the West. Cultural borrowing also took place between Islam and the Far East. In the 9th century, Baghdad was a global seaport connected to the ocean by the canals of Basra, and technology imported from China was employed in the paper mills of the city. With this technology it was possible to mass produce paper. This, in turn, facilitated the dissemination of literature and learning, which would have been impossible with the parchment or vellum used in Europe at the time.[354]

---

[352] Frank, *op. cit.*, note 350.
[353] Hobson, *op. cit.*, note 19, pp. 178-180; J. McGinnis, "Scientific Methodologies in Medieval Islam," *Journal of the History of Philosophy*, Vol. 41, No. 3, 2003, p. 307.
[354] Morgan, *op. cit.*, note 88, p. 59.

Muslim India's own golden age begins with the arrival of the Mughals from Central Asia in the 16th century and lasts to the end of the Mughal Empire in the mid-19th century. One of the descendents of Timur or Tamerlane married a Persian princess, and they invited architects, artists, poets and other scholars from Persia to their court.[355] Indeed, in India the cross fertilisation of two cultures generated a particular Indo-Islamic art form. For example, the Great Mosque in Dehli, which dates back to 1193, was conceived by Muslims and then constructed by Indian masons and sculptors who infused it with distinctly Indian decorative features mixed with Arab calligraphic designs. This fusion reached an apogee in the 18th century by which time it became almost impossible to distinguish between Hindu and Islamic art.[356]

Morgan identifies a part of "lost history" that produced a cross fertilisation of Chinese, Islamic and European thought. For the most part associated with indiscriminate killing and the sacking of cities, the Mongols also established new cities in Persia, Central Asia and India that played a part in an intellectual renaissance in these areas for several hundreds of years. Under Kublai Khan's reign in China, Chinese astronomy filtered West into Persia. Cultural exchange was two-way. Muslim knowledge also flowed East to China.[357] The Muslim scholar Jamal Al-Din introduced a Persian calendar that spans 10,000 years, astronomical tools and a wooden globe of the Earth (terrestrial globe). The engineers and astronomers employed at Kublai Khan's court also helped to contribute to the development of new observatories and mapmaking techniques, all of which helped to give China supremacy at sea in the 15th century.[358]

Al-Biruni (973-1048) worked for most of his life for Sultan Mahmud's court and that of his son, Masud. He joined Mahmud on his campaigns in India in the early 11th century, where he studied Sanskrit and produced what is considered one of the most authoritative accounts of medieval India.[359] He was also an astronomer, astrologist, mathematician, geographer and geologist, immersed himself

---

[355] *Ibid.*, pp. 77-78.
[356] Braudel, *op. cit.*, note 2, p. 80.
[357] Morgan, *op. cit.*, note 88, pp. 138-147.
[358] *Ibid.*, pp. 147-148.
[359] FSTC Limited, "Al-Biruni," *MuslimHeritage.Com*, 6 May 2007, http://www.muslimheritage.com/day_life/default.cfm?ArticleI=690&Oldpage=1.

in Hindu philosophy and religion and passed on some Muslim and Greek knowledge.[360]

3. Innovation

The Arab-Islamic world has also introduced a number of ideas and innovations to the West. Yet, the names of the great contributors to the Scientific Revolution are usually cited as Roger Bacon (1220-1292), Galileo Galilei (1564-1642), Newton and Leibniz (1646-1716). However, these are not the only eminent thinkers who contributed to innovations and new fields of knowledge. Outside influence is sometimes acknowledged in the West, but it is usually identified as originating from Ancient Greek, Latin scholars and the Renaissance.[361] Yet, the golden ages of the Arab-Islamic world reveal that the Scientific Revolution is built on wider foundations.

Algorithms – sets of numerical calculations and instructions, and the basis of today's computer technology, commerce and science – have their origin in the 9th century. A vital figure in their creation was Mohamed Al-Khwarizmi (mentioned above). He was born in Khiva, a small trading post on the Silk Road which acted as a crossroads between East and West. In 832, when the House of Wisdom in Baghdad was established, Al-Khwarizmi was one of the brilliant minds that the caliph, Al-Mamun, brought to his centre of learning. At this university, there were people decoding the formulas of Euclid, Pythagoras and Ptolemy as well as studying and translating the works of Aristotle and Socrates. In an old text brought from India and translated from Sanskrit into Arabic, Al-Khwarizmi discovered the symbol known today as zero from which numerous mathematical paths were suddenly possible.[362]

In Al-Khwarizmi's time, three methods of calculation existed. The first was finger counting, which was suitable for easy calculations. The second allowed more complicated calculations using Arabic letter characters. The third was the Hindu decimal system, which employed the characters representing zero to nine and enabled one to count to positive and negative infinity. This system was vital to calculating angles and curves, the relationship of the Earth to the Sun and

---

[360] Morgan, *op. cit.*, note 88, p. 169.
[361] *Ibid.*, p. 3.
[362] *Ibid.*, pp. 85-87, 89.

the stars, and to locating Mecca accurately thereby allowing Muslims to pray in its direction with certainty. Al-Khwarizmi's works on algebra, astronomy and astronomical tables, as well as his revision of Ptolemy's theories and maps of the world, were only translated for European use 300 years later. Algebra constituted the detachment of calculation from the physical to the purely abstract. Before that, Ancient Greeks had been fascinated by geometry – the calculation of spaces that are reducible to things in the physical world, such as plots of land.[363] Following in the footsteps of Al-Khwarizmi, Al-Nayrizi, who was born in the 9th century, employed trigonometry to calculate the direction of the Kaaba in Mecca in order help Muslims face the correct direction during payer. His work paved the way for more complex calculations of geolocation using trigonometry.[364]

Also at the House of Wisdom in Baghdad, Al-Battani (853-929) calculated the length of the year as 365 days, 5 hours, 48 minutes and 24 seconds, within minutes of what was later calculated with the use of telescopes and atomic clocks. He also identified the equinoxes and the tilt of the Earth's axis of rotation vis-à-vis the plane in which the orbit of the Sun cuts the celestial sphere,[365] and popularised, and perhaps discovered, the basics of trigonometrical ratios, making significant corrections to Ptolemy's work.[366]

In the 10th century, Al-Uqlidisi, who worked in Damascus, is thought to have been the first person to use decimal fractions in Arab-Islamic mathematics. Before this time, non-decimal fractions were used dating back to Babylon and Ancient Egypt and other earlier cultures. In the same century, the foundations were laid for mathematical and optical theories that later enabled Galileo and Copernicus to make breakthrough discoveries about the relationship of the Earth to other heavenly bodies and the shape of the Earth itself.[367]

Researchers in the US have recently discovered 15th century examples of the use of the concept of quasicrystalline geometry, involving complex mathematical formulae, represented through Islamic

---

[363] *Ibid.*, pp. 89-90.
[364] *Ibid.*, p. 95.
[365] *Ibid.*, p. 94.
[366] "An Overview of Muslim Astronomers," *MuslimHeritage.Com*, http://muslimheritage.com/topics/default.cfm?ArticleID=232#Al-Battani.
[367] Morgan, *op. cit.*, note 88, pp. 95, 97.

art. The principles of quasicrystalline geometry were previously thought to have been formulated several centuries later.[368]

In the 11th century, the House of Knowledge in Cairo became the beacon to which the best thinkers of the period were attracted. There, Ibn Al-Haytham (965-1039) developed theories of optics and is believed to have been one of the first scholars to argue for the use of strict empiricism. This contrasted with the Ancient Greeks, who had also applied empiricism but tended to prove their theories by abstract theorising. Fascinated by light and what happens when light enters the eye, Ibn Al-Haytham's dissections of the eyeball laid the foundation for later work that led to modern understandings of human vision. His discoveries furthered theories of light and optics, which created the path for later European scholars such as Leeuwenhoek hundreds of years later. His work also set the stage for greater understanding of the magnifying power of the lens, which was later used to find the stars and microbes, and the stage for early calculus. According to Morgan, he was also aware of gravity some 600 years before Galileo and Newton made their major breakthroughs and his endeavours indeed influenced their studies. His mathematical works were also inspirational to other great thinkers, such as Roger Bacon, Descartes, Frederick of Fribourg, Kepler and Christiaan Huygens (1629-1695). In the 12th century, Al-Khazini hypothesised that the gravity of bodies differs according to their distance from the centre of the Earth.[369]

Ghiyath Al-Din Abu'l-Fath Omar Ibn Ibrahim Al-Nisaburi Khayyami, known as Omar Kayyam, calculated the length of the year as 365.24219858156 days. Using the Hubble telescope, atomic clocks and computers it would later be calculated as 365.242190 days. Thus, in the 11th century, Omar Kayyam was just fractions of a second wrong. He also demonstrated that the Earth rotates on its axis rather than the heavens moving around it.[370]

---

[368] BBC News, Americas, "Advanced Geometry of Islamic Art," 23 February 2007, http://news.bbc.co.uk/2/hi/mid dle_east/6389157.stm.
[369] Morgan, *op. cit.*, note 88, pp. 74, 103-105; J. Al-Khalili, "The 'First True Scientist'," BBC News, http://news.bbc.co.uk/2/hi/science/nature/7810846.stm; G. Hatfield, "René Descartes," *Standford Encyclopedia of Philosophy*, First Published 3 December 2008, http://plato.stanford.edu/entries/descartes/; FSTC Limited, "Al-Khazini – Merv's Physicist," *MuslimHeritage.Com*, 11 March 2005, http://muslimheritage.com/topics/default.cfmArticle ID=493.
[370] Morgan, *ibid.*, p. 112.

The zenith of Arab-Islamic astrology was in the 9th century, supported by Baghdad's House of Wisdom and several observatories established by Al-Mamun. Arab-Islamic astronomers of this time developed a more accurate way of measuring the Meridian – the theoretical line running North-South on the Earth's surface – than that devised by ancient Greeks. They also calculated the diameter of the Earth, the distance around the equator and the precession equinoxes, for example. These constitute some of the most important calculations of the Middle Ages. The Chinese had of course been star-gazers for many centuries before them.[371] The Arab-Islamic astronomer of the 8th century, Ibrahim Al-Fazari, wrote a treatise on the astrolabe, an instrument for sky-based navigation that had Greek and Ptolemic roots but was perfected by Muslims. An early example of an Arab-Islamic astrolabe is depicted in Figure 3. Such astrolabes found their way to Al-Andalus and from there to England in the 13th and 14th centuries. At Oxford University in England, scholars built their own astrolabes. They even maintained the Arabic names of the stars in their new tools. These names have endured in contemporary times and experiments in space.[372]

The Arab-Islamic world also excelled in medicine. Hospitals were constructed and in 931 an examining and licensing system was established. Ibn Sina made one of the most well-known and significant contributions of the time with his *Canon of Medicine*. It quickly became a classic and was translated into Latin in 1175 and subsequently into a number of other languages. It continued to be used for almost six centuries.[373] In the 13th century, Ibn Al-Nafis (1213-1288) argued that the Greek physician, Galen, was mistaken about how blood moves around the body. Ibn Al-Nafis argued that blood is pumped from the heart, through the lungs to the body and back again.[374] This was some 350 years before William Harvey's work.[375]

---

[371] *Ibid.*, p. 126.
[372] *Ibid.*, pp. 124-125.
[373] R.D. Smith, "Avicenna and the Canon of Medicine: A Millennial Tribute," *The Western Journal of Medicine*, Vol. 133, No. 4, 1980, pp. 367-368.
[374] *Ibid.*, p. 74.
[375] Hobson, *op. cit.*, note 346, pp. 159.

Figure 3: Arab-Islamic Astrolabe, 1090 A.D.

Source: Photo by Eric Long, National Air and Space Museum, Smithsonian Institution (SI 2001-5336)

Moreover, the general principles of medicine and hygiene expounded at the dawn of Islam were added to the traditions of Greek, Persian and Indian medicine to produce a synthetic body of knowledge, which was taught in the West up to the 19th century.[376] As early as the 9th century, Al-Jahiz introduced the idea of the food chain, and explicitly outlined an evolutionary theory premised on natural selection, the influence of the environment and perhaps inheritance. As mentioned earlier, the 10th century Ikhwăn Al-Safă' or "Brethren of Purity" are also thought to have perhaps influenced both Lamark and Darwin, and Al-Khazini, who lived in the 12th century, is credited with developing an early theory of evolution.[377]

Chemical and alchemical works of Arab-Islamic scholars also influenced the West through Latin translations. In fact, the name alchemy as well as chemistry derive from the Arabic al-kimiya. Having experimented in alchemy early on – the greatest 8th-century Muslim alchemist being Jabir Ibn Hayyan (Geber) (721-815) – alchemy was transformed into the science of chemistry by Al-Razi (Rhazes) (865-925).[378]

East to West

The Arab-Islamic world was also crucial to the rise of the trading networks that stretched from the Mediterranean to the Indian Ocean, and thus to Europe's commercial revolution.[379] As Sigrid Hunke notes, as early as the 10th century, Venetian and Genoese merchants made regular trips by sea to Syria and Egypt. Each year, at the beginning of September they would leave their Italian ports for the East, where they would stay until the spring of the following year. They therefore spent all winter in the East, travelling to Baghdad or even to the Persian Gulf and India. Exchanges through trade were thus substantial even at

---

[376] R. El-Diwani, "Islamic Contributions to the West," http://www.lssu.edu/faculty/jswedene/FULBRIGHT_FILES/Islamic%20Contributions%20to%20the%20West.doc, pp. 10-11.
[377] P.S. Agutter and D.N. Wheatly, *Thinking About Life: The History and Philosophy of Biology and Other Sciences* (Springer Verlag, 2008), pp. 43, 161; "M. Hamad, "Islamic Roots to the Theory of Evolution: The Ignored History," Viewpoints, *Biology Forum 100* (2007), p. 173; AbsoluteAstronomy.com, *op. cit.*, note 114.
[378] University of California, *op. cit.*, note 373.
[379] Hobson, *op. cit.*, note 346, pp. 159, p. 156.

this early date. Indeed, the rise of Venice, for example, is thought to have depended critically on trade with the Arab-Islamic world.[380] Within Western historical narratives this connection is often discussed in so far as the waning power of the Arab-Islamic world is thought to make way for the rise of Italian commercial and financial revolutions. Hobson argues that this interpretation neglects the continued vitality of the Arab-Islamic world's role in the global economy up to the 19th century and, moreover, that it obscures the sense in which Italy's success was only enabled by its connection to the Arab-Islamic world. While the Venetians dominated European trade, their involvement in the global trading system was undertaken on the terms set out by West Asian Arab-Islamic lands and North Africa.

The southern route connected Alexandria-Cairo and the Red Sea, with the Arabian Sea and the Indian Ocean. When Baghdad fell in 1258 to the Mongols the capital of the Arab-Islamic world shifted to Cairo and it was Cairo that then took on a central role in the global trading system up to the 16th century. Cairo controlled the sea route to the East and therefore could set the terms of trade for Europeans. According to Hobson, "Venice and Genoa were not the 'pioneers' of global trade but *adaptors* and *intermediaries*, operating within the interstices of the Afro-Asian-led global economy and entering the global economy very much on the strict terms laid down by the West Asian Arab Muslims and especially the Egyptians."[381]

These trading routes acted as "transmission" routes for technologies, ideas, techniques and institutions from East to West. The trading partnership institution, the collegantzia, is usually attributed to the Italians. However, it was a replica of qirad trading partnerships developed centuries earlier by Arab Muslims. All other financial institutions, such as banks, bills of exchange, cheques and insurance schemes, were developed in Sumer and Sassanid Persia before they were developed further by the Arab-Islamic world.[382]

A myriad of key innovations and know-how that assisted the rise of the West came from the East. The British industrial revolution relied on a number of crucial Chinese inventions. The Chinese method

---

[380] S. Hunke, *Le Soleil d'Allah brille sur l'Occident: Notre Héritage Arabe*, Translated from German by S. and G. de Lalène (Éditions Albin Michel, 1963), Author's Translation, pp. 23-26.
[381] Hobson, *op. cit.*, note 346, p. 156.
[382] *Ibid.*, pp. 156-157.

of iron and steel production was studied by the British as they sought to develop their own steel manufacturing methods. Cotton manufacturing, which was central to the industrial revolution in Britain, was pioneered in China centuries before. The silk machines used in Britain were copied from Italian machines, which were, in turn, copies of machines from China.[383] Even ideas on steam engines appear to have been diffused to the West from the East.[384]

Another innovation mentioned earlier that had an enormous impact on the West was the manufacture of paper. Parchment had been used by the scribes before the mass production of paper in Europe. According to Hunke, it was brought from Egypt to the port of Marseille. Yet, parchment was more expensive than paper. Samples of paper appear to have made their way to Latin Christendom through Muslim Spain around the 11th century. The replacement of parchment with the a less expensive material represented a significant innovation, enabling the diffusion of ideas and information as well as record keeping. The source of this new material came from the East. Muslim forces had imprisoned Chinese soldiers in Samarkand in 751. When these prisoners were given the opportunity to buy their freedom through the practice of a trade, a number of them became specialists in paper production. The manufacture of paper spread through the Arab-Islamic world, eventually reaching Europe.[385]

Flavio Gioja of Amalfi, Italy, was for some time believed to have invented the compass. However, it is now known that he must have learned of this instrument from the Arab-Islamic world, because other Europeans were aware of it before him. By the 11th century, the Chinese already had some of the know-how with which to make a compass. At that time, sea-faring commerce was dominated by the Arab-Islamic world. Records suggest that they borrowed and built on Chinese know-how to construct compasses, which they appear to have used on their ships. Knowledge of the compass reached Europe through the Crusades. Pierre de Maricourt brought back to France the knowledge of the compass and magnetism he had acquired in 1269. It

---

[383] J.M. Hobson, "The Eurocentric Clash of Civilizations," in M. Hall and P.T. Jackson (eds.) *Civilizational Identity: The Production and Reproduction of 'Civilizations' in International Relations* (New York: Palgrave Macmillan, 2007), pp. 156-158, 161-163.
[384] Hobson, *op. cit.*, note 19, p. 303.
[385] Hunke, *op. cit.*, note 380, pp. 30-32.

was 33 years later that Gioja was attributed with having invented the instrument.[386]

The stirrup, the water mill and the windmill too enabled the economic and political evolution of medieval Europe. The rise of European trade was intimately linked to prior developments in the Arab-Islamic world, including, as is mentioned above, the qirad trading system which had been developed by Muslims hundreds of years before. Significant inventions, such as the sternpost rudder, the triple mast system, and maps all came from either China or the Arab-Islamic world. Travel across oceans would not have been possible without these inventions. Textile manufacturing, sugar refining and the production of iron were all based on technologies that reached medieval Europe from the East.[387]

The development of music in the West also has some Eastern roots. It is possible that Charlemagne in the 9th century enabled the development of church music through the use of musical instruments that originated from the Arab-Islamic world through the transmission points of Spain and Sicily. The lute and the guitar are the most clearly identifiable instruments that derive from the East, brought back by European pilgrims, merchants and others. The popular poetry of the troubadours also spread to Europe from Arab-Islamic lands.[388]

Brett Bowden makes the point that major elements of the Western canon of political thought have reinforced the idea that the East has been incapable of contributing anything of value to the history of ideas:[389] "In essence, the story runs along lines to the effect that the West has led this particular race from the start, and that no other peoples, race, culture, civilisation or whatever have come close to the West in the hierarchy of world civilisations."[390] The overlooked foundations of the West that lie in the East are testimony to a great deal of racism and chauvinism, as well as a misunderstanding of how the torch has been passed on.[391] When Europe finally began the Renaissance and the golden ages of Islam were drawing to a close, a

---

[386] *Ibid.*, p. 33.
[387] Hobson, *op. cit.*, note 19, pp. 301-302.
[388] R. Saoud, "The Arab Contribution to Music of the Western World," Foundation for Science Technology and Civilisation, March 2004, http://www.muslimheritage.com/uploads/Music2.pdf.
[389] Bowden, *op. cit.*, note 334, p. 1360.
[390] *Ibid.*, p. 1361.
[391] *Ibid.*, p. 1361-62.

Eurocentric writing of history would attribute advances in mathematics, astronomy, medicine, science, technology, statecraft and pluralism to the West.[392] While seminal Western thinkers may be acknowledged as indebted to one another, they are rarely thought to be indebted to Arabs and Muslims.[393] Yet, as Bowden identifies, a number of Arabic-Islamic discoveries were essential scientific reading for centuries of European scholarship. Muslim mathematicians and astronomers had, for example, argued that the Earth was spherical and calculated its circumference with amazing accuracy by the 9th century.[394]

The European Renaissance has an Eastern heritage that is seldom recognised. Muslim scholars not only translated Ancient Greek texts and methods, but also went beyond them, also drawing on Persian, Indian, African and Chinese bodies of knowledge.[395] The European Enlightenment's love of reason was, its seems, not without Eastern influence. Ibn Tufayl's book *Hayy Ibn Yaqzan*, which tells the story of a child who grew up on an uninhabited desert island and alone became enlightened, learning how to become a physician, a biologist, an astronomer, a physicist, a psychologist and a philosopher, thereby heralding rationality and self-realisation was published around 1160 or 1170 and is believed to have inspired the thinking of both Locke and Voltaire.[396] A known Sinophile, Voltaire is also thought to have been inspired by Chinese conceptions of politics, religion and philosophy, all of which emphasise rationality.[397] Al-Ghazali's philosophical works are also believed to have influenced the ideas of Descartes, particularly those expounded in the *Discourse on Method*.[398] Spinoza too is thought to have been influenced by Ibn Tufayl and the philosopher Al-Ghazali.[399] The works of Al-Kindi, Al-Farabi, Ibn Sina and Ibn Rushd also influenced the development of Western philosophical thought.

The Arabic division of the sciences also had an impact on the Latin West, primarily through Domincus Gundisalvi's treatise *Divi-*

---

[392] Morgan, *op. cit.*, note 88, p. 33.
[393] Attar, *op. cit.*, note 256, p. 2.
[394] Bowden, *op. cit.*, note 334, p. 1366.
[395] Hobson, *op. cit.*, note 383, p. 159.
[396] See Attar, *op. cit.*, note 256, pp. 4-8.
[397] Hobson, *op. cit.*, note 383, p. 163.
[398] K. Nakamura, "Al-Ghazali, Abu Hamid (1058-1111)," *Al-Ghazali Website*, http://www.ghazali.org/articles/gz1.htm.
[399] Attar, *op. cit.*, note 256, pp. 4-8.

sion of Philosophy. Gundisalvi's own work is heavily influenced by Al-Farabi's *Enumeration of the Sciences* or *Ihsâ Al-'Ulûm*. Together, these works were instrumental in producing a systematic division of the sciences, based on Aristotle's works and a wide range of sciences, some of which were at the time new to the Latin West.[400]

Ibn Khaldūn was born in Tunisia in 1332 into an Andalusian family that fled Spain when Seville fell to Spanish Reconquista forces in the mid-13th century. Late in his career, having at the beginning been involved in politics, Ibn Khaldūn wrote a history of the world or *Kitab Al-'Ibar* (mentioned earlier). In the *Muqaddimah*, he produces an early thesis on the nature of history. Other books in the *Kitab Al-'Ibar* deal with the history of the Arabs and the history of the Berbers. His aim was to explore the conditions of civilisations in general and to examine the history of the Maghreb in particular from the 11th to the 14th centuries. History and historical change are understood through the transformation of primitive societies into more sophisticated societies that eventually collapse, with the Maghreb being used as a specific case study. Some argue that Ibn Khaldūn's work anticipated Marx's historical dialectic, Machiavelli's notion of virtù and Montesquieu's ideas on the environment as well as Darwin's theory evolution and Durkheim's concept of organic versus mechanical solidarity.[401]

Thus, when we consider the sources and influences of Arab-Islamic philosophy, we can see that it has been built on foundations provided by Greek and Roman philosophy, as is mentioned above, as well as Persian, Chinese, Hindu and Syriac Christian philosophies. Arab-Islamic philosophy as well as translations of Greek philosophy from Arabic to Latin, in turn, helped to shape European philosophy. This is, of course, just one example of cultural borrowing.

In 10th century Spain, in the city known today as Madrid, Al-Majriti (b. Madrid, d. 1007 or 1008) started one of the most important cross-cultural diffusions of ideas. Based on eastern Arab advances in the development of the astralobe, Al-Majriti, along with his colleague Al-Saffar, developed and improved on the methods the Romans used to survey land. The same measurements made using the astrolabe

---

[400] D.N. Hasse, "Influence of Arabic and Islamic Philosophy on the Latin West," *Stanford Encyclopedia of Philosophy*, First Published 19 September 2008, http://plato.stanford.edu/entries/arabic-islamic-influence/, pp. 3-4.
[401] Hughes-Warrington, *op. cit.*, note 13, pp. 188-194.

were used in Al-Andalus to build canals to irrigate the land.[402] In 12th century Toledo, Al-Bitruji (d. circa 1204) of Morocco was one of the Arab-Islamic scholars who contributed, as mentioned earlier, to proving that Ptolemy's work was flawed. His work was translated into Latin by a Scotsman, Michael Scot, who was based in Arab Islamic Sicily. The Jewish intellectual community of Seville translated his work into Hebrew. Al-Bitruji's work was studied in Europe a century later and was cited by Copernicus when writing his heliocentric theory in the 16th century.[403]

As the Arab-Islamic authority structures of the Iberian Peninsula slowly disappeared with the break-up of the caliphate and the decline of the remaining taifas (independent Muslim-ruled principalities), translation from Arabic to Latin increased as non-Arabic speakers sought to access the many texts written in Arabic. When Toledo fell to Alfonso VI in 1085, so too did its libraries. The people of Toledo were multilingual, especially the Mozarabs and the Jews, and some were capable of translating many of the books housed in those libraries. Latin Christians became increasingly aware of their richness in terms of technology and philosophy.[404] From the 11th century, thousands of volumes written in Arabic were translated into Latin. Indeed, a culture of translation began to flourish, which provided the perfect environment for large translation projects.[405]

In Toledo, after the city fell to Latin Christendom in 1085, one of the largest projects in the translation of scientific texts was undertaken. Spaniards such as Hugh of Santalla worked under the patronage of King Alfonso, and many other Europeans came to Toledo to engage in translations. The better known among these were Herman of Dalmatia, Rudolph of Bruges and Henry Bate from Flanders, as well as a number of translators from the South of France, including Armengaud son of Blaise, Jacob Anatoli, Moses Ibn Tibbon and Jacob Ben Mahir as well as translators such as Plato of Tivoli, Gerard of Cremona, Salio of Padua and John of Brescia. Translators also came from the British Isles. These included Robert of Chester, Daniel of Morley and

---

[402] Morgan, *op. cit.*, note 88, p. 131.
[403] *Ibid.*, p. 135.
[404] M.R. Menocal, *The Ornament of the World: How Muslims, Jews, and Christians Created a Culture of Tolerance in Medieval Spain* (New York: Back Bay Books, 2002), pp. 194-195.
[405] *Ibid.*, pp. 193-197.

perhaps Adelard of Bath. Among these gifted translators, Gerard of Cremona was one of the most prolific, translating 87 works, according to one source, including those of Al-Khwarizmi and Ibn Al-Haytham. Among the works translated by John of Seville, a Jew who converted to Christianity, were those of Al-Battani, Al-Majriti and Al-Ghazali.[406]

Sicily and southern Italy were important transmission points. Arab-Norman culture in Sicily provided a shining example of cultural borrowing. From 965 to 1061, the island fell under Arab-Islamic rule. After controlling a significant part of southern Italy, Norman forces under the leadership of Roger I of Sicily took control of Messina in 1061. They did not, however, succeed in reaching Palermo until 1071, and the whole island did not fall under Norman rule until 1087. From 1061 until 1250, a great deal of interaction between Arab and Norman cultures took place. This was evident in a myriad of fields. A Norman-Arab style of architecture was born that represented a unique blend of Byzantine, Moorish and northern European influences.[407] Built in 1132, the Cappella Palatina at Palermo is a wonderful example of this fusion of styles, with a Norman nave, a Byzantine Cupola and an Arabic wooden ceiling and arches. Roger II was the sponsor of one of Islam's great geographers, Al-Idrisi, who produced *The Book of Roger* in 1154, which is considered one of the foremost geographical treaties of the Middle Ages.[408] Al-Idrisi's maps are considered to be some of the greatest contributions to geography, one of which is depicted in Figure 4.

---

[406] FSTC Limited, "The Impact of Translations of Muslim Sciences on the West," *MuslimHeritage.Com*, 4 March 2003, http://www.muslimheritage.com/topics/default.cfm?TaxonomyTypeID=22&TaxonomySubTypeID=114&TaxonomyThirdLevelID=1&ArticleID=344.
[407] V. Salerno, "Sicilian Peoples: The Normans," *Best of Sicily Magazine*, 2005, http://www.bestofsicily.com/mag/art171.htm.
[408] L. Inturrisi, "Tracing the Norman Rulers of Sicily," *New York Times*, 7 January 2009; V. Salerno, "King Roger II," *Best of Sicily Magazine*, 2004, http://www.bestofsicily.com/mag/art124.htm.

SUSTAINABLE HISTORY AND THE DIGNITY OF MAN   159

Figure 4: Al-Idrisi World Map

Source: Wikipedia describes the image as having been taken from a manuscript copied by 'Ali Îbn Hasan Al-Hûfî Al-Qasîmî in Cairo, 1456, now preserved in the Bodleian Library in Oxford.
http://en.wikipedia.org/wiki/File:Al-Idrisi%27s_world_map.JPG.

Equally important was the fact that the Normans retained as well as adapted the existing Arab institutions on the island. Indeed, in the Norman era, which lasted until approximately 1200, Sicilian society was characterised by ethnic and religious tolerance, the likes of which most of Medieval Europe never experienced. The Norman system of government included Muslim officials. According to Jeremy Johns, part of the explanation for this incorporation was that Muslim communities entered into pacts with the Norman conquerors that ensured their inclusion within the Norman administration. In return for this, as well as protection, Muslims along with Jews paid a tribute in the form of a "distinguishing tax" to the Norman rulers. The terms of these negotiated settlements are thought to have provided the roots from which the Arab-Norman administration grew.[409] The Norman judicial system also allowed distinct, but equal, jurisdictions based on Shari'a law for Muslims, Judaic law for Jews, Byzantine Greek law for Byzantines and Norman feudal law for Normans.[410]

Arab-Islamic law significantly influenced the development of Norman law, the concepts of which are also believed to have influenced English common law.[411] It has been suggested that the influence of Islamic law on the English legal system may help to explain why English common law is significantly different from classical Roman legal systems found elsewhere in Europe. While there is no undisputable evidence of this possible connection, Medieval England did have a number of legal principles, such as trial by jury, that resemble those of Islamic law, and there are a number of factors that suggest a connection between the two. Only one other place in Europe had similar legal principles at the time, and that was Sicily. The Normans in Sicily were relations of King Henry II of England, who is recognised as having introduced English common law. King Henry's son, Richard I, "The Lionheart", went through Sicily on his way to Palestine during the Crusades. In addition, an Englishman, Thomas Brown, who was Roger II's treasurer in Sicily, returned to England and worked for King Henry II when common law was instituted. As crusaders, The

---

[409] J. Johns, *Arabic Administration in Norman Sicily: The Royal Dīwān* (Cambridge: Cambridge University Press, 2002), pp. 34-35, 63; A. Metcalfe, *Muslims and Christians in Norman Sicily: Arabic Speakers and the End of Islam* (New York: Routledge-Curzon, 2003), p. 34.
[410] See Salerno, *op. cit.*, note 407.
[411] See J.A. Makdisi, "The Islamic Origins of the Common Law," *North Carolina Law Review*, Vol. 77, No. 5, 1999.

Knights Templar, are also thought to have played a role in introducing some aspects of Islamic law into England, such as certain forms of financial contract. The legal mechanism of the waqf or perpetual endowment under which Medieval institutions of learning were established is also believed to have been the source of trusts in England. Perhaps tellingly, Merton College was established by Walter de Merton with a 1264 legal document that appears to have resembled a waqf. De Merton was himself a businessman with connections to The Knights Templar.[412]

The Arab-Islamic presence in Sicily also had an impact on the linguistic history of the island. Prior to the Norman conquest of Sicily, Arabic was employed in the administration, literary culture and in the practice of religion. After the Norman conquest, Arabic continued to be used. Roger II was himself fluent in Arabic, which was the dominant language of his court.[413] Moreover, important official documents were multilingual until Sicily became more Latinised under the rule of Frederick II.[414]

At the end of the Muslim rebellion (1190-1224), Frederick II (the grandson of Roger II) forcibly relocated the Muslims of Sicily to Lucera in southern Italy, where they formed a small Muslim community that survived for 75 years.[415]

Intellectual vitality in Italian universities and the patronage of Italian scholars educated in these universities provided a cultural climate ideal for this kind of work.[416] Scot settled in early 13th century Sicily when it was under the rule of Frederick II, emperor of Sicily, Holy Roman Emperor and King of Jerusalem. Scot was a physician, astrologer, necromancer and translator of Arabic and Hebrew. Under Frederick II's patronage, Scot translated Ibn Sina's significant work on natural history, *On Animals*, as well as Aristotle's multivolume

---

[412] M. Devichand, "Is English Law Related to Muslim Law?," BBC News, 24 September 2008, http://news.bbc.co.uk/2/hi/uk_news/magazine/7631388.stm; M. Lima, "English Common Law and Islam: A Sicilian Connection," *Best of Sicily Magazine*, 2008, http://www.bestofsicily.com/mag/art283.htm.
[413] Johns, *op. cit.*, note 409, p. 4; Salerno, *op. cit.*, note 407; S. Zaimeche, "Sicily," Foundation for Science Technology and Civilisation, November 2004, http://www.muslimheritage.com/uploads/Sicily1.pdf, p. 8.
[414] Salerno, *op. cit.*, note 407.
[415] See J. Taylor, *Muslims in Medieval Italy: The Colony at Lucera* (Lanham, MD: Lexington Books, 2003).
[416] Hasse, *op. cit.*, note 400, p. 3.

work of the same name, which influenced Frederick II's own work, *The Art of Hunting with Birds*. Towards the end of Frederick II's life, he made many contemporary Arabic works available to institutions outside Sicily, most having been translated by Scot. Among these translated manuscripts were the philosophical works of two almost contemporary Andalusians: Ibn Rushd and Maimonides.[417]

According to Howard Miller, Christopher Marlowe's character Tamburlaine the Great is strikingly similar to Arabic descriptions of Timur. He surmises that Marlowe may have come into contact with translations of such descriptions while studying at Cambridge University.[418]

Hobson notably argues that the term "Renaissance" used to refer to a period in European history is problematic since it overemphasises its Ancient Greek foundations, while obscuring the extent to which its foundations were also Eastern.[419]

4. More Reason, Less Dogma

The great Arab-Islamic thinkers, scientists and artists who contributed to world civilisation flourished in a context very different from today's. While all were versed in the tenets of their faith, whether Islam, Buddhism, Hinduism, Christianity or Judaism, none was a dogmatic or doctrinaire thinker. According to Morgan, "The Muslim quest for knowledge often drove even the most devout rulers and religious scholars to support freethinking and empirical scientific inquiry."[420] Indeed, the tradition of Islamic learning and the Islamic education system is believed to have influenced the West. The oldest degree-granting university, the University of Al-Karaouine, is in Fez, Morocco. Even the term chair in a university derives from the practice of teachers sitting to teach students in madrasahs.[421]

Islamic theology developed during the Abassid Caliphate, centred in Baghdad, but various paradigms were becoming apparent in the later Umayyad Caliphate. What was important during this time

---

[417] Menocal, *op. cit.,* note 404, pp. 189-193.
[418] H. Miller, "Tamburlaine: The Migration and Translation of Marlowe's Arabic Sources," in C.G. Di Biase (ed.) *Travel and Translation in the Early Modern Period* (Amsterdam: Rodopi, 2006), p. 255.
[419] Hobson, *op. cit.*, note 346, p. 159.
[420] Morgan, *op. cit.*, note 88, p. xiv.
[421] University of California, *op. cit.*, note 373.

was the reconciliation of traditional science (the hadith scholars) and rational theology. The problem of divine revelation and human capacity for reason preoccupied many thinkers. On one side, there were the traditionalists and those who called for a literal interpretation of the texts and believed that no logical methods could be used to treat legalistic and theological questions. On the other side were those who believed that reason could help to interpret and increase understanding of the Koran and the Sunnah. The latter school of rational theology of the so-called Mu'tazilah was popular within urban intellectual circles.[422]

The Mu'tazilah embraced Greek philosophy and the sciences. They engaged in discussions about physics, anthropology and the Koran, including on the reliability of the tradition about the Prophet, as well as legal questions and the problems of analogy and consensus. This does not mean that the Mu'tazilites wished to base theology on something other than the Koran.[423] Indeed, the concepts of knowledge (ilm) and reason, wisdom and intelligence (aql) also appear in the Koran.[424] They were not pure rationalists, but emphasised the need for more reason.[425]

Indeed, the Koran itself outlines the possibility of interpreting and reasoning through the use of analogy where the Koran and Sunnah are unable to provide guidance. Ijtihad is a term that refers to "the exertion of mental energy in the search for a legal opinion to the extent that the faculties of the jurist become incapable of further efforts. In other words . . . the maximum effort expended by the jurist to master and apply the principles and rules of *Usul Al-Fiqh* [legal theory] for the purpose of discovering God's law."[426] The practice of Ijtihad not only enabled or required adaptation in times of rapid change, it also facilitated an openness to innovation and learning that played such a central role in the rise of the Arab-Islamic world.

In the early 9th century, Caliph Al-Mamun saw no contradiction between reason and divine revelation, but there was opposition to the Mu'tazilites in Baghdad. Ironically, perhaps in an effort to prevent

---

[422] H. Küng, *Islam: Past, Present & Future*, Translated by J. Bowden (Oxford: Oneworld, 2007), pp. 278-280.
[423] *Ibid.*, pp. 283-284.
[424] Morgan, *op. cit.*, note 88, p. 52.
[425] Küng, *op. cit.*, note 422, p. 284.
[426] W. B. Hallaq, "Was the Gate of Ijtihad Closed?" *International Journal of Middle East Studies*, Vol. 16, No. 1, 1984, p. 3.

a spiritual and political crisis, Al-Mamun began a form of religious inquisition in Baghdad and in other provinces. In the mid-9th century, the inquisition ended in victory for the traditionalists. Towards the end of the 10th century, the Ash'arite school of theology gained predominance, under which rationalism was subsumed within traditionalism.[427]

As a result of the disagreement between Arab-Islamic "rationalists", who were committed to preaching divine truth through the use of reason, and "literalists", who believed in remaining true to the statements and teachings of the Prophet, the high place given to non-religious learning came under attack.[428] Morocco and Spain, which had once provided an open environment for non-religious learning under the Umayyad dynasty, came under the harsher rule of the Almoravid dynasty and then the similarly harsh Almohad dynasty. Under the second Almohad ruler, Ibn Rushd fell out of favour with the court and was banished from Cordoba in 1195. His philosophical works were burned and banned. While Ibn Rushd was respected as a grand judge in Cordoba, his attachment to logic and philosophy aroused criticism from religious legal scholars who argued that he would undermine the authority of the revelation, leading to unrest and religious confusion.[429] A certain approach to the relationship between revelation and reason thus won the day in that particular historical context.

5. Mutual Respect and Tolerance of Diversity

It is often assumed in the West that Islam is inherently intolerant. However, this assumption does not stand up to historical scrutiny. Within the history of the Arab-Islamic world there can be found quite remarkable examples of coexistence between people of different ethnicities and people belonging to the Abrahamic religions. The original Muslims originated from the Arabian peninsula. However, as the conquest advanced, a greater number of people learned and spoke Arabic, although they had no Arab blood. What united this group was not their "Arabness" – Arabs constituted only a part of the armies that conquered the Maghreb, Spain and Central Asia – but their shared devo-

---

[427] Küng, *op. cit.*, note 422, pp. 290, 293, 296.
[428] Morgan, *op. cit.*, note 88, p. xv.
[429] Küng, *op. cit.*, note 422, pp. 371-372.

tion to Islam. Their religious identity was more important than their ethnic identity.[430]

Muslims also have a tradition of coexistence with Christians, Jews, Hindus and other religions.[431] Part of the reason for this was that the expansion of the Islamic state meant the extension of Islam as a religion.[432] Braudel surmises that the overwhelming responsibilities that ruling over vast territories, including parts of Europe, North Africa and Asia, required Muslims to govern with a degree of tolerance unknown at the time in the West.[433] Conquered lands were provided with military and financial protection and political stability was sought through the establishment of taxation and the development of legislation. Two different forms of taxation existed: Kharaj, a land tax; and jizya, a poll tax. Islam's special relationship with Jews and Christians – other people of the book or dhimmi – was recognised. Under Muslim rule, Jews and Christians were not obliged to convert to Islam. They could continue to practice their own religions and to partake in many aspects of Muslim social and economic life. However, in return, they were expected to pay the jizya, which Muslims did not pay.[434] Thus, in the early years of expansion, conquered territories did enjoy some form of tolerance of diversity with regard to faith, albeit not by today's standards. Dhimmi occupied a secure status so long as they refrained proselytising and attempts to destabilise Islam.[435] Some Syrians, Egyptians, Persians and others did choose to become Muslim. Similarly, non-Arabs within the conquered territories were not forced to speak Arabic, although many chose to. Local administrative customs, languages and even bureaucracies were also retained, given the small number of Arabs[436] and their lack of administrative experience due to the nomadic background of many of the conquering Arab forces. Non-Arabs and Arabs began to mix as the conquests included a

---

[430] H. Kennedy, *The Great Arab Conquests: How the Spread of Islam Changed the World We Live In* (London: Weidenfeld and Nicolson, 2007), p. 7.
[431] Morgan, *op. cit.*, note 88, p. 17.
[432] Küng, *op. cit.*, note 422, p. 172.
[433] Braudel, *op. cit.*, note 2, p. 61.
[434] Menocal, *op. cit.*, note 404, pp. 72-73.
[435] Morgan, *op. cit.*, note 88, p. 70; *Ibid.*, pp. 29-30.
[436] D.J. Gerner and J. Schedler (eds.) *Understanding the Contemporary Middle East*, Second Edition (Boulder, CO.: Lynne Rienner, 2004), p. 41.

greater number of different ethnicities, and Muslim societies became more diverse.[437]

Arab-Islamic Spain provided a pertinent example of interfaith coexistence. As power in Damascus passed from the Umayyad dynasty to the Abbasid dynasty in a bloody coup, the surviving Umayyad heir, Abd Al-Rahman, fled to the far west of the empire and established his own rule in Al-Andalus. In Cordoba, the city where Abd Al-Rahman was based, a hybrid culture developed. The Umayyad princes had married brides from the old Christian families of Iberia as well as from the North. The population was also mixed as a result of mixed marriages. After 100 years of Umayyad rule in Al-Andalus, Jews found themselves able to benefit from upward mobility, whereas a century before they had largely been reduced to poverty and slavery.[438] Indeed, the leader of the Sefarad (Andalusian) Jews, Hasdai Ibn Shaprut, rose to the rank of foreign minister to the successor of the first Umayyad prince.[439] In Malaga some years later, the Jewish Samuel Ibn Nagrila, born in 993, rose from the rank of wealthy merchant to vizier of the taifa of Granada. Like Hasdai Ibn Shaprut, he was also a leader of his community in Granada.[440]

Jews found a more tolerant environment under Islam than under Christian, Roman or West Gothic empires.[441] In the 9th and 10th centuries, exchanges between Jews and Muslims burgeoned in Baghdad. Jews faired particularly well in Arab-Islamic Spain, where Jewish arts and sciences blossomed.[442] However, as the position of Jews in society in Al-Andalus dramatically improved, that of Christians declined. This can perhaps partly be explained by one of the criteria for religious tolerance of the other dhimmi. Whereas Judaism had long been a domestic or private matter that had survived generations, Christianity was a faith that relied more on its presence in the public domain. This perhaps partly explains why Christians became a declining minority, and why many Christians converted to Islam.[443]

The Ottoman Empire was also, according to some, marked by religious and ethnic toleration. The Ottoman state was an Islamic state

---

[437] Küng, *op. cit.*, note 422, pp. 214-215.
[438] Menocal, *op. cit.*, note 404, pp. 67-68.
[439] *Ibid.*, p. 80.
[440] *Ibid.*, pp. 103-105.
[441] Küng, *op. cit.*, note 422, p. 374.
[442] *Ibid.*, p. 375.
[443] Menocal, *op. cit.*, note 404, pp. 72-74.

that elevated its administrative and political interests over religion. Moreover, according to Karen Barkey, the empire was aware that tolerance was needed in order to prevent fragmentation. She argues that four factors created a particular relationship between the state, religion and the politics of difference that created the conditions for coexistence between people of different faiths. First, Islam at the outset of the Ottoman Empire adapted to the needs of the state. Second, religious diversity and the relatively weaker identification with Islam among rulers created the conditions for openness. Third, the empire was marked by divisions in religious institutions and practices that made it easier for the state to dominate the incorporation of religion into the empire. Finally, the millet system, an ad hoc system employed to facilitate the integration of non-Muslim communities into the empire, is also thought to have played a role and the system itself was enabled by a particular understanding of Islam.[444]

Within such a system, the relationship between the state and religion meant that different strands of Islam could exist as long as they were subordinate to the state. A certain degree of tolerance of diversity was also facilitated by an administrative system established to rule over diverse religious and ethnic communities. The millet system was used to organise and administer religious and communal rule by institutionalising boundaries between them, but allowing enough space for diversity to coexist with some degree of unity. Imperial society was thus, according to Barkey, divided but cohesive. Interlocutors existed for each different community and it was their job to maintain inter-religious and inter-ethnic peace.[445]

Yet, the fact that the different communities were separated and that efforts were made to maintain the cultural homogeneity of each of them suggests that ethnicity was more prominent in this period than in earlier times. Indeed, we would expect that the very fact of organising people into such communities heightened awareness of cultural boundaries. It is therefore possible that ethnicity became more important as a marker of difference between people than in the early days of the spread of Islam. A greater discrimination between People

---

[444] K. Barkey, "Islam and Toleration: Studying the Ottoman Imperial Model," *International Journal of Politics, Culture and Society*, Vol. 19, 2005, pp. 8-9.
[445] *Ibid.*, pp. 15, 17.

of the Book also appears to have been inscribed in the millet system.[446]

6. Commonalities in the Rise, Decline and Fall of Geo-cultural Domains

A number of factors appear to have contributed to the demise of the Islamic Empire. The first was poor governance and the collapse of organised society. The Umayyad dynasty had attempted to legitimise the idea of hereditary empire, which was contrary to the teachings of Islam. For many Muslims, the succession of caliphs should have been submitted to an electoral process. The Umayyads were therefore accused of perverting Islamic principles. Moreover, the official policy of privileging Arab Muslims during this period not surprisingly generated resentment among non-Arabs who had converted to Islam. Further, Arabs themselves began to grow dissatisfied with the social stratification that had emerged. Land was granted to the members of the Umayyad dynasty. The accumulation of grievances and dissatisfaction with Umayyad rule contributed to the numerous rebellions that culminated in the collapse of the dynasty in 750 and their replacement by the Abassids.[447]

While the Abassids justified their takeover by the need for reform, they failed to undo the ills of the previous dynasty.[448] The collapse of the Islamic Empire in the Near East in the 9th and 10th centuries was partly the result of governance problems linked to a crisis in its fundamental institutions. The empire split at this point into regional part-empires. According to Hans Küng, the institutional crisis was due to a number of identifiable factors. First, the complex bureaucratic system could no longer be controlled by the caliph. Second, the empire was militarily overstretched. The areas bordering Central Asia and the Indus valley were unsafe and successive military interventions were undertaken. This, along with wars with Christian Byzantium, implied ever increasing expenditure. Enlisting slaves and prisoners from bordering regions, such as Slavs and Turks, is also thought to have been particularly ruinous. Troops would often be more loyal to commanders of the same ethnic group than to the caliph. Third, taxes

---

[446] *Ibid.*, p. 16.
[447] Chapra, *op. cit.*, note 336, pp. 58-59, 72.
[448] *Ibid.*, p. 59.

had to be raised in order to cover the increasing military costs. The growing independence of the provinces reduced the finances available to the caliph. Institutionalised corruption went hand-in-hand with this problem. All these difficulties contributed to economic decline.[449] At the same time, centrifugal forces in the provinces placed pressure on the unity of the empire.[450]

Governance problems also plagued the Ottoman Empire and contributed to its eventual collapsed. The growing power of the military and corruption resulted in military decline and government corruption. Taxes increased along with economic stagnation, partly due to the declining centrality of the trade routes in the Middle East for commerce between Europe and Asia.[451] The financing of military campaigns also reduced the revenue available for education and the construction of infrastructure. The Ottoman elite also awarded large land grants.

Under the Mongols, land grants were also made, leading to a situation not dissimilar to that of feudalism. Irrigation systems were also neglected and allowed to decay, contributing to difficulties in agriculture in rural areas.[452]

In Al-Andalus, internal rebellion by the Arab nobility and its militia in the Maghreb was one factor that contributed to the collapse of the caliphate in Cordoba in 1031. As a result, central control was replaced by local taifas.[453] The second was the decline of Ijtihad, which enabled critique and reform of Islam. Education was highly valued during the periods in which the Arab-Islamic world flourished. While critical thinking was encouraged when the Arab-Islamic world was on the rise, the open-mindedness this led to was compromised in later periods. This was intimately connected to a conflict between the rationalists who had arisen in the 8th century and conservatives. The rationalist movement, according to M. Umer Chapra, emerged as a result of the swift spread of Islam in lands that were materially and intellectually advanced. Their objective was to demonstrate that God is systematic and methodical, and that He operates according to principles that human beings may discover and understand. They therefore

---

[449] Küng, *op. cit.*, note 422, pp. 299-302.
[450] *Ibid.*, p. 302.
[451] Chapra, *op. cit.*, note 336, pp. 60-61, 76, 84.
[452] *Ibid.*, pp. 72-73.
[453] Küng, *op. cit.*, note 422, p. 377.

established the foundations on which science and technology could advance alongside faith. However, the rationalist emphasis on reason, when it became extreme, threatened to sideline Revelation.[454]

Elite fear of corruption of the faith led to the closure of the gates Ijtihad in the 10th century,[455] in order to minimize deviation from the "true faith" in the absence of an overarching theological authority supported by the political elite. As a result, the focus of the best minds available shifted from the search for knowledge supported by a lack of dogmatism to religious learning advanced in the hope of protecting the faith. While this led to the preservation of the faith, despite the disintegration of society in the subsequent centuries, it also led to a decline in the non-religious learning that had flourished in earlier times. The decline in non-religious learning contributed to the decline of the Arab Islamic Empire. Thus, the dynamic culture of learning that gave rise to tremendous contributions in a plethora of disciplines gradually gave way to a more conservative and restricted intellectual climate.

As is outlined above, one of the factors that contributed to the rise of the Arab-Islamic Empire was the degree of tolerance and respect for diversity, which was remarkable when one considers the historical period of which we are speaking as well as the practices common in other geo-cultural domains at that time. Yet, a third factor that contributed to the decline of the Arab-Islamic Empire was increased intolerance and an emphasis on ethnicity. While initially no significant discrimination with respect to ethnicity and social class was present, with notable exceptions under the Umayyads, this emphasis on tolerance decreased. External pressure from the crusades contributed to greater exclusion and increased defensiveness in Muslim societies. Greater emphasis on ethnicity re-emerged. Under the Ottomans, for example, the millet system, while allowing communities some degree of autonomy and self-governance, maintained and encouraged the establishment of clear boundaries between different communities. Internal divisions facilitated by the millet system served to strengthen the hold of the Ottomans over their subject peoples.[456]

---

[454] Chapra, *op. cit.*, note 336, pp. 101-110.
[455] C. Catherwood, *A Brief History of the Middle East: From Abraham to Arafat* (London: Constable & Robinson, 2006), p. 115.
[456] Gerner and Schedler, *op. cit.*, note 436, p. 46.

Finally, at the same time, external powers were gaining in strength and exerting pressure on the empire. The Arab Islamic Empire came increasingly under attack from Latin Christendom in the form of the crusades. When the crusaders captured what is today Palestine, Lebanon and the coastal areas of Syria in 1099, divisions existed within the Arab-Islamic world on which they were encroaching, notably between the Abbasid caliphate and the Fatimid caliphs in Egypt.[457]

In 1242, the Mongol armies reached Muslim lands. The Mongol armies of Ghengis Khan captured Central Asia and Persia in the early 13th century and later, under the leadership of his grandson, Hülegü, advanced further into Persia and Mesopotamia, capturing Baghdad in 1258. The Mongols, nomads from the Asian steppe, destroyed the irrigation systems in Persia, Mesopotamia and Syria, thereby destroying livelihoods.[458]

By that time, Latin Christendom had begun to take parts of Muslim Spain.[459] In Al-Andalus, Latin Christendom encroached to an ever greater extent on the part of the Iberian Peninsula under the rule of the Almohads.[460]

Commonalities with Other Geo-cultural Domains
Almost every golden age of geo-cultural domains has been characterised by good governance, exchanges, borrowing, innovation and the adaptation of earlier contributions to forms of knowledge, and rationalism. The West's rise was also characterised by an emphasis on rationality as well as the scientific and technological innovation that this facilitated. Its rise also depended on the forms of knowledge that the high point of the Arab-Islamic world and through it the Ancient Greeks contributed to civilisation. One of the distinguishing characteristics of the rise of the Arab-Islamic world was tolerance of diversity. This is perhaps one of the most important lessons that can be drawn from the Arab-Islamic Empire. Indeed, today the need for tolerance and respect for diversity is paramount. We live in a highly interconnected world in which cultural arrogance and exceptionalism may very rapidly translate into confrontation and even violence, par-

---

[457] Catherwood, *op. cit.*, note 455, p. 103.
[458] Gerner and Schedler, *op. cit.*, note 436, p. 42.
[459] Catherwood, *op. cit.*, note 455, p. 111.
[460] Küng, *op. cit.*, note 422, p. 377.

ticularly when instrumentalised by those who wish to propagate tension and instability. Moreover, the vast majority of societies in today's world comprise a variety of cultures, religions and ethnicities. A lack of tolerance and respect for diversity in such contexts serves only to generate anxiety, tension and a lack of trust. Increased awareness of other traditions and values, as well as of inclusive national identities, are essential ingredients for stability, security and prosperity.

7. The Challenges

A number of challenges exist to the creation of conditions conducive to the triumph of geo-cultural domains in relation to governance, the promotion of reason and tolerance, and respect for diversity. Some of these challenges are outlined below.

The minimum criteria for good governance are discussed in the chapters below. Suffice it to say here that good governance requires some degree of self-governance in order to enable people to have an impact on the decisions that affect their lives. Patterns of political competition and political authority are believed to be critical for a country's political stability. Institutional arrangements must encourage political parties to seek support from a wide variety of social groups. Effective legal and institutional checks need to be in place in order to prevent abuses of executive authority.[461] Political accountability is critical in order to ensure the well-being of society and so that critical public services are maintained and the infrastructure exists to support economic development. Lack of corruption among the political and administrative elite is also essential for economic development.

Endeavours to promote good governance may be viewed as hollow geopolitical manoeuvring by dominant Western powers. Moreover, when good governance is equated with Western-style democracy, some people argue that it is a cultural and historical concept that is inapplicable outside the West. Yet, it is easy to find instances of democracy or democratic practices in different places and times in history. ***One challenge is to agree on minimum criteria of good governance that are not perceived as a threat to cultural traditions and***

---

[461] J.A. Goldstone and J. Ulfelder, "How to Construct Stable Democracies," *Washington Quarterly*, Vol. 28, No. 1, 2004-05.

to draw on moral concepts that are indigenous to specific cultural settings.

Another challenge is to engage those who maintain and propagate dogmatic ideas, since excluding them only risks generating more extreme views, increasing isolation and reducing exposure to dialogue and self-critique. As is discussed above in relation to knowledge, we know very little with absolute certainty, which means that it is highly unlikely that any single viewpoint possesses the absolute truth. The contingency of our knowledge and the positions it informs needs to be recognised. Moreover, while everything has a certain physicality, some things may be unobservable. This means that positivism needs to be applied in a qualified way. There may be critical aspects of the world and the universe that we cannot see or measure. Yet, the fact that we cannot observe them does not mean that they do not exist.

A further contemporary challenge that we face is to uncover from the dust the many examples of coexistence and cross-cultural fertilisation that represent parts of our common history, which was marked not by conflict but by tolerance of diversity and mutual sharing. This is important not only from a historical point of view, but also as a source of inspiration for the present and the future. Efforts that seek to bring back to life these "forgotten histories" will be vital to current efforts to construct an inclusive narrative that is capable of transcending binary ways of thinking, which fuel ignorance and the more ugly sides of what we have to offer. It constitutes an important part of broader efforts to increase awareness of other people's cultures, as well as their pains and fears. It is also an important part of building greater trust between people of different cultures and improving relations between geo-cultural domains.

8. The Way Forward

Self-governance has existed in all geo-cultural domains as they have appeared at various times. Democracy is sometimes considered a distinctly Western idea. However, this is a misconception that adds fuel to arguments that democracy is something imposed on cultures, which have no such traditions in their histories. Bowden demonstrates that democracy and the fundamental principles underlying it are not solely Western. Democracy is usually traced back to Ancient Greece and most notably to ancient Athens. Yet, democratic-like practices are now thought to have emerged in the Late Bronze Age (c. 1600-1100 BCE) around Mycenae in the north-east of the Peloponnese. Moreover, self-governing assemblies may have been established in what is now Iraq and Iran, and from there spread to the Indian subcontinent and west to the Phoenician ports before arriving in ancient Athens. According to Bowden, one of the reasons for the sidelining of democratic practices outside the West is the obsession with the state as the principal political institution in the Western canon of political thought.

Furthermore, the idea of democracy has not only been taken up in Western scholarship. The ideals of democracy are not the preserve of the West. Chinese philosopher, Meng-tzu promoted ideas similar to Locke regarding good government. Moreover, Confucianism, Buddhism and Tonghak, a religion native to Korea, have profoundly democratic foundations. In ancient India, small city-state-like republics and regional federations were prevalent, and religious scriptures – the Vedas and Brahmanas – reflect this democratic tradition. Africa has a tradition of democratic local governance at the village level.[462]

Within the Arab-Islamic world, the debates that took place following the Prophet's death touched on the ideas of majority opinion in decision making, sometimes as ijma (consensus), jumhur (majority) and shura (consultation).[463] Indeed, one of the reasons for the decline of the Arab-Islamic Empire was, as is mentioned above, the lack of political accountability. While the shura (consultative councils) continued to exist in later periods of the Arab-Islamic Empire, they no longer played their intended role and they failed to restrain arbitrary rule.[464]

Debates among Muslim thinkers have attempted to overcome this stalemate.[465] Some argue that Islam in fact contains the fundamental facets of democracy. Others believe that Islam and politics are not compatible with one another. Between these two extremes lie a number of other positions, which, according to Ehteshami, either seek to evaluate the contribution of the golden age of Islam to contemporary

---

[462] Bowden, *op. cit.*, note 334, pp. 1367-1370.
[463] Morgan, *op. cit.*, note 88, p. 13.
[464] Chapra, *op. cit.*, note 336, p. 60.
[465] A. Ehteshami, "Islam, Muslim Polities and Democracy," *Democratization*, Vol. 11, No. 4, 2004, p. 95.

issues in today's Muslim countries or attempt to delineate a compromise between Islam and democracy.[466]

As is highlighted above, a noteworthy factor that contributed to the flourishing of learning was the practice of Ijtihad or the critique and reform of Islam according to circumstances and need. When Ijtihad was stopped in the 10th century, the focus shifted from interpretations of Islam based on reasoned argumentation to more dogmatic approaches. This increased emphasis on dogmatic learning was accompanied by a decline in exploration of other forms of knowledge. At the same time, the patrons of learning were at pains to protect the faith by reducing the space for the free flow of ideas, as was the case with the second Almohad ruler in the Maghreb in the 12th century. The conditions under which intellectual pursuits took place thus gradually altered. A distinct lack of dogma had contributed to the Golden Age of Islam. The end of this age of splendour was at least partly due to an increase in dogma.

The increase in dogma may be understood as a defensive response to protect what was perceived as the "true" faith. Yet, defensive reactions tend to entail closure and an end to dialogue, critique and reform, which rarely contribute to the long-term health of what people wish to protect. More reason and the necessary space within which to critique ideas, institutions and beliefs is in the long-term interest of the things that people hold dear.

The shining example of Al-Andalus is testimony to the capacity of people of the three Abrahamic religions to live together and to engage in fruitful exchanges. As Küng aptly remarks, "instead of the excommunication often practised elsewhere in Europe, there was living communication. Even under medieval conditions, a 'dialogue of civilisations' rather than a 'clash of civilisations' was possible."[467] Some of the contributions to Islam's Golden Age and translations of these works came from non-Arabs as well as Jews and Christians. The initial lack of emphasis on ethnicity and the protected status of dhimmis directly contributed to the Arab-Islamic world's achievements, which others, including the West, benefited from later.[468] Diversity and toleration were thus important factors that enabled advances in various forms of knowledge. The strength of diversity needs to be

---

[466] *Ibid.*, pp. 95-97.
[467] Küng, *op. cit.*, note 422, p. 376.
[468] Bulliet, *op. cit.*, note 67, p. 31.

remembered and recognised today. Our societies are built on the contribution of everyone, regardless of how long they have been there. Diversity must be viewed as a strength to be embraced rather than as a weakness to be feared.

Another look at the history of relations between the Arab-Islamic and Latin Christian worlds calls into question the notion that their relations have been marked by blood and conquest. Conflict certainly existed, but there have also been mutually enriching exchanges that have helped to shape the world we live in today. We need therefore to engage in individual and collective efforts to salvage these more hopeful parts of our common history in order to construct a narrative that is not marked by the division between "us" and "them", but is testimony to our capacity to coexist peacefully.

We also need to ask ourselves what it was that enabled periods of peaceful coexistence, and to identify that which may be required in the contemporary era. Recognition of the tremendous cultural, philosophical, scientific and technological transfers from the Arab-Islamic world to the West would also serve to do justice to the contribution of the Arab-Islamic world to the "rise of the West". The East's contribution to the West of course did not stop with the Middle Ages. Contributions to building contemporary societies are ongoing and this needs to be acknowledged at the political level. Octagon 1 summarises the prerequisites of civilisational triumph.

SUSTAINABLE HISTORY AND THE DIGNITY OF MAN   177

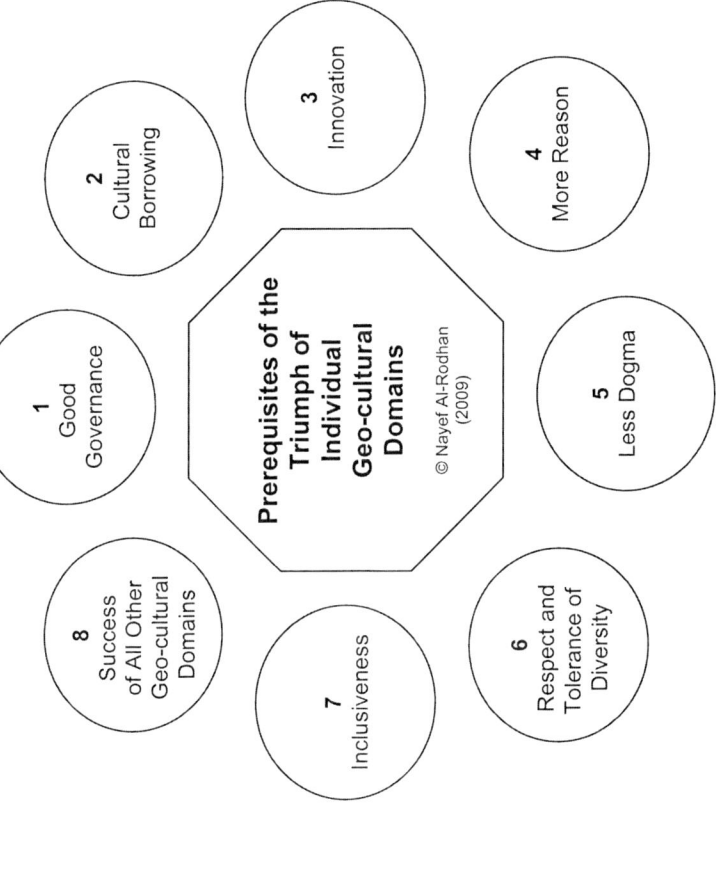

Octagon 1: Prerequisites of the Triumph of Individual Geo-cultural Domains

9. Conclusion

This chapter identified the factors that contributed to the golden ages of the Arab-Islamic world, as well as those that led to the end of that period. It illustrated the way in which the Arab-Islamic world borrowed from and built on the achievements of others, such as the Ancient Greeks, Hindus and Chinese, and how the contributions to forms of knowledge later influenced European science, technology and philosophy, helping to build the foundations for the rise of the West – something that is unfortunately infrequently acknowledged. Such exchanges and hybridity demonstrate that human civilisation has depended on multiple contributions, which were able to flourish due to a specific set of historical, social, cultural and political circumstances. My own cursory examination of *the golden ages of the Arab-Islamic world suggests that good governance, a high value placed on learning, an openness to critique, toleration and respect for diversity are vital ingredients for enabling innovation of all forms to flourish. Good governance is therefore a vital component of sustainable history.*

CHAPTER 7

HOW CAN DIGNITY BE ATTAINED?
MINIMUM CRITERIA OF HUMAN NEEDS AND DIGNITY

Ensuring human dignity is a vital component of sustainable history, because it is central to human well-being. Yet, poverty, disease, discrimination and various kinds of conflict continue to be sources of human misery, despite the era of unprecedented wealth, education and technological advance in which we live. Today, we have no excuse for allowing continued suffering. We cannot claim that we are unaware of the divide that exists between the rich and the poor, the powerful and the powerless, and the included and the marginalised. There is, nevertheless, a general lack of solidarity with those outside our immediate communities. We need to better harness the positive aspects of globalisation in order to forge greater inclusiveness and solidarity. A globalisation capable of serving this objective is a globalisation that has the promotion and protection of human rights at its heart.[469] Human dignity lies at the heart of the Universal Declaration of Human Rights.[470] The idea that human dignity ought to inform human practices and relations seems to the vast majority of people commonsensical. Yet, what we mean by dignity is unclear.[471]

This chapter sets out by looking at how human dignity has been defined. It also attempts to discern what is understood by the concept of dignity. It then outlines minimum criteria of human dignity on which the majority of humanity could agree. While these minimum criteria, against which can be assessed whether human needs are being

---

[469] S. Vieira de Mello, "A World of Dignity," 11 November 2002 Lecture on the Universal Character of Human Dignity," *OpenDemocracy*, http://www.open democracy.net/democracy-un_iraq/article_1449.jsp.
[470] Universal Declaration of Human Rights, 10 December 1948, Office of the High Commissioner of Human Rights, http://www.unhchr.ch /udhr/lang/eng.htm.
[471] G. Zúñiga, "An Ontology of Dignity," Originally Published in German as "Eine Ontologie der Würde" in R. Stoeker (ed.) *Menschenwürde: Annäherung an einen Begriff* (Wien: öbv&hpt, 2003), p. 115

met, need to be universal, they must also be sensitive to cultural and historical specificities.[472] Finally, some of the challenges to establishing minimum criteria of human dignity are identified, and some suggestions made on how these might be overcome. Above all, reason, security, human rights, accountability, transparency, justice, opportunity, innovation and inclusiveness are essential to meeting human dignity needs.

1. The Concept of Human Dignity

While the concept of human dignity is frequently employed in political discourse, the concept of dignity on which it rests remains ill-defined. Etymologically, dignity stems from the Latin noun decus, which means ornament, distinction, honour or glory.[473] In Roman times, dignity had moral, political, legal and social connotations. It could imply indifference to profit, those in high public office, greater or lesser in relation to rank and social background, as well as social rank. Dignity was therefore not thought to be distributed equally.[474] The modern conception of dignity as applying to all humankind developed much later.[475] In a somewhat similar way, Hobbes associated it with power or a man's "price".[476] Dignity, understood in this way, may be thought of as *attributed* dignity. It is derived from the worth that others confer on someone. As D.P. Sulmasy notes, this kind of dignity is created and can equally be lost.[477] The problem with this notion is that it denies that, for instance, the unemployed, the mentally ill or the handicapped have dignity.[478]

Gloria Zúñiga identifies three other types of dignity: a) the ostensive definition; b) the rationality criterion; and c) the social ac-

---

[472] H.C. Kelman, "The Conditions, Criteria, and Dialectics of Human Dignity: A Transnational Perspective," *International Studies Quarterly*, Vol. 21, No. 3, 1977, p. 543.
[473] M. Lebech, "What is Human Dignity?" *Maynooth Philosophical Papers*, 2004, available at http://eprints.nuim.ie/ 392/1/Human_Dignity.pdf.
[474] J. Malpas, "Human Dignity and Human Being," in J. Malpas and N. Lickiss (eds.) *Perspectives on Human Dignity: A Conversation* (Dordrecht: Spinger, 2007), p. 93.
[475] D. Chalmers and R. Ida, "On the International Legal Aspects of Human Dignity," in Malpas and Lickiss, *ibid.*, p. 158.
[476] Hobbes, *op. cit.*, note 151, Part 1: of Man.
[477] D.P. Sulmasy, "Human Dignity and Human Worth," in Malpas and Lickiss, *op. cit.*, note 474, p. 12.
[478] *Ibid.*, p. 13.

count.[479] In the ostensive definition, the intelligibility of human dignity stems from the intersubjective recognition that each human being is connected to an eternal being. Thus, human dignity stems from the likeness of humankind to an eternal being. If the existence of God is acknowledged, then the apparent dignity of the human being is proven. However, this definition depends on knowledge of God, which may be different across religions and belief systems, and, therefore, is not universal. The philosophy of religion has employed this definition of dignity, although it has not been employed to such a great extent in the sphere of ethics in which secular discussions of dignity are carried out.[480]

In Catholic theology, for example, one may understand a person only in the context of that person's relationship to God and the rest of Creation. The Catholic Church's emphasis on human dignity, according to Marc Guerra, may be interpreted as their effort to convey to a modern audience the idea that humankind is created in God's image. The Catholic Church, for example, played an important role in opposing actually existing socialism by emphasising the way in which communist totalitarian regimes denied human dignity, especially during the period of Pope John Paul II.[481] Italian Catholic priest and philosopher Thomas Aquinas conceived of human dignity as the value that something has in relation to its place in the great chain of being. Animals have, for example, more dignity than plants, human beings more than animals, and so on.[482]

The association of dignity with rationality has its roots in the Enlightenment and it suggests that human dignity is connected to autonomy.[483] The best known contribution to the rational definition of dignity is Kant's moral philosophy. Kant infrequently refers to human dignity, but more often uses the term dignity, which he understands as the ultimate target of respect.[484] In Kant's thought, a person is endowed with dignity because of his/her capacity for reason. The ability to reason about ends signifies the highest form of rationality, since it can lead a person to decipher what is good and to choose what ought

---

[479] Zúñiga, *op. cit*, note 471, p. 115.
[480] *Ibid.*, p. 116.
[481] M.D. Guerra, The Affirmation of Genuine Human Dignity," *Journal of Markets & Morality*, Vol. 4, No. 2, 2001, p. 1.
[482] Sulmasy, *op. cit.*, note 477, p. 11.
[483] Malpas, *op. cit.*, note 474, p. 20.
[484] Lebech, *op. cit.*, note 473, p. 6.

to be pursued. These two criteria – the good and the duty to do good – are fundamental to Kant's moral thinking. However, as Zúñiga notes, Kant does not explain how dignity may be obtained by all persons. In his thinking the intrinsic nature of the dignity of other persons stems from recognition that they are rational beings. That is, since a person is an end in his or herself and does not depend on material attributes, his or her dignity is an eternal given. According to Zúñiga, the notion that people are capable of reasoning between different alternatives is not problematic. However, the idea that reason necessarily leads people to do good is problematic. Sometimes people do not recognise what is good and others may consciously fail to do what is good. Moreover, knowledge of what is good may not be derived through reasoning. Indeed, sometimes we immediately recognise something as unjust just as we immediately recognise beauty. In such instances, this judgement is not arrived at by deliberation. Furthermore, if rationality is an essential criterion for intrinsic dignity, infants, children and the elderly suffering from dementia would not possess dignity.[485] We need to reconcile the notion of dignity with "amoral emotional egoism", which indicates that people are emotionally rather than rationally driven.

Others, such as Guerra, argue that Kantian moral philosophy and notions of dignity are circular: "Human dignity and human autonomy are fused together to form a perfect circle: Human dignity is seen to require the exercise of human autonomy and the exercise of human autonomy is seen as definitive proof of human dignity."[486] According to Guerra, Rawls's *Theory of Justice* (1971) is premised on Kantian moral philosophy and is therefore flawed. He takes issue with the Kantian approach to human dignity because it takes human autonomy to an extreme and consequently sees a moral order of divine origin as illegitimate.[487]

Too great a stress on autonomy also relies on a conception of humanness that is too narrow. As Jeff Malpas remarks:

> Who and what we are is not determined solely by our existence as independent beings, but is instead intertwined with the being of those others in relation to whom our lives are shaped, as well as with respect to the wider world in which our lives are played out. This is not merely a point that derives from the

---

[485] Zúñiga, *op. cit.*, note 471, pp. 117-120.
[486] Guerra, *op. cit.*, note 481, p. 3.
[487] *Ibid.*, p. 3.

pragmatic reliance on others that is part of our socialised mode of existence – the fact that, practically speaking, human life depends on cooperative relations with other human beings in order to satisfy basic needs of food, shelter, and security – but rather reflects the way in which, at an even more fundamental level, the very possibility of grasping one's own individual being, and so understanding oneself as having a life of one's own . . . itself depends on grasping the being of others and the being of things around one.[488]

Such a relational account of humanness suggests a relational account of human dignity. Dignity, Malpas argues, is something that has relevance within structures of relations. This relational quality appears to give dignity a number of facets. For example, a person may continue to retain his or her dignity even when others demean it. This dignity that one has in relation to oneself and others can overcome others' attempts to deny or diminish it. Interestingly, Malpas suggests that a person may never really lose his or her dignity. What may be lost is the will to express or assert it. If we accept this to be the case, only respect for dignity can be lost, but not dignity itself. This is why perhaps restraint in the face of assault often seems to capture the meaning of dignity. Malpas also suggests that lack of recognition for the dignity of others in some way reduces one's own dignity.[489]

Notions of dignity that are based on autonomy are unlikely to be universally acceptable,[490] because dignity is not necessarily conceived in this way in a variety of non-Western contexts. Dignity occupies an important position within the Arab-Islamic worldview, which is composed of a fusion of values with a traditional cultural base and those with theological foundations. The importance of honour within the Arab-Islamic world is, for example, linked to pre-Islamic Arabian society. The pre-Islamic social system was premised on tribal law and a code of morality centred on the notion of dignity (karama) through which individuals perceived their worth. The code of tribal law and morality later became incorporated into broader Islamic law (shari'a). Accordingly, concepts of honour, genealogy, paternalism and eloquence were expressed in the Islamic values of Tawhid (Allah is the only God), Iman (belief), umma (community) and ibadah (worship)

---

[488] Malpas, *op. cit.*, note 474, p. 21.
[489] *Ibid.*, pp. 22-23.
[490] Chalmers and Ida, *op. cit.*, note 475, p. 159.

and ilm (knowledge).[491] Thus, dignity-based Arab-Islamic values are not informed by notions of individual autonomy.

Both Hinduism and Buddhism also place the community before the individual, although both recognise and value human dignity. The idea of human dignity is also present in Confucianism.[492] As Andrew Brennan and Y.S. Lo note, the Confucian canon of self-cultivation suggests that dignity is related to developing certain abilities and aspects of character. Dignity, in this sense, is connected to feeling and behaving in particular ways. It is generated by the capacity to feel self-esteem and to gain the esteem of others. It is also dependent on carrying out the rules and duties expected of someone worthy of esteem. Self-cultivation in Confucianism cannot be separated from the idea of hierarchy. Yet, dignity-relevant hierarchy operates on the moral rather than the material plane. Someone who earns their living honestly is more dignified than a corrupt official or a tyrant. Thus, dignity may be cultivated and enhanced, as well as neglected and lost.[493] Don Chalmers and Ryuichi Ida note also that the idea of human dignity appears to have played a role in the modern constitution of Japanese society. The idea of Jinkaku refers to the moral worth of a person that makes that person worthy of respect within society.[494] However, in all these cases, dignity is understood in a context in which the whole is of greater significance than the individual. The Confucian canon of self-cultivation, which Brennan and Lo refer to as a meritocratic idea of dignity, relates to something bigger than the individual.[495]

Lastly, there is the social account of dignity. Here, dignity is thought to stem from the interaction between persons. In this account, a person's dignity depends on the recognition by other's of his/her personhood and their attitude of compassion and respect shown towards him or her as a member of the same group/class. The emphasis on beliefs, according to Zúñiga, does not help to define the nature of dignity. It is also problematic because it does not recognise those who

---

[491] M.I. Ayish, "Beyond Western-Oriented Communication Theories: A Normative Arab-Islamic Perspective," *The Public*, Vol. 10, No. 2, 2003, http://www.javnost-thepublic.org/media/datoteke/ayish-2-2003-5.pdf, pp. 81-85.
[492] Malpas, *op. cit.*, note 474, pp. 95-96.
[493] A. Brennan and Y.S. Lo, "Two Conceptions of Dignity: Honour and Self-Determination," in Malpas and Lickiss, *op. cit.*, note 474, pp. 45-46.
[494] Chalmers and Ida, *op. cit.*, note 475, p. 159.
[495] Brennan and Lo, *op. cit.*, note 493, p. 46.

do not belong to the human social world, such as those with autism, as being invested with dignity. Moreover, according to Zúñiga, the social account is susceptible to relativism and renders dignity vulnerable to wrong beliefs.[496]

Zúñiga's own position is that dignity belongs to ontology and not ethics. In her view, it is not a moral quality, but an individual substance. In epistemic terms, this implies that every person possesses a sense of dignity. Dignity endures through time and is not necessarily bound up with a person's real existence. The dignity of a person may, for example, continue even when a person has ceased to exist. Otherwise, we would not have memorials commemorating fallen heroes or the like.[497] From this perspective, dignity is not something that is fragile and can be easily lost.[498] Dignity is ontological because the value that it implies is constitutive of personal and collective identity. It implies recognition of one's value.[499] It is only in relations with other human beings – in kinship, friendship and love – that we begin to comprehend or feel what dignity is.

Thus, when "human" and "dignity" are combined to form "human dignity" we are referring to the status of human beings that warrants respect. This status is to be taken for granted. This implies that their value is presupposed.[500] It assumes something about *humanness*, which, indeed, does make it an ontological concern.[501] Someone has dignity, simply because he or she is human – because he or she is *someone*. This conception of dignity is independent of the attributions of others.[502] This suggests that dignity is intrinsic.[503] In axiological terms, intrinsic value implies value within itself. Here, something or someone is valuable independent of the valuers' desires, beliefs or interests. This stands in contrast to attributed value, which is dependent on the attribution of the valuer. This conception of human dignity as intrinsic is the basis of human rights.[504] Claiming that there is a connection between human dignity and humanness does not, however,

---

[496] Zúñiga, *op. cit.*, note 471, pp. 121-122.
[497] Lebech, *op. cit.*, note 473, p. 1.
[498] Brennan and Lo, *op. cit.*, note 493, p. 47.
[499] Lebech, *op. cit.*, note 473, p. 1.
[500] *Ibid.*
[501] Malpas, *op. cit.*, note 474, p. 19.
[502] Sulmasy, *op. cit.*, note 477, pp. 14-15.
[503] *Ibid.*, p. 12.
[504] *Ibid.*, pp. 15-16.

mean that dignity is restricted to humans.[505] However, what it is that gives us equal intrinsic value in the absence of God remains fuzzy.

Brennan and Lo point out that the modern notion of dignity as an intrinsic value does not provide a solution to the problem of equality in relation to dignity. They suggest that instead of expressing a reality, the notion of dignity or a priori equal worth expresses a normative ideal that garners widespread support. They argue that it can only be fully understood against the backdrop of a monotheistic past and the accompanying idea that human beings are endowed with a God-given worth. Attempts to provide a secular solution to the equality problem runs into problems. The capacity for rational agency may not be equally distributed. If the capacity for autonomy is the basis for dignity, then people will have dignity even when their ability to exercise that capacity is restrained, that is, in the case of unjust imprisonment. The modern conception of dignity, Brennan and Lo conclude, suggests that the possession (or loss) of dignity appears to be determined by having (or lacking) a particular quality and being able (or unable) to employ it. Their way of reconciling the Universal Declaration of Human Rights with the complex modern conception of dignity is to view the declaration as a normative ideal.[506]

We may link this normative ideal with humanness and subsequent needs. In *"emotional amoral egoism": A Neurophilosophical Theory of Human Nature and its Universal Security Implications* (2008), I set out a theory of human nature that emphasises the emotionally driven character of human nature rather than the capacity for rationality. **Human beings are largely motivated by their emotional repertoire, manifested through their need for attachment, physical security, a sense of belonging and a positive personal and collective identity.**[507] Practices that infringe on our sense of dignity – premised on our value in and of ourselves – negatively impact on vital human needs, that is, the need for a positive sense of self and for respect for the communities to which we belong and in relation to which we define ourselves. Understanding and providing for such human needs are likely to help to protect human dignity. Reconciling the predisposition of human nature to emotionally self-interested behaviour, which may have positive or negative consequences depending on the circum-

---

[505] Malpas, *op. cit.*, note 474, p. 19.
[506] Brennan and Lo, *op. cit.*, note 493, pp. 48-52, 58.
[507] Al-Rodhan, *"emotional amoral egoism," op. cit.*, note 119.

stances, with the imperative of human dignity is central to sustainable history.

2. Minimum Criteria of Human Dignity at the National Level

According to Kelman, "The overarching indicator of human dignity in a society is the worth attached to an individual's life."[508] People need to have a sense of their own dignity, which enables them to feel self worth, and to feel that they are valued by others and treated accordingly. If a stable identity and a sense of community are two of the minimum criteria of human dignity, we may assess the success of a state in this domain by evaluating its institutional mechanisms and societal capacity to ensure that people feel included and are able to maintain a positive and stable identity. Kelman suggests that the provision of identity may be assessed by the level of social justice within a state,[509] defined in broad terms.

Basic Needs
Policymakers must take into account the emotional nature of human beings rather than simply assuming that they are rational beings above all else. If we take the needs for a stable identity and community to form the basis of human dignity, a minimum criterion of human dignity would be the provision of basic needs. This implies that the institutions of the state must be capable of ensuring that the population has adequate access to food, housing, clothing, health care, education and security. This means that governments must be committed to protecting society as a whole against violence, starvation and hunger, disease and the effects of disasters. Moreover, it also implies protecting people with disabilities resulting from disadvantages, sickness and old age. People from all sections of society should enjoy access to basic welfare provision and security. Groups that are systematically discriminated against in their access to economic opportunities and social benefits are deprived of the exercise of individual freedom on a collective basis, as well as of personal and group identity. In addition, these

---

[508] Kelman, *op. cit.*, note 472, p. 532.
[509] *Ibid.*, p. 532.

groups do not have the means or power to resist oppression and violations of their rights.[510]

Inclusiveness and Participation
Policies instituted by the majority within particular societies may reflect and reinforce discrimination through unequal treatment; denial of access to jobs, housing and schooling in particular areas, and so on. This kind of discrimination may be not be explicit: it may be subtle, reflecting integration on the basis of inequality.[511] Yet, in order for people to have a sense of identity, they need not only to feel valued as individuals, but also that the communities to which they belong are recognised and valued. This requires tolerance and respect for religious, ethnic and cultural diversity. Lack of respect for people's cultural heritage or religious affiliations is often accompanied by socio-economic inequalities.[512] States need to be able to successfully manage cultural pluralism[513] in order to ensure the well-being of their population, prosperity and stability. Whether they are succeeding in these endeavours may be evaluated by the absence or presence of marginalised communities.

Societies that do not ensure the free expression of diverse views, enable participation in decision-making processes or protect the rights of minorities and those who challenge official positions will fall short in the fulfilment of minimum criteria of human dignity because as long as all members of society cannot express their views and have a say in the policies that affect them, social, political and cultural justice will not be achieved. In this type of climate, dissenters and those belonging to minority groups may be vulnerable to repression and arbitrary acts, and society will have failed to provide basic welfare and security for all. Yet, if people are not sufficiently free to express their views they will be unable to evaluate the capacity of institutions to provide the required conditions for basic human dignity, making

---
[510] *Ibid.*, pp. 532-534.
[511] A. Eide, "Good Governance, Human Rights, and the Rights of Minorities and Indigenous Peoples," in H-O Sano and G. Alfredsson, With the Collaboration of R. Clapp, *Human Rights and Good Governance* (The Hague: KLuwer Law International, 2002), p. 55.
[512] N.R.F. Al-Rodhan, *The Five Dimensions of Global Security: Proposal for a Multi-sum Security Principle* (Berlin: LIT, 2007), pp. 119-120.
[513] Al-Rodhan and Watanabe, *A Proposal for* Inclusive *Peace and Security, op. cit.*, note 1, p. 72.

reform unlikely or limited.[514] This may be especially the case, given that those who are excluded from the process of evaluating the functioning of institutions are likely to be those who suffer most from their inadequacies and therefore understand their limits. Inclusiveness and the opportunity to participate in society and to participate in government are essential if human dignity needs are to be met.

Socio-economic Justice
Social injustices help to reduce human dignity. Socio-economic injustice can also frustrate basic needs, such as access to health care, adequate food and clean water, as well as the need for a positive identity and sense of belonging.[515] Communities need to have equal access to scarce resources within their country. Potential tensions and conflict stemming from unequal access to such resources can become especially acute against the backdrop of population growth. Where scarce resources are shared with neighbouring states, governments must work cooperatively with their neighbours to manage their use.[516]

Greater harmonisation of national laws governing tariffs, financing, competition, labour rights, environmental protection, and so on, are also required, since variations allow transnational corporations to play one state off against another.[517] This can result in a "race to the bottom" in terms of standards as states attempt to make their national economic situations more attractive for foreign companies seeking to invest in their country. The consequences for individuals may be lower labour standards and perhaps lower wages as well as increased job insecurity in those sectors affected. Corporate activities may also affect the environment in ways that threaten human well-being and dignity.

Gender Equality
Gender inequalities may also have a negative impact on human dignity. One of the most common forms of violence is domestic violence, from which women disproportionately suffer. Moreover, harsh economic conditions are likely to affect women more than men, given

---

[514] Kelman, *op. cit.*, note 472, p. 534.
[515] Al-Rodhan and Watanabe, *A Proposal for* Inclusive *Peace and Security, op. cit.,* note 1, p. 47.
[516] *Ibid.*, p. 73.
[517] Al-Rodhan, *Symbiotic Realism, op. cit.*, note 78, p. 128.

that they take on greater responsibilities in the "private family realm" than men, and that they are seldom as well represented in decision-making mechanisms. Within a globalising economy, women may be particularly vulnerable to poor and unsafe working conditions within unregulated sectors, given that their work is often unskilled work, and some may be vulnerable to human trafficking, finding themselves working as domestic help in an informal economy or as prostitutes in the sex industry.[518] Those women who work in the "public sphere" are likely to be paid less than their male counterparts for doing the same or similar jobs. They may also encounter a "glass ceiling", which their male counterparts do not, which limits the degree of freedom they have to make the most of their skills and abilities. Women may also experience a lack of access to education, which may, in turn, affect their ability to benefit from health care opportunities where they exist, as well as their capacity to participate in decision making.

Human Rights
The protection and promotion of human rights, which include civil, political, social as well as cultural rights, is also an important means of meeting human dignity needs. The difficulty of identifying minimum criteria of human dignity is that they need to be universal but, at the same time, they must be sensitive to cultural and historical particularities. Some commentators have made a great deal of the incommensurability of cultural differences, as is mentioned above in the context of Asian values and similar debates related to other regions of the world. Yet, as Kelman notes:

> The dilemma here may turn out to be less severe than might be anticipated, because there are many such criteria that are in fact accepted – at least at the level of general principle – by a virtually universal consensus. These are criteria that are derivable from all major ethical systems and acknowledged in many national constitutions. They are formalized in international agreements, such as the Universal Declaration of Human Rights. . . . The existing consensus can at least serve as a starting point for continuing transnational exploration and specification of criteria that would have universal validity.[519]

---

[518] Al-Rodhan and Watanabe, *A Proposal for* Inclusive *Peace and Security, op. cit.*, note 1, p. 112.
[519] Kelman, *op. cit.*, note 472, p. 543.

However, assessing specific institutional practices may present more difficulties.[520]

Protection of the Environment and the Ecological Balance
Environmental degradation may have an impact on people's quality of life, health and livelihoods. Some people, because of their race or income, may suffer disproportionately from environmental degradation and its impact. Waste disposal or transit routes, for instance, may be more likely to affect some groups than others. In some countries, there are also sharp disparities in access to safe and clean resources. Discrimination in relation to a safe, clean, productive and sustainable environment may occur on the basis of race, income and even age.[521] Yet, structural inequalities may mean that these very people have little say over decisions that effect the environment. At the national level, states need to ensure fair treatment in relation to environmental issues, disclosure of information and opportunities to participate.

3. Minimum Criteria of Human Dignity at the Global Level

Human dignity is not something that can be achieved solely on a national basis. The broader global system may be partly responsible for the limits placed on human dignity, which means that minimum criteria of dignity should also be sought at the global level. Indeed, Kelman stated as far back as 1977 that "the achievement, extension, and preservation of human dignity are to a large extent a world-wide, transnational enterprise."[522] Thus, even then there was a recognition that meeting human dignity needs had to be global as a result of increased interdependence. Kelman also conceived of the protection and extension of human dignity as a dialectical process in that it requires the fulfilment and constraint of nationalistic demands.[523] We therefore need to ask what are the criteria against which institutions and policies may be evaluated vis-à-vis the fulfilment of human dignity, and how these criteria can be met.

---

[520] *Ibid.*
[521] H. Dillingham, "Determining the Current Status of the Environmental Justice Movement: Analysis of Revolutionary Actions," *Harvard Journal of African American Public Policy*, Vol. 14, 2008, p. 38.
[522] Kelman, *op. cit.*, note 472, p. 535.
[523] *Ibid.*

Avoidance of Conflict
Violence and armed conflict affect civilian populations more now than in the past. Human dignity is diminished by conditions under which the survival of the self, family or groups is compromised. At one level, this requires the avoidance of large-scale, collective violence as well as reassurance that such violence is unlikely. War threatens human dignity not only because it brings with it killing and injury, but also because it can result in hunger, illness, homelessness, displacement and fear. It may also destroy cities and places of cultural importance, and pose both immediate and enduring dangers to the economic base of a group or society. It also creates conditions under which limitations on freedom may be more easily justified and people's human rights more easily violated.[524]

States need to foster a national identity and societal structure in which everyone feels they have a stake. The marginalisation and subsequent alienation of some cultural, ethnic or religious groups can occur as a result of a lack of awareness and respect for their lifeworlds, and a lack of trust can create ghettoised communities, discrimination and unrest, not least because individual identities are intertwined with the collective identities of the communities to which people belong. Respect and toleration of difference, therefore, constitute important conflict prevention measures and should be promoted at all levels. Social, environmental and political justice must also be promoted as a means of preventing conflict.

Provision of Basic Needs
The 2002 United Nations World Summit on Sustainable Development emphasised that the majority of the world's population still lacks clean water, satisfactory sanitation and electricity.[525] Multilateral institutions must make it one of their priorities to promote the understanding of and respect for people's sense of dignity. Since poverty, disease and marginalisation all diminish human dignity, multilateral institutions, in cooperation with states, should endeavour to reduce the structural bases of inequalities and alienation within and between states, as well

---

[524] *Ibid.*, pp. 536-537.
[525] A. Shah, "World Summit on Sustainable Development," Updated 7 September 2002, *Global Issues*, http://www.globalissues.org/article/366/world-summit-onsustainable-development.

as across regions of the globe, that result in widespread suffering.[526] Basic education is likely to play a critical role in enabling people to provide for basic needs, such as basic health care.

Participation
Political participation is essential for ensuring that everyone is entitled to particular benefits. Rights and opportunities must be distributed on an equal basis. Some of the institutions at the heart of global governance are not representative. The membership of the United Nations Security Council (UNSC), for example, is skewed in favour of the victors of the Second World War, namely the Soviet Union (now Russia), the United Kingdom (UK), France, the US and China, and is in radical need of reform. Any one of them has the right to veto a resolution which they perceive to be in conflict with their interests, even if it is in compliance with human dignity needs. Enlarging membership of the UN Security Council and altering veto rights may at least decrease the likelihood of the national interests of one state overriding the greater good. The issue of lack of adequate representation extends to other international institutions established in the immediate aftermath of the Second World War, such as the World Bank and the International Monetary Fund (IMF), and this is similarly reflected in their decision-making arrangements.[527]

Socio-economic Justice
At the global level, the absolute gap between developed and developing countries resulting from 200 years of industrialisation in the West and colonisation in the South is an ongoing problem for human dignity. There are continuing disparities in resources and power in the global political economy.[528] While the liberalisation of trade has created opportunities for developing countries, it remains the case that developed countries maintain high tariffs in areas such as agriculture, in which developing countries have a comparative advantage. The multilateral trading system is therefore not serving these countries as it should. A more level playing field is required in order to ensure that

---

[526] Al-Rodhan, *The Five Dimensions of Global Security*, op. cit., note 512, p. 95.
[527] N.R.F. Al-Rodhan, M. Finaud, E. Palazzolo, L. Watanabe, L. Nazaruk and L. Rurarz-Huygens, *Multilateralism and Transnational Security: A Synthesis of Win-Win Solutions* (Genève: Éditions Slatkine, 2009), pp. 302-306.
[528] Al-Rodhan, *The Five Dimensions of Global Security*, op. cit., note 512, p. 125.

the conditions for human dignity are able to be met. Yet, the issue of unequal representation in key multilateral institutions frustrates this effort.

Gender Equality
Gender inequality affects human dignity in a number of ways. It is intimately linked to family context, social institutions, the state and the global political economy. In some instances, being a women may affect one's life expectancy, level of education and general well-being. Moreover, deterioration in the provision of basic public services and a worsening of economic conditions may be disproportionately felt by women since they tend to take on the greatest responsibility within the private/family sphere and to experience greater economic vulnerability. As mentioned, women's labour, for example, is often perceived as low-skilled and temporary labour, which typically implies greater job insecurity and lower wages. Poverty, as well as security, is gendered. Women are also comparatively more exposed to regular forms of physical violence, often at the hands of a spouse or male relative. They are also more vulnerable in situations of conflict than men. In such situations, they are vulnerable to particular forms of violence, including sexual violence.[529]

Protection of Human Rights
Discrimination negatively affects the dignity of those discriminated against, because those who engage in discriminatory practices deny their equal worth as a human being.[530] Human dignity requires individual worth to be recognised. Moreover, the promotion and protection of human rights at the global level is necessary due to the transnational nature of groups that may suffer from human rights abuses. The violation of the human rights of a group in one country may be felt as a violation of fellow group members elsewhere, and may form part of a group's struggle for the protection and the extension of the rights of a whole group whose members are geographically scattered. Human rights struggles in one place are also influenced by those in another place. Moreover, the increased connectedness of today's world makes human rights violations in any country a matter of global concern.[531]

---

[529] Al-Rodhan, *Symbiotic Realism*, *op. cit.*, note 78, p. 112.
[530] Al-Rodhan, *The Five Dimensions of Global Security*, *op. cit.*, note 512, p. 91.
[531] Kelman, *op. cit.*, note 472, pp. 541-542.

Protection of the Environment and the Ecological Balance
Growth in the worlds population and increased economic activity, particularly over the past century, has placed considerable stress on the environment and the ecological balance. The particularity of our time is characterised by the long period of growth through which we are living.[532] The impact of environmental damage and the disruption of ecosystems may affect human dignity as a result of the damage wreaked by natural disasters promoted by changes in weather patterns connected to global climate change. Water scarcity leading to food shortage, and disease caused by air and water pollution will also impinge on human dignity.

Environmental and social justice are interrelated. Social justice, writes Kelman, should be conceived within a total world system due to increased global interdependence. Scarce resources, regardless of their geographic location, belong to all of humankind. Their use ought therefore to be subject to joint control and planning. This, of course, requires pooled sovereignty. It implies that each society has a responsibility to consider how it is using such resources and how that use affects other societies.[533]

4. The Challenges

Challenges to dignity stem largely from structural inequalities within societies and between states, which result in inequalities of power and representation. Corporate power and the lack of public regulation of the private sector also pose considerable challenges to human dignity.

Basic Needs
Some states do not meet the majority of their population's basic needs. Moreover, some states are reducing the size of the public sphere. Given that the state's social role may in the past have helped to protect people from the vagaries of the market, this trend risks leaving the vulnerable even more vulnerable. The state is also increasingly unable to protect their populations from health risks resulting from the internationalisation of food supplies, and increased travel and migration. Providing for the needs of the population in economic and social terms is perhaps the biggest challenge, although ensuring the popula-

---

[532] Al-Rodhan, *The Five Dimensions of Global Security, op. cit.*, note 512, p. 51
[533] Kelman, *op. cit.*, note 472, p. 538.

tion's health in the face of infectious disease, as well as a clean environment are also challenges that states increasingly face in an era of globalisation. All this makes promoting the economic and social dimensions of human rights an increasing challenge. Yet, the machinery with which to implement human rights is fairly weak.[534] An additional challenge to ensuring that people's basic needs do not go unmet is the problem of poor governance and, in the worst case scenario, state failure. In such instances, the resources and the level of responsiveness necessary to ensure the provision of basic needs are unlikely to be available.

Inclusiveness and Participation
Today, many states are multi-ethnic and comprise groups whose identities are not solely connected to the societies in which they live. Instead, they have multiple, overlapping identities. These segments of the population often encounter discrimination and other exclusionary practices so that their needs on various levels are not met.[535] At the national level, policymakers must take into consideration the emotional needs of the population, which includes the need for a positive personal identity. Given that identity is defined to a significant extent by our relations with others and the communities that we belong to, promoting inclusiveness is central to satisfying human needs and ensuring that the structure of society protects and promotes human dignity.[536] However, in some societies, conflict dynamics between governments and minority groups make accommodation of cultural pluralism very difficult. "Conflict entrepreneurs" risk reducing the space in which those interested in cultural coexistence can explore the opportunities to do so in a positive emotional climate.[537]

Within states, obstacles to participation may be connected to ethnicity, race or gender. Breaking down these barriers requires a concerted effort on the part of the state to better represent women and minorities, as well as active engagement on the part of those concerned. At the global level, all states, in whatever region they are located, need to have adequate opportunities to participate in decision

---

[534] M. Lewis, "A Brief History of Human Dignity: Idea and Application," in Malpas and Lickiss, *op. cit.*, note 474, p. 104.
[535] Kelman, *op. cit.*, note 472, p. 548.
[536] Al-Rodhan, *"emotional amoral egoism,"* *op. cit.*, note 119, p. 173.
[537] Eide, *op. cit.*, note 511, p. 62.

making in order to even out unequal power relations between states and societies. The membership of the G8 is too narrow and ought to better represent all the regions of the world. The UN, as is mentioned above, reinforces unequal power relations between its member states.[538]

Social Justice
Poor governance at the national level leads, among other things, to resources not being distributed in the interests of social justice and to a lack of transparency and accountability. Social injustices and political instability may be mutually reinforcing, particularly when increases in wealth inequalities take place very rapidly, leading poorer members of society to call for a redistribution of wealth.[539] Kelman notes that:

> Social justice in the face of such inequality can be achieved only if the have nations assume some responsibility for the welfare of the have nots. This responsibility, as a matter of justice, becomes even more apparent when we recall that the existing inequalities are often the outcomes of long histories of exploitation of the have nots by the haves.[540]

Continued protectionism practiced by developed states denies market access to developing countries. While average tariff rates may be low in general terms in developed countries, tariffs remain in areas where developing countries have a comparative advantage. Agriculture is the prime example but there is a similar situation in relation to labour-intensive manufactures.[541]

Corporate Regulation
Increased difficulties in regulation using traditional legal means have been accompanied by a global trend towards corporate self-regulation and standard setting. As Amiram Gill explains, corporate governance has traditionally referred to rules governing business decision making internal to firms. However, as companies have increasingly sought to reassure investors and regulating agencies, corporate governance has come to be associated with a broader set of issues including disclosure

---
[538] Al-Rodhan, *Symbiotic Realism, op. cit.*, note 78, p. 110.
[539] N.R.F. Al-Rodhan and S. Kuepfer, *Stability of States: The Nexus Between Transnational Threats, Globalization, and Internal Resilience* (Genève: Éditions Slatkine, 2007), pp. 49-50.
[540] Kelman, *op. cit.*, note 472, p. 539.
[541] Al-Rodhan, *The Five Dimensions of Global Security, op. cit.*, note 512, p. 126.

and accountability. Moreover, the corporate social responsibility movement has attempted to associate corporate governance with a broader set of ethical issues, including social and environmental concerns. As a result, large companies have increasingly attempted to respond to corporate social responsibility concerns by establishing corporate social responsibility committees, mechanisms for dialogue with "stakeholders", and so on. However, they have done so on a voluntary basis and "stakeholders" such as NGOs, institutional investors and social groups have, for their part, sought to make corporate social responsibility self-regulation more enforceable and effective. Meta-regulation through corporate social responsibility indexes, for instance, has also emerged. According to Gill, self-regulation and meta-regulation are converging. Companies are thus subject to a mixture of "hard" law and "soft" standards and codes of conduct.[542]

The merging of corporate governance and corporate social responsibility may result in less hard law and more soft law guiding business practices, reducing the role of the legislature and increasing that of coalitions composed of a variety of stakeholders.[543] This could affect the behaviour of corporations. However, whether this is enough to counterbalance the benefits that companies accrue as a result of cross-border transactions, which occur with much greater speed than in the past as a result of technological advances and the ability of transnational corporations to operate in several legal jurisdictions simultaneously,[544] is far from clear. The question is whether this helps government and broader efforts at regulation or whether it hinders them.

Gender Equality
Since the precise structures that sustain gender inequality are likely to depend on specific family contexts, social institutions and the role of the state and the market, sensitivity to the local environment is required in order to effectively mitigate gender-based discrimination and to promote gender equality. For example, women's sexual and reproductive rights are not perceived and protected by the state as rights per se. This can make family planning difficult, and protection from sexu-

---

[542] A. Gill, "Corporate Governance as Social Responsibility: A Research Agenda," *Berkeley Journal of International Law*, Vol. 26, No. 2, 2008, pp. 453-455, 470.
[543] *Ibid.*, p. 476.
[544] Al-Rodhan, *Symbiotic Realism, op. cit.*, note 78, p. 127.

ally transmitted diseases problematic.[545] Such needs must be met, but in ways that are culturally sensitive. Some issues may be so emotionally charged that only those who understand the social structure and culture of a particular situation are adequately equipped to constructively and effectively promote gender equality.

Protection of the Environment and the Ecological Balance
Unequal power relations have implications for the joint management and regulation of scarce resources. For states that are relatively equal, managing the interdependence of scarce resources to their satisfaction may be fairly unproblematic. However, when states are unequal in terms of resources, the outcome may be very different.[546] Given that environmental degradation and disruption of the ecological balance often have a transnational quality to them, national responses alone will be insufficient to manage these problems successfully. Factors contributing to the destruction of rain forests and global climate change, for example, do not originate in one state alone. Moreover, the consequences of these phenomena affect a number of states and their populations.[547]

One of the difficulties of coordinating approaches to managing scarce resources and protecting the biosphere is the lack of adequate capacity in some states to do so.[548] Some practices that contribute to environmental degradation and disrupt the ecological balance may be embedded in the reproduction of the global system and linked to the generation and distribution of wealth, knowledge and power, and to energy consumption. An additional difficulty in reducing environmental damage is that many of the actors that contribute to it are non-state actors and, as a result, difficult to regulate.[549]

---

[545] *Ibid.*, p. 129.
[546] Kelman, *op. cit.*, note 472, p. 539.
[547] Al-Rodhan, *Symbiotic Realism, op. cit.*, note 78, p. 113.
[548] A. Hurrell, *On Global Order: Power, Values, and the Constitution of International Society* (Oxford: Oxford University Press, 2007), p. 217.
[549] Al-Rodhan and Watanabe, *A Proposal for* Inclusive *Peace and Security, op. cit.*, note 1, pp. 113-114.

5. The Way Forward

While there may be disagreements over context, the debate must continue. Where no international consensus exists, either because national actors do not agree on the criteria or their appropriateness, or because they are reticent to take a clear position for political reasons, it is critical to begin a worldwide debate in an attempt to generate such consensus. The distinction between practices that are culturally legitimate and those which violate international norms is a fine one and cannot always be clearly drawn.[550] Yet, the concept of *just power*, which is introduced in the publication Neo-*statecraft and* Meta-*geopolitics: Reconciliation of Power, Interests and Justice in the 21st Century* (2009),[551] has a critical role to play in ensuring dignity, given the importance of justice to human dignity.

Avoidance of Conflict
Human dignity in many respects depends on security. Efforts to avoid war include arms reductions, reductions in arms sales and the establishment of crisis management and conflict resolution mechanisms.[552] Conflict may also occur as a result of unequal access to scarce resources, such as water. Governments must therefore ensure equal access to scarce resources. When such resources straddle state boundaries, transnational cooperation is necessary for their successful management. At the global level, multilateral arrangements must be put in place to prevent the unilateral use of force to gain control of scarce resources.

So-called soft power is essential to conflict prevention. This is, for example, visible in both the North Atlantic Treaty Organization (NATO) and the European Union (EU) enlargement processes. In the case of the EU, for example, the accession process is also a process of institutional reform and norm diffusion. In relation to conflict prevention, the latter implies an acceptance that pooling of sovereignty offers a more effective means of addressing challenges than acting alone. NATO enlargement, in turn, facilitates security sector reform in pro-

---

[550] Kelman, *op. cit.*, note 472, pp. 546-547.
[551] Al-Rodhan, Neo-*statecraft and* Meta-*geopolitics*, *op. cit.*, note 185.
[552] Kelman, *op. cit.*, note 472, pp. 537-538.

spective member states.[553] When conflict prevention fails, the application of just power will be critical.

Human Security
A focus on human dignity highlights the relevance and importance of the concept of human security. Human security is defined in the United Nations Development Programme's 1994 Human Development Report, *New Dimensions of Human Security*, as "freedom from fear and freedom from want."[554] Human security would be achieved through efforts to eradicate hunger, poverty, homelessness and violent conflict, and the promotion and protection of human rights – all of which are necessary in order to meet a minimum criteria of human dignity. Employing the concept of human security is all the more urgent in the present context. Globalisation has amplified the extent to which state and state-based paradigms are unable to adequately respond to the security needs of state populations either because the threats faced are transnational in nature or because states are withdrawing more and more from their public roles.[555] The education system, the mass media, health care and welfare measures are all central to the promotion of human needs, broadly conceived, and thus to human dignity. The former Japanese secretary of state for foreign affairs, Keizo Takemi, noted that a lack of basic education sometimes prevents the community, especially women, from accessing health care provision in an optimal way.[556] The gender dimension of human security therefore needs to be understood and to form part of efforts to promote human security. Yet, we need to know more about how human security is being conceived of and operationalised in different regions of the world.

Caitlin Mahoney and Tatiana Pinedo suggest that in assessing what may be missing from standard notions of human security, entailing freedom from want and peace, it may be helpful to distinguish between immediate personal security and more long-term assessments of security, which depend on the community in which people live and

---

[553] Al-Rodhan, *Symbiotic Realism, op. cit.*, note 78, p. 126.
[554] UNDP, "New Dimensions of Human Security," *UNDP Human Development Report 1994* (New York: UNDP, 1994), p. 24.
[555] Al-Rodhan, *Symbiotic Realism, op. cit.*, note 78, p. 117.
[556] "Capacity Building for Human Dignity: The Essence of the International Order in the 21st Century," Address by Japanese State Secretary Keizo Takemi to the Asia Society, New York, 1 September 1999, www.asiasociety.org/ speeches/takemi.html.

not simply on the state. They suggest that personal security in the latter case is related to networks of support and the relative absence of a negative emotional climate in the society in which we live.[557]

Gender Equality
Gender equality need not simply be promoted at the national and regional levels, but also at the global level. International conferences, such as the Seventh Women's Health Meeting in Uganda in 1993, the International Conference on Population and Development in Egypt in 1994, the Social Summit and the Fourth World Women's Conference in China in 1995, have played an important role in raising consciousness and facilitating dialogue. International instruments, such as the 1979 Convention on the Elimination of All Forms of Discrimination Against Women and the UN General Assembly's 1993 Declaration on the Elimination of Violence Against Women, have acted as important foundations for such activism.

Since gender and poverty are often interlinked, the notion of gender justice ought to be addressed in relation to development. In the 1990s, the World Bank's focus on gender inequality was piecemeal at best. However, the Bank's development reports have increasingly recognised the linkage between gender disparities and economic growth and the Bank has adopted a broader, more social approach to development in recent years with an emphasis on empowerment. While these reports do not constitute policy papers as such, they do help to inform policy formulation. However, it is important that social and economic policy recommendations comprehensively address the question of gender inequality. The perceived lack of such a coordinated approach has prompted criticism. Susanne Schech and Sanjugta Vas Dev, for example, argue that the World Bank has a dual discourse of "soft" social protection and "hard-nosed" economic policies. Gender empowerment is, in their view, diluted and depoliticised in the Bank's approach. Integrating gender issues into existing development paradigms may not be enough; new approaches to development may be needed if gender inequality is to be addressed in an optimal way in the context of development.[558]

---

[557] C.O. Mahoney and T. Pinedo, "Human Security in Communities in Costa Rica and the United States," *Journal of Social Issues*, Vol. 63, No. 2, 2007, pp. 360-366.
[558] S. Schech and S. Vas Dev, "Gender Justice: The World Bank's New Approach to the Poor?" *Development in Practice*, Vol. 17, No. 1, 2007, pp. 15-16, 24.

Human Rights

Meeting human dignity requirements clearly involves the promotion and protection of human rights. The Universal Declaration of Human Rights lists the rights that are the most universally accepted thus far, including the right to life; the right to nationality; the right to recognition under the law; the right to protection against cruel and degrading treatment; the right to protection against racial, ethnic, sexual or religious discrimination; the presumption of innocence; the guarantee of a free trial; prohibition of ex post facto laws; protection against arbitrary arrest, detention or exile; and against arbitrary interference in one's home, or of one's family or reputation. Civil liberties set down in the declaration include the rights to freedom of thought, conscience and religion, opinion and association. Political rights include the right to take part in government and to periodic and genuine elections with universal and equal suffrage.[559] Participation in decision making, however, requires accountability and the availability of timely and relevant information. Economic, social and cultural rights include the right to food and a standard of living adequate for the health and well-being of oneself and one's family; the right to work, rest and leisure and to social security; and the right to education and to participation in the cultural life of the community.[560] All of these are vital to giving people the opportunity for people to participate, to question dogma and to feel fully engaged in their communities.

Facilitating these rights implies that public resources are allocated in support of them. Steps also need to be made to improve the representation of underrepresented groups in society. This ought to be ensured through a number of measures, including legislation, establishing institutions and mechanisms, the freedom to establish political parties and access to state funding where relevant. The main means through which to counteract racial discrimination, exclusion and various restrictions is through the 1969 International Covenant on the Elimination of All Forms of Racial Discrimination (ICERD). The group identity of members of minorities must also be protected. Some of the central dimensions of the preservation of group identity include the right to organise as a group, the right to speak a minority language, and to be able to protect and maintain a minority culture. To this end, Article 27 of the International Covenant on Civil and Political Rights

---

[559] Office of the High Commissioner of Human Rights, *op. cit.*, note 470.
[560] *Ibid.*

has been interpreted as obliging states to respect the rights of minorities. This has been further strengthened by the Declaration on the Rights of Persons Belonging to National or Ethnic, Religious or Linguistic Minorities, which was adopted by the United Nations General Assembly in 1992. It calls on states to protect minorities and their group identity. Whether governments and minority groups are able to find workable solutions to the reality of culturally pluralistic societies will depend on arriving at a workable mix of a multilayered society that includes an overarching public domain and several separate communitarian domains. In some instances, this may imply power-sharing. It may also depend on the role played by the international community.[561]

However, some of these rights may be more problematic than others in some societies, or may be operationalised in ways specific to the cultural and political context. It is therefore important to understand this if we are to develop standards by which we can judge whether institutions and practices are capable of meeting human dignity needs.

A Global Ethic
According to Küng, "A global ethic is nothing but the necessary minimum of common values, standards and basic attitudes. In other words, a minimum basic consensus relating to binding values, irrevocable standards and moral attitudes, which can be affirmed by all religions despite their 'dogmatic' differences and can also be supported by non-believers."[562]

Several documents specifically talk about human rights and human responsibilities and call for a global ethic. These include the 1995 report by the UN Commission for Global Governance, and the 1995 report by the World Commission on Culture and Development; and this request also found support in the UNESCO Universal Ethics Project of 1997, the World Economic Forum at Davos in 1997 and the Indira Ghandi Conference held in Dehli in 1997. Efforts to clearly

---

[561] Eide, *op. cit.*, note 511, pp. 50-51, 57, 59, 62, 65; International Convention on the Elimination of All Forms of Racial Discrimination, 4 January 1969, http://www.hrcr.org/docs/_CERD/cerd2.html; Declaration on the Rights of Persons Belonging to National or Ethnic, Religious or Linguistic Minorities, 18 December 1992, http://www.unhchr.ch/html/menu3/b/d_minori.htm.
[562] H. Küng, "A Global Ethic: Development and Goals," *Interreligious Insight*, January, 2003 Edition, p. 3.

formulate human responsibilities appeared in the Parliament of World Religions 1993 report *Towards a Global Ethic: An Initial Declaration*, in a 1997 proposal by the InterAction Council, comprised of former heads of state, for a Universal Declaration of Human Responsibilities, and in 1999, in the Third Parliament of the World's Religions' *A Call to Our Guiding Institutions*.[563] According to Küng, a global ethic should contain ethical values and standards such as non-violence and respect for life, justice and solidarity, truthfulness and tolerance, and partnership, mutual respect and love.[564]

International Organisations
Multilateral institutions must endeavour to be impartial. This means eliminating the special advantages that some states enjoy. As is mentioned in Chapter 6, the UN must continue with reforms to make the organisation more representative. It cannot continue to reflect the distribution of global power at the close of the Second World War. It also needs to be more representative – and reform is clearly needed. In an effort to augment its institutional impartiality, the veto system requires reform and the permanent membership of the UNSC should be enlarged. While the need for the latter is largely accepted, a lack of consensus about which states should receive permanent seats on the UNSC, and on whether they should be given veto rights continues to hamper progress on reform.[565] The World Bank and the IMF also need to be more representative. Member states of both institutions are represented on their executive boards. Yet, only the biggest member states – the US, France, Germany, Japan, the UK, Saudi Arabia, Russia and China – enjoy direct representation. All other states are represented within constituencies, giving them only a diluted capacity to influence decision making and discussions.[566]

Multilateral institutions and NGOs, in cooperation with other groups, also have a role to play in addressing problems related to regional and intra-state conflicts from the perspective of human security. Their capacity to deal with the root causes of such conflicts through

---

[563] *Ibid.*, p. 4.
[564] *Ibid.*, p. 9.
[565] Al-Rodhan, *Symbiotic Realism, op. cit.*, note 78, p. 125.
[566] N. Woods, "Unelected Government: Making the IMF and the World Bank More Accountable," The Brookings Institution, Spring 2003, http://www.brookings.edu/articles/2003/spring_globaleconomics_woods.aspx.

efforts to reduce social inequalities, related discrimination and poverty will be an important dimension of conflict prevention and post-conflict rehabilitation.[567]

Michael Tate notes that recognition of human dignity has advanced in the current era following legal processes to hold people personally accountable for violations of International Humanitarian Law, most notably the trials of Augusto Pinochet and Slobodan Milosevic and the subsequent questioning of the doctrine of "Sovereign Immunity", which traditionally protected leaders from being tried under the criminal law in a foreign state, and former heads of state from legal processes related to their period in office. The International Criminal Tribunal for the Former Yugoslavia, established by a UNSC resolution in 1993, has enormous symbolic importance in relation to establishing serious violations of human dignity as crimes against humanity, and also in the prosecution of violations of the human dignity of women committed during conflict situations. The tribunal has, for instance, tried and punished commanders in the Yugoslav conflict. A similar tribunal addressing crimes committed during the conflict in Rwanda has also prosecuted local commanders. Thus, the highest political authority of the international community has decided that some activities constitute crimes because they represent attacks on human dignity.[568]

Corporate Ethics

Corporate governance failures can affect a wide array of people, such as retirees. Good local corporate governance is of great importance for the long-term development of economies. Formal and informal rules, accepted practices and enforcement mechanisms comprise corporate governance systems as opposed to highly personalised and relationship-based practices. The latter risk creating an environment in which resources may be more easily diverted from investment in the creation of new wealth. It is not only corporate governance rules that are needed, but also their effective enforcement. The latter requires, inter alia, strong monitoring capacities and a functioning judiciary.[569]

---

[567] Takemi, *op. cit.*, note 556.
[568] M. Tate, "Human Dignity: The New Phase of International Law," in Malpas and Lickiss, *op. cit.*, note 474, pp. 183-184.
[569] C. Oman and D. Blume, "Corporate Governance: The Development Challenge," *Economic Perspectives*, February 2005, pp. 17-19.

In the area of finance, regulation and the importance of rules-based systems are essential. This has been demonstrated in the latest and ongoing financial crisis. In late 2008 and early 2009, governments found it necessary in some cases to intervene to shore up banking systems and markets. The roots of the present crisis are partly discernable. In the UK and the US, where deregulation of banking systems was forged a generation ago, some financial firms have now become partly state-owned. The UK and the US were pioneers of market deregulation, but continental Europe and Japan followed suit.

The current problems have their genesis in the suspension of the dollar's convertibility to gold in the early 1970s and the subsequent shift to a system of floating exchange rates. Once capital became mobile, companies with costs in one currency and revenues in another, required a means of hedging against exchange rate risk. The creation of financial futures to do just that marked the beginning of the development of complex derivatives.

Against the backdrop of an ideological emphasis on market liberalisation, prospective home owners obtained mortgages more easily. The need to raise more capital translated into more complex banking structures. These began to distinguish between different types of risk and to trade them. The increasingly complicated nature of risk made it difficult for regulators to calculate firms' exposure. As a result, regulators focused on ensuring that deals were thoroughly documented. Yet, banks remained vulnerable to the disparity between assets and liabilities. In order to deal with the possibility of large creditors defaulting, the Basel Accord required banks to reserve capital for such an eventuality. However, in order to circumvent this requirement, banks removed assets from their balance sheets using a number of "tools", such as credit-default swaps, securitisation and structured investment vehicles which contained sub-prime-mortgage assets.[570]

Thus, rapid financial innovation outstripped the capacity of regulators. Moreover, the sheer complexity of the market created by these new tools also posed a challenge to regulators. Better regulatory mechanisms are therefore required to restrain the financial industry and to restore confidence in the financial system. Capital and liquidity requirements need to be set at adequate levels, and given the role of credit-rating agencies in approving bad assets, they must also come

---

[570] "Link by Link," *The Economist*, 18 October 2008, pp. 75-77.

under stricter regulatory standards.[571] Transparency needs to be a bedrock of the global economic system. Greater oversight ought to be facilitated through requirements for making an institution's financial situation publicly known through regular reporting according to agreed upon norms.

Greater effort is needed to regulate the activities of transnational enterprises in order to better serve security at all levels. In order to avoid regulation arbitrage, efforts to regulate the activities of transnational corporations need to be global and the norms related to standards need to be universal. This requires states to give up some degree of sovereignty to gain better control over transnational corporations and to protect their populations against a gradual decrease in standards and increased job insecurity.[572] Efforts to increase the accountability of transnational corporations could focus on reputational costs by establishing partnerships with public global governance institutions and establishing a set of minimum standards.

Protection of the Environment and the Ecological Balance
Protecting the environment and promoting sustainable development necessitate cooperation between a variety of actors, including states, international organisations, NGOs, socio-economic actors and the scientific community. On the positive side, as Andrew Hurrell notes, global environmental governance has grown in scope and complexity in recent decades. At the heart of this complex structure are a considerable number of multilateral environmental agreements. The international community also has a variety of international legal concepts, such as legal obligations to prevent environmental harm and duties to carry out environmental assessments. These developments reflect the evolution of a normative consensus on which to protect the environment and ecological balance, which will undoubtedly grow. Yet, this normative shift needs to form the basis of an extended emphasis on common interests rather than focus on fairly limited understandings of state sovereignty.[573] Furthermore, the role of money and corporate influence in politics and electoral processes must be reduced if the

---

[571] A. Shah, "Global Financial Crisis 2008," *Global Issues*, Updated 4 February 2009, http://www.globalissues.org/article/768/globalfinancialcrisis#Rethinkingtheinternatio nafinancial system.
[572] Al-Rodhan, *Symbiotic Realism, op. cit.*, note 78, p. 128.
[573] Hurrell, *op. cit.*, note 548, p. 225

power of industrial lobbies is to be diminished. Clear and accurate scientific evidence on the causes, extent and consequences of environmental damage is also required. Finally, mechanisms that are capable of assessing and enforcing measures aimed at reducing harm of the environment are also required at the global level.[574]

Octagon 2 summarises the minimum criteria of human needs and dignity.

---

[574] Al-Rodhan, *Symbiotic Realism, op. cit.*, note 78, p. 132.

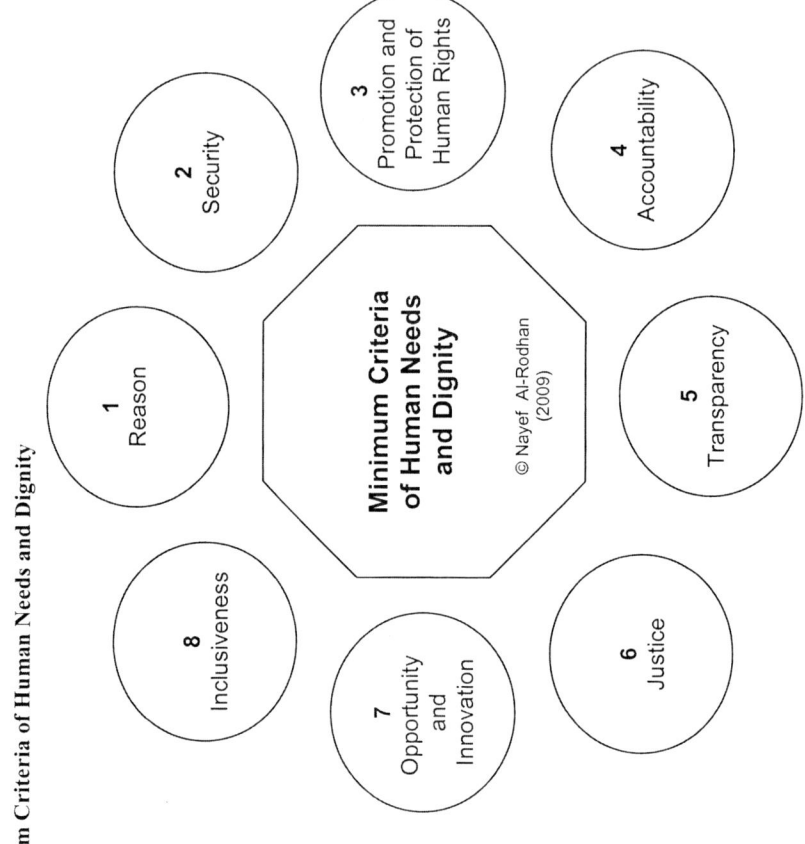

Octagon 2: Minimum Criteria of Human Needs and Dignity

6. Conclusion

Human dignity is vital to achieving a sustainable history, because it is a human need. This chapter has clarified what is meant by human dignity – a concept that is frequently invoked but rarely explained. Based on our understanding of human dignity, we set out minimum criteria of dignity – reason, security, human rights, accountability, transparency, justice, opportunity, innovation and inclusiveness – against which institutions and practices should be assessed at both the national and the global levels. Because of the transnational nature of the factors affecting human dignity, the state may not in many instances be the best actor to ensure its provision. The persistence of state-centric paradigms to address many of the policy areas critical to meeting the minimum criteria of human dignity, such as health care, environmental protection, and so on, is likely to hinder the development of adequate institutional mechanisms and capacities with which to promote and protect human dignity. Greater interdependence and instant connectedness mean that minimum criteria of dignity must apply at the global level as well as the national level. Structural inequalities and disparities between the priorities of public and private sector actors are the greatest challenges to human dignity and efforts to ensure that people have a sense of self-worth. It is also possible that tensions may arise between concerns about the environment and ecological balance, on the one hand, and economic growth, on the other. The question of justice is therefore critical to enhancing human dignity. I turn to this in Chapter 8.

CHAPTER 8

HOW CAN WE ACHIEVE JUSTICE?
MINIMUM CRITERIA OF GLOBAL JUSTICE

As explained in the previous chapter, human well-being is heavily dependent on human dignity and, as a result, on sustainable history. The human need for dignity requires attention to the question of justice linked both to specific agendas and to global justice. In the past, the success of one geo-cultural domain would have been largely unaffected by the decline and problems of others, except in terms of benefiting from them. Contact between people living in diverse geo-cultural domains would have been relatively infrequent, with the exception of points of crossroads between them and through trade. Today, interconnectedness between people is far more commonplace than in the past. *Civilisational triumph is thus not a zero-sum enterprise that favours one geo-cultural domain over another.* I refer to geo-cultural domains because thinking in terms of separate and multiple civilisations obscures the extent to which what might normally be thought of as separate civilisations overlap and influence each other, and ultimately contribute to a broader human civilisation. The fate of those belonging to one geo-cultural domain cannot but affect those of another in the present period. Global justice and security are vital considerations if human civilisation is to triumph.

These issues are therefore addressed in the present chapter, which discusses the concept of civilisation and the importance of civilisational triumph – which depends on the success of each geo-cultural domain. Two central elements of civilisational triumph are global justice and security, both of which are interconnected. The chapter discusses the challenges and the means of achieving these objectives.

1. Civilisational Triumph

Justice is central to ensuring the success of geo-cultural domains and the dominant culture of the day. I therefore discuss what is likely to be required for the overall health of human civilisation, which, as is explained earlier, is made up of the contributions of all geo-cultural domains.

The Concept of Civilisation: The Ocean Model of One Human Civilisation

The term civilisation has been used in a number of different ways. It can be employed in a normative sense. As is noted above, the term civilisation was originally used to denote a stage of societal evolution. It was contrasted with the barbarism associated with more primitive peoples. This conception of civilisation is informed by a linear notion of history in which progress was believed to have reached its summit in modern Europe.[575] This understanding of civilisation was related to European imperialism and the civilising mission it took on itself. The assumption was that non-Europeans encountered by Europeans would and should become like them.[576]

Civilisation is sometimes discussed in essentialist terms. Huntington's clash of civilisation thesis, for example, is informed by an essentialist view of civilisations that assumes that they have fixed properties.[577] The seven, possibly eight, civilisations he identifies are viewed as distinct from one another because of differences in blood, language, religion and way of life. He, thus, identifies multiple civilisations that are marked by their separateness, neglecting mutual influences and cross-fertilisation[578] Huntington's account of civilisations shares an essentialist dimension with Oswald Spengler's earlier work on civilisations. Both Spengler and Huntington view civilisations as self-contained, homogeneous entities.[579] Martin Hall and Patrick Thaddeus Jackson note that Huntington views civilisations as "akin to billiard balls, bouncing off of one another in much the same way that

---

[575] Braudel, *op. cit.*, note 2, pp. 3-7.
[576] Cox with Schecter, *op. cit.*, note 4, pp. 176-177.
[577] Huntington, *op. cit.*, note 46.
[578] M. Hall and P.T. Jackson (eds.) *Civilizational Identity: The Production and Reproduction of "Civilizations" in International Relations* (New York: Palgrave Macmillan, 2007), pp. 4-5.
[579] *Ibid.*, p. 5.

states were thought to do in old realist international relations theory."[580] Huntington's thesis does, however, have the advantage of highlighting the relevance of torn and cleft states in today's world.[581]

Against accounts that see geo-cultural domains as separate homogeneous entities, Schmuel Eisenstadt emphasises the divisions *within* geo-cultural domains rather than between them. He understands civilisations as a relationship between a cosmological vision and the institutional life of people, which contains internal tensions. He also emphasises the potential for transformation that exchange and interaction between civilisations may have. Eisenstadt therefore begins to problematise the assumption that civilisations are homogeneous and closed entities. Within modernising civilisations, confrontation between principles conceived in the West and those associated with traditional life and local cultures are thought to be negotiated in different ways, producing multiple modernities. Thus, there are a number of different civilisations that have the adoption of modern values in common but differ in the way that the tension between modernity and tradition has been resolved.[582]

Robert W. Cox views civilisation as a configuration of social forces and ideas that has reached a certain coherence, but is constantly changing in response to internal and external challenges.[583] External stimuli are thought, for example, to come in the form of pressure and invasion from external powers as well as from marginal peoples and mass migration. Internal challenges may appear in the form of the status of women, for instance, although the form that emancipation takes will be shaped by specific cultural settings.[584]

In both Eisenstadt's and Cox's understanding of civilisations, the emphasis is not simply on ideas, but also on material conditions. Efforts to maintain a coherence between ideational and material aspects of life are for these authors what endows civilisations with a certain fluidity. However, Hall and Jackson share with Huntington the conviction that geo-cultural domains are different from one another.[585] They suggest that geo-cultural domains should be thought of as ongo-

---

[580] *Ibid.*
[581] See Bassin, *op. cit.*, note 58.
[582] Hall and Jackson, *op. cit.*, note 578, p. 5.
[583] *Ibid.*, p. 5.
[584] Cox with Schecter, *op. cit.*, note 4, pp. 144-145.
[585] Hall and Jackson, *op. cit.*, note 578, p. 6.

ing processes of boundary delimitation. In their view, geo-cultural domains are only "weakly bounded" entities that are better perceived as socio-spatial networks that overlap and intersect, and therefore lack overall coherence. Tensions and contradictions as well as coherence may be found within them. They are also heterarchical (i.e. a unified network) and not centralised. As a result of these factors, Hall and Jackson argue that geo-cultural domains are contested and constantly in flux. They suggest that we need to start thinking about them as a set of relations and processes and stop thinking about them as structures or entities;[586] and that the focus should be on how geo-cultural domains appear as "real" entities that are distinct from one another. This leads one to ask how civilisational identities are (re)produced,[587] rather than how to define them.

Working from a post-essentialist perspective, Jacinta O'Hagan suggests that civilisation is

> synonymous with community; with societal evolution; with particular ontologies or intersubjective frameworks; with systems of governance; with the heritage of humankind. Yet, at the same time, "civilisation" remains a distinct concept, first, in the breadth of its associated meaning, and second, in the way the concept suggests a blend of material and ideational dimensions to human existence.[588]

As she points out, the term civilisation has always been employed as a boundary marker. She argues that discourses on civilisations and civilisational identities help to frame identities and interests at various levels and to differentiate between actors and actions in the world. As a result, the focus, in her view, ought to be on the discourses of civilisational identity rather than on defining civilisations.[589]

In addition to how geo-cultural domains ought to be studied, another question that animates discussions of civilisations is whether we attribute agency to them.[590] There are several ways of answering this question. First, one can argue that geo-cultural domains are not actors, given that someone or something is acting on their behalf. However, as Jackson points out, this could be said of states or other

---

[586] *Ibid.*, pp. 6-8.
[587] *Ibid.*, p. 10.
[588] J. O'Hagan, "Discourses of Civilizational Identity," in Hall and Jackson, *op. cit.*, note 578, p. 15.
[589] *Ibid.*, pp. 15-16.
[590] *Ibid.*, p. 18.

entities to which we regularly ascribe agency. Second, geo-cultural domains may be viewed in essentialist terms as social actors with "real" properties. Finally, one can adopt a transactional approach that examines patterns of social relations and social practices, which serve to create and maintain socially relevant boundaries. This latter account, Jackson argues, allows one to look at geo-cultural domains as actors while retaining human agency.[591]

Another issue encountered in the literature is the nature of interaction between geo-cultural domains. Perceptions of incommensurability between political values and institutions, for example, have important implications. They help to fuel tensions, and they can also help to create and maintain a hierarchy between civilisational forms through comparison and ensuing evaluations of different societies. They may be used, for example, to frame who belongs in a particular community and who does not. They may also be used to evaluate the governance norms, practices and institutions of particular societies in comparison to the self. Finally, they may be employed to help locate the self or evaluate the other. Discourses on civilisations can also help to (re)define self-identity in civilisational terms.[592]

John M. Hobson views civilisations as co-constitutive and embedded in one another. He sees them as being "amalgams" in that they are never pure, but hybrid. They are overlapping and permeable. He therefore argues that civilisations co-exist rather than clash as Huntington would suggest. He usefully points out that Huntington's zones of conflict where civilisations meet are better understood as zones of contact that produce "polycivilisational hybridity". Indeed, there is a need to highlight the peaceful contact and mutual enrichment that has taken place between East and West. He argues that there is a need to re-imagine the West along "polycivilisational lines" by recognising the contact, connections and mutual exchanges that have taken place and continue to take place.[593]

According to Yale H. Ferguson, "one reason civilisation as a concept refuses to go away is that it carries just enough empirical sub-

---

[591] P.T. Jackson, "Civilizations as Actors: A Transactional Account," in Hall and Jackson, *op. cit.*, note 578, p. 34.
[592] O'Hagan, *op. cit.*, note 588, p. 19-22, 24.
[593] J.M. Hobson, "Reconstructing the Eurocentric Clash of Civilizations: De-Westernizing the West by Acknowledging the Dialogue of Civilizations," in Hall and Jackson, *op. cit.*, note 578, p. 150.

stance to be credible and, thus anchored, is available for further construction for good or ill. Put bluntly, there is a sufficient range of intersubjective consensus about the term that it can be used with effect, manipulated in all sorts of ways, to inspire concrete human action, and have plainly visible consequences."[594] The latter point helps to explain why geo-cultural domains may be encountered as real entities. When people act on intersubjective meanings, they help to produce patterns of relations and processes that are experienced as structures that, in turn, help to shape people's lives.

Yet, rather than thinking in terms of multiple civilisations, we need to employ the ocean analogy. Human civilisation is more fruitfully conceived of as a great ocean, joined by many rivers that contribute to its overall growth. These rivers represent different geo-cultural domains that flourish at different points within the larger flow of human history due to mutual borrowing and encounters. The middle of the ocean is characterised by a mixture of different cultural influences, although often weighted towards the dominant culture of the day (see Diagram 3 on page 37).

Civilisational Triumph
If we conceive of civilisation as an ocean into which various geo-cultural domains add depth whenever a particular historical conjuncture provides conditions under which the most advanced forms of human enterprise can thrive, then civilisational triumph refers to a situation in which all component geo-cultural domains can flourish, albeit to varying degrees. Since a geo-cultural domain is best understood in both ideational and material terms, this implies that achieving civilisational triumph requires an attention to the relationship between boundary marking practices and concrete situations. Those geo-cultural domains constructed on the basis of narratives that emphasise confrontational relations between geo-cultural domains can only cause tension and conflict, both of which work against the success of the human civilisation as a whole. Civilisational triumph depends on co-existence between geo-cultural domains and a recognition that they belong to one human civilisation.

Moreover, if the construction of civilisational identities is understood as a process of boundary marking rather than a reflection of

---
[594] Y.H. Ferguson, "Pathways to Civilization," in Hall and Jackson, *op. cit.*, note 578, p. 191.

incommensurability, the challenge is to discern the real cleavages in world politics that prompt the civilisational identities to be the most prominent identities that individuals have as well as the securitisation of civilisation(s). The material dimension may be linked to socio-economic inequalities. Ferguson suggests that the relevant divisions are between those who gain from the processes of globalisation and those who do not as well as those who fall between these two extremes.[595] Civilisational triumph requires some degree of socio-economic equality. Domestically, this implies that socio-economic inequalities are minimised. At the global level, it implies at the very least that multilateral institutions and arrangements are premised on rules and practices that are perceived to be fair. It also implies the protection of human dignity and the alleviation of suffering in the world. Civilisational triumph requires the creation of conditions under which innovation and learning can thrive.

Civilisational triumph is important because if it is not actively sought, conflictual relations between members of geo-cultural domains may become a self-fulfilling prophecy. In today's world, geo-cultural domains cannot flourish at the expense of others over the long-term – their interrelated nature has come into sharp relief in recent years as the West's stability and well-being has come to depend on other geo-cultural domains, and vice versa. As a result, there needs to be an emphasis on expanding the boundaries of civilisational identities and an acceptance of the existence of multiple and overlapping identities.

2. Global Justice

Justice is paramount to civilisational triumph because of its centrality to human dignity needs, the success of individual geo-cultural domains and the well-being of human civilisation. In broad terms, justice may be defined as the morally correct distribution of benefits and burdens. In non-contractarian conceptions, justice is a matter of truth. This approach is premised on particular conceptions of human nature as well as normative ideals. Pre-Socratic philosophers treated justice as a question of natural harmony.[596] Similarly, moral cos-

---

[595] *Ibid.*, p. 194.
[596] D. Heyd, "Justice and Solidarity: The Contractarian Case Against Global Justice," *Journal of Social Philosophy*, Vol. 38, No. 1, 2007, p. 115.

mopolitanism holds that human beings have an intrinsic moral worth and that we have an obligation to recognise one another's worth, which implies mutual recognition and respect, David Held, for example, maintains that human beings rather than states are the ultimate moral subjects and that we have a moral duty to respect the inherent worth of human beings. This duty implies, in turn, mutual recognition.[597]

However, in contractarian conceptions of justice, the latter is a matter of consent. Justice in this view arises out of a collective will generated by specific constraints. For Locke, Peter Singer (b. 1946), Rawls and Thomas Pogge (b. 1953), for example, justice is the outcome of a contractual relationship. Justice is thus a question of social cooperation.[598] In Locke's notion of the social contract, governments' authority is restricted to that which is entrusted to it by the people.[599]

Singer is a significant figure in the internationalist movement in philosophy. He argues that a radical reinterpretation of moral obligations is required – if it is in our power to prevent people from suffering by not being able to meet their basic needs, such as for food, shelter and medical assistance, we have a moral duty to do so, as long as doing so does not violate other moral values that we possess. Yet, global justice would be very limited were it simply to concern avoiding the death of strangers.[600]

Rawls argues that a political conception of justice is required in order to construct principles of social justice. This does not mean that a concept of justice should be developed that is intended for application to political matters, but that a concept of justice is required on which the majority of people can agree outside of any particular ethical theory or religion.[601]

Rawls's political conception of justice is intended to evaluate the basic structure of society resulting from economic, social and political institutions. This is because the basic structure of society shapes both our life chances and our identities and, as such, it has ethical importance. In addition, members of a society have no choice but to

---

[597] D. Held, "Cosmopolitanism: Globalisation Tamed?" *Review of International Studies*, Vol. 29, 2003, p. 478.
[598] Heyd, *op. cit.*, note 596, p. 115.
[599] Russell, *op. cit.*, note 154, pp. 574-575.
[600] M. Blake, "International Justice," *Stanford Encyclopedia of Philosophy*, First Published 8 July 2008, http:// www.science.uva.nl/~seop/entries international-justice/.
[601] See Rawls, *op. cit.*, note 159.

share its basic structure with others whether they agree with it or not. Thus, the basic structure of society ought to be justified according to terms that reasonable people can accept regardless of their religion, faith or ethical principles. Hence the need for a political conception of justice, which requires that the state remain agnostic with regard to religious and ethical doctrines. However, this does not mean that individuals must be agnostic with regard to such doctrines.[602]

Central to Rawls's political conception of justice is what he calls the "Original Position", occupied from behind a "veil of ignorance". This is a hypothetical situation in which people have no knowledge of their capacities, status or relations. This veil of ignorance is believed to be necessary to establish a just political arrangement among self-interested actors.[603] Rawls writes:

> In justice as fairness the original position of equality corresponds to the state of nature in the traditional theory of social contract. This original position is not, of course, thought of as an actual historical state of affairs, much less as a primitive condition of culture. It is understood as a purely hypothetical situation characterised so as to lead to a certain conception of justice.[604]

A "Second Original Position" that pertains to the international context is outlined. The veil of ignorance under which participants in this international society would conceive of just principles and norms of international law would mean that members of this society would have no prior knowledge of factors that may skew their judgement. Diverse collectivities that constitute "peoples" (not individuals) should be governed by a "Law of the Peoples" corresponding to the basic principles of political justice. He imagines the extension of the Law of the Peoples.[605] Obligations would include non-aggression and the honouring of treaties as well as some development assistance to people living in countries where conditions are less favourable to social political justice,[606] as well as respect for human rights. Yet, the distributive principles that are implicit in his conception of justice are not perceived to be as demanding in the global context as in the domestic setting, given that if they were, agreement would be extremely

---

[602] J. Mandle, *Global Justice* (Cambridge: Polity Press, 2006), pp. 20, 23, 25.
[603] R. Jackson, *Classical and Modern Thought on International Relations: From Anarchy to Cosmopolis* (New York: Palgrave Macmillan, 2005), pp. 157-158.
[604] See Rawls, *op. cit.*, note 159, p. 11.
[605] Jackson, *op. cit.*, note 603, pp. 158, 164, 169.
[606] See J. Rawls, "The Law of Peoples," *Critical Inquiry*, Vol. 20, No. 1., 1993.

difficult to reach in political communities.[607] This is a useful starting point for examining the contributions to the debate on global justice.

What justice is taken to assess and what its contents should be in the domestic setting has generally been explored to a greater extent than its implications at the global level. There are perhaps several reasons for this. The discipline of international relations and the field of international security have tended to neglect the question of justice. This is partly due to the predominance of realism among academics and practitioners in the Anglo-Saxon world in the post-Second World War period. This has led to an overwhelming focus on the state, and the presumed need to ensure state security through the accumulation of power. In such an environment, little room is left for the pursuit of ethical considerations.[608]

Much of the conceptual debate that has taken place on global justice is centred on whether it is possible to apply Rawls's conception of justice to the global sphere, and whether Rawls was correct in his assertion that it can only be applied in a limited way on a global scale.[609] Among those more sceptical about the application of Rawls's concept of justice is Robert Jackson, who argues that a conception of political justice based on a hypothetical veil of ignorance risks neglecting the potential limits of our moral commitments.[610] He also remarks that the normative question of who qualifies as "Peoples" is similar to the "standard of civilisation" that Europeans used to judge non-Europeans with whom they came into contact.[611] In the political conception of justice, a society that violates human rights does not have the moral status that allows them to be treated with respect, equality and non-interference. This does not apply to a theocratic society that holds elections, as long as it does not mistreat minorities and respects the due process of the law.[612]

Jackson contends that by employing the intellectual tool of the "Original Position" and the "veil of ignorance", Rawls, while appearing to address the question of diversity, in reality bypasses it. He argues that it is based on an idealised notion of human beings and not on

---

[607] Blake, *op. cit.*, note 600.
[608] Al-Rodhan, *"emotional amoral egoism,"* *op. cit.*, note 119, p. 149.
[609] Heyd, *op. cit.*, note 596, p. 24.
[610] Jackson, *op. cit.*, note 603, p. 159.
[611] *Ibid.*, p. 170.
[612] T. Nagel, "The Problem of Global Justice," *Philosophy & Public Affairs*, Vol. 33, No. 2, 2005, p. 135.

human beings as they are in existing realities. Moreover, according to Jackson, Rawls neglects the question of order. His theory is also believed to fail to acknowledge pluralism in international society. Rawls's notion of international society represents a thick conception of community among humankind, which, according to Jackson, risks underestimating the limits of ethics in international affairs. It is premised on the notion that human beings are perfectible.[613]

A thinner notion of moral community is put forward by David Heyd, who maintains that such cooperation has to be examined in the light of the specific circumstances that make it possible. The positive aspects of limited sympathy – expressed as care and concern for others – are, in Heyd's view, a necessary condition for justice. He argues that contractual theorists overlook the extent to which the desire to cooperate with others motivates individuals to engage in cooperative relations, not simply self-interest driven by the need to survive.[614] Yet, solidarity is believed to be different from familial love, camaraderie or tribal loyalty; it is something that is chosen. Thus, rather than applying universally, solidarity can only apply to the group which has been chosen. The state, according to Heyd, is the natural site for distributive norms, because it is able to enforce them as a result of its sovereignty. When solidarity stretches beyond the nation it does not do so on a contractual basis. There is, therefore, no duty of justice or equality between human beings in a general sense. This does not mean that human rights, for instance, should not be respected, because they are premised on conceptions of human nature.[615] This latter point seems somewhat contradictory. As is demonstrated in Chapter 7, human rights are better thought of as normative ideals required to meet human dignity needs.

Pogge's position is that Rawls's idea of moral obligation is too limited in relation to the global sphere. His conception of a Rawlsian basic structure is that any rules known in advance inform interactions between individuals in the public sphere. Pogge believes that the "Original Position" can be applied to the global arena.[616] He points out that Rawls's conception of justice was thought to be applicable because the national system appeared to be the only existing self-

---

[613] Jackson, *op. cit.*, note 603, pp. 175-178.
[614] Heyd, *op. cit.*, note 596, p. 16.
[615] *Ibid.*, pp. 118, 122-123, 125-127.
[616] Blake, *op. cit.*, note 600, p. 9.

sufficient or relatively "closed" system to which it could be applied. Yet, as Pogge notes in *Realizing Rawls* (1989), national systems are not self-sufficient and the only closed system that exists today is the global system – hence, his justification for applying a Rawlsian concept of justice to the global system. In contrast to Rawls, national borders are not thought to mark moral boundaries, and are not believed to shelter us from the moral claims of strangers.[617]

Jon Mandle, also believes that the methods of establishing justice at the domestic level are also applicable at the global level. His position is premised on the fact that a basic structure at the global level is also imposed on its members whether they agree with it or not, and that this is done in a context of religious and ethical diversity. There is, however, a clear difference between the basic structure of the global system and domestic society: the global order is not a state. This has implications for the detailed principles of global justice.[618]

Rawls's political conception of justice raises the question of what is to be evaluated at the global level. Given that it is designed to be acceptable to all reasonable people, a political conception of justice implies some sort of equality. The question is what to be equalised. Mandle suggests that this equalisation would require resources or capabilities that can be used for a significant number of ends. He points out that the principles ensuring this are likely to be broadly liberal, guaranteeing a number of civil and political rights as well as some measure of the fair distribution of resources.[619]

The content of global justice, according to Pogge, includes obligations to the most disadvantaged and, consequently, some form of global social justice. Moreover, he contends that creating a peaceful and ecologically sustainable future that meets the basic social and economic needs of the world's population will require growing supranationalism, although this should not be equated with world government.[620]

To the question of whether global justice requires a sovereign world government, Hobbes would have replied that the coordinated conduct of large numbers of people cannot be ensured without a sov-

---

[617] T. Pogge, *Realizing Rawls* (Ithaca, NY: Cornell University Press, 1989), pp. 7, 10.
[618] Mandle, *op. cit.*, note 602, pp. 26-27.
[619] *Ibid.*, pp. 25-26.
[620] C. Lu, "World Government," *Stanford Encylopedia of Philosophy*, First Published 4 December 2006, http://www.science.uva.nl/~seop/entries/ world-government/.

ereign state with a monopoly on the legitimate use of force to coerce them. In this view, we cannot rely on human motivation alone to accept certain constraints. Without a state that is capable of mobilising legitimate force, individuals are believed to revert back to self-regarding behaviour in the pursuit of survival.[621]

According to Thomas Nagel, even if we assume motives that show a concern for others, such as global social justice, only a sovereign world state would be capable of enforcing what is judged to be just. Two central claims underpin his argument. First, only within a sovereign state is justice possible, because people do not choose to live within a state. Thus, global social justice necessitates a world state. Second, egalitarian distributive social justice through shared institutions is something that we owe only to those with whom we have close political connections. We therefore do not have a moral obligation to ensure global social justice since we may only have very distant political relations with some populations.[622] Justice can only arise when a political authority has the legitimate authority and force to impose it. The basis of Nagel's argument is, thus, that the state as an involuntary association must provide its members with terms of membership that they can accept.[623]

Nagel argues that if the majority within states accept the political conception of justice, it cannot but have an impact on global affairs. He reminds us also that we share a broader pre-political moral community, which implies that we have a duty to protect those outside our own state. Nevertheless, global justice requires less of us than domestic justice. Nagel, therefore, holds a multilayered conception of morality.[624] While there are some institutional arrangements that seek to ensure international justice at this level, actual requirements for justice are less substantial than in the domestic realm.[625]

Other commentators, however, maintain that a global Leviathan is not a prerequisite for global social justice. Michael Plendlebury maintains that Nagel and political philosophy in general tend to place too much emphasis on the sovereign state and its concomitant monop-

---

[621] Nagel, *op. cit.*, note 612, p. 132.
[622] *Ibid.*
[623] M. Plendlebury, "Global Justice and the Specter of Leviathan," *Philosophical Forum*, Vol. 38, No. 1, 2007, p. 51.
[624] Nagel, *op. cit.*, note 612, p. 132.
[625] *Ibid.*

oly on the legitimate use of force. In his view, questions of global social justice arise in the absence of a sovereign world state.[626]

According to Plendlebury, Hobbes holds out the possibility of sources of external incentives for seeking justice other than the power of a sovereign state. Hobbes also cites the church as a power of authority that can induce people to act in particular ways. In the present historical context, there are many other sources of authority, in addition to the state and the church, that encourage individuals and states to conform to particular forms of behaviour. International organizations, for example, can and do have the authority to promote conformity and, in some instances, do so where individual states fail. Just behaviour may also be induced by networks of institutions and organizations, and not simply by sovereign states. Punishment in the sense of deployment of the legitimate use of force is not a prerequisite for conformity. Social norms can also produce conformity. Moreover, while strong standards of justice may depend on the authority of a sovereign state, weaker standards may be provided outside the state. A global system similar to the one that exists at present could, in Plendlebury's view, promote a greater degree of fairness and equality. Global economic inequalities, for example, could be reduced through stricter international labour standards, fiscal measures to fund development, coordinated liberalisation of immigration policies and mechanisms designed to shift the externalities of pollution to those responsible for producing it. Plendlebury suggests that a complex, multilayered authority structure rather than a sovereign global state may provide the best way to ensure greater equality at the global level. This would include multiple authority structures at the city, province, country, regional and global levels but also functional authority structures that operate in a variety of different spheres.[627]

So, what should be done in terms of ensuring global justice in the absence of a sovereign world state? Humanitarian assistance to help people in desperate need is a prerequisite of global justice. Yet, injustice can exist without the same immediate need being present. As Nagel points out, how we answer this depends on our understanding of the relationship between justice and the institutions of a sovereign authority.[628]

---
[626] Plendlebury, *op. cit.*, note 623, p. 44.
[627] *Ibid.*, pp. 45-47, 49, 55.
[628] Nagel, *op. cit.*, note 612, pp. 119.

Nagel suggests that justice is not something that we owe only to those with whom we have a strong political relationship. He states that "[t]he full standards of justice, although they can be known by moral reasoning, apply only within the boundaries of the sovereign state, however arbitrary these boundaries may be. Internationally, there may well be standards, but they do not merit the full name of justice."[629] The minimum criteria of global justice might include a universal duty to provide humanitarian assistance. Obligations that go beyond such a requirement would exist if there were a strong political relationship or associative responsibility such as that created by fellow citizenship. But, is the humanitarian requirement the only universal principle that ought to underpin the pursuit of global justice? Does global justice require us to be concerned with relative as well as absolute deprivation? Negative rights under the sovereign power of the state, such as the right to freedom of expression, freedom of religion and bodily inviolability, do not depend on associative obligations, for example.[630]

Some of the basic rights that people currently enjoy are universal, such as the right to asylum. They do not depend on an institutional relationship between peoples. According to Nagel, only requirements connected to equal treatment are contingent on associative arrangements. At the state level, the legal framework regulating relations is subject to considerations of social justice.[631] While global institutions are charged with the protection of human rights, the delivery of humanitarian aid and the provision of public goods such as free trade and protection of the environment, they are not intended to advance democratic legitimacy or socio-economic justice. According to Nagel, this is because these institutions do not perform the same functions as a state:[632]

> They are not collectively enacted and coercively imposed in the name of all individuals whose lives they affect; and they do not ask for the same kind of authorization by individuals that carries with it a responsibility to treat all those individuals in some sense equally. Instead, they are set up by bargaining among mutually self-interested sovereign parties. International institutions act not in the name of individuals, but in the name of states or state instruments

---

[629] *Ibid.*, pp. 121-122.
[630] *Ibid.*, pp. 125-127.
[631] *Ibid.*, p. 130.
[632] *Ibid.*, p. 137.

and agencies that have created them. Hence the responsibility of those institutions towards individuals is filtered through the states that represent and bear primary responsibility for those individuals.[633]

However, Nagel argues that minimum moral requirements include the obligation to protect human rights. Again, it seems important to note that human rights are based on a normative ideal that all individuals should be treated as endowed with equal worth and, thus, dignity.

An appropriate question that needs to be asked is: if the broader moral context is not based on a universal moral relation, what is it based on? Our moral codes may not be as universal as we might like to imagine. As is mentioned above in relation to emotional amoral egoism, our basic moral repertoire has evolved as a result of the environment in which humankind has evolved – that is in an environment in which relationships with kin are the strongest. Only fairly recently have we come into closer contact with people with whom we have no direct linkage. If we have developed moral codes that enable us to come to the aid of only distantly related others, it is because we are also self-aware. We can therefore develop moral codes that help to govern behaviour, that is, normative ideals. Indeed, most of our moral behaviour is learned, although we do have some predilection towards sensitivities under particular conditions.[634] Thus, even if we are emotionally self-interested beings that have no innate moral codes and only morally relevant emotions, we are capable of developing moral norms that help to guide us in our relations with one another.

It is true that international arrangements and institutions may be established by self-interested states rather than individuals, and that they do not amount to a sovereign global state. However, it is not the case that states and their populations can choose whether to be part of the global order. Regardless of whether a world sovereign state exists to enforce the global order, the extent to which states have established a minimal governance structure implies that this structure should be premised on some degree of equality at least among those states if stability and security are to be ensured. Institutions that form part of the global governance structure ought to be largely representative of their members so that the governance framework that they help to institute is generally accepted as fair. Without a world sovereign state,

---

[633] *Ibid.*, p. 138.
[634] Al-Rodhan, *"emotional amoral egoism,"* *op. cit.*, note 119, pp. 189-190.

the requirements of global justice cannot be assessed on the same basis, although it is not the case that greater global justice requires a sovereign world state.

Global Justice and Civilisational Triumph
Justice is paramount to security, but it is all too often neglected in the formulation of policies and actions. One of the reasons for this is that it is often regarded as a philosophical question rather a security concern. Yet, given that human nature is largely emotionally driven, implying that human behaviour is predominantly driven by emotional self-interest and that human beings have emotional needs that are fundamental to their well-being, dignity, to which justice is central, must be ensured. Justice is at the heart of the multi-sum security principle put forward in *The Five Dimensions of Global Security: Proposal for a Multi-sum Security Principle* (2007), in which I identify five facets of security: human, environmental, national, transnational and transcultural; and that one of the major means of promoting security in these five areas is through the pursuit of justice.[635] Justice is central to security because injustice can lead to feelings of humiliation, anger and alienation. When people feel that society and its institutions are responsible for injustice, they may be more likely to seek justice by non-conventional means and to fall prey to those who seek to spread insecurity. Only by promoting justice will extremism, for instance, be mitigated. Military force alone is not enough to ensure long-term security, since it fails to address the root causes of the problem. Indeed, rather than enhancing long-term security, military force is likely to fuel resentment and anger.[636] People whose families and friends have been injured or killed by deployments of force will not forget and will be susceptible to the arguments of those who seek to fuel hatred and violence.

Concern about social justice, compassion and kindness is common to all cultures.[637] This is perhaps because the need for justice is central to human dignity. Injustice violates a fundamental abstract ideal of how people ought to be treated that lays at the heart of notions

---

[635] Al-Rodhan, *The Five Dimensions of Global Security*, op. cit., note 512, especially ch. 4.
[636] *Ibid.*, p. 88.
[637] E. Hatfield and R.L. Rapson, "Social Justice and the Clash of Cultures," *Psychological Inquiry*, Vol. 16, No. 4, 2005, p. 173.

of what we morally owe others in terms of equal dignity for all. Injustice may also cause people to feel alienated from themselves or their own lives because external influences make them act in a way that they are not happy about. Both these factors may contribute to feelings of anger and frustration. Humiliation and alienation stem from undertaking actions that do not fit with one's own sense of worth or potential. In such situations, people suffer from a fractured identity as a result of the way in which people define or treat them. Being treated as inferior or denied agency is likely to lead to attempts to re-establish a positive identity and sense of self-worth. Such efforts might include extreme actions to bring about a betterment of their situation or of that of people belonging to the same group or collective identity.[638]

An important facet of perspectives on global politics within the Arab-Islamic world, as Shahram Akbarzadeh points out, is a sense of unfairness that is linked to concrete issues and the desire to be treated fairly and as equals. Here the importance of injustice rather than religion per se is evident. According to Akbarzadeh, Muslims of various types are concerned with the unequal power relations between the Arab-Islamic world and the West in the contemporary world. They feel alienated from the present global order because they view it as unjust and can find no mechanisms through which to address this.[639] Thus, "The Muslim cry for justice is not so much about restoring the glory of the caliphate, but for dignity and equity in modern times. It rests on tangible grievances and can therefore be addressed with relevant policies."[640] This sense of injustice is, he argues, exacerbated because of the apparent lack of official mechanisms through which to challenge inconsistencies in US policies and sometimes those of other states supporting the US.

The sustainability of a particular global order depends on global justice. The danger is that when people feel that injustices exist and are unable to affect them within established global governance mechanisms, they make seek to effect change outside of them. Those who feel disenfranchised and alienated may develop a resistance identity couched in terms of civilisational conflict. Manuel Castells sug-

---

[638] Al-Rodhan, *The Five Dimensions of Global Security, op. cit.*, note 512, pp. 93-94.
[639] S. Akbarzadeh, "Islam and Global Politics," in L. Elliot, M. Beeson, S. Akbarzadeh, G. Fealy and S. Harris, *Religion, Faith and Global Politics* (Canberra: PSPAS Publishing, 2006), pp. 12-13.
[640] *Ibid.*, p. 13.

gests that resistance identity construction processes are adopted by those who occupy devalued or stigmatised positions. This kind of identity construction, he suggests, may form the most significant type of identity construction today. It may provide a means of resisting oppression and is likely to draw on already clearly defined aspects, such as geography, history or biology.[641]

3. Global Security

The state is attributed paramount importance in realism. The state is assumed to be a unitary, rational and selfish actor that is primarily concerned with ensuring its own survival. Consequently, the state is considered the primary referent of security, making realism state-centric in its outlook. Moreover, achieving greater security is believed to be zero-sum – the more security one state enjoys, the less its neighbours will have – in the absence of a sovereign world state. The "security dilemma" engendered in what is believed to be an anarchical state system is thought to preclude the emergence of stable universal principles.[642]

My classification of global security is intended to provide a more comprehensive view. The "multi-sum security principle" outlined above argues that achieving security in these interrelated areas depends to a great extent on the promotion of justice. The "multi-sum security principle" states that *"In a globalized world, security can no longer be thought of as a zero-sum game involving states alone. Global security, instead, has five dimensions that include human, environmental, national, transnational, and transcultural security, and, therefore, global security and the security of any state or culture cannot be achieved without good governance at all levels that guarantees security through justice for all individuals, states, and cultures."*[643]

Human security refers to the security of individuals and calls into question the traditional focus on the state. The United Nations Development Programme's definition of human security as the "free-

---

[641] M. Castells, *The Power of Identity, The Information Age: Economy, Society and Culture*, Volume II (Malden, Mass.; Blackwell Publishers Inc., 2004), pp. 8-9.
[642] Al-Rodhan, *The Five Dimensions of Global Security, op. cit.*, note 512, pp. 20, 22.
[643] *Ibid.*, pp. 15-16.

dom from fear and freedom from want,"[644] implies freedom from hunger and disease, respect for human rights and the absence of violent conflict.[645] Security should therefore not simply be centred on states, but should also see individuals as important subjects of security. People's basic shelter and personal security must be central to security considerations. It is also important to take into account the security implications of a person's ego needs, most notably the needs to belong and to possess a positive identity.[646] In this sense, human security ought to be broadened beyond freedom from fear and want, and human dignity ought to be at the heart of any such conception of human security.

Global climate change may increase the likelihood of natural disasters connected to floods, cyclones and droughts. Asia and Africa are both likely to be at particular risk of increased flooding, health problems and desertification as a consequence of global warming. Against the backdrop of global climate change, the environment is being increasingly recognised as a security issue. Environmental change may affect individual well-being and national security, as well as the biosphere's capacity to sustain current levels of human enterprise.[647] Global warming may have a significant effect on the world's ecosystems. While the precise implications of climate change are as yet unclear, in some areas increased evaporation, more profuse rainfall and weather patterns that are more favourable to pests could reduce crop yields, thereby affecting people's livelihoods and food supply. This could, in turn, affect global food production and therefore human security.

Threats to security are thus multifaceted and not necessarily military in origin. They may include human- and drug-trafficking, cybercrime and weapons proliferation, for example, and be transnational. National security has economic, societal and political dimensions. These types of security challenge cannot be adequately addressed by any one state alone. Instead, they require cooperation be-

---

[644] UNDP, *op. cit.*, note 554.
[645] *Ibid.*
[646] Al-Rodhan, *Symbiotic Realism*, *op. cit.*, note 78, p. 71.
[647] See, e.g., *Climate Change 2007: Impacts, Adaptation and Vulnerability*, Contribution of Working Group II to the Fourth Assessment Report of the IPCC (Cambridge: Cambridge University Press, 2007).

tween states as well as multi-level cooperation in relation to functional sectors and greater burden-sharing among states.[648]

Cultural questions have tended to be obscured in security policy and in the discipline of international relations, although representatives of the Copenhagen School's concept of societal security such as Barry Buzan, Ole Waever and Jaap de Wilde point out that the state and the collective identities to which people belong do not necessarily fit together. The concept of societal security comprises large collective identities that may function beyond the territorial boundaries of the state.[649] Recent scholarship has also taken up issues of culture and relations between civilisations. As is mentioned above, Huntington's thesis on the clash of civilisations is one of these theses. Other scholars, such as Dieter Senghaas, however, contest this issue by arguing that the clashes are within civilisations as part of the tension between tradition and modernity.[650]

Global Security and Civilisational Triumph
Global security is important for civilisational triumph because poverty, disease and personal insecurity are all factors that contribute to frustration, despair, alienation, negative self-identity and, ultimately, indignity. Human security is important for overall civilisational success because human civilisation can only triumph if people can flourish and contribute to the communities of which they feel a part. At a minimum level, human well-being depends on the fulfilment of basic needs, broadly defined. It therefore depends on people having sufficient food, access to clean water, shelter, physical security, a positive self-identity and a sense of belonging.

Ecosystems, both local and planetary, must be capable of sustaining human activity, making environmental security central to civilisational triumph. As the exploitation of the Earth's resources and population growth have advanced apace, the Earth's carrying capacity is arguably being increasingly strained. The scale of human activity and the growth in the human population means that the future of humanity will depend on sustainable development.

---

[648] Al-Rodhan, *The Five Dimensions of Global Security*, *op. cit.*, note 512, p. 72.
[649] B. Buzan, O. Waever, and J. de Wilde, *Security: A New Framework for Analysis* (Boulder, CO; London: Lynne Rienner, 1998), pp. 22-23, 123.
[650] See Huntington, *op. cit.*, note 46; Senghaas, *op. cit.*, note 26.

Transnational security is also essential for civilisational triumph because states cannot tackle alone many of the security challenges they currently face. Cross-border cooperation is imperative, as most states now recognise, in order to effectively address the vast array of problems such as trafficking in drugs, arms and people, environmental degradation and financial market instability.

Civilisational identities may be emphasised at least in part due to issues related to public policy, such as disputes over religious symbols in France and Turkey. Lorraine Elliot points out that we are currently witnessing an increased securitisation of religion and faith. In its most simplistic and dangerous form, this securitisation succumbs to the dichotomy between "us" and "them" and a struggle between "good" and "evil".[651] The outcomes of perceived conflicts are zero-sum.[652] As is highlighted above, culture and geo-cultural identities may be being securitised at least in part because of a lack of fair treatment and dignity.

4. The Challenges

While there is an increasing recognition that more comprehensive approaches to security are required today, obstacles still exist. Moreover, there is scant recognition of the centrality of justice to achieving global security. Nonetheless, calls for justice in relation to a number of specific and more general problems are intimately connected to enhancing global security.

Obstacles to Global Justice
One of the major challenges, even for a minimalist conception of global justice, is the disparity in power that exists between states in the global order as it currently exists. In this sense there is, as Hurrell suggests, a distortion in who gets to set the rules of international society. Rather than being neutral arenas of bargaining between equal entities, institutions are sites of power and perhaps even dominance. Moreover, some states and societies are better equipped to adapt to the established rules than others. This is clearly demonstrated by the dis-

---

[651] L. Elliot, "Introduction," in L. Elliot, M. Beeson, S. Akbarzadeh, G. Fealy and S. Harris, *Religion, Faith and Global Politics* (Canberra: PSPAS Publishing, 2006), p. 1.
[652] S. Harris, "Religion, Politics and Foreign Policy: A Contemporary Diplomatic Challenge," in Eliot, Beeson, Akbarzadeh, Fealy and Harris, *ibid.*, p. 28.

advantageous position occupied by developing countries in the global political economy,[653] and in the multilateral institutional structures that help to regulate it. Yet, dominant states that benefit from these established and institutionalised inequalities are unlikely to want to alter the status quo, unless it is in their self-interest to do so. Inequalities in power that disadvantage developing counties in particular are likely to continue to generate more strident calls for justice that will need to be addressed.

Given the human need for dignity, calls for greater global justice are also likely to continue from those within societies that are disadvantaged because of the rules set by the more powerful. The most vulnerable members of societies have very little voice both domestically and globally. In most cases, there is a lack both of the opportunity to engage in the decision-making process and the empowerment required to do so. There are, thus, insufficient means for the vulnerable to make demands about justice.[654]

Despite the continued relevance of power relations between states and societies, as well as within societies, there does exist, as Hurrell notes, a normative structure of international society that is enshrined in human rights, humanitarian intervention and the obligations associated with state sovereignty.[655] This means that there is at least some basis on which to build greater global justice in a broader sense. Yet, this normative framework can also reinforce power relations between states, which will contribute to a more visceral sense of injustice. The unfortunate consequence of this is the potential erosion of that normative framework due to mistrust and perceived double standards. The challenge is to ensure that demands for justice can secure authority and include the whole of humanity.[656]

Obstacles to Global Security
One of the principle obstacles to the promotion of human security is the persistence of parochial state interests. The dynamic and interconnected relationship between the environment and human activity is increasingly recognised by a number of actors. However, leading actors in the "environmental sector" tend to focus on specific sets of

---

[653] Hurrell, *op. cit.*, note 548, p. 305.
[654] *Ibid.*, pp. 315-316.
[655] *Ibid.*, p. 296.
[656] *Ibid.*, p. 312.

issues. The diverging interests of various lobbies at the state level also pose a significant obstacle to improving environmental security. Challenges to environmental security sometimes originate with governance problems in the area of environmental management.[657] There is also an ongoing controversy over whether rapidly developing countries should bear significant burdens in relation to reducing the global level of greenhouse gas emissions.

Challenges to meeting national security may be the result of governance problems, engaging in cooperative security arrangements and parochialism.[658] Global security is, for example, compromised by the persistence of power inequalities among states and the institutionalisation of these inequalities within international institutions, such as the UNSC, the IMF and the World Bank. Moreover, many security challenges, such as transnational organised crime, cybercrime and epidemics, are transnational in nature and involve non-state actors. States must work together in order to respond effectively to these challenges. A failure to do so will necessarily make the pursuit of universal security more difficult.

Regional and international organisations and arrangements often focus on short-term solutions to transnational security challenges but long-term strategies to address the root causes of problems are also required. Establishing shared norms on which to base common action is a related challenge. In addition, the persistence of state-centric paradigms for health and the environment, for example, is an obstacle to dealing successfully with transnational threats to security.[659]

One of the greatest challenges facing states today is the problem of how to promote inclusive national identities, a problem that is made all the more acute by the dependence of many states on migration, and in the context of increased and instant global connectedness. Demographic trends in some countries are likely to place pressure on perhaps already overstretched government resources, creating high levels of domestic unemployment and attendant problems, as well as a "brain drain" as the best educated people leave the country in search of better opportunities elsewhere.

---

[657] Al-Rodhan, *The Five Dimensions of Global Security, op. cit.*, note 512, p. 57.
[658] *Ibid.*, p. 72.
[659] *Ibid.*, pp. 78-79.

There are different approaches to sustainable development, although the overall interests and objectives may be broadly the same. Some states may consider it their right to pursue economic development without the constraints implied by agreed limits on greenhouse gas emissions. Meanwhile, developed countries may also resist such regulations, perhaps due to the strength of business interests in politics or the cost of converting to non-fossil fuels.

One of the challenges facing transcultural security is the tendency to see the world in terms of cultural stereotypes, when instead we need to see people in all their complexity and to avoid ascribing people identities as a way of excluding them and drawing a boundary around our own community. Communication can also be difficult without awareness of other cultures and histories. This is connected to trust between cultural groups, which may be lacking if relations have been marked by discrimination and tension.

5. The Way Forward

Promoting universal justice may be achieved by a focus on fair processes and representation. While no sovereign world state exists to ensure or promote global justice, there are, nevertheless, a number of mechanisms and norms that provide a basis on which calls for justice may be addressed. As with the promotion of global justice, the evolving norms that may support universal security are often in tension with state-centric security practices and the traditional divide between the public and the private sectors.

Global Justice

There is common agreement about what constitutes fair process, and all societies need to find a way of adjudicating fairly between claims.[660] Fairness in terms of the participants in dialogue is also a perquisite for the promotion of universal justice. Diplomacy must be based on an openness to hearing and acknowledging the concerns and positions of others. Empathy and an acknowledgment of the grievances of others is also important.[661] It is important to try to understand the complexities behind what may on the surface appear to be a clash of interests, cultures or religions. In relation to the latter, for example,

---

[660] Hurrell, *op. cit.*, note 548, p. 308.
[661] Akbarzadeh, *op. cit.*, note 639, p. 13.

we need to go further and to try to comprehend the socio-cultural, economic and political factors behind problems that may be articulated through appeals to faith or religion.

In addition, all parties that have a stake in a particular issue being addressed need to be involved in negotiations. If they are not, the risk is that they will feel alienated from a process designed to address an issue. Within the context of negotiations, fairness implies ensuring that all parties are treated as equals and thus have an equal "voice". Clear and transparent rules, the parameters of which have been agreed by all parties concerned, are also important elements of ensuring that the interlocutors feel that they are treated fairly.[662] Less powerful countries must also be involved in rule-making. Hedley Bull, in his seminal book, *The Anarchical Society* (1977), argued in as far back as 1977 that non-Western dimensions would need to be included in what he perceived as a nascent cosmopolitan culture if a universal international society were to be attainable.[663] This argument remains valid and is even more urgent today.

The normative basis of greater global justice is in place, even if it exists alongside more traditional power relations. While the law enforcement capacity of the UNSC has its limits, the General Assembly is not a world legislature and the International Criminal Court can only operate when its jurisdiction is accepted by states, they do provide for a minimum degree of global justice that will develop as global norms evolve. In addition to facilitating state-to-state relations and outlawing the use of force except in self-defence or in instances of a breach of the peace, international law also helps to diffuse particular norms and values, such as the peaceful settlement of disputes and arms control. Moreover, international law has also expanded. Although its initial concern was with the rights and duties of sovereign states, international law is now applied to individuals by states. Yet, international law relies on the voluntary commitment of states. All states, no matter how powerful, need to be bound by international law and its obligations. When some appear to be above international law, operating with impunity, this only feeds sentiments of a lack of equal-

---

[662] C. Albin, "Getting to Fairness: Negotiations over Global Public Goods," Netherlands Institute of International Relations 'Clingendael', Discussion Paper in Diplomacy, 2002, p. 11.
[663] H. Bull, *The Anarchical Society*, Second Edition (Basingstoke: Macmillan, 1977), p. 305.

ity in global politics. In the absence of a sovereign world state, international law plays a significant role in the pursuit of global justice. The established body of international law helps to forge a normative consensus on state behaviour, and it is constantly evolving.[664]

According to Hurrell, the creation of a moral community in which claims about justice are able to secure authority and be accessible to humanity as a whole will be based on a minimum agreement about fair process. This ought to be embedded in the institutions of international society and fostered within an international political culture that values deliberation.[665]

Global Security

There are a number of apparent obstacles to promoting human security. The increased emphasis on individual dignity and individual security, reflected in the evolution of intervention as well as recent efforts to convict those responsible for crimes against humanity, obviously conflicts with traditional conceptions of state sovereignty. It is also susceptible to being employed for power political reasons, given the unequal power relations in the global system. In the arena of development, efforts to promote ends favourable to human security, such as empowerment, may come into conflict with more neo-liberal-driven market agendas.

Efforts to protect the biosphere encounter problems connected to the conflict between short- and long-term interests and where the burden falls. In order to promote sustainable development, governments need to provide incentives to the private sector to encourage it to help meet environmental policy goals. However, governments also need to level the playing field on which companies compete while helping to meet public policy objectives.[666] As is mentioned above, the debate over whether the rising powers should share the burden of reducing greenhouse gases is ongoing.

Today, national security strategies need to be underpinned by a broad conception of security that enables policymakers to under-

---

[664] Al-Rodhan and Watanabe, *A Proposal for* Inclusive *Peace and Security, op. cit.*, note 1, pp. 84-85.
[665] Hurrell, *op. cit.*, note 548, pp. 312, 314.
[666] M. Strong, Chairman, the Earth Council, Special Report, *The Rocky Road to Johannesburg: We Need a More Sustainable Civilization,* European Affairs, Summer 2002.

stand the variety of actors and the complexity of interrelated issues. If such a strategy is to be applied effectively, state institutional capacities must reflect the broad scope of security threats. In *The Three Pillars of* Sustainable National Security *in a Transnational World* (2008), I suggested that national security councils (NSC) need to be structured to be able to deal with a wide range of security issues, including likely future issues, and to be guided by ethical standards.[667]

Since many threats to security are transnational, multilateral cooperative frameworks and arrangements are vital means for effectively responding to challenges. The advantages to states derived from mutually beneficial security relationships are many. This is apparent in the increasingly dense governance networks that exist today in a variety of issue areas.

Transcultural security requires not simply coexistence but synergy, which is discussed in Chapter 14. States need to promote tolerance and respect for diversity, as well as awareness of the "other"; and to empower underrepresented communities to make their voices heard and to participate in society.[668] Knowledge of other cultures, religions and histories, as well as the numerous examples of coexistence and exchange, should be included in school curricula.

We need to recognise the diversity in different societies that share a particular faith or religion rather than depicting them as monolithic wholes. Just as complexity exists at this level it also exists within loosely bounded geo-cultural domains, and it is essential that we recognise this since depicting geo-cultural domains as homogenous, easily definable entities necessarily ascribes qualities to their constituent parts, often with the result of encouraging people to define themselves primarily in terms of civilisational identities. It is also critical that calls for justice are taken seriously and that concrete grievances are recognised and addressed.

Octagon 3 summarises the minimum criteria of global justice.

---

[667] N.R.F. Al-Rodhan, *The Three Pillars of* Sustainable National Security *in a Transnational World* (Berlin: LIT, 2008).
[668] Al-Rodhan, *The Five Dimensions of Global Security*, *op. cit.*, note 512, p. 83.

SUSTAINABLE HISTORY AND THE DIGNITY OF MAN 241

Octagon 3: Minimum Criteria of Global Justice

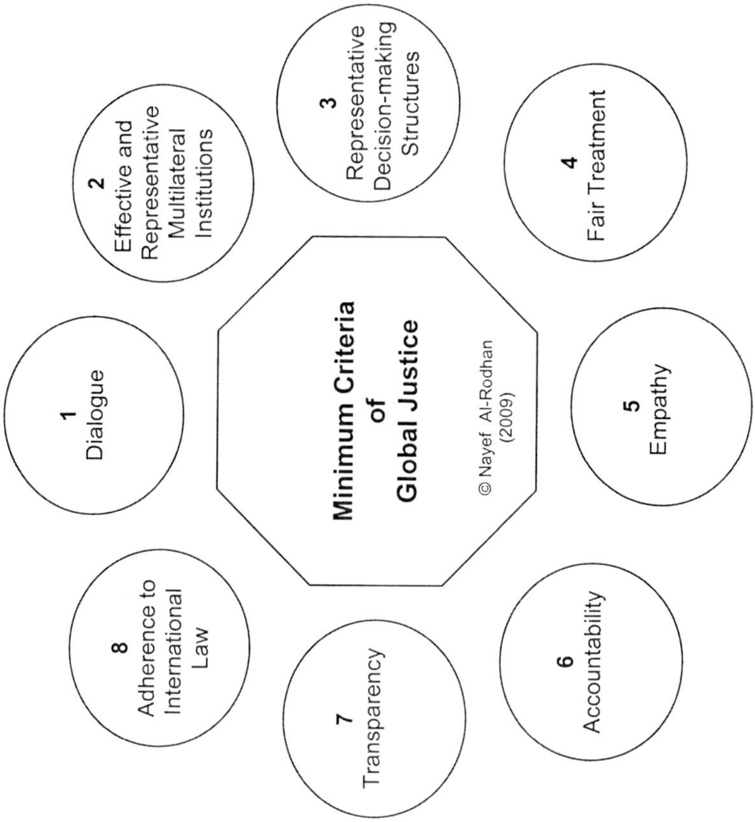

6. Conclusion

This chapter has examined the issue of global justice, because of its importance to human dignity. The different approaches to civilisation range from normative to post-essentialist accounts. I suggested that it is unhelpful to think in terms of multiple civilisations and their separateness, which is not to say that geo-cultural domains do not have their own specificities and do not appear real and distinctive. They are experienced as real entities because intersubjective and material "resources" fit together in particular ways that give rise to separate geo-cultural domains in which civilisational characteristics and memory exist. To this end, we can talk about geo-cultural domains. However, these geo-cultural domains are only loosely bounded and it must be understood that their boundaries appear impermeable despite numerous mutual influences and synergies. I suggested that a sense of injustice, understood primarily as unfairness, is an important contributory factor to the rise of exclusionary civilisational identities and efforts to bring about transformations outside of regular channels. Injustice damages humankind's dignity needs and, as long this is the case, people will proactively seek redress and recognition through whatever means are available. Thus, injustice does not contribute to overall civilisational triumph, which rests on non-zero sum relations between co-constitutive geo-cultural domains. Hence the need for the application of universal minimum requirements for justice and universal security, which are based on promoting greater justice for individuals, cultural collectivities and states. Global justice and global security are therefore essential to the triumph of human civilisation.

CHAPTER 9

WHAT IS NEEDED FOR GOOD NATIONAL GOVERNANCE?
MINIMUM CRITERIA OF INCLUSIVE, EFFECTIVE AND
GOOD *NATIONAL* GOVERNANCE

Sustainable history depends mostly on good governance, because human nature attributes need to be balanced against human dignity needs. Given that the state is still the principle political unit within the global system, good *national* governance is a vital ingredient of sustainable history. Yet, the normative and structural agenda of democratisation is often understood in the Global South as masking the political, economic and even military ambitions of the Global North. Some argue that democracy is specific to Western cultural and historical contexts and cannot be transposed elsewhere.[669] Indeed, the incommensurability of democracy with non-Western societies is often taken up in the Asian or Islamic values debates. Whether these discourses exaggerate the differences that exist between fundamental values is discussed in this chapter. The greatest agreement may, however, be in relation to good governance. Certain facets of good governance are expressions of the fundamental values of democracy and a more liberal type of constitutionalism, and for the most part they already exist in most countries, although how they are articulated is likely to be context-specific. Contemporary debates on governance do not adequately address the need for intercultural dialogue and the identification of common values and governance structures. Yet, if we are to discern which aspects of governance have the widest universal application, we need to ask how political constitutions and governance arrangements are conceived across the world. This chapter identifies what may be considered to be the key facets or minimum criteria of

---

[669] Al-Rodhan and Watanabe, *A Proposal for* Inclusive *Peace and Security, op. cit.*, note 1, p. 63.

good governance. It also outlines some key challenges to achieving good governance and suggests how these may be overcome.

1. The Concept of Good Governance

The concept of good governance has been employed by development donors to encourage institutional reform in countries that receive development aid. The concept began to be deployed among the development community in the early 1990s after the end of the Cold War.[670] Its attractiveness to policymakers stemmed from its focus on political processes in the context of broader structures. As such, it seemed capable of linking political and administrative spheres, and also appeared to provide neutral criteria on which to base reforms. However, as a concept it is extremely vague.[671] Governance is not one and the same as government.[672] The term good governance has been employed in different ways and for different purposes.[673] However, it has generally been used to refer to the exercise of authority within a specific domain and to denote efficient management. International financial institutions, such as the World Bank and the IMF, emphasise in their definitions of governance the way in which resources are used to promote political power and development. The role of governments is highlighted by this definition.[674]

The United Nations Development Programme (UNDP) defines governance as "the exercise of economic, political and administrative authority to manage a country's affairs at all levels. It comprises mechanisms, processes and institutions through which citizens and groups articulate their interests, exercise their legal rights, meet

---

[670] M. Doornbos, "'Good Governance': The Metamorphosis of a Policy Metaphor," *Journal of International Affairs*, Fall 2003, Vol. 57, No. 1, 2003, p. 3.
[671] *Ibid.*, p. 5.
[672] J. Graham, B. Amos and T. Plumptre, "Principles for Good Governance in the 21st," Institute on Governance, Policy Brief 15, August 2003, http://www.roadmap.depkeu.go.id/Ina/Files/pustaka006.pdf, p. 1.
[673] A.M. Abdellatif, "Good Governance and Its Relationship to Democracy and Economic Development," Workshop IV, Democracy, Economic Development, and Culture, Global Forum III on Fighting Corruption and Safeguarding Integrity, 20-31 May 2003, p. 3.
[674] S. Kataoka, "The Plight of African States and Good Governance," The Japan Institute of International Affairs, January 2003, http://www.jiia.or.jp/pdf/working_paper/h14_kataoka-e.pdf, pp. 1-2.

their obligations and mediate their differences."[675] What is important to note is that in this definition not only the state, but also the private sector and civil society are considered important governance actors. The state is perceived as providing the political and legal framework within which sustained development and civil society institutions can flourish and facilitate the participation of individuals and groups in politics.[676] In this sense, it also allows for both formal and informal actors to shape decision making and the implementation of decisions. In addition, the UNDP definition recognises that governance may take place in the institutional, local, national or global spheres. [677] Thus, the concept of governance may be conceived of as a new approach to the notion of governing where the boundaries between public, private and non-profit sectors are unclear.[678]

The concept of good governance, according to the United Nations Economic and Social Commission for Asia and the Pacific (UNESCAP), has eight major facets: participation, the rule of law, transparency, responsiveness, a consensus oriented approach, equity and inclusiveness, effectiveness and efficiency, and accountability.[679] According to the 2002 Human Development Report, good governance depends on building the appropriate institutions, which may be achieved through creating an environment in which participation can take place through representation through political parties and elections, promoting the participation of minorities and women, developing electoral systems and limiting the influence of money in politics. Strengthening checks on power and the separation of power between the executive, the judiciary and parliament are considered vital, as is the creation of independent bodies. It also recommends decentralisation through the devolution of power from the central government to provinces and villages, supported by local democratic institutions and

---

[675] "Governance for a Sustainable Human Development," A UNDP policy paper, UNDP 1997, pp. 2-3.
[676] Abdellatif, *op. cit.*, note 673, pp. 4-5.
[677] ESCAP, "What Is Good Governance," http://www.unescap.org/pdd/prs/Project Activities/Ongoing/gg/governance.asp.
[678] V. Pettai and E. Illing, "Governance and Good Governance," Introduction to the Special Issue of *TRAMES: A Journal of Humanities and Social Sciences*, Vol. 8, No. 4, 2004, p. 348.
[679] ESCAP, *op. cit.*, note 677.

practices. The development of a free and independent media is also considered essential.[680]

From the human development perspective, good governance is taken to be democratic governance.[681] Democratic governance comprises efficient institutions, a stable economic and political environment, and effective public services. However, democratic governance is also concerned with political and human rights, as well as the elimination of discrimination. Reforms aimed at democratic governance involve the establishment of rules and institutions that are efficient, fair and conceived as a result of an inclusive democratic process in which everyone had a voice. Democratic governance, therefore, implies a concern with good governance for development, democratic processes and institutions, and securing political and civil rights as well as human rights.[682] Democratic governance may be distinguished from good governance in that it is based on the premise that political and civil freedoms and participation are essential for development.[683] Regular, free and fair elections, for example, are thought to encourage responsiveness from a governing elite. Democracy, it is argued, also allows citizens to monitor those elected and to try to influence the policymaking process through civil society institutions. In addition, increased public participation in the political debate may endow governments with a greater degree of legitimacy.[684]

Despite the widespread employment of the term, its promotion has had a mixed record. The recommended reforms associated with the concept of good governance were not always adopted in the way the international donor community may have hoped. The types of reforms required by the set of standards implied changes to existing power relations and for those with stakes in local political contexts. Several aspects of the good governance discourse deserve attention in this respect. First, in relation to democratisation and pluralism, the danger is that pluralism may emerge without any significant change in the political system. In Ethiopia, Zimbabwe and Zambia a dominant political party representing the existing regime emerged but little else

---

[680] UNDP, *Deepening Democracy in a Fragmented World*. Human Development Report 2002 (New York, Oxford: UNDP and Oxford University Press, 2002).
[681] *Ibid.*, p. 51.
[682] Abdellatif, *op. cit.*, note 673, p. 10.
[683] *Ibid.*, p. 11.
[684] *Ibid.*, p. 13.

changed. In other instances, authoritarian regimes, such as that in Uganda, argued that political pluralism was a product of Western culture and therefore not applicable outside the West. Second, given the vagueness of the concept of good governance, efforts to alter what was defined by aid donors as poor governance practices into good governance produced few results.[685]

2. Universal Standards of Good Governance?

One of the fundamental questions that has to be addressed in relation to the promotion of good governance is whether it does, indeed, comprise a neutral set of standards that can be applied outside the West. In recent years, there has been a reinvigoration of autochthonous cultural traditions. This "revival" of tradition and reassertion of cultural identities has been important in Asia, the Pacific, the Middle East and Africa, as well as in Europe at the sub-state, state and supra-state levels. These debates are likely to be significant for governance issues.[686] Yet, the good governance debates have failed to adequately question the universality of the standards often linked with the concept. In the policy community, criteria for good governance are likely to reflect the priorities and perceptions of the world held by donor organisations or states. When particular standards are promoted globally, this is likely to be because they accord with those setting the preferences or those setting the standards.[687]

If good governance is taken to imply the protection of political and human rights as well as civil rights, advocates may encounter appeals to traditionalism. The principal argument in the Asian values discourse employed by political elites is that the outstanding levels of economic growth, the increasing standards of living and the low crime rates in cities in South East Asia are primarily the result of a specifically Asian culture. Goh Chok Tong, the Prime Minister of Singapore, for example, has argued in relation to his own country's economic success that the correct economic policies and good governance practices are not enough in themselves to explain Singapore's high stan-

---

[685] Doornbos, *op. cit.*, note 670, pp. 10-11.
[686] S. Lawson, "Cultural Traditions and Identity Politics: Some Implications for Democratic Governance," *State and Society and Governance in Melanesia*, Discussion Paper, 1997, http://www.clg.uts.edu.au/pdfs/Helu.pdf, pp. 1-2.
[687] Doornbos, *op. cit.*, note 670, pp. 8-9.

dard of living. A strong sense of community and family, a hard working and disciplined people and robust moral values are considered essential to explaining and maintaining Singapore's success.[688]

This debate has been particularly animated in relation to the issues of human rights and democracy. "Traditionalism" as expressed in the Asian values argument posits that democracy is something that is a cultural product of the West and, as such, is not necessarily suitable for other cultures.[689] The Asian values argument, for example, emphasises that ethical practices determined by traditions and conventions rather than specific governmental principles designed to guard against the abuse of power are important sources of order and public morale in Asian cultures. In such traditions and conventions, legitimate forms of resistance are recognised in instances where rule is considered despotic or at odds with public welfare.[690]

Similar efforts at cultural construction are also evident in the South Pacific. Stephanie Lawson views traditionalism as an ideology. In her view, in the South Pacific, appeals to tradition tend to take the form of notions of the "Pacific Way". In some instances, a more specific cultural representation is appealed to in the "Melanesian Way".[691] Within these discourses, autochthonous cultural traditions are held in opposition to the West. The achievements of South East Asian countries within the Asian values discourse are contrasted with an image of the West as decadent and in social and economic decline, which is posited as linked to an "excess" of democracy.[692]

Yet, it is important to note that Western political traditions were hostile towards democracy until relatively recently.[693] Democratic and liberal democratic thought emerged in Europe from the 15th to the 18th centuries in the context of absolutist paradigms in which authority was linked to the notion of supreme or sovereign power. As the state's sovereign power and administrative powers expanded, opposition movements sought to limit the powers of the state in the form of constitutionalism.[694] Constitutions set out the organisation of gov-

---

[688] Lawson, *op. cit.*, note 686, p. 3.
[689] *Ibid.*, p. 7.
[690] Senghaas, *op. cit.*, note 26, p. 93.
[691] Lawson, *op. cit.*, note 686, p. 2.
[692] *Ibid.*, pp. 2-3.
[693] *Ibid.*, p. 7.
[694] D. Held, *Models of Democracy*, Second Edition (Stanford, CA.: Stanford University Press, 1996), pp. 70-72.

ernment and the powers attributed to its various parts as a form of protection against the arbitrary rule of the monarchy.[695] These developments took place against the backdrop of liberal thought, which aimed to limit the power of both the church and the state and to demarcate a private sphere distinct from both. This gradually developed into the idea that individuals should be able to pursue their own religious, economic and political preferences, which, in turn, led to a belief in the constitutional state, private property and the competitive market economy as the key vehicles for coordinating the interests of private individuals.[696]

Liberalism and democracy were initially two separate tendencies. Liberals often viewed democracy as a threat to liberty and individual rights. Limitations on the government's powers by way of a fundamental law (i.e. constitutionalism), the separation of powers, legal protections and a bill of rights are all legacies of an undemocratic past. Indeed, constitutionalism is in some senses undemocratic in that it cannot easily be amended and is interpreted by a non-elected, independent judicial authority.[697] These developments were underpinned by liberal doctrines, in which individuals were considered free and equal and endowed with natural rights.[698] Popular sovereignty was only gradually embraced. Fundamental qualities and rights were, moreover, ascribed to men and not women and were largely for property-owning men.[699] In the US, for example, democracy was viewed as a threat auguring a "tyranny of the majority". The US constitution is partly designed to prevent this perceived danger.[700] To this end, liberalism was a stronger motivating force for change in the West than democracy. Democratic governance has only taken a firm hold in Western Europe in the past 50 years.[701]

These discourses are also problematic because they assume that Asia and the West are homogeneous entities that can easily be defined and generalised about, when in fact both are heterogeneous

---

[695] J. Markoff, "Where and When Was Democracy Invented," *Comparative Studies in Society & History*, Vol. 41, No. 4, 1999, p. 665.
[696] Held, *op. cit.*, note 694, pp. 74.
[697] R.N. Stromberg, *Democracy: A Short Analytical History* (Armonk, N.Y.: M.E. Sharpe, 1996), p. 9.
[698] Held, *op. cit.*, note 694, pp. 74.
[699] *Ibid.*
[700] Lawson, *op. cit.*, note 686, p. 7.
[701] *Ibid.*

and complex. Asian values debates succumb to an inverted form of Orientalism or Occidentalism.[702] Traditionalism as represented by the Asian values debates also fails to recognise the plurality of "insiders", when it may be difficult to speak of a people or nation as a uniform authentic unit.[703] The argument that "excessive democracy" is "too Western" also serves as a way of externalising internal critics.[704] In relation to appeals to the "Pacific Way" or the "Melanesian Way", Lawson argues that traditionalism invoked by political elites often has a political motive. In Tonga, for instance, where pro-democracy activists challenged existing power structures, particularly the Tongan nobility, opponents have responded by invoking Tongan tradition.[705]

As an ideological stance, traditionalism may reduce the space that might otherwise exist for dialogue and a focus on common values. The fundamental facets of democracy do, in fact, exist in non-Western societies, although they are articulated differently. At the core of the democratic ideal is the idea that sovereignty lies with the people and that the necessary institutions and resources are available to allow them to govern themselves. Mohammed Khatami, former President of the Islamic Republic of Iran, remarks that:

> The main features of democracy – which should be clearly distinguished from its various manifestations – include people's right to determine their destinies; the emanation of authority, particularly political authority from the free will and choice of the people and its submission to their continued scrutiny; and the institutionalization of such accountability. No one form of democracy can be prescribed as the one and final version. Hence unfolding efforts to formulate democracy in the context of spirituality and morality may usher in yet another model of democratic life.[706]

In the Middle East, for example, democratic – but not liberal democratic – institutions already exist. Some monarchies have consultative assemblies.[707] In the Gulf states, such as Bahrain, Qatar, Saudi Arabia and Oman, institutional reform is being introduced through the deliberate use of traditional forums for consultation (the *Majlis Al-*

---

[702] *Ibid.*, p. 5.
[703] *Ibid.*, p. 9.
[704] *Ibid.*, p. 10.
[705] *Ibid.*, p. 6.
[706] Seyyed Mohammed Khatemi, quoted in UNDP, *op. cit.*, note 680, p. 64.
[707] Gerner and Schedler, *op. cit.*, note 436, p. 89.

Shura).⁷⁰⁸ The transition from liberalisation to democratisation is extremely difficult. Ehteshami argues that "the pursuit of the agenda of constitutionalism and good governance, which largely avoid some of the ideological underpinnings of the western 'democratic model', might still bear fruit."⁷⁰⁹ Other commentators argue that democratic institutions alone are not enough to secure democracy. Without "good governance" – the rule of law, an active civil society and a political culture of inclusiveness, consultation and circulation of power – democratic institutions could simply lead to a situation of rule by a powerful few. Therefore, constitutional liberty is offered as a better way of ensuring wide-ranging reforms.⁷¹⁰

There are those who argue that a reinterpretation and an updated application of divine texts would leave room for the emergence of democracy in the Muslim world. The Shura (a consultative assembly) is believed to provide an institutional basis for accountable government. While such bodies may be in danger of monopolisation by unelected officials or "wise men", other sources of divine knowledge, such as the Hadith (the Prophet's traditions) are thought to provide authoritative means to guard against this through their support for the de-monopolisation of power. In addition, it is argued that doctrines central to Islam such as ijtihad (independent reasoning) and ijma (consensus) encourage the practice of consultation.⁷¹¹

The Muslim world should not be viewed as a homogeneous whole. Muslim societies and polities have their own specificities linked to their culture and political systems. Moreover, few countries, in fact, adhere to Islamic teachings in the application of law and forms of political organisation. Most Muslim countries have Western-style written constitutions and secular approaches to political institutions and these countries interact with other countries first and foremost as members of a wider international community and not necessarily as a result of religion. For this reason, they themselves cannot develop a common basis for an ideal-type Islamic state, let alone one which could be presented to the world as an Islamic democracy. Moreover, pluralism is taking hold in many parts of the Arab world. It is increas-

---

⁷⁰⁸ Ehteshami, *op. cit.*, note 465, p. 101.
⁷⁰⁹ *Ibid.*, p. 107.
⁷¹⁰ *Ibid.*, p. 97.
⁷¹¹ *Ibid.*, p. 93.

ingly the case that popular elections are being held, which are not sufficient, but certainly necessary for democracy.[712]

Equally, in relation to human rights, common ground may exist that is obscured by ideologies of traditionalism captured by the Asian or Pacific values arguments. The development of the concept of human rights is associated with Western philosophical and political principles. In the commonplace account of the Western origins of human rights, the human rights tradition has its roots in the *Magna Carta* of 1215, between King John of England and the barons who were protesting the level of taxes being levied against them by the King. The right contained in the document, however, was simply the right to trial by jury for men with property. Similarly, the 1689 *English Bill of Rights*, which is also sometimes considered to be a precursor to human rights, was a political settlement between Parliament and the monarch.[713]

Moreover, it is possible to identify principles linked to mass education, self-fulfilment, respect for others and a concern to enhance the well-being of others in the Confucian, Hindu or Buddhist traditions. Andrew Clapham argues that the Bible and the Koran may be interpreted as creating rights as well as duties. The need to protect human freedom and human dignity was recognised in the Hammurabi Code of ancient Babylon as far back as c.1780 BCE, as well as in natural law, which drew on Stoic philosophy and Roman legal traditions.[714] At the heart of many such concerns with obligations towards fellow human beings is the concept of dignity.

3. Minimum Criteria of Good Governance

Good governance requires effective mechanisms and institutions to ensure that the long-term needs of all of those in society are met. Minimum criteria for good governance are set out below: (1) participation, equality and inclusiveness; (2) the rule of law and the separation of powers; (3) accountability and transparency; (4) limiting the distorting effect of money in politics; and (5) a free and independent

---

[712] *Ibid.*, pp. 98-99.
[713] A. Clapham, *Human Rights: A Very Short Introduction* (Oxford: Oxford University Press, 2007), pp. 6-7.
[714] *Ibid.*, p. 5.

media. All these elements can be moulded and developed in ways that are in keeping with local cultures and traditions.

Participation, Equality and Inclusiveness
Universal and equal suffrage is required for good governance. Free and fair elections should also be ensured.[715] Participation, which may be either direct or through intermediary institutions or representatives, depends on freedom of expression and of association. Given that people should be informed and organised, participation also implies a civil society. Inclusiveness is also listed by UNESCAP as central facets of good governance, given that a "healthy" society depends on all of its members having a stake in it. Mediation of diverse interests within society with the aim of reaching a broad consensus based on the long-term needs of a society is therefore also considered an important dimension of good governance. UNESCAP notes that "This can only result from an understanding of the historical, cultural and social contexts of a given society or community."[716] All groups, especially those which include the most vulnerable in society, should feel that they have the opportunity to influence the decisions that affect them. In order for ethno-cultural minorities to participate effectively in society, political rights to participation are not enough. Specific arrangements are required to ensure that national minorities are fully included in public life and are able to be so while maintaining their identity.[717]

As is noted above, the 2002 Human Development Report recommends decentralisation through the devolution of power from central government to the provinces and villages, supported by local democratic institutions and practices, in order to allow people to participate more directly in the political process. This is, however, only one aspect of increasing participation. The empowerment of the most marginalised groups in society is also important in this context. In Bolivia, the 1994 Popular Participation Law brought about an increase in participation and devolved fiscal decision making. Municipalities were created in areas where no state institutions existed. According to the

---

[715] Al-Rodhan and Watanabe, *A Proposal for Inclusive Peace and Security*, *op. cit.*, note 1, p. 64.
[716] ESCAP, *op. cit.*, note 677.
[717] F. Palermo and J. Woelk, "No Representation without Recognition: The Right to Political Participation of (National) Minorities," *Journal of European Integration*, Vol. 25, No. 3, 2003.

2002 Human Development Report, this had the effect of redistributing fiscal resources in accordance with population density. It also officially increased recognition of local grassroots organisations. The law gave local governments a greater degree of control over resources by devolving responsibility for health care, education and infrastructure such as roads as well as cultural issues. The result was positive empowerment in some communities, but not in every community. Critics of the initiative argue that the law did not do anything to reduce patronage structures in local parties or to reduce local corruption.[718] This highlights the importance of understanding the local context and addressing practices that prevent participation, equality and inclusiveness.

The Rule of Law and the Separation of Powers
The separation of powers between the executive, an independent judiciary and the legislature is essential for good governance. In India, for example, the judiciary has consistently sought to fight corruption and to maintain its independence.[719] When the separation of powers is not functioning as it should, judiciaries are vulnerable to influence from the politically powerful. Even when a separation between the executive, the legislature and the judiciary is guaranteed by the constitution, judiciaries may be subject to undue influence by the executive or the legislative assembly. This may be the case in countries where the rule of law has historically lacked robustness. Where the judiciary is weak, judges may feel greater pressure to acquiesce to politically powerful or connected individuals. In some instances, the executive branch has the power to select, appoint and promote judges. Where procedures for doing so are not transparent, the independence of judges may be in danger.[720] When judiciaries lack independence, their ability to protect the civil liberties of citizens is likely to be compromised.

If legal and judicial systems are not functioning well, non-compliance with laws and corruption are likely too, which will ultimately reduce respect for the rule of law, and lead to a degeneration of societal norms and of sustainable development due to a lack of confi-

---

[718] UNDP, *op. cit.*, note 680, pp. 74-75.
[719] *Ibid.*, p. 72.
[720] M.N. Pepys, "Corruption within the Judiciary: Causes and Remedies," in *Transparency International, Global Corruption Report 2007* (New York: Cambridge University Press, 2007), p. 4.

dence on the part of economic actors and societal instability.[721] An independent judiciary and an impartial and incorruptible police force are also necessary.[722] Fair treatment under the law may be compromised where corruption in the judiciary is a systemic problem. In such instances, improper application of the law may result from bribery, fear of retribution and inadequate procedures for monitoring judges.[723]

Government Legitimacy, Accountability and Transparency
Accountability and transparency are both central to ensuring participation and responsive institutions. They are also required for good governance. In the first instance, this implies accountability of governments to citizens, the reduction of corruption and the sound use of resources. Accountability and transparency apply not only to public institutions, but also to organisations in the private and non-profit sectors. All must be accountable to the public and their stakeholders. In order to ensure accountability, elections need to be free and fair. Accountability itself depends on the rule of law and transparency.[724] Accountability in the administration of elections is also critical to people's right to legitimate government and is important in order to prevent the ruling elite from using elections for their own ends.[725]

Transparency is an essential element of good governance. Decisions and their enforcement should be carried out in ways that comply with rules and regulations. People must have the ability to hold their governments to account. This implies having access to the information necessary to be in a position to monitor the activities of government. People therefore need to have access to timely and reliable information,[726] which ought to be easy to understand.[727]

---

[721] S. Morito and D. Zaelke, "Rule of Law, Good Governance and Sustainable Development," *Conference Proceedings of the Seventh International Conference on Environmental Compliance and Enforcement*, Marrakech, Morocco, 9-15 April 2005, Vol. 1, p. 15.
[722] ESCAP, *op. cit.*, note 677.
[723] Pepys, *op. cit.*, note 720.
[724] Al-Rodhan and Watanabe, *A Proposal for* Inclusive *Peace and Security*, *op. cit.*, note 1, pp. 69-70.
[725] M. Suksi, "Good Government in the Electoral Process," in Sano and Alfredsson, With the Collaboration of R. Clapp, *op. cit.*, note 511, p. 217.
[726] Al-Rodhan and Watanabe, *A Proposal for* Inclusive *Peace and Security*, *op. cit.*, note 1, p. 70.
[727] ESCAP, *op. cit.*, note 677.

Limiting the Distorting Effect of Money in Politics

If good governance implies fair elections in which political parties compete for power, adequate resources with which to fund campaigns need to be at the disposal of those parties. Yet this requirement can risk distorting electoral processes or corrupting elected officials within a country. In the former case, money can distort the electoral process by creating an uneven playing field between political parties as they compete for power. When sufficient accountability mechanisms are lacking, resources may be open to abuse. State resources, for example, may be improperly used by an incumbent politician to finance his or her campaign for re-election. Abuse is likely to occur in situations of low accountability. Once elections have taken place, financing can also influence the policymaking process. This may be more prevalent when candidates are funded rather than parties. Money may influence decisions related to both domestic and foreign policies.[728]

A Free, Independent and Responsible Media

A diverse and pluralistic media that is free and independent is fundamental to good governance. Mass access to and widespread diffusion of unbiased information are also vital to enabling citizens and decision makers to make informed decisions. Such a media enables different segments of society to be heard and various viewpoints to be debated, and serves to mobilise diverse parts of society to become politically engaged. It may also reinforce transparency and accountability by monitoring government activities and helping to hold public officials to account, and help to strengthen constitutional and legal guarantees of freedom of speech. In many countries, restrictive press laws have been abolished and increased privatisation and deregulation of the media has facilitated greater competition and a pluralistic mass media. The Internet and other information technologies have increased the diversity and scale of mass communication.[729]

The fusion of entertainment and information can also be viewed as detrimental to democracy or good governance. The challenge is to make a free and independent media accountable and responsible. A higher degree of media professionalism and responsibility may be achieved by setting up independent media commissions

---

[728] Transparency International, "Accountability and Transparency in Political Finance: Why, How and What For?" Working Paper 01/2008, www.transparency.org, pp. 1-2.
[729] UNDP, *op. cit.*, note 680, p. 76.

empowered to raise the level of responsible journalistic skills. Self-regulation can also help to ensure that certain ethical guidelines are followed by journalists and news agencies. The level of professionalism can be improved using internal guidelines, training and education.[730]

4. The Challenges

Entrenched interests may prevent the strengthening of legal and judicial institutions or distort the electoral and political process. Unequal power relations also create obstacles to participation by all individuals and groups in political decision-making processes, making accountability extremely difficult.

Participation, Equality and Inclusiveness
In some countries, formal democracy may exist but the ability of people to influence their life chances remains extremely low. This may be because political parties are unresponsive to articulating the new political concerns often expressed by new actors such as indigenous peoples, environmentalists and the landless. The elites in these countries increasingly represent a shrinking part of the population.[731]

Decentralisation of the political decision-making process in some countries may represent little more than rhetoric. In some African states, for example, lower-level structures are often disabled by a lack of adequate funding, and local revenue raised through taxation is minimal. Even when countries are formally democratic, powerful individuals often decide who has access to resources, government offices and government funds. Parliaments are also challenged in their capacity to monitor government.[732]

The issues of ethnic, cultural and religious minorities need to be addressed in order that everyone can contribute to society and feel that they are a valued member. This, as is pointed out above, is related to the basic human needs to have a positive self identity and to feel a sense of belonging. Yet, ensuring that this is the case remains a chal-

---

[730] *Ibid.*, p. 78.
[731] German Development Institute, "Statehood and Governance: Challenges in Latin America," Briefing Paper No. 1, 2007, pp. 1-2.
[732] German Development Institute, "Statehood and Governance: Challenges in Sub-Saharan Africa," Briefing Paper No. 3, 2007, p. 3.

lenge for the majority of multicultural countries. There are texts on which protection of the right to maintain cultural, ethnic and religious identities may be based, such as the Universal Declaration of Human Rights,[733] Article 27 of the International Covenant on Civil and Political Rights and the 1992 UN Assembly Minority Declaration.[734] In the Arab-Islamic world, the Koran is also very clear about the right to freedom of religion. It outlines that compulsion should not be used in relation to religion and makes clear that no one is obliged to adopt Islam. Once someone has decided to follow Islam, however, he or she should not be compelled to follow anyone else's beliefs. The death penalty for apostasy is therefore argued by some to be against the teachings of the Koran.[735]

While devolution may be a preferred option in some instances, in culturally and religiously heterogeneous societies some mixture of integration and functional autonomy may be preferable. For example, when members of a cultural group are not concentrated in a specific geographic location in a country, the state may grant them separate treatment with regard to some facets of their collective life, such as the separate management of places of worship. The education system, which ought to foster national consciousness as well as the preservation of collective identities, may be the cause of tension regarding the use of language. Where members of a cultural group are not territorially dispersed, territorial separation may be sought. However, this solution is unlikely to be successful if it occurs on the basis of dominant separation, where the aim is to keep groups separated on the basis of a hierarchical ranking.[736]

The Rule of Law
United Nations agencies are increasingly directing resources to the reform of legal and judicial institutions. However, as Sachiko Morita and Durwood Zaelke note, these have tended to be devoted largely to the creation of new laws and institutions rather than building capacity to enforce existing laws, which means that non-compliance continues to pose a problem and can generate a general lack of respect for the

---

[733] Office of the High Commissioner of Human Rights, *op. cit.*, note 470.
[734] Eide, *op. cit.*, note 511, p. 59.
[735] N.A. Shah, "Freedom of Religion: Koranic and Human Rights Perspectives," *Asia-Pacific Journal on Human Rights and Law*, Vol. 6, Nos. 1 & 2, 2005, pp. 71, 74.
[736] Eide, *op. cit.*, note 511, pp. 55-56.

rule of law. Many developing countries and countries in transition have weak legal and judicial systems.[737] In most Latin American countries, for example, the rule of law is imperfect.[738]

Government Legitimacy, Accountability and Transparency
Governments may have to exist alongside other institutions that are perceived to be legitimate, such as religious or traditional authority structures. In sub-Saharan Africa in some instances the latter are active in the distribution of land, and there is civil law at the local level.[739] Political power in Central Asia is highly personalised and political parties play only a minimal role. Legitimate behaviour or political legitimacy may be perceived as stemming less from the result of democratic procedures than traditional and personal forms of authority. In such a context, formal elections may either enhance or decrease political legitimacy.[740] In many African countries people feel that they do not have effective means to hold their governments to account.[741] Lack of information, which may be compounded by an absence of a free and independent media, is also a hindrance to accountability and transparency.

Mitigating the Distorting Role of Money in Politics
Modern democracies attempt to limit the distorting and corrupting influence of finance in politics through the enactment of laws and the creation of regulatory mechanisms. Caps on campaign financing, bans on particular kinds of contributions and the use of public subsidies have, for example, been instituted in some countries. However, while legislation aimed at regulating the role of money in election campaigns is often in place, it is often either not rigorously enforced or not rigorous enough. One way in which the distorting role of money in election campaigns may be minimised is through publicly financing them.

Yet, in order for these mechanisms to be effective, transparency is needed across a number of interrelated levels of activity. Transparency International suggests that accountability is first re-

---

[737] Morito and Zaelke, *op. cit.*, note 721, p. 15.
[738] German Development Institute, Briefing Paper No. 1, *op. cit.*, note 731, p. 1.
[739] German Development Institute, Briefing Paper No. 3, *op. cit.*, note 732, p. 2.
[740] *Ibid.*, p. 2.
[741] *Ibid.*

quired within political parties. This includes employing correct methods of accounting and keeping party members well informed. Second, it suggests that political parties and candidates as well as donors and those providing services should be held accountable to the state through the reporting of political finance transactions. Finally, political candidates and parties should be accountable to the public through the disclosure of financial contributions to campaigns.[742]

Corruption
Corruption affects many aspects of society, including income levels, education, security, and so on. We may think of corruption as the misuse of public office for the purpose of private gain, in which the private sector is, of course, deeply implicated. Corruption is a challenge to good and effective governance because it compromises economic justice and may result in a diminution of human dignity. One difficulty in addressing corruption is that is may be intertwined with cultural norms and practices. Curbing corruption depends on checks and balances involving the judiciary, the media, NGOs, free electoral processes, police forces and public opinion.[743]

Corruption in the judicial system endangers protection of the civil liberties of citizens as well as the guarantee of a fair trial in an independent court of law. When judiciaries are corrupt, the right to equal treatment under the law is compromised. In many countries, there are procedures in place to ensure transparency in the judicial system and accountability of the police and of judges. However, in some countries corruption of the judicial system is endemic, because of the vulnerability of judges to negative influence and the low risk of being caught and punished.[744]

Mary Noel Pepys identifies several factors that make corruption more likely. First, the separation of powers may not be functioning as it should. Even when a separation between the executive, the legislative branch and the judiciary is guaranteed by the constitution, judiciaries may be subject to undue influence by the executive or the legislative assembly. This may be the case in countries where the rule

---

[742] Al-Rodhan and Watanabe, *A Proposal for* Inclusive *Peace and Security*, *op. cit.*, note 1, pp. 64-65; Transparency International, *op. cit.*, note 728, p. 2.
[743] M. Buckley, "Anti-Corruption Initiatives and Human Rights," in Sano and Alfredsson, With the Collaboration of R. Clapp, *op. cit.*, note 511, pp. 174-176.
[744] Pepys, *op. cit.*, note 720, p. 3.

of law has historically lacked robustness. Where the judiciary is weak, judges may feel greater pressure to acquiesce to politically connected individuals. Judges who have attempted to retain their independence and impartiality have been known to receive death threats. Vilification by the media may also cause some judges to apply the law incorrectly when deciding the outcome of a case. In some instances, judges fearful of public retribution may alter the verdict. In some instances, the executive branch has the power to select, appoint and promote judges. Where the procedures for doing so are not transparent, the independence of judges is in danger.[745]

Second, there may be a higher social tolerance for corruption in some contexts than in others. This may be the case in contexts where interactions are shaped less by formal legal rules than by familial codes of conduct or local customs. In some countries, bribery may be perceived as necessary in order to obtain access to legal services. In countries where judicial processes are particularly slow, bribery may buy quicker services. Third, when the salaries of court staff and judges are particularly low, the likelihood of bribery becoming widespread is higher than in cases where members of the judiciary can support themselves and their families.[746]

Fourth, ethical behaviour may not always be rewarded in some judicial systems. Indeed, in some cases ethical behaviour may be punished rather than rewarded. The decisions of judges in lower courts of law may be overturned by those in higher courts, making the former appear incompetent. Ethical judges may also be punished by receiving unusually heavy caseloads, which may cause delays in treating cases and lead to a subsequent reprimand. Judges that vehemently retain their independence may be asked to retire early or be subject to false charges of misconduct. Where corruption is rife within a judicial system, judges may collude among themselves to favour decisions from which they will personally benefit. Moreover, when the procedures with which to monitor the behaviour of judges are unclear or in the process of change, this ambiguity may be exploited by judges and court staff. This may present a particular danger where court files are not computerised, and are therefore open to the abuse of individual discretion.[747]

---

[745] Ibid., p. 5.
[746] Ibid., pp. 4-5.
[747] Ibid., pp. 6-7.

5. The Way Forward

Improving governance requires adequate opportunities to participate in societal structures and political decision making through inclusive political and societal structures, reducing the role of money in politics and electoral processes, and improving access to the information required to hold governments to account.

Participation, Equality and Inclusiveness
Civil and political rights are essential if participation is to be ensured. Yet, even where these formal rights are present, women and members of minority groups must also be adequately represented within decision-making mechanisms. Given that the objectives of fostering national unity and group identities can lead to considerable tension within culturally and religiously heterogeneous societies, it is critical that the right balance is found. Territorial separation achieved through political devolution within a federal state can provide a solution to the tension between separateness and equality in cases where members of cultural groups are not territorially dispersed within a country. This solution, however, must be voluntary – no hierarchy can exist between groups, common resources must be shared equally and there can be no practices of exclusion or privilege in relation to treatment and interaction.[748]

    Members of minorities must have the means available to them to preserve their collective identity. This implies the right to organise as a group, to speak their own language, to maintain and reproduce their culture and, thus, to have some input into the education of new generations. Article 27 of the International Covenant on Civil and Political Rights, which is mentioned above, provides that ethnic, religious and linguistic minorities should not be denied the right to benefit from their own culture, to practice their own religion and to use their own language. Yet, these rights are formulated in a negative way. States must also ensure the conditions for members of minorities to preserve and reproduce their identities. Here, the 1992 UN Assembly Minority Declaration sets out a more proactive role for the state in this regard, calling on the state to protect ethnic, cultural, linguistic and

---

[748] Eide, *op. cit.*, note 511, p. 56.

religious minorities and to facilitate conditions conducive to the maintenance of their identities.[749]

The Rule of Law
Efforts to improve the rule of law must focus above all on training and capacity building.[750] Strengthening legal and judicial institutions takes time, however. Changes in practices and norms need to take place and clearly this requires a long-term commitment on the part of both governments and donors hoping to improve the rule of law in particular countries. Institutionalised interests that hinder changes in existing practices also need to be addressed.[751]

Government Legitimacy, Accountability and Transparency
Government accountability and legitimacy are dependent on adequate access to understandable and accurate information published by the government. A free and independent media also plays a critical role in improving transparency and holding governments to account through the provision of information to the public and by questioning government practices and performance. NGOs such as Transparency International are also critical to consciousness raising and improving standards in countries. Accountability in election administration is central to ensuring government legitimacy, and may be ensured through, for instance, independent administrators as well as the establishment of a mechanism for checks involving participant parties.[752]

Transparency is also critical in relation to corporate dealings as the 2008/2009 financial crisis demonstrates. In addition to ensuring that deals of various kinds are properly documented, corporate bodies need to be made more accountable through increased, although not stifling, regulation and transparency requirements. In rapidly developing markets, such as those in the financial sector, governments need to stay one step ahead of economic actors and innovations in their surveillance of developments and their regulatory mechanisms.

---

[749] *Ibid.*, p. 59.
[750] Morito and Zaelke, *op. cit.*, note 721, p. 15.
[751] *Ibid.*, p. 16.
[752] Suksi, *op. cit.*, note 725, p. 217.

Mitigating the Distorting Role of Money in Politics

The reform of political financing is under debate in a number of countries, involving efforts to place limits on contributions to and spending by political parties, increase transparency and encourage grassroots contributions rather than corporate contributions. New laws have been introduced in France, the US and India. Aspects of these laws concern spending limits, contribution limits, disclosure requirements, bans on particular types of donation, direct and indirect subsidies for political broadcasting and subsidies for parties and their candidates.[753] Transparency International argues that public, civil society and media oversight can help to complement laws and formal regulatory mechanisms.

Almost all countries have placed a ban on contributions to political parties and candidates from public institutions in an effort to prevent the misuse of public resources. Yet, abuse of state finances for election campaigning is still a problem in some countries. As a means of dealing with this problem some countries put a limit on public spending during election campaigns. Many countries have also established rules related to public procurement, the employment of government employees and government publicity during election periods as well as general rules on fiscal responsibility. Efforts have also been made to limit the level of private donations to political parties or candidates. Methods to control secret contributions from corporations or private individuals include bans on these forms of financing and caps on campaign expenditure. However, despite such measures private finance continues to play a significant role in political funding, due either to lack of restraints or lax oversight.[754]

Public funding for election campaigns exists in some countries in an attempt to limit the influence of private donors on election processes. It is also employed as a means of strengthening political parties. According to Transparency International, most EU member states provide public support for their respective political parties. Israel and Mexico publicly fund up to 80 percent of the election expenses of political parties.[755]

Regulating the role of the media in campaigns has in some instances been central to reforms aimed at promoting fair competition between political parties or candidates as well as keeping the public

---

[753] UNDP, *op. cit.*, note 680, p. 71.
[754] Transparency International, *op. cit.*, note 728, p. 3.
[755] *Ibid.*

informed. In some cases, limits on spending on campaign advertisements have been set. This is a means of reducing the pressure on political parties or candidates to find sources of funding and, as a result, become subject to undue influence. Equal and free airtime and, in some cases, banning paid publicity in the media are also used as means of facilitating fair competition. The type of advertisements permitted during electoral campaigns can also be delimited.[756]

The distorting role of finance in election campaigns may also be controlled by establishing independent state agencies designed to monitor whether political finance rules are being followed. These agencies require adequate financial resources and legal powers to investigate and impose sanctions where necessary. In order to be effective they also require adequate resources to facilitate technical preparation. Their independence is also essential. In many countries, such agencies remain under the control of the president or the political party in office.[757]

Citizens and NGOs also have an important role to play in monitoring and limiting the role of money in politics. Some organisations are established specifically to monitor elections, while others monitor advertising expenses. Citizens need to be sufficiently empowered to hold the holders of elected offices accountable for the use of public resources as a means of controlling abuse of state finances. As with other forms of oversight, citizens need to have access to the necessary information with which to monitor campaign contributions and state expenditure. Where public subsidies exist, citizens also require access to information on any independently raised funds.[758]

Anti-Corruption
During the 1990s, a concerted international effort to combat corruption got under way, with organisations such as Transparency International taking a lead role. This effort took the form of anti-corruption campaigns, consciousness raising, lobbying, the establishment of new laws and the promotion of best practices. Corruption is now a recognised concern of many leading institutions, such as the World Bank, the Organisation for Economic Co-operation and Development (OECD) and other development donors, including governments.

---
[756] *Ibid.*, pp 3-4.
[757] *Ibid.*, p. 4.
[758] *Ibid.*, p. 5.

However, as Marella Buckley points out, enduring anti-corruption control depends on high levels of public integrity. Basic civil and political rights are critical to controlling corruption. Free and fair elections; an impartial judiciary, police service and military; NGOs and an independent media help to provide systems of checks and balances that can foster public integrity and reduce corruption.

Laws on freedom of information are extremely important in advancing anti-corruption efforts. It is important that people have the fullest information possible about government contracting, procurement procedures and funding. Access to the most complete information possible is in the interest not only of private citizens, but also of the public sector, journalists, professionals and social workers. Yet, for access to information as a legal right to help to reduce corruption, there must also be other rights, such as freedom of expression and freedom of assembly.[759]

Ensuring an independent judiciary is also critical. Measures to mitigate judicial corruption should take account of the national and local factors that contribute to corruption, and ought to form part of an overall reform initiative. Anti-corruption measures need to incorporate not only judges, but also the police, prosecutors, court staff and the agencies charged with enforcing court decisions. However, in general a number of measures may help to reduce corruption in the judiciary. First, the independence of the judiciary must be ensured. The administration and budget of the judiciary ought to be independent of both the executive and the legislature. The independence of the judiciary may be facilitated by judicial councils responsible for the appointment and promotion of judges. Ensuring that judiciaries have control over the judicial budget is also a way of insulating the judiciary from political considerations and undue influence. Corruption of judges may also be mitigated by encouraging ethical behaviour through the introduction of stringent, transparent and fair measures to punish unethical conduct. Professionalising the judicial career through tenuring judges may also serve to protect them against negative influence. Judges and court staff should also receive salaries that reflect their responsibilities and the cost of living in order to reduce the temptation to accept bribes in order to supplement inadequate salaries. A final way to guard against corruption in the judiciary is to ensure that the public has full

---

[759] Buckley, *op. cit.*, note 743, pp. 184-186, 189.

access to the applicability of the law and are therefore able to judge when the law is being improperly applied.[760]

Checks on abuses of executive power may also rely on judiciaries and legislatures having adequate equipment, trained staff and access to information. Independent entities, such as ombudsmen, electoral committees and human rights committees, should also be strengthened. Electoral committees can play a significant role in ensuring free and fair elections.[761]

Octagon 4 summarises the minimum criteria for good national governance.

---

[760] Pepys, *op. cit.*, note 720, p. 8.
[761] UNDP, *op. cit.*, note 680, p. 73.

268 NAYEF R.F. AL-RODHAN

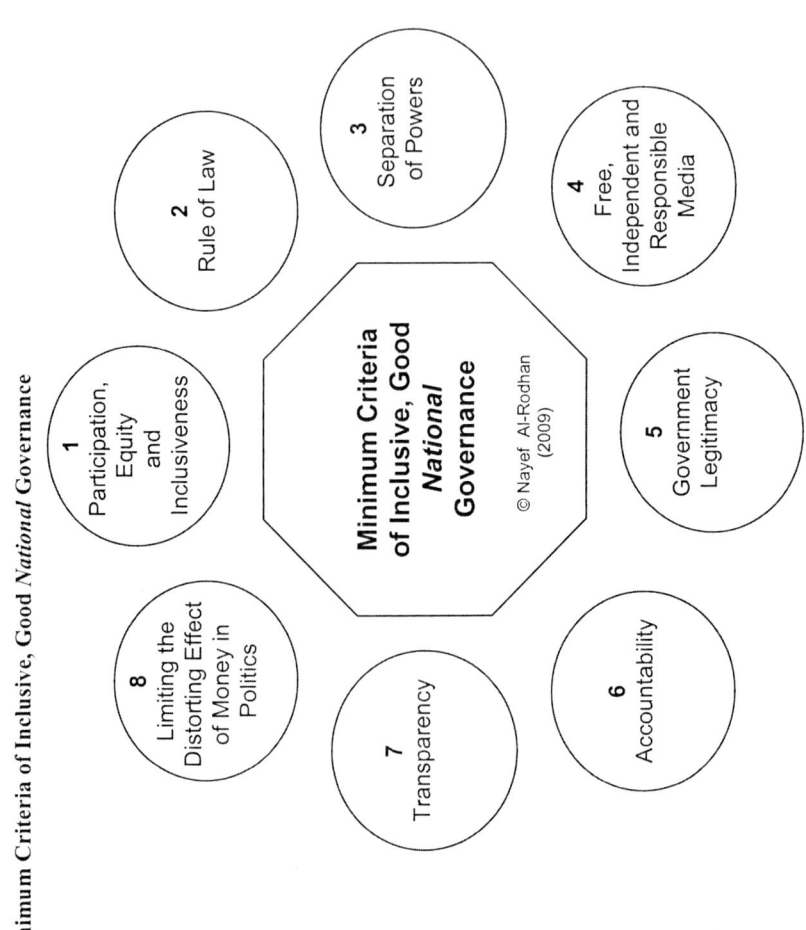

Octagon 4: Minimum Criteria of Inclusive, Good *National* Governance

6. Conclusion

Efforts to improve governance standards have taken a number of forms, some of which are susceptible to accusations of Western bias and hegemonic machinations. It is therefore important that some minimum criteria for inclusive and effective national governance can be agreed as essential means of advancing shared fundamental values. As such, I have suggested that there is a need to identify which aspects of good governance have the widest application. Ultimately, this will depend on increased dialogue with regard to what good governance is, despite the fact that this may be articulated differently in local contexts. In my view, participation, equality and inclusiveness, the rule of law, the separation of powers, government legitimacy, accountability and transparency, a free and independent media, and measures to limit the distorting effect of money in politics and electoral systems are criteria by which human dignity can be ensured and promoted, and a broad consensus achieved. However, the precise institutional forms through which they are implemented and mediated may differ, depending on specific histories and cultures.

CHAPTER 10

WHAT IS NEEDED FOR GOOD GLOBAL *GOVERNANCE?*
MINIMUM CRITERIA OF INCLUSIVE, EFFECTIVE AND
GOOD *GLOBAL* GOVERNANCE

Global governance is not a novel phenomenon, but its scope is thought to be increasing.[762] Given that good national governance cannot be fully achieved without taking into account the global context in which the state exists, good *global* governance also forms a vital dimension of bringing about a sustainable history. James N. Rosenau defines governance "[at] a very abstract level as spheres of authority at all levels of human activity – from the household to the demanding public to the international organization – that amount to systems of control."[763] A broad definition of governance is required in a highly interdependent and interconnected world. Spheres of authority do not exist only in relation to formal institutions at the national, regional and global levels. While multilateral institutions and national governments are still central to governance in today's world, other actors that frame objectives, make demands and influence policymaking are also central to governance.[764] Simultaneous globalising and localising processes have contributed to a shift in the location of spheres of authority across different sectors and levels. This has an effect on the governance mechanisms of sovereign states. While a great deal of governance continues to be carried out through traditional state mechanisms, states are increasingly engaging in more extensive as well as narrower governance mechanisms.[765] Global governance comprises the UN system, public and private legal institutions, and transnational regimes

---

[762] B.K. Woodward, "Global Civil Society and International Law in Global Governance: Some Contemporary Issues," *International Community Law Review*, Vol. 8, Nos. 2 & 3, 2006, p. 254.
[763] J.N. Rosenau, *Along the Domestic-Foreign Frontier: Exploring Governance in a Turbulent World* (Cambridge: Cambridge University Press, 1997), p. 145.
[764] *Ibid.*
[765] *Ibid.*, p. 154.

and networks.[766] A focus on global governance helps us to understand how power operates and the organising principles of global governance.[767] Yet, a great deal of interest in global governance also stems from concerns about how to make it more representative and inclusive, and more capable of enhancing global justice.

This chapter outlines the existing framework of global governance and discusses the major challenges it faces. I then suggest how more effective global governance may be achieved. At the most basic level, global governance mechanisms need to be more representative, more transparent and more accountable. Private interests and networks that also play a governance role need to be more transparent and accountable as well as more responsive. This implies a need to empower civil society representatives in order to make both public and private forms of governance accountable, and to raise issues that the market alone cannot handle.

1. The Existing Global Governance Framework

An exhaustive description of the global governance mechanisms and associated actors would be impossible, given that many are private and difficult to identify. Nevertheless, it is possible provide an overview of the main public governance mechanisms that together constitute an important dimension of global governance. The most visible aspects of global governance are thus represented by the multilateral system. Multilateralism may be defined in narrow terms as interaction among three or more states. In broader terms, multilateralism has been defined as coordination among three or more countries regulated by a particular set of principles.[768] The latter wider definition highlights the normative dimension of multilateralism. This is important since multilateralism facilitates the creation not only of formalised, legal rules but also of informal norms that help to shape the behaviour of states.[769]

---

[766] Woodward, *op. cit.*, note 762, p. 247.
[767] M. Hewson and T. Sinclair, *Approaches to Global Governance Theory* (Albany: State University of New York Press, 1999), p. 3.
[768] J.G. Ruggie, "Multilateralism: The Anatomy of An Institution," in P.R. Viotti and M.V. Kauppi (eds.) *International Relations Theory: Realism, Pluralism, Globalism, and Beyond*, Third Edition (Boston: Allyn and Bacon, 1999), p. 333.
[769] Al-Rodhan and Watanabe, *A Proposal for* Inclusive *Peace and Security*, *op. cit.*, note 1, p. 103.

While multilateralism has a long history dating back as far as Ancient Greece, the multilateral system with which we are concerned today is that of the post-Second World War period. This is most readily associated with the UN, which has been vital in establishing rules that help to regulate relations between states. It has also played a central role in diffusing the norms of sovereignty. The Bretton Woods institutions also form a central part of post-war multilateralism.[770]

The most transparent of global governance mechanisms is the UN system, its agencies, affiliated bodies, programmes and funds.[771] The UN provides a global forum in which states can discuss and develop common approaches to challenges. The UN Charter also provides the basis for international law and plays a central role in establishing international norms and standards.[772] Its funds, programmes, offices and departments address all dimensions of peace, security and human well-being. The principal Programmes and Funds include the UN Capital Development Fund (UNCDF), the UN Children's Fund (UNICEF), the UN Conference on Trade and Development (UNCTAD), the UN Development Fund for Women (UNIFEM), the UN Development Programme (UNDP), the UN International Drug Control Programme (UNDCP), the UN Environment Programme (UNEP), the UN High Commissioner for Refugees (UNHCR), the UN Human Settlements Programme (UN-HABITAT), the UN Population Fund (UNFPA), the UN Relief and Works Agency for Palestinian Refugees in the Near East (UNWRA), the UN Volunteers (UNV) and the World Food Programme (WFP).[773] Subsidiary bodies include the UN Peacebuilding Commission, the Sanctions Committee, the Counterterrorism Committee (CTC), and the International Criminal Tribunal for the Former Yugoslavia (ICTY), among others.[774] Specialised agencies created by the UN include the International Labour Organization (ILO), the IMF, the World Bank, the United Nations Scientific, Educational and Cultural Organization (UNESCO), the World Health Organization and the WTO.[775]

---

[770] *Ibid.*, pp. 103-104.
[771] Woodward, *op. cit.*, note 762, pp. 156-257.
[772] Al-Rodhan, Finaud, Palazzolo, Watanabe, Nazaruk and Rurarz-Huygens, *Multilateralism and Transnational Security*, *op. cit.*, note 527, p. 38.
[773] *Ibid.*, pp. 41-46.
[774] *Ibid.*, pp. 48-49.
[775] *Ibid.*, pp. 59-65.

Regional concerns have also prompted states to seek cooperation, and this has become the basis for new authority structures.[776] A number of regional arrangements therefore contribute to global governance. In Europe, the post-Second World War period saw the establishment of a number of multilateral institutions aimed at contributing to many facets of security and stability. The "security architecture" in the region comprised the Western European Union (WEU), the Council of Europe (CoE), the EU, NATO and the Organization for Security and Co-operation in Europe (OSCE).[777] Multilateralism in the context of the EU in particular profoundly shapes relations between member states, altering the very nature of their sovereignty.[778]

Recent decades have also witnessed increased cooperative efforts in the Americas and the establishment of regional arrangements aimed at the promotion of peace, prosperity, equality, justice, democracy and environmental protection. The two main institutions are the Organization of American States (OAS) and the Southern Common Market (Mercosur). The former is primarily committed to the promotion and defence of democracy, human rights, justice and peace. The OAS has made an important contribution to monitoring elections and strengthening a democratic culture in the region. It also serves as a forum for addressing common regional concerns, such as sustained growth, the reduction of poverty and combating crime. It is in the process of developing its disaster response capacities. Agreements on common external tariffs and the establishment of a customs union in the context of Mecosur have facilitated regional integration.[779]

The African continent remains war-torn and much of its population suffers from extreme poverty, leading to ill-health and pandemics. A number of regional and sub-regional arrangements exist. The two major organisations that play a stabilising role in the region are the African Union (AU) and the Economic Community of West African States (ECOWAS), the aims of which are to promote cooperation and economic integration. The AU has become the major forum for advancing regional integration and the promotion of peace, democracy

---

[776] Rosenau, *op. cit.*, note 763, p. 162.
[777] Al-Rodhan, Finaud, Palazzolo, Watanabe, Nazaruk and Rurarz-Huygens, *Multilateralism and Transnational Security*, *op. cit.*, note 527, pp. 66-97.
[778] Al-Rodhan and Watanabe, *A Proposal for* Inclusive *Peace and Security*, *op. cit.*, note 1, p. 105.
[779] Al-Rodhan, Finaud, Palazzolo, Watanabe, Nazaruk and Rurarz-Huygens, *Multilateralism and Transnational Security*, *op. cit.*, note 527, pp. 98-103.

and development, and addressing economic, social and political concerns.[780] In addition to efforts to promote good governance, human rights and democracy, the AU has also expanded its activities in the form of the New Partnership for Africa's Development (NEPAD), a Comprehensive African Agricultural Development Plan, as well as a number of infrastructural projects. Mechanisms to encourage peer review and other soft law mechanisms have helped progress in these areas.[781] The AU has also contributed significantly to the promotion of peace and security. In relation to the Burundian peace process (in conjunction with ECOWAS) it facilitated stabilisation and national reconciliation until the UN took over in 2004. It also successfully engaged in the conflict in Côte d'Ivoire, along with the UN and ECOWAS, and has recently engaged in the Darfur crisis, demonstrating its capacity for collective action. The AU is in the process of developing a rapid deployment capability in the form of an African Standby Force (ASF). ECOWAS has contributed to increased economic integration, and has contributed to regional peace and stability through the development of a legal framework and declared moratorium on the import, export and manufacturing of light weapons, and, for instance, contributions to peace support operations in Liberia and Sierra Leone.[782]

In the Middle East, a number of efforts have been made to encourage regional integration through the establishment of multilateral institutions and arrangements. The region is nevertheless less integrated with the outside world in terms of trade and capital flows, and less integration has taken place between the states of the region than elsewhere. This situation is linked to the Arab-Israeli conflict, the fragility of regional institutions and the prevalence of narrowly defined national interests. The most robust regional organisations are the Gulf Cooperation Council (GCC), the League of Arab States (LAS, formerly the Arab League) and the Organisation of the Islamic Con-

---

[780] "African Union in a Nutshell," African Union, http://www.africa-union.org/root/au/AboutAu/au_in_a_nutshell_en.htm.
[781] *Ibid.*; African Leadership Forum, "Origins of the Conference on Stability, Security, Development and Cooperation," http://www.africaleadership.org/CSSDCA.htm.
[782] Economic Community of West African States, *Silver Jubilee Anniversary: Achievements & Prospects* (Abuja, 2000), Ch. 1, http://www.sec.ecowas.int/sitecedeao/english/publicat-2.htm; T. Murithi, "The African Union's Evolving Role in Peace Operations: The African Union Mission in Burundi, the African Union Mission in Sudan and the African Union Mission in Somalia," *African Security Review*, Vol. 17, No. 1, 2008, pp. 74-76.

ference (OIC). The GCC has contributed in particular to progress in the areas of foreign policy coordination, security cooperation, the development of crisis management capabilities, cooperation in the areas of law enforcement and the creation of a free trade area and a customs union. The LAS has contributed to conflict resolution and management among its member states. The LAS has also been active in the economic, social and cultural domains. The Organisation of the Islamic Conference was established to foster unity and solidarity between its member states in all areas.[783]

Multilateralism has also gained momentum in Asia in recent decades. The main regional organisations are the Association of Southeast Asian Nations (ASEAN), the Shanghai Cooperation Organisation (SCO) and the South Asian Association for Regional Cooperation (SAARC). The creation of ASEAN has helped to reduce tensions between its members. Regional peace and stability are sought through political and security dialogue. ASEAN has played a mediation role in the Cambodian civil war,[784] and intensified dialogue with the countries of the Asia Pacific region, which has resulted in the creation of the ASEAN Regional Forum (ARF). ASEAN has also contributed to regional economic integration with the adoption of the ASEAN Free Trade Area (AFTA) and the construction of trans-ASEAN transport and energy networks. ASEAN member states are also collectively undertaking efforts to prevent the spread of diseases and pandemics, most notably in relation to HIV/AIDS and Avian Influenza. The Shanghai Cooperation Organisation (formerly the Shanghai Five) was originally set up to deal with border issues and instability in Afghanistan. It now addresses an array of economic, political, cultural, military, energy and environmental issues. Its most pressing challenge is in the area of counterterrorism. It has developed institutional bodies and a legal framework with which to deal with this problem on a region-wide basis. SAARC emerged in the 1980s in order to enhance the welfare of the people of the region. It has advanced regional economic integration through the Agreement on the SAARC Preferential Trading Arrangement (SAPTA) and the Agree-

---

[783] Al-Rodhan, Finaud, Palazzolo, Watanabe, Nazaruk and Rurarz-Huygens, *Multilateralism and Transnational Security*, op. cit., note 527, pp. 109-116.
[784] United States Institute for Peace, "Agreement on a Comprehensive Political Settlement of the Cambodia Conflict," 23 October 1991, http:// www.usip.org/library/ pa/cambodia/agree_comppol_10231991_toc.html.

ment on the South Asian Free Trade Area (SAFTA). Significantly, SAARC has adopted a Social Charter to address social concerns. It has also developed an open and distance learning forum. Other important developments include the conventions on the Suppression of Terrorism, Narcotic Drugs and Psychotropic Substances, Trafficking of Women and Children and on Child Welfare in South Asia as well as the Agreement on a Food Security Reserve.[785]

These forums are supplemented by a number of sub-regional organisations, such as the Economic Cooperation Organization (ECO), and the Pacific Islands Forum Secretariat (PIFS).[786]

Transnational institutions and networks also contribute to global governance. These include, for example, the Basel Committee on Banking Supervision, the Group of 8 (G8), the Paris Club and the OECD. Some have legal status while others do not. The G8, for example, is a network of heads of state and ministers of finance, which makes key decisions on how to respond to financial crises, debt relief and so on. The G20 is also a network established to help avert future crises. It is comprised of the finance ministers of 20 developed and developing countries. Organisations such as the Trilateral Commission have also proliferated in the private sector, including bond-rating agencies and private sector NGOs. Some regulatory mechanisms exist for multinational enterprises (MNEs), such as the UN Global Pact, the OECD Guidelines for Multinational Enterprises and the International Labour Organization's Tripartite Declaration of Principles Concerning Multilateral Enterprises and Social Policy. Some international conferences and ad hoc forums may become formal legal processes if convened through International Governmental Organizations (IGOs), such as UN summits.[787]

The political authority that multilateral institutions embody is that of states, but some do not adequately represent the concerns of the greatest part of their populations. Thus, in addition to the formal governance mechanisms and powerful financial and commercial interest groups, members of global civil society, such as NGOs, are now actively involved in the process of global governance as well as social

---

[785] Al-Rodhan, Finaud, Palazzolo, Watanabe, Nazaruk and Rurarz-Huygens, *Multilateralism and Transnational Security*, *op. cit.*, note 527, p. 125.
[786] *Ibid.*
[787] Woodward, *op. cit.*, note 762, pp. 262-263.

movements of all types.[788] NGOs are traditionally thought of as non-profit private organisations. Among the best known of the NGOs are the World Alliance of YMCAs, the Carnegie Endowment for International Peace, the International Federation of Trade Unions and the International Committee of the Red Cross (ICRC). In the 1990s, NGOs played a role in advancing the development of international conventions as well as soft law such as Agenda 21. The UN embraced the idea of drawing on their expertise in the early 1990s, and the participation of NGOs in UN activities prompted a review of the UN's relations with NGOs and civil society in 1993. A number of NGOs now have observer status in the UN. NGOs have also become involved in influencing international judicial proceedings, and they are considered an important source of information in the area of international criminal justice. The lack of formal regulatory mechanisms has meant that global civil society actors have sometimes contributed to law-making processes, and to establishing best practices and the informal rules that have developed as a result of soft law. A substantial NGO campaign helped to bring about the 1997 Landmines Treaty (Ottawa Convention).[789] The WTO has also made a concerted effort to engage with NGOs.

Social movements are also sometimes perceived as nascent control mechanisms that have no defined membership or authority structures: they exclude nobody and include all those who wish to be involved; they are organised around an issue or set of issues; and they are transnational and fill a governance gap, as far as those involved are concerned.[790]

While many actors have been able to accommodate shifts in the loci of spheres of authority, other spheres of authority are contested. For example, some members of ethnic minorities and of different sub-groups seek to leave their authority sphere. The attempt by Greenpeace to prevent France from carrying out a nuclear test in the South Pacific is also illustrative of this point. The subsequent protests and boycotts of French products resulted in the French government reducing the number of tests from eight to six. Actors engaged in organised crime have also established contested spheres of authority.[791]

---

[788] Ibid., p. 265.
[789] Ibid., pp. 267, 308, 313-314, 328-331.
[790] Rosenau, op. cit., note 763, p. 166.
[791] Ibid., p. 169.

For example, terrorists, arms traffickers, money launderers, drug traffickers, and traffickers in women and children also function through global networks.[792]

2. Problems of Global Governance

Globalisation is an asymmetrical, unequal and incomplete process. It is asymmetrical in that it affects different areas of life in different ways. It is unequal because it affects different countries differently. While the countries in highly industrialised areas are at the centre of globalising trends, others, such as those in sub-Saharan Africa, remain on the periphery of these trends. It is incomplete in so far as it is ongoing. For some, globalisation is an expression of social and economic modernisation, whereas for others it is a danger to social cohesion and planetary governance. Therefore, globalisation is a process that encompasses both opportunities and threats.[793] The opening up of economies, for example, may provide the means for increased dynamism. However, it also brings with it instability due to increased vulnerability to international speculation and market contagion. Moreover, globalising forces reduce the capacity of the state to regulate the national economy through domestic public policy. External pressures also oblige national governments to justify interventions in the economy. Thus, while globalisation may increase expectations of growth and prosperity, it also reduces public social spending – suggesting increased inequality. The more negative aspects of globalisation need to be mitigated by public policies.[794]

Many problems require multilateral action and multilateral institutions provide a framework for dialogue and collective and coordinated action. This is necessary given the transnational nature of many concerns – from economic and financial stability to health and the environment. In order for successful coordination to occur multilateral institutions need to be able to effectively facilitate global dialogue and

---

[792] A. Slaughter, *A New World Order* (Princeton, N.J.: Princeton University Press, 2004), p. 1.
[793] J.A. Alonso, "Globalisation, Civil Society, and the Multilateral System," *Development in Practice*, Vol. 10, Nos. 3 & 4, 2000, p. 349.
[794] *Ibid.*, p. 350.

facilitate joint management of global concerns. This implies addressing the problems of global governance.[795]

The multilateral system has a role to play in the management of international public goods. Political and financial stability, environmental and ecological policies and basic public health cannot be left to the market and require organisational structures to ensure individual contributions. Moreover, problems that may have previously been considered local now have transnational and/or global consequences. Environmental degradation, the pressure exerted on scarce resources by population growth, the spread of disease, migration and humanitarian crises, among other concerns, can be mentioned in this regard.[796]

Effective multilateralism may be thought of as a system of global governance which ensures that citizens have access to fundamental public goods provided domestically by states. Such goods include physical security and stability, an enforceable legal order, an open and inclusive economic order and ensuring well-being, which extends to access to health care, education and a clean environment, for example.[797]

Representation
One of the challenges for all multilateral institutions in an era of globalisation is whether organisations with a small number of dominant member states can effectively respond to global problems that concern the broader global community.[798] This issue is one of the main factors motivating efforts to reform the multilateral system. The international multilateral system is skewed in favour the victorious great powers of the post-Second World War period.[799] While a number of international and regional organisations have been established after the creation of the UN and the Bretton Woods institutions, much remains the same in terms of the basic structure of the institutions at the heart of the public

---

[795] *Ibid.*, p. 352.
[796] *Ibid.*, pp. 353-354.
[797] S. Biscop and V. Arnould, "Global Public Goods: An Integrative Agenda for EU External Action," in B.E. Espen (ed.) "'Effective Multilateralism': Europe, Regional Security and a Revitalized UN," Global Europe Report 1, The Foreign Policy Centre, 2004, http://fpc.org.uk/fsblob/350.pdf, pp. 22-23.
[798] Al-Rodhan, Finaud, Palazzolo, Watanabe, Nazaruk and Rurarz-Huygens, *Multilateralism and Transnational Security, op. cit.*, note 527, p. 310.
[799] Alonso, *op. cit.*, note 793, p. 355.

dimension of global governance. The UN, the IMF, the World Bank and the G8 are all organisations that are unrepresentative, are not as effective as they might be and have legitimacy problems.[800] Developing countries had no part in their design and were integrated into them on a subordinate basis.[801]

Greater inclusion and coordination are necessary in order to meet many of today's global challenges.[802] Effective multilateralism implies the need to ensure that multilateral institutions are representative, rather than being dominated by the will of the few. The lack of representation of developing countries in particular leads to the view that multilateral institutions are the instruments of powerful states, which leads developing countries to prefer participation within regional forums. This is reflected in the decision-making structures of major multilateral institutions, such as the UNSC, the IMF and the World Bank.[803] Reform of the core multinational institutions needs to focus on making them more representative. This means giving an adequate role to the major countries and giving smaller countries an effective voice.[804]

The UN was designed by the US, the UK, Russia and China at the Dumbarton Oaks conference of 1944. Its charter is based on that of the League of Nations. While core states aimed to create something more robust than the League, they nevertheless sought to protect what they perceived to be their vital interests through the UN's institutional design. This was provided by giving the great powers of the time the right of veto as the permanent members of the UNSC. The five powers that received permanent seats on the UNSC (the P5) were the four countries that met at Dumbarton Oaks and France.[805]

The right to veto has not radically changed since 1945 but the political dynamics in the UNSC have changed to reflect changes in the broader environment. The Russian Federation is weaker than the Soviet Union, the UK and France have become less prominent, and the

---

[800] C.I. Bradford, Jr. and J.F. Linn, "Reform of Global Governance: Priorities for Action," *Brookings Institution Policy Brief*, No. 163, p. 1.
[801] Alonso, *op. cit.*, note 793, p. 355.
[802] *Ibid.*, p. 357.
[803] Al-Rodhan, Finaud, Palazzolo, Watanabe, Nazaruk and Rurarz-Huygens, *Multilateralism and Transnational Security*, *op. cit.*, note 527, p. 313.
[804] Bradford and Linn, *op. cit.*, note 800, p. 3.
[805] Al-Rodhan and Watanabe, *A Proposal for* Inclusive *Peace and Security*, *op. cit.*, note 1, p. 108.

US has become pre-eminent. Other members of the UNSC are now concerned with constraining the US. Increasing pressure is coming from Japan and Germany to become permanent members in order to reflect their more active global roles. Several developing countries, notably India and Brazil, are also pushing for permanent membership.

The Open-ended Working Group on the Question of Equitable Representation and Increase in the Membership in the Security Council and Other Matters Related to the Security Council was established in 2003. The expansion of UNSC membership and the extension of veto powers, however, cannot be easily resolved. Two possible options for making the UNSC more representative were suggested by the then UN Secretary-General Kofi Annan in the 2005 report *In Larger Freedom: Towards Development, Security and Human Rights for All*.[806] Plan A envisaged the creation of six new permanent member seats, without veto rights, plus three non-permanent members elected for two-year terms. In Plan B, the creation of eight new Security Council members was proposed, with four-year terms that would be subject to renewal. In addition, one two-year non-permanent member seat would be established. These plans, however, floundered just before the World Summit in 2005, when the US suggested its own proposals for reform that differed from those suggested in the report. The document resulting from the summit contained a less ambitious reform agenda, the outcome of which is still unclear.[807]

The veto system should be reformed to become a majority veto system. The current P5 should keep their veto rights. However, Germany and Japan should also be given the right of veto. Regional veto rights should also be instituted, which may be invoked when fundamental interests are at stake. These veto rights would be subject to unanimity among the member states of the region concerned as well as a majority of the permanent members of the UNSC.[808] The *2005 World Summit Outcome Document*[809] is the basis for continued efforts at reform.

---

[806] *In Larger Freedom: Towards Development, Security and Human Rights for All*, Report of the Secretary-General, 21 March 2005, A/59/2005.
[807] Global Policy Forum, "UN Reform," http://www.global policy.org.
[808] Al-Rodhan and Watanabe, *A Proposal for Inclusive Peace and Security*, op. cit., note 1, p. 110.
[809] United Nations, "2005 World Summit Outcome," 24 October 2005, http://www.un.org/summit2005/ documents.html.

One important factor to remember when discussing reform of the UN is the relationship between the UN and the US. The Bush administration claimed that the US government is the largest single financial contributor to the UN. It has also been a strong proponent of UN reform in recent decades. Moreover, the US has advanced the argument that collective action and collective security do not necessarily require multilateralism.[810] The US preference for forming coalitions of the willing demonstrates its ongoing reticence about being bound by multilateral institutions.

The IMF was established to support a system of fixed exchange rates for currencies, and the WTO's predecessor, GATT, was established to promote trade liberalisation and commerce.[811] The IMF suffers from a lack of legitimacy resulting from the distribution of ownership shares and votes, too few of which belong to the rapidly growing Asian countries; a limited leadership selection process; and an unstable way of financing its activities. Some progress was made in 2006 towards rebalancing the distribution of shares and votes, with China, South Korea, Mexico and Turkey receiving small increases.[812] The two main objectives of negotiations were to create a formula that would give emerging economies more votes, and to prevent the share of the votes of developing countries from falling. However, according to a number of experts, the new formula is an insufficient basis on which to rebalance quotas and voting shares.[813]

The World Bank requires an unrestricted, merit-based procedure for choosing its president. Greater representation needs to be given to new recipient and donor countries, while maintaining a leading role for the significant donor countries. The relevance and effectiveness of the institution could also benefit from simpler lending instruments for middle-income countries, providing greater access to sub-national government entities, as well as providing loans in the local currencies of recipient countries.[814]

---

[810] Al-Rodhan, Finaud, Palazzolo, Watanabe, Nazaruk and Rurarz-Huygens, *Multilateralism and Transnational Security*, *op. cit.*, note 527, p. 316.
[811] Alonso, *op. cit.*, note 793, p. 355.
[812] Bradford and Linn, *op. cit.*, note 800, p. 4.
[813] J.F. Linn, "Experts Critique Proposal for International Monetary Fund Quota Reform," The Brookings Institute, 09 April 2008, http://www.brookings.edu/opinions/2008/0409_imf_linn.aspx.
[814] Bradford and Linn, *op. cit.*, note 800, p. 5.

The geopolitically altered post-Second World War reality requires a rebalancing among the "stakeholders of globalisation".[815] The WTO does, however, have a flexible structure. Decisions at the WTO are consensus-based and there is no Security Council or Board of Directors. Within the WTO, member states work in coalitions.[816] The Global South has managed to form the caucus G20 Plus. At the 2005 Hong Kong Ministerial Conference of the WTO, Argentina, Brazil, Egypt, India, Indonesia, Namibia, the Philippines, South Africa, Tunisia and Venezuela formed the so-called NAMA 11 and together called for an end to tariff peaks (i.e. high tariffs on sensitive products when general tariffs levels are low), high tariffs and increases in tariffs in the developed world.[817] Other influential coalitions of developing countries include the G33, the African Group, the ACP group and the LDC group. However, Director-General of the WTO Pascal Lamy recognises that there remains work to be done. The poorest countries need to be able to actively participate in deliberations. The WTO has in this respect established a "Geneva Week" during which non-Geneva resident members can engage in twice-yearly intensive updates on the status of negotiations as well as on other concerns.[818]

In the view of some, the G8 no longer serves as an effective forum for global consultation and coordination, particularly as the group's focus has shifted from coordination to broader economic and political issues. Moreover, economic and demographic changes mean that key states are not represented in the G8. Some therefore argue that the there is an urgent need for a more effective high-level global forum; and the momentum for reform of the G8 is growing. In 2007, under the German Presidency, the leaders of selected non-G8 countries were invited to parts of the G8 summit in an "outreach process". The President of France, Nicolas Sarkozy, and the Prime Minister of Russia, Vladimir Putin, have both called for an expansion of G8 membership. Calls were also made by the former prime minister of the UK, Tony Blair and the former Prime Minister of Canada, Paul Martin. Broadening the forum's membership will, however, require lead-

---

[815] P. Lamy, "60 Years of the Multilateral Trading System: What Have We Learnt?" *The Geneva Lectures on Global Economic Governance*, 6 February 2008, p. 5.
[816] *Ibid.*, pp. 5-6.
[817] E. Sidiropoulos, "Toward More Inclusive Informal Global Governance: A View from South Africa," *Global Governance*, Vol. 13, 2007, p. 316.
[818] Lamy, *op. cit.*, note 815, pp. 5-6.

ership from the US, and this is thought to be unlikely even though it is in the interests of the US to seek to address global challenges through broader partnerships.[819]

The seeming deadlocks on climate change, multilateral trade, disease control, UN reform, among others, have prompted proposals for a new architecture for global governance. Paul Martin launched the idea of a high-level group of 20 leaders – the so-called L20. Kofi Annan's High-level Panel on Threats, Challenges and Change and the International Task Force on Global Public Goods also called for similar apparatuses to be set up.[820] The L20 would be a summit that brings together 20 major states representing all regions of the world. According to Martin, it would be an effective mechanism for advancing the developments needed in global public policy. The L20 would, in his view, build on the benefits of informality and flexibility provided by the G8 and complement the UN.[821]

In Martin's view, an L20 is needed primarily as a result of globalisation. A global public policy is required for the well-being of humanity and particularly to ensure that globalisation benefits all countries. While international organisations are essential for addressing global issues, they are dependent on their member states' political will and financing. The most powerful states have a special responsibility to round off the sharp edges of globalisation. This new group of states, however, has to be more representative and inclusive than the G8, which gathers only the advanced industrialised countries and the Russian Federation, meaning that major emerging economic powers as well as a number of the world's regions are not represented.[822] According to Martin, the fundamental criteria for L20 membership are as follows: first, the countries chosen must include the G8 and other leading economies. Second, members must possess the requisite social and political stability. Finally, the major regional powers should be included regardless of economic ranking. The membership of the L20 should be the same for all issues. It should not have a "variable geometry", with a different combination of leaders to deal with different

---

[819] Bradford and Linn, *op. cit.*, note 800, p. 6.
[820] "A Symposium: Global Summit Reform and the L-20," Editorial, Global Insights, *Global Governance*, Vol. 13, 2007, p. 299.
[821] P. Martin, "Breaking Deadlocks in Global Governance: The L-20 Proposal," Global Insights, *Global Governance*, Vol. 13, 2007, p. 301.
[822] *Ibid.*, pp. 301-302.

topics because the personal chemistry that will drive positive outcomes can be developed only if the same people meet repeatedly (subject, of course, to the exigencies of each country's electoral system).[823]

Martin admits that an L20 would not be without its potential problems. One of the major issues would be who gets to be a member.[824] Some have suggested that key candidates would be China, India, Brazil, South Africa and Mexico. As Marcos de Azambuja argues, a country from the Muslim world would be a welcome addition, helping to better include the over 50 countries and 2 billion people that belong to Islamic culture and the Islamic faith. De Azambuja argues that the G8 should be enlarged selectively, which may result in something less than an L20 – perhaps an L14.[825] There remains the question of which Muslim-majority country would be selected.

Martin also concedes that an L20 would face legitimacy issues. It would have legitimacy if it were established with a mandate that supports the formal multilateral architecture and is committed to facilitating the reform of public global governance institutions. It is also essential that it be a joint North-South initiative rather than a forum created by the North from which membership is extended to the South. It would also be important that the rules determining the operation of such a forum be developed together by all members.[826]

In terms of citizen involvement, Martin argues that each leader in the L20 can and should be held accountable by their own country's civil society and legislative bodies. Both before and after L20 meetings, governments should engage in consultation processes that they have developed with their civil society and legislative bodies.[827]

However, as Lan Xue notes, breaking the deadlocks in global governance is extremely difficult, particularly because the priorities of the highly industrialised countries and those of the less developed countries are likely to be disparate: "The major developed economies place issues like terrorism, climate change, nuclear non-proliferation, intellectual property protection, drug traffic, and trade negotiations at

---

[823] *Ibid*, p. 303.
[824] *Ibid.*, p. 304.
[825] M. de Azambuja, "Responses to Paul Martin's Proposal for the L-20," Global Insights, *Global Governance*, Vol. 13, 2007, pp. 309-310.
[826] Sidiropoulos, *op. cit.*, note 817, pp. 317-318.
[827] Martin, *op. cit.*, note 821, p. 303.

the top of their agenda. In contrast, major developing countries are more concerned about issues that mean life or death for millions, such as extreme poverty, huge financial debt, pandemic diseases, corruption, crime, and social upheavals."[828] This would make the agenda addressed by such a forum difficult to define in a selective manner.

The role played by the Group of Twenty Finance Ministers and Central Bank Governors in the 2008/2009 economic crisis is perhaps indicative of a recognition that global economic governance needs to be more inclusive. Having been created in response to the Asian financial crisis of the late 1990s, the G20 endorsed a 47-point plan to introduce new measures to help make the global financial system more stable in the future. Proposed safeguards include mechanisms to facilitate regulatory cooperation between countries, means of highlighting risky investments practices, the eventual standardisation of accounting rules regarding the valuation of assets, and so on.[829]

Accountability
According to Robert Keohane, rather than aspiring to some sort of participatory democracy, we should limit our ambitions in relation to the global democratic deficit and seek simply to limit abuses of power. Accordingly, the focus of this endeavour should be entities, such as multinational enterprises, states and multinational organisations. A pluralistic accountability system should be devised, comprising of legal, fiscal, supervisory, peer and reputational accountability mechanisms.[830]

With regard to states, the doctrine of sovereignty has, at least to some extent, prevented leaders from being held externally accountable for their actions, and has permitted resort to war and other means of coercion. Multilateral organisations aim to hold states accountable for their actions. Yet, in the face of the most powerful states these institutions often appear weak. The US is the most prominent example

---

[828] L. Xue, "Breaking Deadlocks in Global Governance: How to Make the L-20 Work," *Global Governance* 13, 2007, p. 321.
[829] CBC News, "G20 Leaders Promise Action on Economic Crisis," 15 November 2008, http://www.cbc.ca/world/story/2008/11/15/eco-summit.html?ref=rss; see also the G20's website: http://www.g20.org/G20/.
[830] R.O. Keohane, "Accountability in World Politics," *Scandinavian Political Studies*, Vol. 29, No. 2, 2006.

of the most powerful state refusing to accept to be held to account by multinational institutions.[831]

Peer accountability may also act to constrain states. Organisations may exert peer accountability on similar organisations. Similarly, states may hold each other to account for their policies in the context of multilateral organisations such as the OECD. Governmental and nongovernmental networks also help to establish peer accountability by setting minimum standards or establishing best practices. Reputational accountability also helps to encourage what is considered to be appropriate behaviour.[832]

While Keohane is convinced that we cannot rely on a domestic analogy when seeking to address the accountability issue at the global level, he nevertheless recognises that power needs to be constrained in order to benefit from governance at the global level rather than suffer as a result of it.[833] He distinguishes between internal and external accountability. Internal accountability problems may occur within an international organisation, for example, as the oil-for-food scandals at the UN have shown. Accountability gaps are more easily dealt with in relation to intergovernmental organisations. Supervisory mechanisms can help to oversee the activities of states and major multilateral organisations. Fiscal mechanisms also serve to supervise the exercise of power by such entities. Legal accountability mechanisms are also expanding; for example, an expanding body of law helps to hold states accountable for violations of international treaties, and the International Criminal Court represents an important expansion of legal accountability.[834]

Yet, the problems related to external accountability are even more significant. The majority of people affected by the policies and activities of the IMF, the World Bank and the WTO, for example, have no way of holding those organisations to account. In response to the activities of NGOs, some international organisations have made an effort to become more transparent and therefore more accountable. But international organisations are accountable to governments rather than those whose lives are affected by their practices. Moreover, NGOs that claim to speak on behalf of the most vulnerable people

---

[831] Ibid., p. 82.
[832] Ibid., pp. 83-84.
[833] Ibid., p. 78.
[834] Ibid., pp. 82-83.

tend to represent liberal elites rather than the poorest in societies. NGOs accuse international organisations, rather than the governments that they represent, of being unaccountable, which only serves to weaken international organisations further.[835] The real question, Keohane suggests, is whether multilateral institutions are accountable to the right people.[836] Unless good governance exists within states, the mechanisms to hold international organisations accountable will be inadequate.

Multilateral institutions have nevertheless made efforts to increase their transparency. The WTO, as is noted above, has made a conscious effort to engage NGOs. As Lamy explains:

> In Seattle, the WTO received a stern warning that it ignores the concerns of civil society at its peril. Since then, the interests of civil society related to labour, business, poverty reduction, the environment or democracy, are represented in Geneva and dialogue with the WTO in various fora. We now also have an annual symposium for civil society. This is more than just a dialogue. Civil society has been instrumental in bringing to the negotiating table issues such as subsidies to fisheries or cotton farmers and access to essential medicines.[837]

This does not, however, imply that the WTO is accountable to the people most affected by its activities, given that there is no global demos as such.

Similarly, multinational enterprises may be accountable to their shareholders, but their actions affect a huge number of people who have very little opportunity to place constraints on their activities. Measures aimed at increasing the accountability of multinational enterprises could help to increase reputational costs, according to Keohane. The UN's Global Compact represents an effort to institutionalise the relationship between the UN and some of the biggest multinationals in the hope of rewarding those enterprises that exercise corporate responsibility and punish those that need to improve. However, how effective these types of endeavours will be is as yet unclear,[838] and whether they actually contribute to the ongoing reduction in formal regulation remains open to question.

---

[835] *Ibid.*, p. 80.
[836] *Ibid.*, p. 81
[837] Lamy, *op. cit.*, note 815, p. 6.
[838] Keohane, *op. cit.*, note 830, pp. 81-82.

3. Adapting to New Circumstances

There is a discrepancy between the emergence of global problems and the emergence of adequate governance mechanisms with which to effectively address these problems.[839] Multilateral institutions need to act in a coherent and coordinated manner.[840] They are a reflection of their member states, in that they are what their members want them to be. The common challenge for multilateral institutions is whether those with a small number of dominant states can effectively act in the interests of the wider international community.[841] Multilateral institutions offer opportunities to address transnational concerns in a broader and more comprehensive manner than any single state could. The will and enforcement mechanisms are required to ensure effective multilateral responses.

Effective multilateralism must be able to address governance problems in their multidimensionality. There is a need for a global agenda that allows the market to function freely in areas where proven benefits result, to ensure that public governance mechanisms can operate effectively in order to protect the most vulnerable and the most disadvantaged sectors, and to ensure the provision of public goods, such as basic health care, education and a clean environment, economic and political stability, and international development.[842]

Regional organisations also need to improve their capacities to address existing challenges. In some instances, they currently lack the financial resources with which to do so. The AU is in need of international support in order to strengthen its crisis management capacity, and its programmes aimed at advancing good governance.[843] In some instances, institutional capacity needs to be strengthened. For instance, countries in the Asia Pacific should strengthen cooperation. The need for institutional capacity to respond to the challenges faced by the region was demonstrated by the 2004 Tsunami and earthquakes, and this capacity needs to be improved. A regional disaster response capacity would contribute significantly to the preparedness of the re-

---

[839] Alonso, *op. cit.*, note 793, p. 357.
[840] Bradford and Linn, *op. cit.*, note 800, p. 3.
[841] Al-Rodhan, Finaud, Palazzolo, Watanabe, Nazaruk and Rurarz-Huygens, *Multilateralism and Transnational Security, op. cit.*, note 527, p. 310.
[842] Alonso, *op. cit.*, note 793, p. 358.
[843] Al-Rodhan, Finaud, Palazzolo, Watanabe, Nazaruk and Rurarz-Huygens, *Multilateralism and Transnational Security, op. cit.*, note 527, p. 107.

gion.[844] The ability to deal effectively with challenges in a coordinated manner may also be hampered by a lack of institutional capacity in member states. In Africa, ECOWAS has faced challenges in its promotion of integration among the states of West Africa related to political instability, weak economies and a lack of diversification, poor infrastructure, lack of institutional capacity and financial problems.[845] Like multilateral institutions, regional organisations need to engage more with civil society in order to develop comprehensive responses to common concerns.

The increased integration of markets, which is particularly marked in the area of finance, has resulted in increased instability which affects all countries.[846] There is, thus, a need for a governance structure to deal with global macroeconomic management as well as global finance. As is mentioned above, the IMF was created to supervise fixed exchange rates. However, fixed exchange rates have since been replaced by floating exchange rates, resulting in the growth of international finance. Combined with increased openness and interdependence, this has increased the impact of contagion and the potential for global financial crises. There is thus a need for an institutional architecture capable of preventing and managing such crises. Such institutional mechanisms should facilitate consultation and the surveillance of states' macroeconomic policies. Resources for emergency financing also need to be available before international reserves are exhausted. Provisions for debt arrangements would help to stabilise debtor countries. Some argue that only an institution that has the power to regulate, intervene and enforce could meet global financial governance needs.[847] Deepak Nayyar and Julius Court suggest that a World Financial Authority could offer the possibility of managing the risks linked with international financial liberalisation and coordinate national responses to market abuse and failure.[848]

Moreover, the economic dimensions of globalisation affect how power and wealth are distributed, making a discussion of global

---

[844] *Ibid.* p. 126.
[845] *Ibid.*, p. 109.
[846] Alonso, *op. cit.*, note 793, p. 356.
[847] D. Nayyar and J. Court, "Governing Globalization: Issues and Institutions," *World Institute for Development Economics Research Policy Brief* No. 5, 2002, pp. 21, 23.
[848] *Ibid.*, p. 23.

social justice necessary.[849] Anti-globalisation movements call for greater social justice and solidarity through decentered and decentralised movements and have a deep suspicion of mediated and institutionalised authority.[850] Yet, as Alejandro Colas notes, "successful struggles for the democratisation of global governance... must be attentive to both the mediating power of political institutions in the reproduction of capital, and to the centrality of representation in the legitimation of such a democratic politics."[851] Civil society mechanisms have the advantage of not being mediated by states and thus not potentially subject to the narrow definitions of national interest that undermine efforts to develop effective coordination mechanisms with which to deal with global problems. Ultimately, multilateral agencies need to be reformed so that they work in a consensual way with non-state governance mechanisms.[852] As is indicated above, this is already under way, however imperfectly.

According to the UN High Commissioner for Human Rights, a fundamental indicator of good governance is whether the relevant institutions of governance are able to effectively ensure the protection of civil, cultural, economic, political and social rights through health care, housing, food security, education, justice and personal security.[853] Yet, José Antonio Alonso argues that the source of a more effective and new form of multilateralism is civil society. Dynamism needs to be injected into this process by some sort of universal citizens' charter that is premised on human rights, which are conceived not simply as civil and political rights but also basic social rights.[854] Alonso suggests that acting to ensure these rights would be a duty of the international community rather than individual states. Universal human rights also serve as a source of empowerment for civil society and therefore have the benefit of contributing to greater inclusiveness and more representative and legitimate global governance.[855]

---

[849] G. Collste, "Globalisation and Global Justice," *Studia Theologica*, Vol. 59, No. 1, 2005, p. 57.
[850] A. Colas, "The Power of Representation: Democratic Politics and Global Governance," *Review of International Studies*, Vol. 29, 2003, p. 102.
[851] *Ibid.*, p. 101.
[852] Alonso, *op. cit.*, note 793, p. 357.
[853] Abdellatif, *op. cit.*, note 673, p. 6.
[854] Alonso, *op. cit.*, note 793, p. 358.
[855] *Ibid.*, p. 358.

The notion of burden-sharing is central to symbiotic realism, which is discussed in greater detail in Chapter 12. Symbiotic realism recognises that state-centric paradigms are inadequate frameworks with which to understand the complex and interrelated nature of the global system. While states are still considered the major actors in global affairs, symbiotic realism moves beyond the realist paradigm of international relations by identifying a number of significant global actors, including international organisations and NGOs, in a "globally anarchic world of instant connectivity and interdependence."[856] It also recognises that the capacity of states to ensure the security and well-being of their populations requires a new paradigm that captures the complex relations between issues, sectors of activity and a variety of actors. Addressing global challenges in a timely and effective way depends on a shift away from state-centric thinking and the implementation of a broader conception of the global system, as well as a more cooperative approach to international affairs focused on human dignity needs. Multilateralism is therefore considered an essential means of creating a just and sustainable global order.[857]

Octagon 5 summarises the minimum criteria of good global governance.

---

[856] Al-Rodhan, *Symbiotic Realism, op. cit.*, note 78, pp. 11, 14.
[857] *Ibid.*, pp. 120, 139.

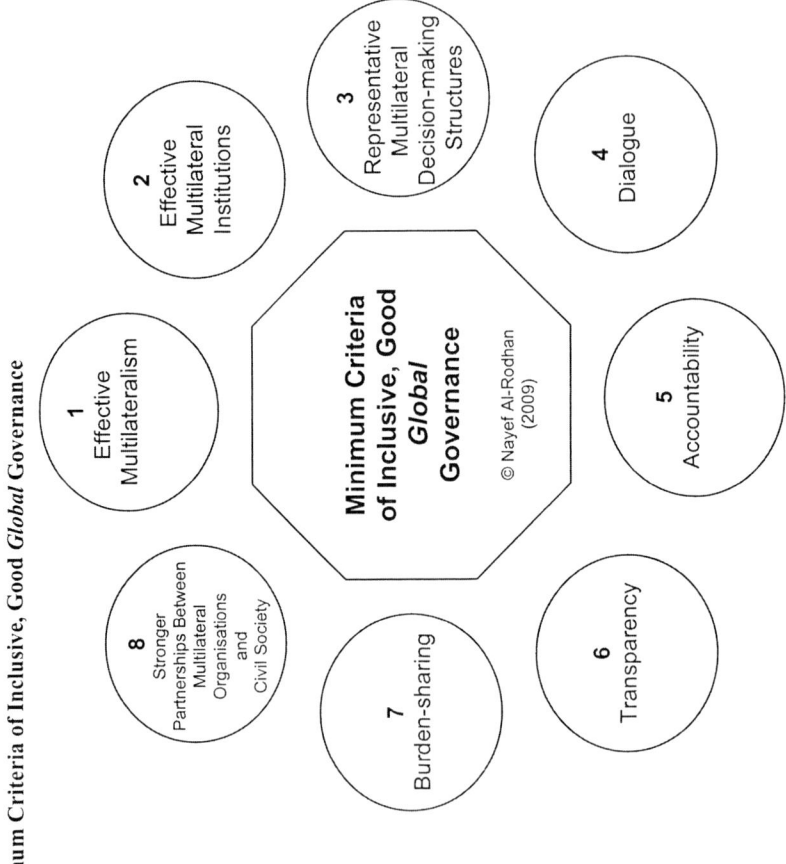

Octagon 5: Minimum Criteria of Inclusive, Good *Global* Governance

4. Conclusion

This chapter has looked at global governance, which is central to sustainable history due to its role in balancing the attributes of human nature with the need for human dignity. I identified some of the major problems with the current structures of global governance. Since multilateral institutions are accountable to states, and states are not always representative or accountable to their citizens, I argued that civil society needs to be empowered not simply through partnerships with multilateral institutions, but also through a universal citizens' charter premised, in the first instance, on a broad conception of human rights – one that includes not only political, civil, gender and cultural rights but also basic social rights.

CHAPTER 11

HOW CAN WE ACHIEVE SUSTAINABLE SECURITY?
THE MULTI-SUM SECURITY PRINCIPLE AND
SUSTAINABLE SECURITY

Given human nature attributes (i.e., emotionality, amorality and egoisms), security is critical for achieving a sustainable history. The realist paradigm has traditionally been dominant in Security Studies. As is discussed in greater detail in the next chapter, its focus is largely state-centric and militaristic. However, it is increasingly apparent to both academics and practitioners that approaches and responses to contemporary security challenges cannot be limited to a narrow focus on the state and the military. Today, major security challenges may come in a variety of forms – ranging from major disruption to information systems, to the release of pathogens and toxins to rising sea levels – and may often originate from non-state actors. These are threats on a number of levels, from the individual to humankind as a whole, and they affect a number of interconnected sectors and systems. Given the complex and interconnected nature of challenges to security – many of which are transnational and linked to the processes of globalisation – there is a need to develop a new approach to security.[858] Security is multifaceted and therefore requires a multidimensional approach.

This chapter classifies global security into five dimensions: human, environmental, national, transnational and transcultural security. Each of these dimensions is discussed in turn. I then illustrate how these dimensions are interconnected by discussing cyber, biological and space security. I end by discussing how the Multi-sum Security Principle may be employed as a framework for achieving sustainable security.

---

[858] S. Werthes and S. Härtig, "Human Security: New Threats, New Responsibilities," *Military Technology*, Vol. 31, No. 6, 2007, p. 147.

1. The Multidimensional Nature of Security

According to the realist worldview, states are both the source of threats and the means of security. They are the primary source of insecurity because the international system is an anarchical system in the sense that there is no overarching authority capable of enforcing order. Given that states are assumed to be rationally calculating entities, the lack of a sovereign authority capable of providing security guarantees means that insecurity is endemic, since all states will decide to accrue power in order to ensure their survival thereby producing the "security dilemma". In this so-called self-help system, states are the principal vehicles for security. Increases in security in this framework are zero-sum in the sense that one state's security, measured mostly in terms of military power, is other states' insecurity.[859]

Attempts to overcome the limitations of realism have taken a number of forms. Liberal or idealist approaches to the study of international relations argue that the absence of a sovereign global authority does not result in the security dilemma. They suggest instead that other governance mechanisms, such as rules and norms, can help to alter the nature of international anarchy. This approach, nevertheless, privileges the state and fails to adequately address the increasing concern with transnational security challenges, such as environmental degradation, drugs and arms trafficking and pandemics.

The rising concern about non-traditional security challenges prompted a debate within Security Studies about the appropriate subjects of security. This debate led some to argue in favour of a broader approach to security, that is, one that expands its scope beyond military threats to include a wide variety of largely cross-border issues.[860] Others attempted to offer a new sectoral approach to security:[861] a clear move away from a state-centred perspective, arguing that human

---

[859] J.H. Herz, "Idealist Internationalism and the Security Dilemma," *World Politics*, Vol. 2, No. 2, 1950, pp. 157-158.
[860] See, for example, S. Walt, "The Renaissance of Security Studies," *International Studies Quarterly*, Vol. 35, No. 2, 1991, pp. 211-239; E.A. Kolodziej, "Renaissance of Security Studies? Caneat Lector!" *International Studies Quarterly*, Vol. 36, No. 4, 1992, pp. 421-438; S. Dalby, "Contesting an Essential Concept: Reading the Dilemmas in Contemporary Security Discourse," in K. Krause and M.C. Williams (eds.) *Critical Security Studies: Concepts and Cases* (Minneapolis: University of Minnesota Press, 1997).
[861] Buzan, Waever and de Wilde, *op. cit.*, note 649.

beings rather than states should be considered the subjects of security. Thus, the question of who or what is to be secured was answered very differently.[862]

As these efforts suggest, security is increasingly recognised as being multi-dimensional. A more comprehensive view of security is, therefore, necessary. In *The Five Dimensions of Global Security: Proposal for a Multi-sum Security Principle* (2007), I put forward a classification of five dimensions of global security: human, environmental, national, transnational and transcultural security.[863]

Human Security
Intra-state conflicts, state failure, genocide, the spread of disease, famine and the devastating impact of natural disasters all suggest that a new approach to security that places a different referent-object of security at its centre is sorely needed.[864] The UNDP's 1994 Human Development Report, *New Dimensions of Human Security*, signalled that such a realisation was taking place among practitioners.

In 1999, Canada, in its capacity as chair of the UN Security Council, initiated a debate on "Civilians in armed conflict". This was followed in 2000 by another gathering of "like-minded states" in the "human security network" organised by Norway, Canada and Switzerland. This "Lysoen network" is still in existence.[865]

While there is no agreement on the appropriate scope of human security, there is general agreement about the implications of the concept. First, security of the individual implies a concern with development and other policy fields. Responses to security must therefore be multifaceted, employing instruments from a variety of different policy domains. Second, a multilateral approach to security is necessary; and, third, national security ought not to trump human security, but act as a vehicle for it.[866]

Some, however, would go further: *The Responsibility to Protect*, published by the International Commission on Intervention and

---
[862] See UNDP, *op. cit.*, note 554; K. Derghoukassian, "Human Security: A Brief Report of the State of the Art," The Dante B. Fascell North-South Center, Working Paper No. 3, November 2001, pp. 2-3.
[863] Al-Rodhan, *The Five Dimensions of Global Security*, *op. cit.*, note 512.
[864] Werthes and Härtig, *op. cit.*, note 858, p. 147.
[865] J. Matlary, "Much Ado about Little: The EU and Human Security," *International Affairs*, Vol. 84, No. 1, 2008, pp. 135-136.
[866] Werthes and Härtig, *op. cit.*, note 858, p. 148.

State Sovereignty (ICISS) in 2001, attempts to reformulate state sovereignty as a responsibility to protect citizens' lives and their human rights. This implies a responsibility to prevent violent conflicts and human rights abuses, and to assist states in their efforts to do so. It also implies a responsibility to take action when preventive measures fail, including the use of coercive measures and even military force as a last resort.[867] This stands in contrast to the 1994 UNDP Report, which outlined human security as a purely civilian concept. The ICISS report potentially has military implications. The debate lost momentum, however, after the 2001 terrorist attacks in New York and Washington, DC.

The work by ICISS on the responsibility to protect was continued by the UN High-level Panel on Security. In 2004, it issued a report arguing that state sovereignty is understood today to imply the state's obligation to protect the well-being of its citizens and to fulfil its obligations to the wider international community. The UN General Assembly endorsed the panel's report in 2005. The question of whether military force was justified, however, was left vague.[868]

In the European context, the EU has commissioned a report for the EU security strategy on the implications of human security, entitled "A Human Security Doctrine for Europe".[869] According to the former deputy foreign minister of Norway, Janne Haaland Matlary, it represents the first attempt to develop a notion of the right to intervene in support of individual rights to security, in terms of establishing both the need for civil-military integration and legal principles.[870]

Environmental Security
Environmental security refers to the security of the biosphere. A number of threats to environmental security are clearly identifiable. Climate change has the capacity to affect world food production and to

---

[867] International Commission on Intervention and State Sovereignty, *The Responsibility to Protect: Research, Bibliography and Background, Supplementary Volume to the Report of the International Commission on Intervention and State Sovereignty* (Ottawa: International Development Research Centre, 2001), p. 11.
[868] Matlary, *op. cit.*, note 865, pp. 135-137.
[869] "A Human Security Doctrine for Europe: The Barcelona Report for the Study Group on Europe's Security Capabilities," presented to the EU High Representative for Common Foreign and Security Policy Javier Solana, Barcelona, 15 September 2004.
[870] *Ibid.*, p. 139.

make currently inhabited areas of the globe uninhabitable, affecting the lives of innumerable people. Civil violence, ethnic conflict and state failure are also possible outcomes of global climate change.[871] Climate change may lead to mass migration of people fleeing from drought, floods or failed states, which may cause instability and perhaps even conflict. Shifts in demographic balances may, for instance, alter ethnic or religious balances. National security may be negatively affected by global climate change as a result.[872]

One source of tension and possible conflict is the reduction in the supply of essential resources. Michael Klare identifies four major changes in the resources equation. First, there is likely to be reduced rainfall in tropical and temperate areas, resulting in prolonged droughts. Second, river flows are likely to be less significant due to the retreat of glaciers, contributing to increased water scarcity. Third, sea levels are set to rise, leading to flooding in coastal cities and farmlands. Finally, occurrences of severe weather such as storms are likely to increase, affecting regions of the world in different ways.[873]

Africa is expected to suffer disproportionately from the effects of global warming, particularly from enduring drought and water scarcity. At the same time, African states have perhaps the least capacity to adapt to and manage these effects. South and Central Asia are also likely to be significantly affected by rising temperatures and a reduction in available water. According to Michael Klare, land and fresh water will be the most severely affected vital resources, leading to a reduction in arable land in Africa and South and Central Asia. The Sahel – the southern part of the Sahara, which stretches across central Africa – is thought to demonstrate some of the first signs of the potential security impact of global climate change. This area incorporates Senegal, Mauritania, Niger, Chad, Sudan, Eritrea and Ethiopia. The southern fringe of the Sahara has traditionally been the home of Muslim herdsmen. These herdsmen are increasingly moving south into traditionally non-Muslim areas as the Sahara extends further south, sometimes generating conflict.[874] In northern Nigeria, Sudan and

---

[871] M.T. Klare, "Global Warming Battlefields: How Climate Change Threatens Security," *Current History*, November 2007, p. 355.
[872] S.C. Maybee, "National Security and Global Climate Change," *Joint Force Quarterly*, No. 49, 2008, pp. 99-100.
[873] Klare, *op. cit.*, note 871, p. 356.
[874] *Ibid.*, pp. 356-358.

Kenya, conflicts between herders and farmers have become violent, with the situation in the Darfur region of Sudan being a poignant case in point.[875]

Countries that rely on transboundary water flows are also thought to be vulnerable to the impact of global climate change on water resources. Egypt depends on the Nile for the majority of its fresh water, which originates in Central Africa and Ethiopia. Iraq and Syria rely on freshwater from the Tigris and the Euphrates, which have their sources in Turkey. Israel's principle source of fresh water comes from the Jordan River, which partly originates in Syria and Lebanon. For downstream countries, relations with upstream countries could prove critical.[876]

Klare speculates that another type of threat to security and stability resulting from global climate change could be linked to militia and gang warfare, similar to that which is taking place in Mogadishu, Somalia, where the official government no longer exercises any authority and, in its place, armed gangs control access to vital resources. Where states have not failed but are failing, climate change could strike the blow that leads them to fail.[877]

Increased migratory pressures may also increase the likelihood of conflict as a result of global climate change. This could fuel xenophobic fears and anti-immigrant sentiment, leading to a rise in support for ultra-nationalism and perhaps even for neo-Nazi groups.[878] Yet, migration need not be a destabilising factor, although it may be when people move to areas in which conditions make life only just feasible. In addition to the context in which migration takes place, government responses to migration are also vital in determining whether migration contributes to instability and insecurity.[879]

A combination of poverty and poor governance means that the areas most likely to be hard hit by the effects of global climate change are those least likely to have the capacity to adapt and respond to a changing environment, and are perhaps especially vulnerable to the risk of violent conflict. Dan Smith and Janani Vivekananda identify

---

[875] D. Smith and J. Vivekananda, *A Climate of Conflict: The Links between Climate Change, Peace and War*, (London: International Alert, 2007), p. 13.
[876] Klare, *op. cit.*, note 871, p. 358.
[877] *Ibid.*, p. 359.
[878] *Ibid.*, p. 360.
[879] Smith and Vivekananda, *op. cit.*, note 875, p. 8.

four political and socio-economic factors that are likely to interact with the more immediate effects of climate change in a way that increases the risk of instability and violent conflict: political instability, economic weakness, food insecurity and mass migration.[880]

Political instability and poor governance make it harder for a state to adapt to the more immediate physical changes in the environment that result from climate change. Economic weakness also makes it harder for people whose livelihoods have been negatively affected or destroyed as a result of the physical effects of climate change to find other means of survival. It also means that reductions in state finances will be harder felt than in more wealthy states. This, in turn, means that meeting the basic needs of the population will be all the more challenging. Food insecurity represents a challenge to the ability of people to go on living in a particular place and a challenge to life itself. This and the other factors contributing to instability and insecurity may increase the likelihood of mass migration.[881]

Rising temperatures also imply health risks from waterborne diseases, such as Malaria and Cholera, which could, if badly managed, lead to epidemics that not only cause immediate loss of life, but also contribute to shifts in power balances and increased tensions between communities. Increased natural disasters, heat waves and water shortages can threaten lives and increase pressure on medical resources. Those who suffer most are likely to be the poor and the marginalised.[882]

Global warming also has geopolitical implications. The melting of the Arctic icecap will open up the Arctic ocean to shipping and make available oil and gas deposits, which may significantly increase competition for territory and resources among Russia, Canada, Denmark, Norway and the US – the five Arctic states. Russia has already made claim to 460,000 square miles of Arctic waters. Canada has been manoeuvring to stake its claim to Arctic waters, and Denmark and Norway are also keen to stake their claims. At present, there are no international political and legal frameworks governing the development of the Arctic, making potential disputes over shipping lanes and resources particularly worrisome. The rights of the indigenous

---

[880] *Ibid.*, p. 3.
[881] *Ibid.*
[882] *Ibid.*, p. 15.

peoples of the region may also come into conflict with the development objectives of the Arctic powers.[883]

National Security

Historically, ensuring the right to govern involved the capacity to defend that claim against both internal and external challengers. National security has thus traditionally involved a military and police dimension by virtue of the nature of sovereignty.[884] Yet, it also has political, societal and economic dimensions. In *The Three Pillars of* Sustainable National Security *in a Transnational World* (2008), I argue that the concept of national security requires radical rethinking in the 21st century. Today, states are highly interdependent and the challenges they face are often cross-border in nature and multidimensional. The roles of Information and Communications Technologies (ICT) and the mass media in general have added another dimension to national security, and constitute a critical dimension of the global environment.

The idea of national security has been thought about in a variety of ways. It has familiar physical facets, such as ensuring that the country is safe from physical attack, and ensuring the rule of law within state territory. Yet, there is also a less physical aspect to national security. Buzan, Waever and de Wilde define political security as the organisational stability of a social order. Some threats may have a predominantly political character.[885] At the national level, threats may be posed to the *internal* legitimacy of the regime, which is connected to ideology or constitutive ideas, or its *external* legitimacy, which may involve threats to the sovereignty of the state such as a lack of formal recognition by other states. In weak states that lack internal legitimacy, for example, the basic institutions or ideologies that underpin them may be challenged with the aim of destabilising the established political order. A strong state will be relatively immune to political threats because of the high degree of regime legitimacy.[886]

A country's historical experiences and collective memory also inform its definition of national security. A country that has been sys-

---

[883] S.G. Borgerson, "Arctic Meltdown: The Economic and Security Implications of Global Warming," *Foreign Affairs*, March/April 2008.
[884] Al-Rodhan, *The Five Dimensions of Global Security*, op. cit., note 512, p. 60.
[885] Buzan, Waever and de Wilde, *op. cit.*, note 649.
[886] Al-Rodhan, *The Five Dimensions of Global Security*, op. cit., note 512, pp. 62-63.

tematically attacked and occupied is likely to have a different security culture to one that has never experienced direct attack or occupation. In addition, a country's access to natural resources is likely to affect national security priorities. A country that does not have natural gas or oil reserves is likely to place greater weight on energy security than one that does.

These factors remain relevant to national security. However, the internal and external dimensions of national security that characterised traditional thinking are now becoming blurred.[887] Increasing economic interdependence, the growth of ICT and the ever present mass media, and increased human mobility, as well as the broadening of the security agenda to include issues such as the environment, health and transcultural concerns mean that this domestic/international dichotomy is simply untenable today.

Moreover, as is discussed in Neo-*statecraft and* Meta-*geopolitics: Reconciliation of Power, Interests and Justice in the 21st Century* (2009), geopolitics must now consider a number of elements of state power or "capacities". *Meta*-geopolitics, which expands the scope of traditional geopolitics, ought to include a number of additional determinants of power relations. I suggest a new focus on seven capacities of state power: social and health issues; domestic politics; economics; the environment; science and human potential; military/security; and international diplomacy.[888]

Ensuring national security, therefore, requires cooperation between states on a number of issue areas as well as within global governance frameworks. It is also in a state's national interest to promote justice. Moreover, state diplomacy must reconcile a number of global interests to ensure the well-being of the state and its people.[889] Public diplomacy is also an increasingly important tool for national security because of the growth in ICT and increased access to the media.

Transnational Security
Something is transnational when it crosses national borders. Transnational security, therefore, refers to security against cross-border threats that may have a variety of sources. Transnational threats may take the form of cyber attacks, air and water pollution, global climate change,

---

[887] Al-Rodhan, *The Five Dimensions of Global Security*, op. cit., note 512, pp. 11-12.
[888] Al-Rodhan, Neo-*statecraft and* Meta-*geopolitics*, op. cit., note 185, p. 12.
[889] *Ibid.*, pp. 3-5.

the proliferation of infectious diseases, transnational terrorist networks, and the trafficking of weapons, drugs and human beings, to name but a few. Transnational threats pose a specific challenge because they typically affect a number of states simultaneously and can only be mitigated or resolved through the cooperative efforts of a number of states. Moreover, they often originate with non-state actors, which can make them asymmetric in nature, with no easily identifiable source. An added problem is that many of the frameworks employed to address them are state-based, making them inadequate frameworks with which to guide effective policy responses. Furthermore, such frameworks often emerge over an indefinite time frame, which can mean that threats are not addressed in a timely fashion.[890]

Security policy analysts now count the Internet and cybercrime among their concerns, for example. The power of the Internet derives from its easy access. It is also a vehicle for rapidly bringing people and communities of interest together. As such, it is a medium for the transmission of ideas, information and calls to action. If leveraged, it can create asymmetric capabilities that can be employed without being traceable. Controlled delivery of information may be aimed at exploiting, disrupting or manipulating an opponent's operations. This may not take the form of a single attack, but could be made up of several small attacks that together cause large scale disturbance.[891] Cyber attacks have the capacity to create considerable economic damage. Nationally significant attacks could involve criminal activities, such as organised theft, trespass and terrorist activities, as well as non-state actors who wish to influence political or public opinion, obtain information or engage in intelligence gathering.[892]

Frank J. Cilluffo and J. Paul Nicholas identify three main categories of threats: those posed by individuals, groups and states. They point out that attacks may be mounted by individuals using unsophisticated means, or highly sophisticated carried out by states or alliances of states. Within the range of possible sources of attack, individuals are taking on greater importance. They may use the asymmetrical power of the Internet to launch attacks against systems and even people. Previously, this would have been the preserve of states,

---

[890] Al-Rodhan, *op. cit.*, note 511, p. 73.
[891] F.J. Cilluffo and J. P. Nicholas, "Cyberstrategy 2.0," *The Journal of International Security Affairs*, No. 10, Spring 2006, pp. 23-24.
[892] *Ibid.*, pp. 24, 26.

which alone would have possessed the necessary technology, tools and skill sets for such attacks.[893]

Detecting sophisticated and subtle cyber attacks requires more than identifying which systems are affected. Early warning systems need to be developed. Here, there is a clear role for governments in cooperation with the cyber-security industry. Identifying potential targets of cyber-attacks also requires partnerships between the public and private sector. Deterring cyber-attacks, according to Cillufo and Nicholas, requires the development of capacities to respond as well as the rapid arrest and prosecution of the perpetrators. Legal tools with which to prevent cyber attacks also need to be harmonised.[894]

Creating defensive mechanisms against cyber-crime is likely to involve establishing the tools with which to coordinate responses to potential attacks by individuals, groups and states or alliances of states. Among these potential sources, groups are perhaps the most difficult to identify, break into and deter. States tend to be more cautious about employing information-based attacks. There are a number of reasons for their caution; for instance, they may not wish to reveal their cyber capacities or they may fear a military response by the target.[895]

Biological threats also feature among the concerns of security policy analysts. Like every new technology, biotechnology brings with it tremendous benefits. For example, in the area of medical genomics, biotechnology is making a significant contribution to health. Improvements in DNA sequencing technology, along with better characterisation of genes, is helping experts to discern the genetic basis of disease. The development of genetically modified crops has made some resistant to disease. Biotechnology may also enable the creation of clean biological fuels as well as environmentally friendly forms of breaking down waste. The potential benefits of biotechnology are thus wide-ranging and remarkable.

As is explained in *Global Biosecurity: Towards a New Governance Paradigm* (2008),[896] biosecurity and biosafety are related

---

[893] *Ibid.*, p. 24.
[894] A. Nouri and C.F. Chyba, "Biotechnology and biosecurity," in .N. Bostrom and M. M. Ćirković (eds.) *Global Catastrophic Risks* (Oxford: Oxford University Press, 2008), p. 456.
[895] Cilluffo and Nicholas, *op. cit.*, note 891, pp. 28-30.
[896] N.R.F. Al-Rodhan, L. Nazaruk, M. Finaud and J. Mackby, *Global Biosecurity: Towards a New Governance Paradigm* (Genève: Éditions Slatkine, 2008).

concepts. Biosecurity, broadly defined, implies safety or freedom from fear of disease and sickness from living organisms.[897] However, it has also been employed to refer to personal and international security measures employed to prevent the theft or misuse of pathogens and toxins, as well as the protection of systems supporting people or other living organisms.[898] Biosafety has been employed in a number of different ways, but is generally used in relation to laboratory containment or biotechnology hazards.[899] I employ the term biosecurity in a way that combines both biosecurity and biosafety and ranges from *"the safety of all living organisms, protection from biological harm (diseases, pests or bioterrorism), and risk management practices in defence against any biological threat, to preventing or eliminating the effects of intentional or unintentional misuse of the life sciences and technology."*[900]

Biological risks may result from the spread of disease, the re-emergence of infectious diseases, the unintended results of research, laboratory accidents or deliberate misuse.[901] One biosecurity concern is bioterrorism. For example, the Aum Shinrikyo cult in Japan attempted to carry out a mass-casualty attack by releasing *Bacillus anthracis* from a rooftop in a busy area of Tokyo. It was unsuccessful in its attempt to procure a pathogenic strain of *Bacillus anthracis*, and lacked the capacity to effectively disperse it, but it was later successful in releasing Sarin nerve gas into the Tokyo commuter railway network. Another non-state group that has engaged in biological attacks is the Oregon-based cult Rajneeshees, which spread the bacterium *Salmonella typhimurium* on salad bars, causing illness, to prevent people from voting in local elections in 1984.[902]

While the employment of pathogens as weapons and tools with which to spread terror is not new, the risk has intensified in recent years.[903] Bioterrorism, as Andreas Wenger and Reto Wollenmann

---

[897] The Draft of the National Biosecurity Strategy of the Commonwealth of the Bahamas, http://www.unep.org/biosafety/files/BSNBFrep.pdf, p. 5.
[898] Al-Rodhan, Nazaruk, Finaud and Mackby, *Global Biosecurity*, *op. cit.*, note 896, p. 14.
[899] *Ibid.*, p. 13.
[900] *Ibid.*, p. 28.
[901] *Ibid.*
[902] Nouri and Chyba, *op. cit.*, note 894, p. 466.
[903] A. Wenger and R. Wollenmann, *Bioterrorism: Confronting a Complex Threat* (Boulder, Co.: Lynne Rienner, 2007), p. vii.

explain, is an extremely complex threat.[904] There is no officially agreed definition of bioterrorism. The United States Federal Bureau of Investigation (FBI) defines it as "unlawful use of viruses, bacteria, fungi, toxins or other pathogenic material against a government, the civilian population, livestock, crops or any segment thereof, in furtherance of political, social and/or economic objectives."[905]

Biological risks may also stem from intentional or unintentional misuse of life sciences and technology, and from genetic engineering. Legitimate biological research may also be used for malicious purposes, creating a dual-use dilemma. Some risks occur due to the potential misuse of biotechnology and the ease of transportation of biological materials. UNSC Resolution 1540 calls for more robust export controls related to biological substances, but it remains difficult to enforce. The scientific community has also made efforts to reduce the likelihood of misuse of biological research, but the risk of unintentional misuse and accidents is an ongoing concern and a threat to human, animal and plant life.[906]

Efforts to minimise threats of bio-attacks are making health professionals more aware of counterterrorism measures. Reducing biological threats requires cooperation between public health and security officials, and effective health measures increasingly require transnational cooperation. While efforts tend to be centred on preventing terrorism and activities by extremist groups, infection or exposure may also be due to unsafe research conditions, theft or insufficiently restricted access to biological material. Indeed, the latter category poses a greater risk to public health. Reducing the risk of proliferation of biological substances means a security system that aims to enhance the physical security of buildings, security-screening of personnel authorised to work on pathogens or toxins, and licensing of the trade in and exchange of material and information.

Biological technologies present considerable problems for inspection regimes, given the growing number of laboratories that carry out pathogen research, the expansion of the biotechnology and pharmaceutical sectors, and the increasing number of countries that invest

---

[904] *Ibid.*, p. 1.
[905] J. Mackby, *Strategic Study on Bioterrorism*, Centre for Strategic and International Studies Report, 16 October 2006, p. 12.
[906] Al-Rodhan, Nazaruk, Finaud and Mackby, *Global Biosecurity, op. cit.*, note 896, pp. 41-42.

in biotechnology.[907] In the event that preventive measures fail, preparedness, and rapid and effective response mechanisms must be in place, such as an epidemiological surveillance system that can provide early identification of the proliferation of biological agents, especially disease-causing pathogens, and enforceable and harmonised legislation to criminalise violations of security standards, regulations and export controls.[908] The elements of a comprehensive and harmonised approach to biological risk management include awareness-raising, risk evaluation and oversight.[909]

The consequences of environmental degradation also raise transnational security concerns. Environmental security challenges include global climate change, water and air pollution, and the degradation of scarce resources. As is highlighted in *The Five Dimensions of Global Security: Proposal for a Multi-sum Security Principle* (2007), the threats to environmental security are the result not simply of degradation, but frequently of poor environmental management policies and weak state institutions.[910]

Global climate change could increase the severity of natural disasters.[911] The impacts of tsunamis, earthquakes and hurricanes, for example, damage people's lives and livelihoods, disrupt health care and the provision of clean water, and cause displacement.[912] The consequences, which might include the spread of disease and refugee flows into neighbouring countries, could therefore extend beyond the community immediately affected by the natural disaster.

Ozone depletion is also another major atmospheric issue resulting from environmental damage. In the long-run, increased ultraviolet radiation reaching the Earth's surface could lead to serious environmental consequences such as reduced agricultural yields and disruption to ecosystems. For human beings, ozone depletion implies

---

[907] Nouri and Chyba, *op. cit.*, note 894, pp. 454-455.
[908] F. Kuhlau, "Countering Bio-threats: EU Instruments for Managing Biological Materials, Technology and Knowledge," SIPRI Policy Paper No. 19, August 2007, pp. 5-6.
[909] Al-Rodhan, Nazaruk, Finaud and Mackby, *Global Biosecurity*, *op. cit.*, note 896, p. 29.
[910] Al-Rodhan, *The Five Dimensions of Global Security*, *op. cit.*, note 512.
[911] J.R. McNeil, *An Environmental History of the Twentieth-Century World: Something New under the Sun* (New York: W.W. Norton & Company, 2000), p. 1.
[912] Al-Rodhan, *The Five Dimensions of Global Security*, *op. cit.*, note 512, p. 55.

increased risk of skin cancer, as well as respiratory conditions and other health problems.[913]

Transboundary water pollution is so serious in some areas that it has caused tension between states. Some of the more notable water-management disputes include those between Mexico and the US, and those concerning the Nile basin, the Jordan Basin and the Ganges Basin.[914]

Financial instability may also represent a transnational security challenge. Increased openness and interdependence increase the likelihood of contagion, making financial crises potentially global in character, perhaps leading to economic recessions and a general downturn in the global economy. Indeed, we are witnessing this cycle of events taking place today.

Transcultural Security
The concept of transcultural security is outlined in *The Five Dimensions of Global Security: Proposal for a Multi-sum Security Principle* (2007). Transcultural security is defined as relating to the integrity of cultures and geo-cultural domains. If global security is to be ensured, there needs to be more than simply a coexistence of cultures; synergies are required between different cultural domains. This does not, however, imply that all cultures need to merge into one dominant form. Transcultural synergy implies that the net effect of a plurality of cultures is greater than the sum of those of individual cultural domains. Transcultural security contributes to the end goal of transcultural synergy.[915]

One of the most original contributions to the Copenhagen School's sectoral approach is the concept of "societal security". Buzan, Waever and de Wilde define societal security as the security of large collective identities that may not be coterminous with a state.[916] With intensified migration, in part facilitated by improvements in travel and the global division of labour, many states are pluri-cultural, comprising a number of overlapping collective identities. Issues of

---

[913] *Ibid.*, p. 56.
[914] H. Haftendorn, "Water and International Conflict," Paper Presented at the International Studies Association, 40th Annual Convention, Washington, DC, 16-20 February 1999, p. 1.
[915] Al-Rodhan, *The Five Dimensions of Global Security, op. cit.*, note 512, pp. 78-79.
[916] Buzan, Waever and de Wilde, *op. cit.*, note 649, pp. 22-23.

culture and collective identity, in my view, do not receive enough attention. Yet, in a context of increased human mobility and almost instantaneous connectivity, mutual understanding and mutual recognition are prerequisites for a more secure future.[917]

As I outlined in *"emotional amoral egoism": A Neurophilosophical Theory of Human Nature and its Universal Security Implications* (2008),[918] human nature is such that well-being depends on having a positive identity and a sense of belonging. Part of what constitutes a person's identity is their membership within a broader collective identity, be it national, ethnic or religious. If they feel that this collective identity is not recognised and positively defined, their own identity as a member of that community will be negatively affected. This is only likely to breed tension, the securitization of that collective identity and defensive actions.

At the state level, collective identities may become securitised in states that have failed to promote a national identity in which everyone in society can find a place. Large collective identities may also be securitised when change and processes of transformation prompt renegotiation of fundamental principles within cultural groups.[919]

Unfortunately, media stereotyping of migrants, asylum seekers, refugees and particular ethnic and religious communities is quite prevalent. Such stereotypes may inform how people treat those who are stereotyped as well as the policies they support. A stereotype may be defined as a mental image that represents an oversimplified or prejudiced attitude towards a group or individual. Not surprisingly, negative stereotyping can lead to discrimination and insecurity on the part of those being depicted. It can even contribute to the dynamics of conflict and genocide.[920]

In *Policy Briefs on the* Transcultural *Aspects of Security and Stability* (2006), Katja Flückiger writes that a number of studies suggest that migrants tend to figure more frequently in particular types of news reporting, such as news on crime, than in other types of news

---

[917] Al-Rodhan, *The Five Dimensions of Global Security, op. cit.*, note 512, pp. 80-81.
[918] Al-Rodhan, *"emotional amoral egoism," op. cit.*, note 119, p. 162.
[919] Al-Rodhan, *The Five Dimensions of Global Security, op. cit.*, note 512, pp. 81-82.
[920] K.M. Flückiger, "Xenophobia, Media Stereotyping, and Their Role in Global Insecurity," in N.R.F. Al-Rodhan (ed.) *Policy Briefs on the* Transcultural *Aspects of Security and Stability* (Berlin: LIT, 2006), pp. 21-22.

genres. Moreover, they encompass a standard narrative that depicts migrants in a negative light.[921]

The impact of the media was demonstrated when the Danish newspaper *Jyllandes-Posten* published cartoons satirising the Prophet Mohammed in late 2005. This was followed by attacks on the Danish and Norwegian embassies in Damascus, riots in Cairo, Tehran and Beirut, and protests in London, Paris and Copenhagen. The publication of the cartoons as well as the violent response to them prompted questions about freedoms and responsibilities in Western liberal democratic states.[922]

The mass media and the entertainment industry have a critical role to play in determining whether transcultural security or insecurity prevails. In a period when cultural, ethnic and religious heterogeneity are part of the everyday lives of almost all of us, and in a highly interconnected world, responsibility is required from the mass media, which, along with other opinion formers such as educators, spokespersons and politicians, need to be attuned to the heightened role of public diplomacy and the impact of irresponsible political statements.

2. The Interrelated Nature of Security Threats

Threats to security are multifaceted and typically affect a number of dimensions of security simultaneously. A brief look at a number of selected security challenges helps to demonstrate this.

Biological Threats

Human security: At the level of the individual, biotechnologies have tremendous potential for improving human well-being in areas such as molecular diagnostics, recombinant vaccines, and delivery systems for drugs as well as vaccines. In addition, some biotechnology companies are developing treatments for people in developing countries. The positive application of biotechnology could help to reduce hunger and poverty and, in so doing, contribute to human security.[923] Biotechnol-

---

[921] *Ibid.*, p. 22.
[922] G. Herd and N.R.F. Al-Rodhan, "Danish Cartoons: A Symptom of Global Insecurity," in Al-Rodhan, *Policy Briefs on the* Transcultural *Aspects of Security and Stability*, *op. cit.*, note 920, p. 43.
[923] Al-Rodhan, Nazaruk, Finaud and Mackby, *Global Biosecurity*, *op. cit.*, note 896, pp. 138-139.

ogy could also help to improve air quality through the production of environmentally friendly biofuels.[924]

Yet, biosecurity risks could cause harm to individuals. Intentional release of pathogens or toxins could harm human, animal or plant health or even life. If misused, biotechnology could also negatively affect food security. Viruses could be created that have the capacity to stop regular cellular processes and provoke disease.[925] This could cause an epidemic for which there is no known vaccine. Biological threats also impact national security.

National Security: In relation to national security, governments have a duty to protect public health. Biosecurity threats may also generate public panic and economic harm, as well as reduce confidence in public institutions. In the autumn of 2001, the US was faced with a serious challenge to ensuring public safety when it was discovered that someone or some group had deliberately sent letters contaminated with anthrax spores to public officials and to the media in a number of states and in the District of Columbia. As a result, five people died and thousands were tested. Apart from the damage done to individuals and their families, the incident demonstrated a shortcoming in the public health care system.[926]

The state and public health authorities must be well prepared to prevent, and where prevention fails to respond quickly and effectively in the event of a biological attack. The challenge is to establish a comprehensive legal framework that endows public health authorities with the means to respond to emergencies, while at the same time safeguarding individual and group rights.[927]

Environmental Security: Biotechnology could, as is mentioned above, lead to the development of clean biofuels and improve waste management systems.[928] Yet, along with the potentially beneficial effects, biotechnology may carry with it certain risks. As such, biosecurity also needs to be considered in relation to nature. It is relevant to food safety, animal life and plant life, for example. In this con-

---

[924] Nouri and Chyba, *op. cit.*, note 894, p. 456.
[925] *Ibid.*, pp. 457-458.
[926] J.G. Hodge, Jr. and Lawrence O. Gostin, "Protecting the Public's Health in an Era of Bioterrorism: The Model State Emergency Powers Act," in J.D. Moreno (ed.), With a Foreword by Ford Rowan, *In the Wake of Terror: Medicine and Morality in a Time of Crisis* (Cambridge, Mass.: The MIT Press, 2004), p. 17.
[927] *Ibid.*, p. 18.
[928] Nouri and Chyba, *op. cit.*, note 894, p. 456.

text, biological risks may arise as a result of the introduction of plant and animal pests and diseases, zoonosis, genetically modified organisms (GMOs) and their products, as well as the introduction of alien species, for example.[929] Biosecurity therefore needs to be aimed at ensuring food safety, sustainable agricultural production and the protection of the environment.[930]

Transnational Security: Biological risks, such as the spread of infectious diseases, clearly do not respect formal state borders; as such, they constitute transnational security threats. Illness and disease are carried not only by people, but also by food. Poor hygiene conditions in the place of food preparation could have an impact in another country.

Developing countries may be hardest hit by biological catastrophes, given the lack of available drugs and diagnostic equipment, the existence of densely populated areas and the low level of public health, as well as in some cases, poor infrastructure and the lack of human resources necessary for effective responses to biological attacks. Transnational efforts are needed to improve surveillance, communication and coordination. Apart from the direct health impact, biological attacks, even if regional or local, could affect tourism, trade and travel across a number of states.[931]

Nano-threats

Nanotechnology is the technological product of research at the atomic, molecular or macromolecular levels to create and use structures, devices and systems that have specific applications and properties because of their small size.[932] Most structures produced using nanotechnology are only a nanometre, which is just a few atoms, in width.[933] Nanotechnology development and research involves the manipulation of materials from nano-level structures or their insertion into larger-scale material elements, systems or architectures. Nano-scale research

---

[929] See the website of the Food and Agricultural Organization of the United Nations, http://www.fao.org/biosecurity/.
[930] *Ibid.*
[931] Nouri and Chyba, *op. cit.*, note 894, pp. 473-474.
[932] C.S. Sabulski, "The Emerging Field of Nanotechnology," *Techdirections*, October 2004, p. 18.
[933] C. Phoenix and M. Treder, "Nanotechnology As Global Catastrophic Risk," in .N. Bostrom and M.M. Ćirković (eds.) *Global Catastrophic Risks* (Oxford: Oxford University Press, 2008), p. 481.

could lead to innovations in the areas of manufacturing, medicine, energy, chemicals, biotechnology, agriculture, transportation and electronics.[934]

Some of the major priorities in current nanotechnology research include enabling nanomaterials, nano-biointerfaces, nano-imaging, cell biology, molecular and cellular sensing and signalling, nano-systems design and application, in vivo therapeutics, sensor technologies, prosthetics and bioinformatics for nanotechnology. Research on the environmental and health impacts of nanotechnologies is also being undertaken. Other lines of inquiry include investigations into the production of molecular devices and machines.[935]

Nanotechnology implies more than simply scaling down the functions, for instance, of microtechnology. It enables human beings to work with the building blocks of matter. At present, nanotechnology applications tend to involve the development of small-scale components to be incorporated into larger ones. However, molecular nanotechnology (MNT) will permit the construction of human-size and larger products. MNT has several important properties. First, it enables the control of chemical reactions at the molecular level, which allows molecules to be assembled in useful ways. Second, it is capable of exponential manufacturing by creating fabricators that create more fabricators, with outside assistance, which are not self-replicating.[936]

The potential range of uses of nanotechnology is enormous: from repairing damaged organs, to destroying cancer cells, more rapid identification of infectious diseases, improving energy technologies, building stronger products, and reducing manufacturing costs, to name just a few.[937]

Chris Phoenix and Mike Treder argue that most nanotechnologies do not pose globally catastrophic risks, but that MNT is potentially more problematic. They argue that most nanostructures will be integrated into larger products, which means that the potential damage from nanostructures is likely to be limited to the larger product. They maintain that there are two main types of risk related to

---

[934] Sabulski, *op. cit.*, note 932, p. 18.
[935] See. For example, C. Ruch, "Nanotechnology in the EU – Bioanalytical and Biodiagnostic Techniques," September 2004, www.nanoforum.org.
[936] T.D. Vandermolen, "Molecular Nanotechnology and National Security," *Air and Space Journal*, Fall 2006, p. 97.
[937] Phoenix and Treder, *op. cit.*, note 933, pp. 482, 484.

nanotechnologies. The first results from the availability and application of nanotechnologies, which make products more powerful and potentially more dangerous. The second results from new materials that may cause unintended harm.[938] For instance, the Munich Re Group suggests that it may be conceivable that nano-robots, equipped with constant power sources, could modify organic matter into new substances that could cause damage to crops.[939]

New nano-materials should be tested for toxicology and environmental impact. However, nanotechnology is still in its infancy and little is known at this stage about the health and environmental effects of nano particles, for example.[940]

Human Security: MNT could significantly improve human well-being. At a very basic level, its applications could save many lives and increase life expectancy. Some researchers anticipate that nanotechnology will enable great strides in the area of cancer treatment, for instance. Eventually, it may enable the prevention and control of cancer through the use of tiny devices that deliver anti-cancer vaccines or preventive substances to the relevant areas of the body or where genetic information indicates that cancer might appear. Implanted nano-scale sensors may even be able to identify chemical changes connected to the growth of cancer, and improved diagnostic tools may one day enable doctors to discern which cells are cancerous.[941] Tiny robots could also be sent into the human body to destroy viruses. They could even repair damaged organs. Molecular nanotechnology is likely to endow people with more control over the human body.

National Security: Nanotechnology could play a significant role in a state's economic and industrial growth and a country's economic competitiveness.[942] Yet, intentional misuse of nanotechnology is thought by some to pose a potential threat to national security. Molecular manufacturing will enable anyone to rapidly, and relatively cheaply, construct all manner of weapons. By providing only the design, power and materials, a state could build highly sophisticated

---

[938] *Ibid.*, pp. 481-483.
[939] Munich Re Group, *Nanotechnology: What Is In Store for Us?*, Munich, 2002, p. 4.
[940] Phoenix and Treder, *op. cit.*, note 933, p. 484.
[941] W.S. Bainbridge, *Nanoconvergence: The Unity of Nanoscience, Biotechnology, Information Technology, and Cognitive Science* (Boston: Prentice Hall, 2007), p. 89.
[942] Sabulski, *op. cit.*, note 932, p. 18.

weapons quickly and economically. This could destabilise a region as well as perhaps global stability by generating arms races. Furthermore, individuals may be able to engage in the construction of Weapons of Mass Destruction, thereby creating security concerns for governments. The risk of non-state actors building such weapons could pose a serious threat to national security.

The implications of an MNT-based economy are wide-ranging. Commentators expect them to be similar to the software economy in the sense that the design phase of production would be the most expensive part, with manufacture and distribution being relatively inexpensive. While this may be welcome in some respects, the consequences could pose considerable economic and social problems. Economies that rely heavily on mass production and the mass use of human labour could suffer. MNT could at some point enable home production of products. Consumers may even be able to custom design low-cost, high-quality products at home. Clearly, this would imply a significant restructuring of the economy. The shipping industry may also be negatively affected in the transition to an MNT-based economy, given that the physical transportation of goods would be likely to decline.[943] Many service jobs could also be displaced. The level of social and economic disruption caused by a transition to a nanotechnology-based economy would, however, depend on the rapidity of such a change.[944]

Improvements in energy technologies, while being in the long-term national interest of states, might create short-term difficulties for oil-producing states that have not prepared their economies for a less oil-dependent future, as well as for oil companies.[945] Those states that currently either are oil-dependent or rely on external sources of oil, would gain greater economic and political room for manoeuvre from improvements in energy technologies.

Environmental Security: nanotechnology has the potential to significantly contribute to environmental sustainability.[946] Fewer materials and resources would be required in manufacturing.[947] Impor-

---

[943] Vandermolen, *op. cit.*, note 936, pp. 100-101.
[944] Phoenix and Treder, *op. cit.*, note 933, p. 492.
[945] Vandermolen, *op. cit.*, note 936, p. 101.
[946] T. Shelley, *Nanotechnology: New Promises, New Dangers* (London & New York: Zed Books, 2006), p. 23.
[947] L.B. Lave, "Lifecycle/Sustainability Implications of Nanotechnology," in M.C. Roco, W.S. Bainbridge (eds.) *Societal Implications of Nanoscience and*

tantly, nanotechnology is likely to prove central to addressing climate change, notably through reducing emissions.[948] MNT is set to improve energy technologies that should help to produce sustainable and clean energy sources. For example, it is expected to improve solar power by making solar cells more efficient and more robust.[949] Nanotechnology could improve energy efficiency by making vehicles lighter and stronger.[950]

Moreover, nano-engineering and nano-science could help to improve our molecular understanding of environmental processes. It could help clean polluted land and make available environmentally friendly ways to break down waste.[951]

One of the potential dangers of nanotechnology is the possibility that omnivorous self-replicating nanomachines might overpower the Earth's naturally occurring life forms.[952] Yet, it seems unlikely that such self-replicating assemblers would be required for manufacturing – nano factories may provide more efficient means of doing the job.[953] Nanotechnology and MNT are likely to create a significant amount of nanoparticles and other nanoproducts, the environmental effects of which are not yet known. Some of this nano waste may be tiny enough to penetrate living cells, which could lead to toxic poisoning.[954] The use of nanotechnologies could disrupt the ecosystem before we have time to realise or correct such imbalances.[955]

Transnational Security: A cooperative international strategy is required to maximise the potential benefits offered by nanotechnology, while minimising its potential for human, political, economic and societal disruption. Should non-state actors obtain the means and

---

Nanotechnology (Arlington, Virginia: National Science Foundation, March 2001), p. 162.
[948] Shelley, *op. cit.*, note 946, pp. 23-25.
[949] Vandermolen, *op. cit.*, note 936, p. 101.
[950] M. Scott, "Business and the Environment: Innovative Plans May Be Key for Green Future," *Financial Times*, 17 April 2008, http://www.ft.com/cms/s/0/afa073fa-0b6b-11dd-8ccf-0000779fd2ac.html.
[951] Deliotte Touche Tohmatsu, Technology, Media & Telecommunications, *Technology Predictions: TMT Trends 2008* (United Kingdom: The Creative Studio, 2008), available at http://www.deloitte.com/dtt/article/0%2C1002%2Ccid%25253 D187257%2C00.html, p. 9.
[952] Vandermolen, *op. cit.*, note 936, p. 97.
[953] Phoenix and Treder, *op. cit.*, note 933, p. 495.
[954] Vandermolen, *op. cit.*, note 936, pp. 100-101.
[955] Phoenix and Treder, *op. cit.*, note 933, pp. 494-495.

know-how with which to build their own weapons, the consequences and the required responses would be transnational in nature.[956]

Transcultural Security: The likely disparities in the distribution of the capacity to employ MNT mean that countries in the developed world might be expected to gain a lead in the application and development of this form of technology, while countries in the developing world continue to function without it.[957] The consequence would be a deepening of North-South divide. Furthermore, if MNT enables a reduction in the reliance on human labour, the consequences for economic growth and prosperity could be dire. Potential increases in the already wide gulf in conditions and opportunities between developed and developing countries could aggravate tensions between large-scale communities.

Aerospace Security
The number of actors in space increased during the 1990s, adding another dimension to geopolitics. Moreover, advances in space-related technologies tend to be dual-use, that is, they can be used for both civilian and military ends. Space is no longer the preserve of a few governments. The diversity of actors in space has increased.[958]

Space has not yet been weaponised, but it has been militarised.[959] In general, two kinds of space-based weapons exist: direct energy weapons that destroy their targets by energy transmitted at the speed of light; and kinetic-energy weapons that destroy missiles or surface targets by the kinetic energy of their own speed and mass or stored chemical energy.[960] Were weaponisation to lead to space warfare, global commerce would be severely compromised.[961]

Human Security: Space-based assets also provide critical information related to the weather and are vital to forecasting severe

---

[956] Vandermolen, *op. cit.*, note 936, pp. 97, 100.
[957] *Ibid.*, p. 102.
[958] J. West, "Next Generation Space Security Challenges," in UNIDIR, *Security in Space: The Next Generation*, Conference Report, 31 March – 1 April 2008, p. 42.
[959] UNIDIR, *Safeguarding Space Security: Prevention of an Arms Race in Outer Space, Conference Report*, 21-22 March 2005, p. 1.
[960] R. Preston, D.J. Johnson. S.J.A. Edwards, M.D. Miller and C. Shipbaugh, "Summary," in *Space Weapons Earth Wars*, RAND Corporation, 2002, p. xvi, http://www.rand.org/pubs/monograph_reports/MR1209/.
[961] M. Krepon, "Space Assurance or Space Weapons?" *Georgetown Journal of International Affairs*, Summer/Fall 2004, pp. 3-4.

weather that could put people, their homes and their livelihoods at risk.[962] In relation to the latter, space technologies can help to improve crop and water management, which can improve human well-being. Yet, human security may also require "freedom from space-based threats". This implies the need for a space governance architecture.[963] Space technologies can also help to improve access to health care in remote areas or to disaster relief teams through the use of telemedicine. The latter also helps health care professionals keep up to date with developments in medical procedures.[964]

National Security: Space increasingly supports economic activities and this has implications for national security.[965] Satellite-derived weather forecasts could also facilitate agricultural production by improving crop management and irrigation decisions, improve the management of water resources, and benefit other economic sectors such as commercial aviation, commercial land and sea transportation and commercial fishing. Improved weather forecasting capacities would also have advantages for the tourism and recreation sectors through, for example, more accurate snow forecasts in skiing areas. More accurate forecasts of tropical cyclones and heavy rainfall could assist governments in preparation for such natural harzards.[966]

A state that has satellites in orbit would suffer from an increase in the quantity of space debris.[967] Space capabilities also have direct battlefield relevance by providing real-time information and communication. They may therefore play a role in helping a state to

---

[962] *Ibid.*
[963] "Advancing Human Security: The Role of Technology and Politics," Reports of the Conference Working Groups, Halifax and Pugwash, Nova Scotia, Canada, 14-22 July 2003, http://www.ciaonet.org/pbei-2/pug/dec_03/dec_03.pdf, p. 13.
[964] OECD, "Solutions in Space," *Policy Brief*, October 2005, http://www.ciaonet.org/pbei/oecd/oecd026/oecd026.pdf, p. 6.
[965] UNIDIR, *Security in Space: The Next Generation*, Conference Report, 31 March-1 April 2008, pp. 25-26.
[966] R.A. Williamson and H.R. Hertzfeld, "Future Directions in Satellite-derived Weather and Climate Information for the Electrical Energy Industry: A Workshop Report," Space Policy Institute, The George Washington University, June 2004, http://www.gwu.edu/~spi/, pp. 1-2, 7; R.A. Williamson, H.R. Hertzfeld and J. Cordes, "The Socio-Economic Value of Improved Weather and Climate Information," Space Policy Institute, The George Washington University, Washington DC 20052, December 2002, http://www.gwu.edu/~spi/, pp. 1, 6, 14, 21.
[967] T. Hitchens, "Space Debris: Next Steps," in UNIDIR, *Safeguarding Space for All: Security and Peaceful Uses*, Conference Report, 25-26 March 2004, p. 61.

achieve military objectives and safeguard the lives of military personnel.

Environmental Security: Space technologies can help to monitor climate conditions and, thus, climate change. Space technologies could monitor climate fluctuations in particular areas over time, which could help to identify environmental degradation and provide the information needed to mitigate further damage. Satellite information could also help monitor deforestation and damage to forests due to fire damage, and assist with water resource management.[968]

Transnational Security: One of the key space security concerns is debris.[969] The principle sources of space debris are the accidental break-up of objects in orbit and the testing or employment of anti-satellite (ASAT) weapons.[970] Were space to become weaponised, any country in the line of fire of a space-based weapon would be at risk.[971] Given that a number of national security objectives, including economic performance and civil and military planning, rely on space technologies, there is a common interest in ensuring that threats to space-based assets are minimised. This concern has led some to call for a treaty-based common approach to space security.[972] Space technologies could also increase global transparency. Governments need to develop greater cooperation between space agencies as well as between those state agencies most likely to use space-based capabilities.[973]

Transcultural Security: Advances in satellite technology have helped to connect people across the world, particularly those without access to land-based communications.[974] They have also increased access to foreign media sources, widening the range of information and news sources available to people and their exposure to other cul-

---

[968] OECD, *op. cit.*, note 964, p. 2.
[969] Hitchens, *op. cit.*, note 967, p. 61.
[970] D. Wright, "Space Debris from Antisatellite Weapons," *Bulletin of the Atomic Scientists*, 1 October 2007, http://www.thebulletin.org/web-edition/features/space-debris-antisatellite-weapons.
[971] M. Krepon, "Weapons in the Heavens: A Radical and Reckless Option," *Arms Control Today*, Vol. 34, No. 9, 2004.
[972] See "Space Security" Space Policy Institute, Elliot School of International Affairs, George Washington University, Washington DC, http://www.gwu.edu/~spi/.
[973] OECD, *op. cit.*, note 964, p. 7.
[974] *Ibid.*, p. 2.

tures. Space technologies provide a medium for education about different histories, cultural traditions and values.

Global Justice

Central to security is the question of justice, which has traditionally been considered a domestic concern that is not applicable to the global context. Indeed, as is mentioned above in the discussion of global justice, whether justice can be achieved at the global level is still one of the major debates in the global justice literature, which is partly related to contractarian dimensions of the concept of justice in Western traditions. Some observers, such as Nagel, maintain that the content of justice must be shaped by the type of associative arrangements that exist between people. In line with this argument, global justice promoted by international organisations would include humanitarian assistance, the promotion of human rights and the provision of public goods, such as free trade and a clean and sustainable environment, but would not imply democratic legitimacy or social justice.[975]

Yet, it is not the case that people or states can choose whether to be part of the global system, and even the minimum moral obligations of providing humanitarian assistance and protecting and promoting human rights are premised on normative ideals, given that we have no innate moral repertoire but only some morally relevant emotions. Thus, whatever is implied in global social justice has normative foundations. Even from the point of view of self-interest, global justice is required because of the centrality of human dignity to well-being, security and stability. Yet, ensuring human dignity necessarily implies some degree of socio-economic justice and political legitimacy in those organs most responsible for dispensing global justice.

The centrality of justice to security was outlined in my proposal for a multi-sum security principle (see Diagram 9).

---

[975] Nagel, *op. cit.*, note 612, p. 137.

Diagram 9: The Multi-sum Security Principle

```
                    Human
                   Security

Transcultural    Multi-sum Security    Environmental
  Security           Principle            Security

              "In a globalized world, security can no
              longer be thought of as a zero-sum game
              involving states alone. Global security,
              instead, has five dimensions that include
              human, environmental, national, trans-
              national, and transcultural security,
              and, therefore, global security and the
              security of any state or culture cannot
              be achieved without good governance at
              all levels that guarantees security
              through justice for all individuals,
              states, and cultures."

Transnational     © Nayef R.F. Al-Rodhan     National
   Security              2007                Security
```

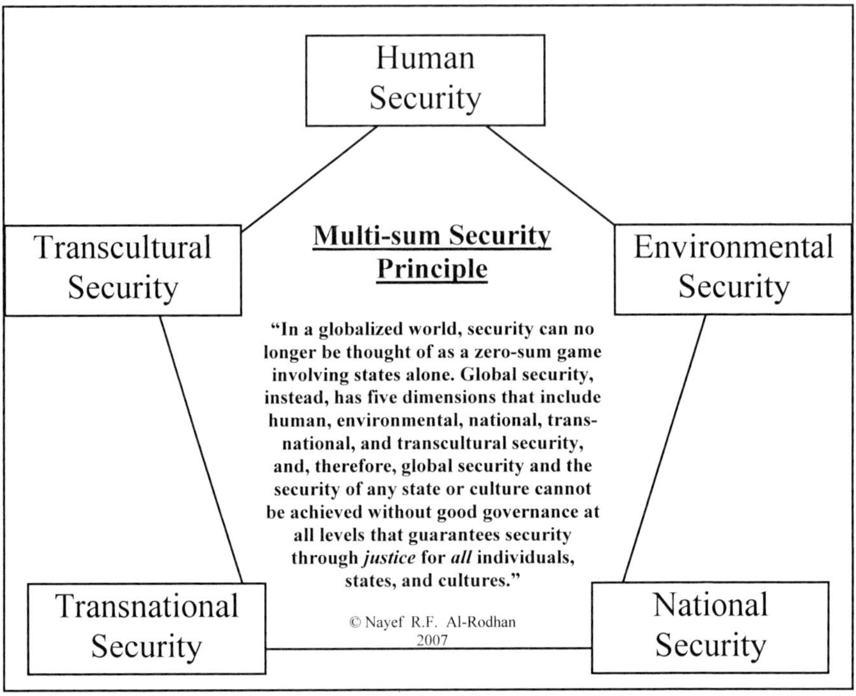

Source: N.R.F. Al-Rodhan, *The Five Dimensions of Global Security: Proposal for a Multi-sum Security Principle* (Berlin: LIT, 2007), p. 31, reprinted with permission from LIT.

3. The Challenges

A number of challenges to achieving sustainable security stem from the tension between emerging universal norms, on the one hand, and the continued importance of traditional conceptions of state sovereignty, national security and neo-liberal market agendas, on the other.

Human Security
Shifting the focus of international law away from state sovereignty in support of human security would prove difficult indeed. This is due to the continued employment of narrow conceptions of national security, even though focusing on human security complements national secu-

rity. This is connected to another difficulty encountered in the promotion and protection of human security – that multilateral institutions and instruments, such as the Ottawa Convention (banning antipersonnel landmines), the International Criminal Court and the Optional Protocol to the Convention on the Rights of the Child, rely on the cooperation of states to achieve human security objectives.[976] The EU has a doctrine of human security, for instance, but joint European Security and Defence Policy (ESDP) operations take place on the basis of unanimity.[977]

The "logic" of neo-liberalism that accompanies globalisation also hinders the promotion of human security. In the area of health, this logic does not work in favour of immunisation against infectious diseases, despite the existence of the necessary technology. In addition, only a fraction of those suffering from HIV/AIDS have access to retroviral therapy. This is largely due to the high cost of such drugs and their protection under intellectual property rights.[978]

Governance problems clearly have a negative effect on human security. At the national level, human security relies on states having the institutional and financial means with which to provide for people's basic health, housing, food, physical security and justice needs. It also requires effective transnational cooperation, given that many threats to human security, such as environmental damage or infectious diseases, are transnational in nature. However, not all states have the capacity to engage effectively in such cooperative efforts. At the global level, the problem, as is indicated above, is that multinational institutions are at the mercy of power political relations in the international system.[979]

Environmental Security

Global climate change is likely to affect different regions differently. At the same time, regions have different capacities to respond to the local effects. How climate change will affect social order will largely depend on the success with which governments respond. When states

---

[976] Al-Rodhan, *The Five Dimensions of Global Security*, *op. cit.*, note 512, pp. 45-46.
[977] Matlary, *op. cit.*, note 865, p. 140.
[978] World Health Organization, UNAIDs, UNICEF, *Towards Universal Access: Scaling Up Priority HIV/AIDs Interventions in the Health Sector: Progress Report*, April 2007, pp. 14, 21.
[979] Al-Rodhan, *The Five Dimensions of Global Security*, *op. cit.*, note 512, pp. 46-47.

cannot provide for their populations' basic needs and security, they may be considered failing states.[980] At present, few governments have the capacity to respond adequately to humanitarian crises or to mitigate the indirect effects of climate change. There is a need to develop resilience and the ability to respond to the effects of global climate change, and this involves good governance.[981] Moreover, in developing countries the resources with which to curb destruction of forests, fisheries, reefs, and so on, may simply not be adequate.[982]

A major factor hindering environmental security is the existence of competing interests at the national level. The strength of business lobbies in particular tends to cause state policy to reflect short-term interests at the expense of long-term ones. The US case is illustrative.[983]

As mentioned earlier, like human security, governance problems also represent obstacles for environmental security. In many cases, environmental degradation is partly the result of bad environmental management policies.[984] At the global level, environmental security governance is hampered by the fact that while all states and societies benefit from measures taken to prevent or reduce environmental damage, individual states and their economies bear the cost. Moreover, some developing countries argue that they have a right to industrialise as the developed world did in the past and should not have to bear the cost of reducing pollution while doing so. This is a contentious point, and the preferential treatment granted to developing countries in the Global South in the Kyoto Protocol is one of the reasons for US objections to it.[985]

National Security
Despite the increased recognition that transnational threats to security are typically multidimensional, state-based paradigms in areas such as health continue to complicate effective and coordinated responses. At

---

[980] Maybee, *op. cit.*, note 872, p. 99.
[981] *Ibid.*, pp. 101-102.
[982] F. McNeil, "Making Sense of Environmental Security," *The North-South Agenda Papers*, No. 39, February 2000, http://www.ciaonet.org/wps/mcf01/39AP.pdf, p. 8.
[983] J. Wallace, "US Environmental Policy and Global Security," in N.R.F. Al-Rodhan (ed.) *Policy Briefs on the* Transnational *Aspects of Security and Stability* (Berlin: LIT, 2007), p. 187.
[984] Al-Rodhan, *The Five Dimensions of Global Security, op. cit.*, note 512, p. 57.
[985] J. Goldstein, *International Relations* (New York: Longman, 1999), pp. 472-473.

a more operational level, the growth in the salience of transnational challenges to national security requires states to have the correct military and civil capacities to respond effectively to them in coordination with other states. This may demand a considerable degree of restructuring in some states as well as the development of civilian capacities. A comprehensive national security architecture may be lacking in many countries.

Transnational Security
Transnational threats to security cannot be effectively responded to through solutions generated by state-based regimes. For example, countering the spread of infectious diseases relies on coordination between health and other public authorities on a transnational basis. In the area of non-proliferation, existing arms control regimes were established to deal with state proliferators, but the number of non-state proliferators is growing. Intelligence also remains a primarily state-based activity, and there is still considerable reluctance to work on a transnational basis.

In addition, the need to establish a common set of norms can make transnational security efforts challenging. Joint activities also require the availability of resources. This may be particularly difficult to achieve when some states lack the institutional and financial capacities to participate effectively in cooperative measures and activities. Moreover, cooperation may be required in areas that are traditionally perceived as at the heart of state sovereignty, such as law enforcement, intelligence and, potentially, defence.[986]

Transcultural Security
A major challenge facing states is to promote a national identity that is inclusive enough for all members of society to feel they are part of it. This is a particularly important task for those countries with declining populations and a growing dependence on the multiple contributions of migrants and immigrants.

In an era of globalisation, tension may be generated by close contact between people of different ethnicities and religions if that contact is marked by a lack of awareness.[987] At all levels, efforts must be made to spread knowledge of "the other". Increasing awareness of

---
[986] Al-Rodhan, *The Five Dimensions of Global Security*, *op. cit.*, note 512, p. 78.
[987] *Ibid.*, p. 83.

one another is vital. Attempting to see the world through other people's belief systems is an important part of awareness of others. As Mark Earls points out, some things take on greater significance than they would in one's own belief system. Equally, things that would be important in one's own system of beliefs may be less important in someone else's.[988]

Irresponsible statements on the part of opinion formers in the media and the education system or by politicians and spokespersons can also fuel negative cultural stereotypes and a culture of fear and alienation. One of the difficulties in relation to ensuring that the media plays a positive role in relation to transcultural security is that responsible practices may largely depend on the establishment of voluntary standards. The Internet poses the added problem of anonymity, as is discussed in my book *The Emergence of Blogs as* a Fifth Estate *and Their Security Implications* (2007).[989]

4. The Way Forward

Challenges to sustainable security exist, but the concepts and values on which to achieve it also exist, even under conditions of formal international anarchy. Norms and governance mechanisms are expanding along with increased interdependence and interconnectedness. Those who prioritise the need for human dignity provide a solid foundation on which to build.

Human Security
Ensuring human security requires that basic civil liberties and human rights be respected and upheld. While human rights are universal, the way in which they are realised in particular cultural settings has to be taken into account. Inclusiveness is also an important means of generating a sense of belonging among all members of society, and of preventing marginalisation and alienation within society. The state has a responsibility to foster an inclusive national identity and environment. Human security also depends on states having the institutional capacities to ensure that people are free from fear and want, and that they

---

[988] M. Earls, *Herd: How to Change Mass Behaviour By Harnessing Our True Nature* (Chichester: John Wiley & Sons Ltd, 2007), p. 320.
[989] N.R.F. Al-Rodhan, *The Emergence of Blogs as* a Fifth Estate *and Their Security Implications* (Genève: Éditions Slatkine, 2007).

have a positive sense of self. As mentioned, corruption and lack of accountability, for example, typically diminish human well-being, resulting in the misallocation of resources and a lack of equal access to public services such as health care and education. In addition to good domestic governance, meeting human security needs depends on cooperation between states in areas of prevention as well as effective management of threats to human security.[990]

Environmental Security
It is not only the UN and its agencies but also regional and sub-regional groupings that need to be mobilised in order to address the consequences of global climate change. Help from neighbours should also be mobilised, and the more affluent states must contribute the resources with which to prepare for the potential consequences of climate change.[991] Burden-sharing is also required since many countries in the Global South may not have the financial resources available to prevent further destruction of natural resources. While a comprehensive "grand strategy" for linking security, the environment and growth might be desirable, it may be much easier in the short term to proceed, as Frank McNeil suggests, with a series of smaller "bargains" to deal with specific problems, perhaps on a regional basis.[992]

Information regarding environmental security needs to be easily accessible and transparent. Studies on climate change need to be clear and scientific.[993] Scientific case studies that demonstrate the connection between environmental security and sustainable economic growth could help to encourage changes in approaches to development and the economy. Equally, environmental security-relevant information compiled by governments needs to be accessible to scientists and the general public.[994]

---

[990] Al-Rodhan, *The Five Dimensions of Global Security, op. cit.*, note 512, pp. 118-121.
[991] Smith and Vivekananda, *op. cit.*, note 875, p. 8.
[992] McNeil, *op. cit.*, note 982, p. 8.
[993] N.R.F. Al-Rodhan, "Editorial of Policy Brief on US Environmental Policy and Global Security," in Al-Rodhan, *Policy Briefs on the* Transnational *Aspects of Security and Stability, op. cit.*, note 983, p. 199.
[994] McNeil, *op. cit.*, note 982, p. 7.

National Security
National security requires a comprehensive approach and a security strategy that addresses the multidimensional character of security challenges. This, in turn, needs to be complemented by a national security council that is able to deal with the broad range and interconnected nature of issues that affect national security in today's world. *The Three Pillars of Sustainable National Security in a Transnational World* (2008) argues that a national security council should be capable of engaging in long-term threat prevention by upholding and promoting ethical standards.[995] The pursuit of justice as fairness is also critical.

Sustainable national security cannot be achieved alone. Given the interdependence between states and sectors, and almost instantaneous interconnectedness, coordination and cooperation across sectors as well as between states are required to prevent, and where they occur, to ensure adequate and timely responses to, security challenges. Mutually advantageous security relationships that imply burden- and capacity-sharing must also be accompanied by a recognition that positive exchanges and interactions between cultures are critical to long-term, sustainable security.

Transnational Security
Effective domestic governance is essential in order to ensure transnational security. However, some states may lack the financial and institutional capacities with which to adequately respond to issues that cannot be contained within their borders. Capacity-building is thus likely to be important in promoting transnational security. This may include training and the exchange of best practices. Effective multilateralism is also needed if states are to collectively prevent, and where this fails, adequately respond to, transnational threats as they emerge. Multilateral institutions have an essential role to play in complementing the efforts of states and regional institutions and arrangements. This means effective and accountable administrative, legislative and executive capacities at the global level. It also means liberating multilateral institutions from power politics as far as is possible, which

---

[995] Al-Rodhan, *The Three Pillars of* Sustainable National Security, *op. cit.*, note 667.

generally implies reform with the aim of making them more representative.[996]

Transcultural Security
Mutual awareness, recognition, respect and exchanges are essential aspects of transcultural security. Increased awareness of other peoples traditions, cultural values and histories has to begin with dialogue. Inter-cultural and inter-faith dialogues are not only means of understanding the bases of differences, but also vehicles for discerning commonalities and the complexity of "the other" that is all too often understood not just in essentialist, but also in homogenous terms.[997] Transcultural security also implies respect for human rights that also have a cultural group dimension. The education system is vital to enhancing awareness of cultural and religious differences. The media and the entertainment industry also need to be aware of the potential positive or negative impact they can have on inter-cultural relations, and ought to continue to develop a set of standards and best practices to help guide their activities. Moreover, minorities within national mass media institutions require better representation in order to help break down stereotypes, increase awareness and promote greater trust between ethnic, cultural and religious communities.

5. Conclusion

Global security is vital to satisfying human needs, including the need for dignity, and is therefore an important ingredient of sustainable history. The five dimensions of security outlined above provide a more comprehensive framework for global security than that provided by a traditional realist approach. While global security may be divided into these five elements for analytical purposes, the five are in reality intertwined. Successfully addressing security challenges in today's world requires a recognition of the multi-dimensional nature of security issues, and a concerted effort to establish the capacity to address such multi-faceted and often transnational challenges. Moreover, there is a need to understand the linkage between security and justice, and to ensure that security policies incorporate a strong justice-based ele-

---
[996] Al-Rodhan, *The Five Dimensions of Global Security, op. cit.*, note 512, pp. 120-121, 124.
[997] *Ibid.*, p. 126.

ment. Given that this is the case, how should we approach international relations? This question is addressed in Chapter 12.

CHAPTER 12

HOW SHOULD WE APPROACH INTERNATIONAL RELATIONS?
SYMBIOTIC REALISM

How we understand international relations will also have an impact on the sustainability of history, given that this will inform how we act in the world. Realism has dominated the study of international relations and a great deal of foreign and security policy thinking. This has meant that the focus has been disproportionately on relations between states. Realism does not constitute a single theory but an orientation. In general, states are assumed to be unitary rational egoists, behaving on the basis of rationally calculated decisions about outcomes that maximise self-interest. In order to ensure their continued survival, a state's primary concern is thought to be to amass power and to form alliances against any state that threatens to upset the established power balance. In this vision of the world, outcomes are zero-sum. States are assumed to be concerned not with absolute gains, but with relative gains. In the absence of an overarching authority capable of enforcing commitments, managing conflict and providing security, morality is believed to have no place in international relations. Interaction between states is not assumed to significantly alter patterns of behaviour.[998]

      This chapter outlines some of the problems with realism. I then briefly outline a theory of international relations that provides a conceptual framework better able to ensure sustainable history than realism. Symbiotic realism is a theory of relations in a globally anarchic world of interdependence and instant connectedness.[999] It is intended to provide an understanding of global politics that overcomes the state-centrism of realism, as well as a guide to action in a complex global system characterised by four interconnected dynamics: a) the

---

[998] Al-Rodhan, *Symbiotic Realism, op. cit.*, note 78, pp. 9-10.
[999] See *Ibid.*

predilections of human nature; b) global anarchy; c) interdependence; and d) instant connectivity.[1000] This chapter discusses the foreign policy challenges that become apparent when the world is viewed through the lens of symbiotic realism rather than realism. Finally, I suggest how these challenges may be met.

1. The Problems of Realism

Human nature in a realist vision of the world is driven by fear, reputation and self-interest, with very little place allotted to free will and, thus, for the capacity to alter one's nature. Any moral behaviour that may be displayed is thought to result from self-interest rather than altruism. Since the state is believed to be the most important political unit, these characteristics are transposed to the level of the state. A state is thought to be above all concerned with its own survival, which it attempts to secure through the accretion of power. However, as one state accumulates power it makes others insecure and encourages them to do the same. In the absence of an overarching authority structure capable of guaranteeing the security of states, a permanent security dilemma is believed to be generated and security competition becomes part of the natural order of things.[1001] Realists believe that the security dilemma can be limited by a balance of power. The neo-realist scholar Kenneth Waltz, for example, contends that wherever two or more major powers exist, a balance of power will prevail. In his view, states tend to balance a growing power in order to prevent it from upsetting the status quo. Indeed, according to Waltz, the correct subject of study for international relations is the study of the balance of power under conditions of international anarchy; and thus "high politics", such as war, military alliances, and so on. The distribution of military power is thought to determine change and transformation in the international system.[1002]

Since states are considered the principal actors in international politics, and they are presumed to be rational egoists, moral values are thought to belong solely to the domestic sphere. The self-interest of states negates agreement on universal moral principles. Similarly,

---

[1000] Al-Rodhan, *Symbiotic Realism*, *op. cit.*, note 78, p. 11.
[1001] Al-Rodhan, *The Five Dimensions of Global Security*, *op. cit.*, note 512, p. 21.
[1002] K.N. Waltz, *The Theory of International Politics* (New York: McGraw-Hill, 1979).

cooperative arrangements between states are thought to survive only for as long as states perceive them to be in their interest,[1003] and multilateral institutions are thought to exist at the whim of the interests of the major powers.

Yet, human nature is composed of a greater number of facets than those emphasised by realism. As is pointed out in Symbiotic Realism, the realist conception of human nature neglects those elements that require an ability to capture the manner in which perceptions and norms may alter behaviour and may, indeed, be at least partly constitutive of self. This indicates that shifts in the distribution of military power may form only one explanation for change and transformation within the international system. Norms and perceptions are also likely to account for change and transformation.

Moreover, states can no longer ensure their security simply through self-help. Many of the threats that they face originate not from other states, but from non-state actors, many of which may act transnationally. The increasing attention devoted to culture, for instance, reflects the importance of large collective identities in global politics. We cannot afford to negate the importance of cultural issues in a world marked by increased human mobility and communications. When images can be broadcast simultaneously in various areas of the globe, the treatment or activities of a group could affect that or those of fellow members of the group in other countries.[1004]

Moreover, as is explained in Chapter 11, the dangers posed by non-state actors are in many instances non-military in nature. Today, national security analysts count the consequences of global warming, such as extreme weather and water shortage, as well as the spread of infectious disease, cyber attacks on critical infrastructure, and so on, as potential threats to security. High politics is therefore not necessarily the most effective focus of global politics. Moreover, events in one area of the world can have an almost immediate impact in another due to the rapidity and availability of information flows. Addressing the dangers posed by non-state actors requires cooperation with other states and a different range of "security tools" – not just military means.

Given that security and prosperity are highly dependent on cooperative relations with other states, we cannot assume that rela-

---

[1003] Al-Rodhan, *The Five Dimensions of Global Security, op. cit.*, note 512, p. 22.
[1004] Al-Rodhan, *Symbiotic Realism, op. cit.*, note 78, p. 14.

tions between states are necessarily principally governed by competition. Increased interdependence means that absolute gains are possible and that global politics ought not to be a priori zero-sum as realism suggests. This implies that even if a state possesses a disproportionate degree of power, other states may not form alliances against it. Indeed, it is far more likely in today's world that they would ally themselves with the most powerful state, if that power were constituted primarily through capacities other than solely military power.

Realists also assume that state power is derived from the control of resources. The need to control resources derives from the assumption that resources are scarce and that there exists no overarching authority to regulate their distribution. Competition for resources is, thus, presumed to be omnipresent. Yet, the validity of this assumption needs to be re-evaluated, given that technological advances may provide alternatives to currently scarce resources.[1005] While natural resources, such as oil, remain highly relevant to a state's situation in the global environment, a number of other "capacities" are also significant, as I explain in Neo-*statecraft and* Meta-*geopolitics: Reconciliation of Power, Interests and Justice in the 21st Century* (2009).[1006] Meta-geopolitics, as I term it, ought to consider a number of facets of state power, including social issues and health, domestic politics, economics, the environment, science and human potential, military and security issues and international diplomacy.

2. Symbiotic Realism

Symbiotic realism attributes an important role to human nature. It adopts a broader conception of human nature informed by the insights of neurobiology. Within this view, people may be driven by basic instincts or higher aspirations. When survival is at stake, basic instincts take precedence. However, once basic needs are satisfied, humankind is capable of acting morally. Yet, it is important to remember that we are referring to the majority of people and that the moral capabilities of individuals also depend on upbringing, education and personal experience.[1007] Clearly, the existence of governance mechanisms makes moral behaviour more likely under international anarchy. In-

---

[1005] Al-Rodhan, *Symbiotic Realism, op. cit.*, note 78, p. 11.
[1006] Al-Rodhan, Neo-*statecraft and* Meta-*geopolitics, op. cit.*, note 185.
[1007] Al-Rodhan, *Symbiotic Realism, op. cit.*, note 78, p. 70.

deed, if people are generally capable of acting according to moral standards only when their basic needs are met, good global governance structures are essential.

In my view, states remain central actors in the global system. Yet, we do not assume that they are unitary actors that base their actions on rationally calculated interests. Some parts of the state may be involved in transnational networks, forming part of a governance structure that goes beyond the boundaries of the state but, at the same time, does not constitute a world state. State interests and preferences may also be modified by the product of repeated interaction with other states. Both of these factors suggest that order may exist even in the absence of a sovereign world state.

In addition, military capabilities alone may not be enough to indicate a threat. There must also be a perception that a state's possession of military capabilities represents a threat. The security dilemma that is thought to exist in an internationally anarchic world order is thus not automatic and is likely to depend as much on threat perceptions as on actual military capabilities.[1008]

However, a focus on states is not sufficient, and a more comprehensive conception of the global system was sought for my theory. I consider large collective identities, whether sub-national, transnational or supranational, to be important actors. They should not be conceived in a static way, but as fluid entities. Moreover, they are not homogenous, but are likely to contain contradictions. Given the degree of human mobility and instant connectivity today, we must be aware of the relevance of large collective identities, for maintaining a stable sense of self, and also for maintaining a sense of community in multicultural societies and on a global level.[1009] A positive self-identity, which is partly related to collective identities, and a sense of belonging are basic human needs which need to be understood as such.

Moreover, a lack of attention to exchanges and instances of borrowing between geo-cultural domains can lead to cultural arrogance and the belief that each geo-cultural domain is self-sufficient, and that encounters with others implies conflict. Yet, if we look at the history of human civilisation it becomes clear that cultures and geo-cultural domains have always overlapped and intersected in ways that

---

[1008] *Ibid.*, pp. 74-75.
[1009] *Ibid.*, p. 78.

cumulatively constructed human civilisation. Awareness of this interconnectivity and mutual debt is essential as a means of undercutting arguments, such as Huntington's clash of civilisations thesis,[1010] that only risk becoming self-fulfilling. It is also a highly useful means of "deconstructing" the exclusionary civilisational identities on which a great deal of history has been written.

In a highly interconnected world, multilateral institutions are important actors. While they are all too frequently held hostage to the whims of the most powerful states, this is often because of the manner in which institutional mechanisms and arrangements reflect power relations within the global political system.[1011] As is noted above, the Bretton Woods institutions and the UN were established by the victors of the Second World War and clearly reflect that fact.

Nevertheless, these institutions have a vital role to play in mediating relations between states as well as providing the means through which to tackle an array of problems that cannot be dealt with by any one state alone or through state-centric paradigms (e.g. health, environmental degradation, migration). They still form the central public elements of global governance and, as such, there is a greater possibility of holding them accountable, at least to their members. Multilateralism is also crucial for burden-sharing between states, and the need to find cooperative solutions to policy challenges. In addition, these institutions have played a key role in diffusing norms and principles.

NGOs also contribute to global governance and their role needs to be captured within a theoretical framework. Their memberships are transnational actors rather than states. This means that they are not subject to the same constraints as multinational institutions and, indeed, can claim to be more capable of representing people or causes that may be neglected by mainstream politics. Yet, NGOs were not only created to represent the less fortunate in society. Companies have come together to help to establish common standards, and professional bodies have developed transnational connections, forming organizational bodies to help them achieve their objectives. In between multilateral institutions and NGOs, there exist hybrid organisations in which states and NGOs work together for particular purposes. These include organisations such as the International Committee of

---

[1010] See Huntington, *op. cit.*, note 46.
[1011] Al-Rodhan, *Symbiotic Realism, op. cit.*, note 78, p. 15.

the Red Cross and the International Air Transport Association, for example.[1012] Such organisations are central to effective and timely responses to, for instance, natural disasters and conflict situations.

Transnational corporations are generally understood to be firms that are based in one country and operate in another. However, they are also understood as companies that have affiliates abroad.[1013] Although they have existed since the 19th century, their phenomenal growth has been under way since the late 20th century and is related to a restructuring of the global political economy. The deregulation of markets and technological advances have created new possibilities for companies wishing to practice regulatory arbitrage. One of the consequences of this is that health and safety standards, and arguably wages, are under downward pressure, contributing to a decline in standards and well-being. This may be especially true of those working in sectors that rely on a heavy presence of foreign companies.[1014]

Symbiotic realism also classifies women as actors in and of themselves in order to make them more visible. Women are affected by and, at the same time, help to shape the global system in ways that may be quite different from those of men. At the most basic level, they have different access to health care and education. A recent Geneva Centre for the Democratic Control of Armed Forces report documents that women's mortality rate is higher due to inadequate access to health care, for example.[1015] Reduced educational opportunities can also affect women's life expectancy. Lack of education could, for instance, increase the risk of death during childbirth as well as that of undernourishment. In short, women are a specific kind of actor and are all too often hidden from view because of what the traditional international relations paradigm has allowed one to "see".[1016]

Symbiotic realism identifies the environment as a "reactive actor", because it responds, albeit in a non-conscious and non-rational way, to human activities. While human beings have affected the environment since the time they first appeared, the past century has been unprecedented in terms of their impact. This degree of human activity,

---

[1012] *Ibid.*, p. 80.
[1013] *Ibid.*, pp. 80-81.
[1014] *Ibid.*, p. 111.
[1015] M. Vlachova and L. Biason (eds.) *Women in an Insecure World: Violence against Women, Facts, Figures and Analysis* (Geneva: Geneva Centre for the Democratic Control of Armed Forces, 2005).
[1016] Al-Rodhan, *Symbiotic Realism, op. cit.*, note 78, pp. 85-87.

particularly economic activity, in conjunction with population increases is prompting the environment to react in specific ways that are presently affecting and are likely to help shape the future global order. It is therefore essential to recognise the role that the environment plays in the international sphere. Indeed, the environment is reacting in ways that may affect the sustainability of the present level of human civilisation.

Global climate change caused, according to the majority opinion in the scientific community, by the emission of greenhouse gases such as carbon dioxide is likely to result in a temperature rise of 2-9 degrees over the next 50 years. This will accelerate the melting of the polar ice caps, causing sea levels to rise. As a result, whole communities could be displaced and island states may disappear completely. A rise in sea levels could also increase the severity of storms, due to altered wave patterns. Global warming is also likely to have an impact on ecosystems in ways that may threaten people's livelihood and affect local and national economies, as well as having much broader global ramifications.

Moreover, the regions of the world are likely to be affected differently by a rise in the global temperature. Africa is thought to be the most vulnerable to global climate change, where it could lead to a further reduction in the availability of water, increased food insecurity and increased health risks. Other regions, such as Latin America, could experience more pronounced variations in climate, affecting biodiversity and crop yields.[1017] Countries such as Canada may gain habitable land in their northern territories, and benefit from the opening up of shipping routes. Climate change is, thus, likely to help shape the security and geopolitical environment of the future.

One of the difficulties of reducing environmental damage is the transnational nature of its impact. Moreover, damage to the environment is connected to practices that are embedded in the global political economy. Many actors that contribute to environmental degradation are the non-state actors which are hardest to regulate, most notably corporations. Successful regulation of the environment will require governance mechanisms that will have to be agreed multilaterally and in some instances transnationally, as well as enforcement mechanisms.[1018]

[1017] *Ibid.*, pp. 83-85.
[1018] *Ibid.*, pp. 113-114.

Natural resources also need to be considered as types of "actors" since they too "react" in ways that affect the global system and have implications for human civilisation as a whole. They constitute resources essential to human life. Industrial wealth creation processes rely on the use of natural resources. As such, they also constitute a source of wealth for states. Energy use, in particular, is likely to have a profound impact on the global system. Economies depended on fossil fuels, such as coal and oil, in the 20th century. The ease of moving away from a dependence on such fuels is likely to depend on advances in technology and those who develop them.

As a subset of technology, ICT is also considered to be a "reactive actor" by symbiotic realism. ICT has altered the rapidity with which information and images can be diffused across the globe. The consequences of advances in this area have been felt in relation to global economic and financial market activities, travel and transportation, the increased relevance of the media and of public diplomacy, and the growth and risks related to cyberspace and the "blogosphere", to name just a few.[1019] Regulation of ICT is difficult because of its widespread accessibility and the decentralised nature and potential anonymity of its users.

3. The Dynamics of the Global System

According to symbiotic realism, the dynamics of the global system are the outcome of four interlocking dynamics – the neurobiological substrates of human nature, global anarchy, interdependence and instant connectivity. Actors thus exist in particular conditions determined by the "state of nature" (SON), depicted in Diagram 10.

[1019] *Ibid.*, pp. 90-91.

Diagram 10: Symbiotic Realism and Governance

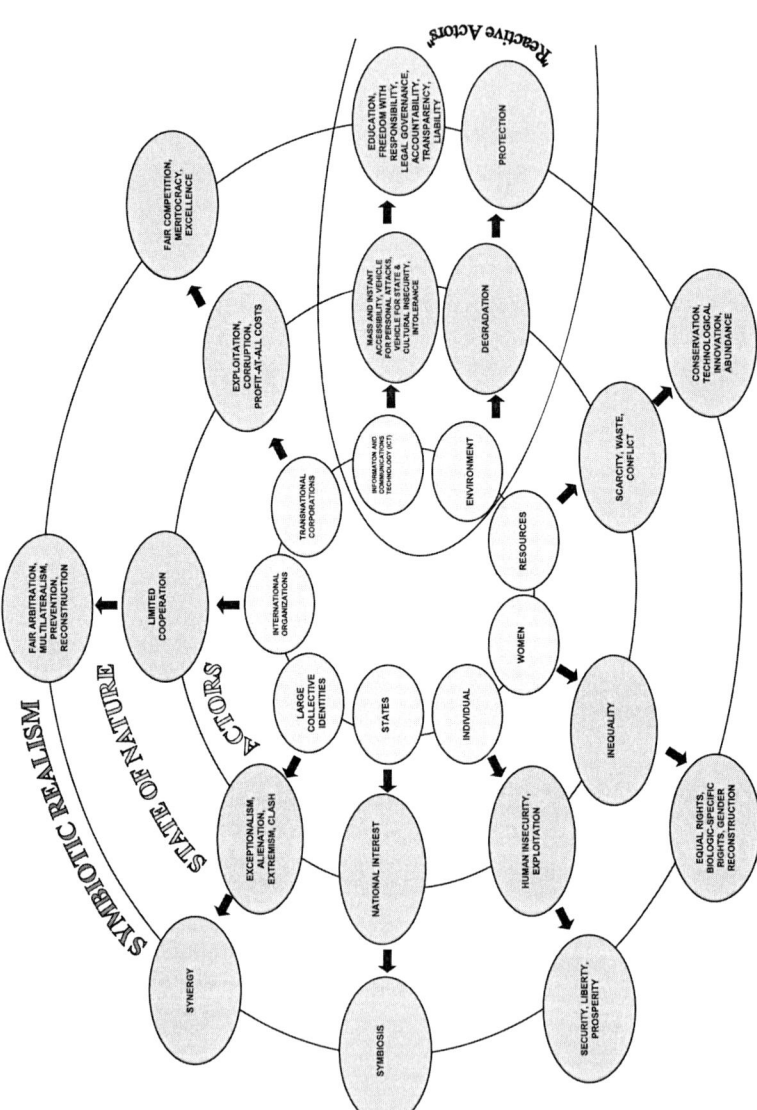

Source: N.R.F. Al-Rodhan, *Symbiotic Realism: A Theory of International Relations in an Instant and an Interdependent World* (Berlin: LIT, 2007), p. 118, reprinted with permission from LIT, appears with modifications.

Individuals
Human beings are driven first and foremost by the satisfaction of their basic needs, including food, shelter, physical security, belonging and a positive self-identity. They are, thus, motivated by their emotional self-interest. Until their basic needs are satisfied, they are unlikely to be guided by conscious moral frameworks. Human insecurity and exploitation are likely to exist in the SON. As is mentioned above, women both affect and are affected by the dynamics of the global system in gender-specific ways determined by their reduced/lack of status in many spheres of life.

States
In an SON, states are likely to pursue their own self-interest, perceived as ensuring their own survival in conditions of international anarchy. National interest may, however, be defined not only by the external environment, but also by domestic actors or "penetration" by other states.[1020] In *Taming American Power: The Global Response to US Primacy* (2005), Stephen Walt argues that "domestic political penetration" by other states helps to shape US foreign policy for the worse.[1021] ICT may also penetrate domestic politics in states and help to shape policy stances. Balancing behaviour as a result of threat perceptions may also constitute part of state behaviour in an SON.

International Organisations
In an SON, cooperation between states within multilateral institutions is limited. States are, moreover, likely to be hostages to major powers, which are over-represented and enjoy privileged positions in multilateral institutions. Cooperation will prevail when it is in the perceived interests of these powers. NGOs have a greater ability to act impartially. They sometimes help to fill the vacuum left by multilateral institutions. They also play a significant role in terms of raising consciousness and agenda-setting.[1022]

[1020] *Ibid.*, p. 100.
[1021] S. Walt, *Taming American Power: The Global Response to US Primacy* (New York: Norton & Company, 2005), p. 216.
[1022] Al-Rodhan, *Symbiotic Realism, op. cit.*, note 78, p. 111.

Large Collective Identities

The basic need of human beings for a positive identity and belonging can, if not met, lead to exceptionalism, exclusion and alienation. The history of imperialism, cultural arrogance and exceptionalism that unfortunately persists today can lead to a sense of injustice and lack or recognition by those who feel pushed to the margins of global history. Increased interdependence and instant connectivity may add another dimension. Migration in the context of the global division of labour may bring people into close contact with "strangers" against a backdrop of socio-economic inequalities. Without sufficient awareness of different traditions and cultural values, this can lead to tension, particularly when exploited by those who wish to breed mistrust and fear for their own personal ends. [1023]

Transnational Corporations

Without rules and regulations that specify otherwise, TNCs practice regulatory arbitrage. By relocating or establishing strategic alliances with other enterprises, they can move from one country to another where conditions are deemed more favourable. This capacity may result in a steady decline in labour conditions as governments seek to attract or keep TNCs on their territories. Thus, in an SON, TNCs may contribute to increased exploitation and to the pursuit of profit at all costs. [1024]

Environment and Natural Resources

In an SON, a legal framework regulating activities that affect the environment is notoriously difficult to negotiate on a multilateral basis. These activities are embedded in the socio-economic and political structures of states. Ensuring economic prosperity forms part of the state's national security considerations, which makes acting on the basis of long-term considerations that may imply short-term costs on the part of companies particularly challenging for states. The scarcity of natural resources may also be aggravated by inadequate management strategies on the part of states. [1025]

[1023] *Ibid.*, pp. 100-103, 107-108.
[1024] *Ibid.*, p. 111.
[1025] *Ibid.*, p. 114.

ICT
The enforced regulation of ICT is particularly difficult because of mass and instant access. Cybercrime is developing faster than the capacity of law enforcement agencies to combat it. As is noted in *The Emergence of Blogs as* a Fifth Estate *and Their Security Implications* (2007), if cyberspace is insufficiently regulated, it can become a vehicle for personal attacks as well as state insecurity and intolerance.[1026]

4. Foreign Policy Challenges

A great many of the foreign policy challenges faced by states today are the result of the emergence of norms that challenge traditional and narrow conceptions of state sovereignty, such as those centred on the individual as a subject of security. In addition, relative power remains a concern for states, but the context in which states act requires cooperation and a considerable degree of burden-sharing. Finally, finding the right balance between peaceful unity and respect for cultural differences is a challenge for states in the present context.

Individuals
The 1948 Universal Declaration of Human Rights extended liberal political and civil rights to include economic and cultural rights. It enjoys widespread support, but people's human rights are still not universally respected.[1027] Challenges are posed by the conflicting principle of state sovereignty. Human rights are conceived as universal rights that belong to all individuals, although the continuation of particularistic national identities continues to compromise such rights, due to a lack of openness to international human rights pressure. The international norms of sovereignty and non-intervention are more vigorously supported than those of human rights. There are, nevertheless, different interpretations of the scope and implications of sovereignty and non-intervention, and it is this fact that is likely to determine the extent to which the leaders of a particular state perceive a contradiction between sovereignty and international human rights norms.[1028]

[1026] Al-Rodhan, *The Emergence of Blogs as* a Fifth Estate, *op. cit.*, note 989.
[1027] Al-Rodhan, *Symbiotic Realism*, *op. cit.*, note 78, p. 116.
[1028] J. Donnelly, "An Overview," in D.P. Forsythe (ed.) *Human Rights and Comparative Foreign Policy* (United Nations University, 2000), pp. 315, 318-319.

Another matter alluded to above is the claim that human rights are not compatible with some non-Western cultures. In some instances, people may not be fully aware of cultural sensitivities, what may be feasible and when, and which actors may be best placed to progress particular rights, such as those of women.

States

As is explained above, states in the realist paradigm are assumed to pursue their own material interests within an anarchical international system. These are, moreover, assumed to be concerned with relative as well as absolute gains. There is a tendency therefore for states to engage in short-term calculations of national interest. These calculations are assumed to be reached by rational assessments of the costs and benefits of various options.[1029] Yet, national interests may be derived through other mechanisms.

In *Taming of American Power: The Global Response to American Primacy* (2005), Walt proposes a slight modification to the realist viewpoint. He stresses the capacity of other states to penetrate the US domestically and influence foreign policy choices. Walt argues that this helps to account for foreign policy decisions that do not further the long-term interests of the US.[1030] The notion of domestic penetration also highlights the way in which big business, for example, may influence domestic political decisions and thus reinforces the importance of taking steps to minimise the role of money in politics. Transnational actors may also succeed in influencing the policies of national governments. Transnational corporations provide the most obvious example of this. What these instances imply is that the boundary between what has traditionally been thought of as "domestic" and "international" is artificial, and that it is no longer helpful to think in these terms.

Walt maintains that, historically, states have tended to try to balance the states that threaten to disrupt the existing balance of power. Yet, the relative absence of attempts by European states to balance the US in the post-Cold War era indicates that this assumption may not hold under all circumstances, and that there is no necessarily systematic nature to it. Walt's answer to this is that rather than focusing on the shifts in power – conceived primarily in military terms –

[1029] Al-Rodhan, *Symbiotic Realism, op. cit.*, note 78, p. 100.
[1030] See Walt, *op. cit.*, note 1021, pp. 194-217.

balance of power theorists ought to place threats at the centre of their analysis. Thus conceived, there is no reason to expect European states to engage in balancing behaviour in relation to the US. In his view, the evidence suggests that states do not demonstrate a tendency to balance against rising powers that are not perceived as threatening. The significance of this should not be overlooked. It implies that if interstate relations are marked by good relations, the accumulation of power by one state need not imply instability. Morcover, it also highlights the importance of confidence-building measures and engagement in international relations. By not equating power with threat, Walt calls for a return to the US strategy of "offshore balancing", which involves convincing others of the legitimacy of one's policies.[1031]

Walt's argument is useful to the extent that it calls into question the realist assumption that changes to and transformations of the international system are caused by shifts in the distribution of military power. Moreover, it also challenges the realist notion that gains are relative and therefore that international politics is a "zero-sum game". Moreover, increased interdependence would tend to buttress this argument, given that states can only make gains in some instance by coordinating their responses.

Liberal international relations theorists would argue that the realist assumption that states are more concerned with relative gains is premised on the assumption that a "game" is played only once. They stress that where a game is repeatedly played cooperative relations may be preferred. This implies that long-term absolute gains are given precedence over short-term relative gains. Iterative relations enable the leaders of states to perceive the long-term absolute gains from cooperative relations as fairly certain.[1032]

Prioritising absolute gains over relative gains within the liberal perspective relies on there already being repeated relations. Where states are poorly integrated into the multilateral arrangements that might provide the means with which to influence outcomes that affect them, we might expect relative gains to be privileged. Where a state uses its resources to engage in bargaining rather than to secure long-term cooperation with other states, relative gains are likely to be emphasised. In such instances, short-term gains are privileged over longer term gains. This may be driven by the domestic political situa-

---

[1031] *Ibid.*, pp. 120-126; 222-223.
[1032] Al-Rodhan, *Symbiotic Realism, op. cit.*, note 78, pp. 100-107.

tion. If a regime or a country's leaders seek to bolster their legitimacy by short-term gains it may be unlikely that gains will be deferred. There is also the variable of the accountability of leaders to their publics. Whether leaders are seeking immediate electoral gains may have an impact on their calculations. It may also be that the long-term gains are small or uncertain. If a state feels that it has little capacity to affect its long-term benefits, it may opt for maximum short-term gains.[1033]

International Organisations
It is important that multilateral solutions are favoured over unilateral solutions. For most states this is likely to be the case given the transnational nature of many policy issues and the futility of trying to address them alone. Yet, this may not be the case for states that are inadequately integrated into the multilateral system and maintain a highly particularistic conception of national interests. Unilateral responses to problems are even more damaging to the credibility of multilateral institutions. An added challenge to multinational institutions stems from their unrepresentative nature. These institutions may therefore be regarded by many as lacking in legitimacy and reflecting the preferences of the dominant states.

Large Collective Identities
Foreign policy choices may negatively affect inter-cultural relations by fuelling the grievances of members of large collective identities. Policies that create or sustain injustices experienced by a group are unlikely to be in the long-term interests of a state. This is because the need for a stable identity and for a sense of community are vital to human dignity. If people or members of one's community suffer persistent humiliation, the appeal of extremism is likely to be greater. Even ordinary citizens may condone terrorism, for example, as a means of punishing those actors that they perceive as responsible for sustaining the status quo.[1034] The difficulty for the state is to achieve the appropriate balance between societal cohesion and solidarity, and the preservation of cultural identities.

[1033] G.J. Ikenberry, "Distant Gains: When do States Make Choices for the Long Term?" Working Paper, Browne Center for International Politics, July 1997.
[1034] M. Tessler and M.D.H. Robbins, "What Leads Some Ordinary Arab Men and Women to Approve of Terrorist Acts Against the United States?" *Journal of Conflict Resolution*, Vol. 51, No. 2, 2007.

Environment and Natural Resources
Environmental degradation does not only affect a country's economic growth, it affects its security too. Environmental degradation may contribute to conflicts over resources, the displacement of people, the destruction of livelihoods and damage to health. The interconnection between the environment, political economy and security means that protection of the environment should form part of a country's policy considerations, not simply in the area of development but also in the area of security. Successful management of the natural resource base on which a country's political stability rests is a foreign policy concern.

ICT
New technologies mean that news can be transmitted at a much faster pace than before – either through 24 hour news channels or using the Internet. This has meant that the media is often used by policymakers to diffuse messages. However, in some instances, this may prompt policymakers to respond too rashly to events. The public may also rely on Internet news sources that are not mediated by journalists who may at least make some effort to corroborate their stories. Policymakers need to be aware of such sources.[1035] Widespread access, anonymity and the speed with which information can be diffused through the Internet also pose challenges to efforts to prevent it from being employed for nefarious means, such as spreading hatred and inciting violence.[1036] Efforts to regulate ICT need to be balanced with the need to allow freedom of expression. Public authorities must find an equilibrium between efforts to prevent violence, hatred and intolerance, and efforts to allow freedom of speech.

5. The Way Forward

Symbiotic realism provides a normative framework to help guide policymakers in a world that is driven by the dynamics created by the substrates of human nature, formal anarchy, interdependence and instant connectivity. The facets of the symbiotic realism framework are shown in Diagram 10 on page 342.

[1035] P. Seib, "Politics of the Fourth Estate," *Harvard International Review*, Vol. 22, No. 3, 2000.
[1036] Al-Rodhan, *Symbiotic Realism, op. cit.*, note 78, p.115.

Individuals
The promotion and protection of human rights must form part of the promotion of security. Yet, this needs to be done in ways that are culturally sensitive and empowering. A people-centred conception of security would provide a framework for the consistent promotion and protection of human rights broadly defined. Human security defined as freedom from want and fear[1037] is broad enough to include political, civil, socio-economic and cultural rights. Yet, human security ought to include the promotion of a positive sense of self as well.

While human rights offer an effective means of promoting the well-being of the individual, efforts to promote human rights may be viewed with suspicion. It is therefore important to remember that "humility, understanding, patience, dialogue, and time are all crucial aspects of encouraging the emergence of endogenous convictions, players, and process that take into account historical and cultural specificities."[1038] Placing the emphasis on human dignity may provide a means of promoting the fundamental principles underlying human rights in a way that is compatible with all moral lexicons.

The State
International anarchy does not have to imply perpetual insecurity, competitive relations and relative rather than absolute gains. Despite the absence of an overarching authority structure, governance mechanisms that regulate state relations do exist, for instance, in the form of international law and soft law comprising good practices and standard setting. There is thus governance without a world government, however imperfect this may be. Moreover, increased interdependence between states means that absolute gains are more likely to be recognised. Indeed, increased interdependence makes symbiotic relations between states possible. Employed in relation to state to state relations, symbiosis may be understood as an interstate relationship in which one party benefits more than the other party, but does not have to imply a serious disadvantage for the less fortunate state let alone an absolute loss.

If there is no "logic" within the international system that implies a perpetual security dilemma, there is no reason to assume that morality has no place in global politics. States often comply with hu-

---

[1037] *Ibid.*, p. 117.
[1038] *Ibid.*, p. 130.

manitarian norms, and have reacted to enforce anti-genocide norms, even in the absence of enforcement mechanisms.[1039] Moreover, as is suggested above, interaction between states is repeated, implying that greater trust and shared norms may help to reduce insecurity in an anarchic international system.

Symbiotic relations do, nevertheless, depend on a prior degree of integration. In terms of political integration, the leaders of states need to calculate that the long-term absolute gains bring more than the short-term relative gains, and that they have the capacity to influence decisions that affect them. This implies that states need to be well-represented in multilateral institutions and arrangements. The accountability of leaders to their public is also likely to reduce short-term calculations. Good governance, which entails accountability, should be promoted, but in a way that is sensitive to local political and cultural structures.

Large Collective Identities
Greater efforts need to be made to construct a shared consciousness based on the compatibility of fundamental moral principles. Synergy is suggested as a guiding principle for states faced with the challenge of successfully managing culturally plural societies. Intra-civilisational synergy should be sought. Synergy occurs where the effect of two entities, influences or agents is greater than that which could have been predicted from the known effects of each.[1040] Synergy relies on there being a certain degree of transcultural understanding. Dialogue and engagement are essential parts of foreign policy. Active measures to promote the spread of knowledge aimed at encouraging peaceful transcultural and intra-civilisational relations should also be employed.

Rapid changes are under way that are altering traditional structures and reference points. However, the focus in the West, particularly in relation to Islam, is often on extremism. Yet, the peaceful and moderate majority should not be confused with extremist groups. Combating extremism will rely on addressing its root causes, and reducing poverty and marginalisation. The appeal of the extremist has to be dented. Solutions to the problems of extremism that are indigenously conceived are likely to be more successful than those imposed

---
[1039] *Ibid.*, pp. 119, 120-121.
[1040] *Ibid.*, p. 124.

from the outside. There should therefore be a constructive effort made to support and help finance local initiatives aimed at reducing the appeal of extremism.

The promotion of justice also needs to form an important part of foreign policy. Injustice can lead people to feel alienated from their societies. Those who seek to propagate extremist ideologies are most likely to be successful wherever injustice exists and there are no apparent mechanisms to remedy that injustice. Greater justice needs to be promoted.[1041]

International Organisations
Multilateral institutions need to be more representative so that all member states feel that they constitute an effective forum in which they can further their interests in a cooperative manner. Similarly, the special privileges attributed to major powers must be eliminated so that multilateral institutions are not perceived as mere instruments of the powerful. It is also important that the less powerful members of an institution are included in the design process for any reforms. In order to encourage such states to opt for cooperative relations, policymakers need to support measures to ensure that all members of multilateral institutions are represented.

The Environment and Natural Resources
Protecting the environment and promoting sustainable development require cooperation and burden-sharing between states, multinational institutions, NGOs, social movements and the scientific community. The scientific community will play a key role in presenting information on the impact of environmental degradation in a clear and scientific manner to policymakers and the general public. States need to publicly fund studies on the environment so that scientists and the public can make informed choices and hold politicians accountable. Yet, the capacity of politicians to curb environmental degradation is sometimes constrained by the role played by money in electoral and political systems. The influence of industrial lobbies needs to be reduced.

Investment in substitutes for natural resources that are likely to run out in the near future needs to be made now. Reducing the de-

---
[1041] Al-Rodhan, *The Five Dimensions of Global Security*, op. cit., note 512, pp. 82-84, 88-89.

pletion of natural resources also requires lifestyle changes, particularly in the developed countries.[1042]

ICT
The 2003 Additional Protocol to the Council of Europe's Convention on Cyber Crime provides a model for enacting legislation that makes the spread of hatred and incitement to violence via the Internet a criminal offence.[1043] Regional efforts to regulate ICT ought to be coordinated with global efforts. There is also a need to engage in dialogue over the normative basis for regulation, as well as what constitutes the "right balance" between efforts to regulate the harmful use of the Internet and the right to freedom of expression. The tools with which to survey and encourage greater responsibility on the part of Internet users, such as bloggers, also need to be developed. Bloggers, for example, could be required to reveal their real name when they register, but use a pseudonym when they write.

6. Conclusion

Symbiotic realism seeks to go beyond the state centrism of realism to focus on: the predilections of human nature; global anarchy, interdependence and instant connectivity. It identifies a number of non-state actors such as large collective identities, international organisations and transnational corporations as important in helping to shape the global system. Foreign policy challenges include overcoming the tension between narrow conceptions of state sovereignty and international norms that shift the focus to the security of the individual. We might also imagine an increasing tension arising between the principle of state sovereignty and concern for the protection of the biosphere. Unequal power relations between states and a continued emphasis on relative gains also pose considerable challenges to the need for cooperative and coordinated responses to today's problems, which require an emphasis on burden-sharing and absolute gains. In addition, there is a need to achieve a correct balance between respect for cultural specificities and the identification of common fundamental values.

[1042] Al-Rodhan, *Symbiotic Realism, op. cit.*, note 78, pp. 132-133.
[1043] M. Finaud, "Information Technology, Terrorism, and Global Security," in Al-Rodhan, *Policy Briefs on the* Transcultural *Aspects of Security and Stability, op. cit.,* note 920, pp. 173-174.

Symbiotic realism's focus on the four dimensions mentioned above offer a paradigm with which to overcome these challenges. It suggests that emphasis should be placed on the promotion of human dignity, symbiotic relations between states premised on absolute gains, the promotion of justice and transcultural synergy.

CHAPTER 13

HOW SHOULD STATECRAFT BE CONDUCTED?
NEO-STATECRAFT AND *META-GEOPOLITICS*

The basis on which statecraft is conducted as well as how it is conducted also has a critical role to play in achieving a sustainable history. Neo-*statecraft and* Meta-*geopolitics: Reconciliation of Power, Interests and Justice in the 21st Century* (2009)[1044] explains that statecraft has to contend with three factors: human nature, conceived as primarily emotionally driven; the need to manage relations with other states and to employ foreign policy tools to ensure that the state flourishes and is secure; and the question of how power should be employed. These are perennial aspects of statecraft, but an increasingly complex environment means that statesmen today need to be concerned with the global as well as the regional context. This means that strategic considerations are also global. With this complexity comes increased connectedness between issues and actors. Responding effectively to this new strategic environment requires the promotion of justice, transcultural synergies and cooperative relations between states, all of which are essential to producing an environment conducive to sustainable interstate relations, which is an important element of sustainable history.

This chapter briefly outlines traditional concepts of statecraft and geopolitics. It then proposes that statecraft should be informed by *neo*-statecraft, an important component of which is *meta*-geopolitics. *Neo*-statecraft will be required to achieve a sustainable history, because it is comprehensive, inclusive, employs just power and promises to reduce conflict. *Neo*-statecraft has four substrates. The first substrate is an expanded concept of geopolitics, *meta*-geopolitics, which takes into account seven interconnected capacities of state power: (1) social and health issues; (2) domestic politics; (3) economics; (4) environment; (5) science and human potential; (6) military and security

---
[1044] Al-Rodhan, Neo-*statecraft and* Meta-*geopolitics, op. cit.*, note 185.

issues; and (7) international diplomacy. The second substrate is sustainable national security, achieved through multilateralism, multi-sum security, symbiotic realism and transcultural synergy. The third is the concept of just power, which is premised on the idea that statecraft today must aim to promote justice not for altruistic reasons, but because it is in the interests of states to do so. Power must not only be smart, but also just. The fourth substrate I put forward is the concept of reconciliation statecraft, which suggests eight global interests that statesmen must reconcile in order to further the well-being of their state and its people; and, finally, I discuss the future of geopolitics in a transnational world.[1045]

1. Traditional Concepts of Statecraft and Geopolitics

Statecraft

Statecraft refers to the use of appropriate policy tools to achieve policy objectives effectively.[1046] History suggests that there are some constants in statecraft across the ages, notably human nature; cooperation and competition among states; and the question of whether to use armed force.[1047] There are a number of tools available to the statesman. Statecraft always involves deploying power. Power is generally defined as the ability to obtain a desired outcome.[1048] Getting others to do what one wishes may be achieved in a variety of ways. In the international realm, state power has tended to be defined rather narrowly in terms of military and sometimes economic capabilities. In Joseph Nye's distinction between "hard" and "soft" power, military and economic power are characterised as hard power. Yet, employing this kind of power is clearly not exhaustive of all the means available to a state to achieve its objectives. Attraction and cooperation are forms of soft power that a statesman may employ.[1049] Soft power stems from

---

[1045] Al-Rodhan, Neo-*statecraft and* Meta-*geopolitics, op. cit.*, note 185, pp. 31-32.
[1046] D. Ross, "Ways and Means," *New Republic* Online, 9 April 2007, http://www.thewashingtoninstitute.org/ templateC06.php?CID=1044.
[1047] P.G. Lauren, G.A. Craig and A.L. George, *Force and Statecraft: Diplomatic Challenges of Our Time,* Fourth Edition (New York and Oxford: Oxford University Press, 2007), p. 270.
[1048] J.S. Nye, Jr., *Soft Power: The Means to Success in World Politics* (New York: Public Affairs, 2004), p. 2.
[1049] Al-Rodhan, Neo-*statecraft and* Meta-*geopolitics, op. cit.*, note 185, p. 17.

the attractiveness of values and the application of these values.[1050] Economic power may be a soft or hard power tool. It can be used to coerce through sanctions or to encourage other states to engage in cooperative relations.[1051] A variety of tools are therefore available to statesmen, such as negotiation, mediation, propaganda, intelligence gathering, incentives, sanctions and coercion. Yet, incentives are likely to have a more positive long-term impact than coercion.[1052]

While often confused with statecraft, diplomacy forms only one part of statecraft. Diplomacy refers to the implementation of a state's foreign and security policy through representation. Jose Calvet de Magalhães sets out a broad definition of diplomacy in *The Pure Concept of Diplomacy* (1988). He writes that diplomacy is a foreign policy instrument that serves the goal of peaceful interaction with other states through recognised intermediaries.[1053]

Some observers maintain that diplomacy needs to be adapted to a changed global environment. In the global information age, the diplomat's role of transmitting information back to the capital of the country they represent is made less vital by email and other ICT.[1054] A greater degree of direct contact between capitals may also make the diplomat's representative function less vital than in the past.

At the same time as these traditional diplomatic functions may be becoming less relevant, there is an increased need for expertise in a number of non-traditional security fields, such as the environment, health and human rights.[1055] Moreover, with the increasingly obscure division between domestic and foreign policy, there is also an increased need for public diplomacy. Greater transparency is required if statesmen wish to win the support and trust of their domestic populations. A state's image abroad is also of growing concern to statesmen. Yet, a country's image is shaped not only by the actions of states and their agencies, but also by an array of non-state actors, ranging from companies to individual bloggers.[1056]

[1050] Nye, *op. cit.*, note 1048, p. 7.
[1051] Al-Rodhan, Neo-*statecraft and* Meta-*geopolitics, op. cit.*, note 185, pp. 17-18.
[1052] *Ibid.*, pp. 19-31.
[1053] J. Calvet de Magalhães, *The Pure Concept of Diplomacy*, translated by B. Futscher Pereira (New York: Greenwood Press, 1988), p. 59.
[1054] S. Riordan, *The New Diplomacy* (Cambridge, UK: Polity Press, 2003), p. 110.
[1055] *Ibid.*, pp. 118-119.
[1056] Al-Rodhan, Neo-*statecraft and* Meta-*geopolitics, op. cit.*, note 185, pp. 27-31.

As a result of these phenomena, traditional statecraft faces a number of challenges. First, a number of actors have to be taken into account by statesmen, including non-state actors such as NGOs, transnational corporations, private security firms, transnational terrorist and drug networks, and so on.[1057] Membership of alliances, such as NATO, and international organisations, such as the WTO, also form part of the framework for action of statesmen.

With increased access to the mass media, statecraft has to take public opinion increasingly into account,[1058] both at home and abroad. Advances in ICT have also introduced a cyber dimension to the international political arena. Whether the cyber world will fundamentally alter political interactions or merely serve as an instrument of international relations is as yet unclear. However, it is the case that the "information revolution" is challenging state-centric conceptions of the world.[1059]

Developments in the area of weapons technology may have a significant impact on statecraft. Some commentators claim that precision-guided weapons will result in an increased use of force. In fact, there are two opposing views about whether modern weaponry will affect a state's option to use war as a tool of policy.[1060] Yet, it seems unlikely that this would come to pass in democratic states. It has also been argued that advances in weapons technology will make wars less controllable, producing unintended results and developing dynamics of their own.[1061] While these are legitimate considerations, one has to remember that serious security challenges are no longer dealt with through traditional forms of warfare. With the rise of transnational threats, cooperation with other states, often through non-military means, is often the chosen response.[1062]

Good statecraft, nevertheless, requires a sound understanding of the global environment and the state's place within it in terms of its position and relative capabilities. I therefore turn to the "macro-picture" to consider how best to conceptualise the dynamics that shape this broader "spatial" context.

[1057] Lauren, Craig, and George, *op. cit.*, note 1047, p. 271.
[1058] *Ibid.*, p. 273.
[1059] Al-Rodhan, Neo-*statecraft and* Meta-*geopolitics*, *op. cit.*, note 185, pp. 28-29.
[1060] W. Saletan, "The Lessons of Kosovo," *Slate*, 22 June 1999, http://www.slate.com/id/30876/.
[1061] J. Shell, *The Fate of the Earth* (New York: Knopf, 1982).
[1062] Al-Rodhan, Neo-*statecraft and* Meta-*geopolitics*, *op. cit.*, note 185, pp. 30-31.

Geopolitics

The spatial dimension of international affairs has traditionally been analysed through the concept of geopolitics. It has been a critical tool for statesmen as they attempt to understand where their state stands in relation to the rest of the world. Neo-*statecraft and* Meta-*geopolitics: Reconciliation of Power, Interests and Justice in the 21st Century* (2009) defines geopolitics as

> the study of how geography, but also economics and demography, impacts politics, and particularly political relationships among states. It looks at the power dynamics among states seeking to control territory and to acquire reliable access to strategically important locations and resources. Looking at international relations from a geopolitical point of view leads to strategic prescriptions that have a strong focus on geographical realities.[1063]

In the past, geopolitics was primarily concerned with geography. Early theorists tended to have backgrounds in the natural sciences and the discipline of geography. However, human action and socio-economic systems have become an increasingly important part of geopolitics and social scientists have come to dominate the field of study,[1064] although geography has made something of a comeback through scholars such as Saul Cohen and Walt.

Classical geopolitical analyses have come under criticism for a number of reasons. The stress on geography is believed to be too deterministic.[1065] Geopolitics, when considered in narrow terms, does not account for the human factor in political and economic relations. Moreover, it does not take adequate account of the contingency of events and processes. For example, technological development may depend on the type of political system, which, in turn, would affect a state's relative position in the world. Religion may also influence how people relate to their natural environment and geographic location.[1066]

[1063] Al-Rodhan, Neo-*statecraft and* Meta-*geopolitics, op. cit.*, note 185, p. 33.
[1064] J.J. Grygiel, *Great Powers and Geopolitical Change* (Baltimore: Johns Hopkins University Press, 2006), p. 15.
[1065] L.K.D. Kristof, "Political Laws in International Relations," *Western Political Quarterly,* XI, 1958, pp. 603-604.
[1066] Al-Rodhan, Neo-*statecraft and* Meta-*geopolitics, op. cit.*, note 185, p. 38.

Globalisation is also believed to be transforming geo-strategy by making territorial state boundaries less significant than they once were.[1067]

The most forceful arguments against classical geopolitical analyses come from the Liberal International School. Its proponents argue that globalisation has collapsed the domestic/international boundary, making distinction between the two spheres obsolete. Moreover, they argue that the information-based economy that currently exists has altered the capacity of states to offer political incentives in order to achieve particular ends.[1068]

These two developments are thought to have a number of consequences. First, the size of a state's territory is no longer a reliable indicator of its economic and political clout.[1069] Second, economic capital is likely to be a more important indicator of a state's power and influence internationally.[1070] Third, regional economic integration engendered by globalisation may result in regional security cooperation.[1071] Fourth, states no longer need to conquer a country territorially in order to further their economic capacities.[1072] Fifth, ideas are more significant factors and more capable of transforming the global system than geography.[1073]

In response to the perceived inadequacies of traditional geopolitics, a new school of thought, Critical Geopolitics, emphasises the role of perceptions and the representation of states and peoples in shaping global dynamics. In the view of contributors to this approach, geographic representations are highly subjective[1074] and constitutive of

---

[1067] See E.L. Frost, "Globalization and National Security," in R.L. Kugler and E. Frost (eds.) *Global Century: Globalisation and National Security* (Washington, DC: National Defense University Press, 2001).

[1068] P.R. Faber, "Thinking about Geography: Some Competing Geopolitical Models for the 21st Century," Academic Research Branch, NATO Defense College, Rome, No. 15, February 2005, p. 3.

[1069] *Ibid.*, p. 3.

[1070] *Ibid.*

[1071] S.G. Brooks, *Producing Security* (Princeton, N.J.: Princeton University Press, 2005), p. 14.

[1072] *Ibid.*, p.3.

[1073] I. Kant, "Perpetual Peace: A Philosophical Proposal," in *Kant's Principles of Politics*, including his essay *Perpetual Peace: A Contribution to Political Science*, Translated by W. Hastie (Edinburgh: Clark, 1891).

[1074] See, e.g, W.A. McDougall, "Why Geography Matters...But Is So Little Learned," *Orbis*, Spring 2003; G.Ó. Tuathail, *Critical Geopolitics: The Politics of Writing Global Space* (Minnesota: University of Minnesota Press, 1996).

global power relations. Geography, seen from this perspective, is not an objective science. Instead, all representations, whether scholarly, practical or popular, are for someone or something, and are shaped by where we are situated.[1075]

Geoffrey Kemp and Robert E. Haravy introduced a new term, "strategic geography", that is concerned with tactical aspects of geography which are relevant to grand strategy.[1076] All areas of modern geography are taken into account including physical geography, human geography, political geography, economic geography and military geography. This more comprehensive approach to geography provides a more nuanced way of analysing how access to or control over physical space may shape power relations between states.[1077]

While there are valid criticisms of classical geopolitics, states remain constrained by their territories, albeit somewhat less so than in the past. To discard geography entirely from the study of international relations would be an error. Even though many environmental and geographic obstacles may be surmountable, a state's control of its coastline or waterways continues to be important.[1078] Access to resources also remains significant, even in a largely knowledge-based economy, and resources are unevenly spatially distributed.[1079] Moreover, despite the increasingly transnational and asymmetric nature of threats today, states remain the most important actors within the global system, as the US "war on terror", which followed the attacks of 11 September 2001, demonstrated.[1080] Furthermore, there is no strong evidence to suggest that mutual economic interdependence makes the cost of war prohibitive.

While technological capacities, knowledge and the capacity to diffuse information can greatly contribute to a state's power, spatial analysis can serve grand strategy if it focuses on the spatial concentration of software and human resources as well as natural resources. So

---

[1075] See Kristof, *op. cit.*, note 1065, p. 45; K. Dodds, *Geopolitics: A Very Short Introduction* (Oxford: Oxford University Press, 2007), p. 45.
[1076] G. Kemp and R.E. Harkavy, *Strategic Geography and the Changing Middle East* (Washington, DC: Brookings Institution Press, 1997), p. 8.
[1077] See *ibid.*
[1078] Grygiel, *op. cit.*, note 1064, pp. 3-5.
[1079] D.E. Streusand, "Geopolitics versus Globalization," Institute for National Strategic Studies (INSS), 2002, http://www.ndu.edu/inss/books/Books_2002/Globalization_and_Maritime_Power_Dec_02/04_ch03.htm.
[1080] Al-Rodhan, Neo-*statecraft and* Meta-*geopolitics, op. cit.*, note 185, p. 47.

long as state power is distributed unevenly, geopolitics will continue to be important. What is required is a new geopolitical framework of analysis that spatially represents the distribution of both soft and hard power in a globalised world.[1081]

2. *Meta*-geopolitics

A spatial analysis of international power relations must consider a number of unevenly distributed "capacities". *Meta*-geopolitics considers seven capacities that determine state power. *Meta*-geopolitics is distinct from traditional geopolitical analyses in that it puts forward a multidimensional conception of power, which includes both the soft and the hard power tools available to states. It also enables an analysis of future power projections.

One thing that it is important to recognise is that the threats faced by states are often transnational in nature. As such, cooperation between states and the active involvement of international institutions are required to effectively address them. Some, such as the threat of pandemics, need to be addressed at their source.

Social Issues and Health
This capacity assesses the societal situation within a state, based on demographic factors, ethnic composition, the extent of social peace and cohesion and health issues.

Demographic Factors
Demographic trends affect the relative strength of any given state. Population increases in areas with few basic resources are likely to lead to greater risk of ethnic tension and social unrest. For wealthier countries, in which the population may be declining, emigration from over-populated areas becomes a serious policy issue. In addition, for many developed countries, declining birth rates and increased life expectancy may imply economic malaise and difficulties in maintaining military strength. Advances in technology that may reduce the need for manpower in both economic and military sectors also affect the impact of demographic trends on a state's power.[1082]

[1081] *Ibid.*, p. 48.
[1082] *Ibid.*, pp. 56-59.

Social Issues
The degree of social cohesion affects a state's capacity to build or maintain a prosperous economy, as well a state's stability. Social cohesion may be defined as the absence of large social and economic divisions within a society.[1083] Ethnic divisions and large disparities in wealth and opportunity can all negatively affect a country's social cohesion. This, in turn, can erode a government's legitimacy and political stability. Conversely, socially cohesive countries are not only likely to be socio-economically and politically more stable; they are also likely to demonstrate greater resilience in the face of adversity.[1084]

Health Issues
The general health of a country's population is an important factor determining the demographic situation of a state. Epidemics in a country can also be an indicator of a country's capacity to contain infectious disease. This, in turn, can have a negative effect on a country's economic and military strength. Severe health problems will therefore affect a state's long-term economic situation and geo-economic standing.[1085]

Domestic Politics
A state's domestic politics have an impact on its foreign policy. Countries with a volatile domestic political scene are likely to experience problems in maintaining a coherent and robust foreign policy. The type of political regime may also have an impact on a state's foreign policy. For example, authoritarian governments may deflect domestic problems to the international realm, taking on a siege mentality.

Governments that only have partial control of their country can also generate regional instability. They may, for instance, find it hard to prevent or contain transnational criminal networks from operating, with the effect spilling over into neighbouring countries. Weak governments may also have a limited capacity to contain infectious diseases or to implement environmental protection measures. Migra-

---

[1083] W. Easterly, J. Ritzen and M. Woolcock, "Social Cohesion, Institutions, and Growth," Working Paper 94, Center for Social Development, November 2005, draft, www.cgdev.org/files/9136_file_WP94.pdf, p. 4.
[1084] Al-Rodhan, Neo-*statecraft and* Meta-*geopolitics, op. cit.*, note 185, pp. 60.
[1085] *Ibid.*, pp. 61-62.

tion and refugee flows from such states may also cause problems for their neighbours.

Stability of States: The Nexus Between Transnational Threats, Globalization, and Internal Resilience (2007) identifies a number of factors that contribute to a state's internal stability.[1086] A stable political system is essential to state stability. Another important factor affecting the resilience of a state is a cohesive civil society infused with a common sense of national purpose and identity. Durable political institutions are vital to ensuring public order. The more mature a state's political institutions, the more likely they are to be durable and the more likely it is that a state will be stable. State institutions critical to stability include a competent and professional police force, a professional civil service, an independent judiciary, a professional military accountable to legitimate civilian authority, and institutions with sufficient autonomy from any one political faction.[1087]

Regimes in which a particular political faction is able to monopolise state institutions are vulnerable to political upheavals. Similarly, those states in which judicial and legislative checks are weak may suffer from potential political instability.[1088] When a country can no longer provide basic public services, can no longer provide law and order, and has lost control of parts of its territory it is considered a failed state.[1089]

Economics

Economic capacity has tremendous geopolitical significance, perhaps beyond that of military strength. States are also vulnerable to the vagaries of the market in a globalised economy. A country's economic situation, as well as its reliance on outside resources, economic aid or a single trading partner, reveals much about its geopolitical position. The distribution of resources among a country's population is also revealing of its stability. As is outlined above, unequal access to resources can lead to societal and political instability. In general, the

---

[1086] Al-Rodhan and Kuepfer, *Stability of States*, *op. cit.*, note 539, p. 25.
[1087] P.H. Baker, "Conflict Resolution: A Methodology for Assessing Internal Collapse and Recovery," Fund for Peace, 2003, http://www.fundforpeace.org/publications/reports/methodology-chapter.pdf, p. 6.
[1088] *Ibid.*, p. 16.
[1089] Al-Rodhan, Neo-*statecraft and* Meta-*geopolitics*, *op. cit.*, note 185, pp. 65.

more evenly distributed a country's resources are within society, the more stable it will be.[1090]

Good infrastructure, including good transportation, communications and financial services networks, reliable utilities and distribution networks as well as a sufficient energy supply are likely to foster economic growth. The above may critically affect a state's capacity to attract foreign direct investment and be particularly critical in transitional states. Economic growth may also be facilitated by the existence of stable political institutions and a transparent and independent legal system. Finally, access to affordable and plentiful oil supplies is central, at least at present, to a country's economic growth.[1091]

Environment
Environmental issues can also affect a country's geopolitical standing. Consumption of natural resources at an unsustainable rate may jeopardise a country's future economic growth. Air and water pollution negatively affect the health of the population, which, as is mentioned above, is also a determinant of a state's relative power. Water scarcity is a serious problem for some countries and may have a number of weakening effects. Insufficient access to clean water and sanitation can contribute to conditions conducive to the spread of waterborne diseases. A lack of water also places strains on industry and agricultural production. A lack of sufficient safe drinking water and food can cause social unrest. Water scarcity may also contribute to regional conflicts.

Global warming will have important geopolitical ramifications. As is noted above, rising sea levels will make parts of many states' territory uninhabitable or infertile or, conversely, may create newly inhabitable fertile land. Some island states may completely disappear. As sea levels rise, legal disputes between maritime states are likely to follow. Low-lying islands and rocks around which the radius of a state's Exclusive Economic Zone (EEZ) would have been drawn will no longer exist. This could cause serious international disputes between some countries.[1092] In addition, severe weather, leading

---
[1090] Al-Rodhan and Kuepfer, *Stability of States, op. cit.*, note 539, p. 27.
[1091] Al-Rodhan, Neo-*statecraft and* Meta-*geopolitics, op. cit.*, note 185, pp. 67.
[1092] A. Dupont, "The Strategic Implications of Climate Change," *Survival*, Vol. 50, No. 3, 1 June 2008, http://www.iiss.org/publications/survival/survival-summaries/2008-volume-50/year-2008-issue-3/, p. 36.

to droughts, floods and storms, is likely to affect crop production, destroy homes and displace people.[1093]

As noted earlier, new maritime passages may be created as a result of the melting of permanent ice sheets. In the event that this transpires, these areas will become important military security considerations for their respective states.[1094] This may become an all the more important consideration, should the melting of permanent ice sheets reveal the presence of natural resources, such as oil, gas and minerals.[1095]

Science and Human Potential

A state's research and development capacity and human resources can significantly affect its geopolitical position in the world. An education system capable of producing highly skilled workers is essential for economic competitiveness. Technological developments that allow a country to keep up with the information-based economies of developed countries are also critical to a country's power relative to other states. Technological capacities have relevance not only for economic growth, but also for military capacity, which is increasingly technology-intensive.[1096] In some instances, technologies may have both civil and military applications, indicating an overlap between sectors.

Military and Security Issues

This category of a state's capacities comprises internal, transnational and external security challenges. The first two types of challenges, in particular, may affect a state's political or social cohesion. They may also make a country a less attractive place for investment and tourism. Internal security challenges that may affect a country's geopolitical standing may include secessionist movements or a high crime rate. Transnational threats include, for example, transnational criminal activities, transnational terrorist networks and insurgency. External security challenges may come in the form of military attacks. The capacity of a state to deter or repel attacks will be critical in assessing its posi-

---

[1093] *Ibid.*, p. 39.
[1094] K. Naumann, J. Shalikashvili, The Lord Inge, J. Lanxade, H. van den Breemen, with B. Bilski and D. Murray, "Towards a Grand Strategy for an Uncertain World: Renewing Transatlantic Partnership," Noaber Foundation, 2007, http://www.csis.org/media/csis/events/080110_grand_strategy.pdf, p. 35.
[1095] Dupont, *op. cit.*, note 1092, p. 37.
[1096] Al-Rodhan, Neo-*statecraft and* Meta-*geopolitics*, *op. cit.*, note 185, pp. 70-71.

tion in international power relations. A state's possession of or capacity to develop nuclear weapons is likely to be important in this respect.

Energy security is also an ever-present concern for states. A good number of states are dependent on oil and gas. Dependence on other countries for the supply of these energy sources makes a state economically vulnerable and reduces its political room for manoeuvre. Oil producing countries possess greater leverage as a consequence of the world's growing demand for oil. This is the case both for "older" oil-producing states, such as Saudi Arabia and Russia, and "newer" ones, such as Kazakhstan. The uneven geographic distribution of oil has profound geopolitical implications.[1097]

International Diplomacy
This final capacity is assessed by a state's involvement in international organisations, as well as the diplomatic challenges it is confronted with. Membership of international organisations is considered a factor affecting a state's geopolitical position in that it may reflect its standing within the international community. Indeed, a state's political clout may be determined as much by the appeal of its values and its strategic location as by its military or economic leverage. In other word's, a country's soft power resources are an important factor, determining its power in the international realm. International credibility can give a country a significant advantage when it wishes to achieve something in international affairs.

States may improve their credibility by participating constructively in international organisations and actively supporting the UN through engagement and participation in reform endeavours. Moreover, the more that states engage in effective multilateralism, the more robust international law will be – of which every state is ultimately the beneficiary.[1098]

3. Sustainable National Security

National security policy forms an integral part of modern statecraft. Security threats today are widely recognised as comprising not only

---

[1097] T.W. O'Donnell, "Global Oil to 2030: A Quantitative Assessment in the Context of International Affairs," International Relations and Security Network, 2 May 2007, http:// www.isn.ethz.ch/pubs/ph/details.cfm?lng=en&id=30696, p. 6.
[1098] Al-Rodhan, Neo-*statecraft and* Meta-*geopolitics, op. cit.*, note 185, pp. 74-75.

military threats from other states, but also transnational security threats that are often non-military in nature. In a previous publication *The Three Pillars of* Sustainable National Security *in a Transnational World* (2008), I outlined 11 major challenges to national security. They include (1) changing global power structures, state failure and regional conflicts; (2) security implications of population growth, migration and refugee flows; (3) the information revolution and national security; (4) transcultural interactions; (5) growing economic cleavages and energy security; (6) transnational organised crime; (7) non-state actors, terrorism and asymmetrical warfare; (8) proliferation; (9) the privatisation of security; (10) health, diseases and biosecurity; and (11) environmental security.[1099]

These challenges are interrelated. As argued in Chapter 11, meeting today's security challenges require a policy framework that is capable of capturing and addressing the multidimensional and interconnected character of security. I suggested that the first pillar of national security should be the multi-sum security principle, since it provides such a framework. Yet, it is important to note that it must be complemented by effective multilateralism, given that states can no longer meet security challenges alone.

Sustainable national security also depends on approaching international relations through the lens of symbiotic realism, as outlined in Chapter 12, which constitutes the second pillar. The third pillar is therefore transcultural synergy as a means of promoting stability and security, which is discussed in greater detail in Chapter 14. While these three pillars of sustainable national security may be achieved through a variety of soft and hard power tools, the use of power should always be in line with the principles of justice if it is to achieve sustainable security outcomes.

4. Just Power

Employing hard power in response to a great deal of today's security challenges may be counterproductive. Yet, reliance on soft power alone may not always be enough. In 2007, a number of US scholars put forward the concept of "smart power" as a means of guiding the

---

[1099] Al-Rodhan, *The Three Pillars of* Sustainable National Security, *op. cit.*, note 667.

US government in the intelligent use of power.[1100] Smart power was outlined in response to the concern that the United States was relying too much on hard power and, in doing so, neglecting to fully exploit its soft power tools. The experts agreed that what was required was a better balance of soft and hard power instruments. The term smart power was adopted to capture the correct balance between these two types of power. The development of the concept of smart power is important in that it signified a recognition that not all security challenges can be adequately addressed through the use of military power, no matter how powerful the military behind its application might be.[1101]

However, as argued in Neo-*statecraft and* Meta-*geopolitics: Reconciliation of Power, Interests and Justice in the 21st Century* (2009), "a state's foreign policy should not just be *smart*, it should also be *just*."[1102] It is only in the application of just power that a state's national interest will be furthered and its influence in the world sustained. Just power argues that military power and coercive economic power may sometimes be justified. Yet, just war principles must be observed. Humanitarian objectives as well as the protection of human rights and human dignity must guide the multilateral use of hard power. Soft power tools are, nevertheless, the preferred foreign and security policy tools used in the service of justice and human dignity.[1103]

5. Reconciliation Statecraft

Statesmen often have to reconcile conflicting loyalties or sources of authority. Eight levels of interests that require reconciliation are depicted in Octagon 6. These interests are not necessarily in conflict, although they may be.[1104]

[1100] R.L. Armitage and J.S. Nye, Jr. (cochairs), "CSIS Commission on Smart Power," Center for Strategic and International Studies, 6 November 2007, http://www.csis.org/comonent/option.com_csis_pubs/task.view/id4156/type.1.
[1101] Al-Rodhan, Neo-*statecraft and* Meta-*geopolitics, op. cit.*, note 185, pp. 142-144.
[1102] *Ibid.*, p. 139.
[1103] *Ibid.*, pp.147-150.
[1104] *Ibid.*, p. 203.

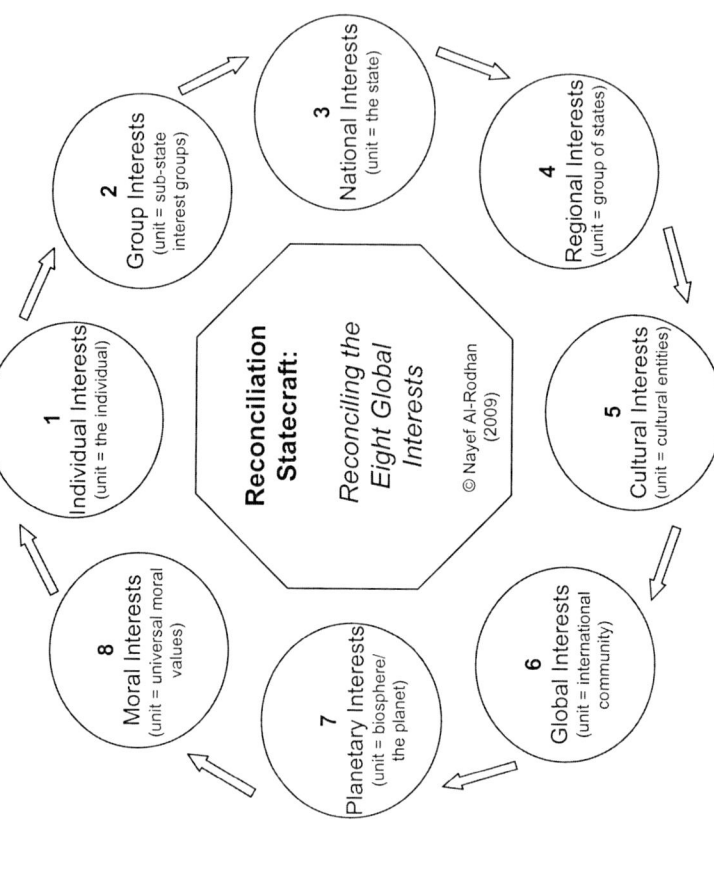

Octagon 6: An Octagon of the Eight Global Interests

Source: N.R.F. Al-Rodhan, *Neo-statecraft and Meta-geopolitics: Reconciliation of Power, Interests and Justice in the 21st Century* (Berlin: LIT, 2009), p. 231, reprinted with permission from LIT.

Individual Interests

Individual interests include ensuring one's livelihood, which may include employment, affordable housing, personal safety, access to quality affordable education, affordable and good quality health care, and perhaps access to state social services. Individuals whose well-being is directly affected by the natural environment are also likely to be concerned with environmental issues. Those who enjoy comfortable lives may also be concerned with environmental protection and their government's capacity to implement measures designed to meet this end. Others may be interested in their state's international image. This may be the case for those concerned with international security issues, as well as those affiliated in some way with international business.

Most individuals do not want external interference in their domestic politics, although this will depend on the domestic situation and is likely to be dependent on the state of human rights in the country and how that individual fares within it. Individuals generally want their human rights protected.

As is noted above, in *"emotional amoral egoism": A Neuro-philosophical Theory of Human Nature and its Universal Security Implications* (2008), I suggest that well-being depends on the satisfaction of basic needs, and also on a positive self-identity and a sense of belonging to a wider community in which the individual's interests are embedded.[1105]

Group Interests

In some instances, international borders are not congruent with ethnic and religious community boundaries. Multi-ethnic states are, thus, commonplace and some ethnic groups may belong to communities found in several different states. Ethnic and religious group interests are recognised by the UN as important rights. Groups may, for example, consider it their right to maintain their language and culture. Moreover, groups that constitute minorities within multi-ethnic and multi-religious states are also concerned that their right to minority protection is respected by the state. In addition to group interests related to ethnicity and religion, women also constitute a group with specific and shared interests in equal treatment concerning both opportunities and reproductive rights, as set out in the 1979 UN Conven-

---

[1105] Al-Rodhan, *"emotional amoral egoism,"* *op. cit.*, note 119, pp. 78-79.

tion on the Elimination of All Forms of Discrimination against Women (CEDAW).[1106]

Children also make up a group with particular interests related to protection of their rights as elaborated in the 1989 UN Convention on the Rights of the Child. These rights include the right to care, protection, education and health care.[1107] The disabled too have particular group interests, such as accessibility to public areas, employment and education, as well as greater safety.

Possible Conflicts with Individual Interests
Individual and group interests may come into conflict in some circumstances. Group practices may, for instance, encroach on some of the human rights and freedoms of individual members of the group. Group and individual interests may be at least partially reconciled if group rights are only extended to the extent that they respect individual human rights. Although tensions between group and individual interests may never be entirely reconciled, conflict can be minimised.[1108]

National Interests
National interests are not necessarily those of a population as a whole, although they may be largely derived from the values of the people and their general well-being. The most basic national interest is protection of the territorial integrity of the state and the security of its population. This particular category of interests may also be shaped by geographic location, access to natural resources, culture and national identity, threat perceptions and the material needs of the population, for example. In some instances, influential lobbies may help to determine what is defined as a national interest.

A country's international image and political clout on the international stage may also form part of what is perceived as in the national interest. In some instances, this may be achieved through constructive participation in the international community. However, in other in-

---

[1106] Convention on the Elimination of All Forms of Discrimination against Women (CEDAW), Division for the Advancement of Women, United Natiosns Department of Economic and Social Affairs, 31 December 2007, http://www.un.org/womenwatch/daw/cedaw/.
[1107] Convention on the Rights of the Child, Office of the High Commissioner for Human Rights, 2003, http://www.unhchr.ch/html/menu3/b/k2crc.htm.
[1108] Al-Rodhan, Neo-*statecraft and* Meta-*geopolitics, op. cit.*, note 185, p. 206.

stances, it may be sought through less constructive measures designed to augment a country's clout. However, the selfish pursuit of narrowly defined national interests is unlikely to serve a state's long-term interests, which are better served by acting as a positive force in the international realm. States' core interests are likely to be best protected through international law and the UN's collective security system, provided that they abide by the international legal framework put in place.

Possible Conflicts with Individual and Group Interests
National interest may conflict with individual interests if its pursuit violates human rights. A country that diverts a great deal of revenue to military spending risks neglecting the needs of its people, denying them access to basic health care and a good education, for example. A state's pursuit of its national interest may also be in tension with group interests in so far as the desire for national cohesion encroaches on group rights.[1109]

Regional Interests
A number of regional groupings were formed in the post-Second World War period (see Chapter 10 for a detailed discussion). Sub-state regions may also pursue specific interests. This may be especially the case in countries that are made up of unevenly developed regions, or in regions that are endowed with scarce natural resources.[1110]

Possible Conflicts with Individual, Group and National Interests
Regional interests may conflict with individual interests when free trade arrangements negotiated by a regional entity contribute to the loss of people's livelihoods, for example. Depending on how well a particular state is able to promote its interests in a region, national interests may be compromised by regional integration efforts.[1111] They may come into conflict with both individual and group interests when a regional group favours non-intervention and adopts a "hard" conception of sovereignty.

[1109] Al-Rodhan, Neo-*statecraft and* Meta-*geopolitics, op. cit.*, note 185, p. 208.
[1110] *Ibid.*, p. 208.
[1111] *Ibid.*, p. 211.

Cultural Interests

Some groups may have specific cultural interests linked to the desire to maintain their cultural practices, language or religion. They may also have an interest in maintaining the economic well-being of their community.[1112] As is mentioned above, cultural group rights are protected rights. In 1966, the International Covenant on Economic, Social and Cultural Rights (ICESCR) was added to the Universal Declaration of Human Rights.[1113]

Possible Conflicts with Individual, Group, National and Regional Interests
A potential conflict between cultural and individual interests could arise in instances of cultural relativism where universal human values are rejected in favour of culturally specific values. Yet, against this, human rights are premised on the applicability of universal values. In terms of cultural and individual interests, the cultural context ought to accommodate individual interests while reducing self-interest.

Cultural interests may also come into conflict with the national interest in fostering national unity. Cultural groups seeking greater autonomy may find themselves in conflict with a state's interest in national unity in so far as national unity is defined as conformism with the dominant culture.[1114]

Global Interests

Global interests are the shared interests of states in the international system and those of the world population. States have a common interest in preserving the interstate system and their sovereignty, although sovereignty may be interpreted in either soft or hard ways. They also share an interest in promoting a stable international environment in which threats to security are minimised. States share a common interest in maintaining access to strategic resources and, on the whole, they share an interest in environmental protection.

States also share an interest in economic prosperity and, therefore, in minimising market instabilities. However, their long-term

---

[1112] *Ibid.*, p. 212.
[1113] International Covenant on Economic, Social and Cultural Rights (ICESCR), Office of the High Commissioner of Human Rights, 1976, http://www.unhchr.ch/html/menu3/b/a_cescr.htm.
[1114] Al-Rodhan, Neo-*statecraft and* Meta-*geopolitics, op. cit.*, note 185, p. 213.

collective interests are best served by attempting to minimise inequalities in the distribution of wealth within countries and within states. Extreme poverty may lead to efforts to seek justice through non-conventional means and therefore increase social unrest, which may affect the international community as a whole. Disparities in wealth between states caused by protectionism are likely to stand in the way of international efforts to enhance prosperity through trade. We may consider the world's population as having an interest in living in a clean and safe environment with an absence of fear and want.[1115]

Possible Conflicts with Individual, Group, National, Regional and Cultural Interests
Long-term individual interests are likely to conform to global interests. While individuals may define their interests in fairly narrow ways in the short term, their long-term interests do not differ radically from global interests. Trade regulations, environmental protection and labour protection are, for example, likely to benefit them in terms of ensuring a clean environment, a stable societal situation, and fair trade and market opportunities further down the line. The global interest in promoting stability and minimising insecurity also serves the individual by providing a more secure environment and perhaps even in saving their lives.

Global and national interests are likely to be congruent over the long run. Long-term interests are served by both international law and norms, and global collective security. The unilateral pursuit of narrowly conceived national interests will not increase a state's long-term prosperity and security. It is likely to generate deep-rooted resentment and instability, and to precipitate an erosion of its international image and credibility.

Global and regional interests may collide at times. A scenario may be imagined in which regional interests as they are conceived involve the establishment of quotas and the protection of certain markets. These interests will come into conflict with global interests, given that such actions can engender and sustain global inequalities. Regions as well as states are likely to view the protection of industries deemed "strategic" as in their core interest. Wealthy states ought to see that it is in their long-term interest to give up some of their trade advantages which harm those of other countries.

[1115] *Ibid.*, pp. 215-216.

Individual, national, perhaps regional, and global interests may come into conflict in situations of humanitarian intervention. A state whose people require humanitarian assistance may not view it as in its national interest to allow intervention on the part of the international community. Furthermore, the region in which such a state belongs may not approve of international intervention. This was the case, for example, when the Burmese government was reluctant to open the county to humanitarian aid in the aftermath of the 2008 cyclone there.

Another potential scenario may be that a wealthy state that has the means to engage in humanitarian or peace support assistance is reluctant to commit its national resources to such an endeavour, when clearly it would be in the interest of those individuals affected as well as the world community. States may only wish to intervene in a crisis situation when their immediate interests are at stake.

Globalisation and increased connectedness may conflict with cultural interests. Cultural groups may view their cultural traditions as coming under threat in the increasingly global context. In some instances, this may generate resistance movements or even extremism.

Planetary Interests
Symbiotic Realism: A Theory of International Relations in an Instant and an Interdependent World (2007) identifies the biosphere as a "reactive actor" endowed with a "non-conscious form of agency" and "reacting to human activities in such a way as to call into question current levels of civilisation and to transform aspects of the global system, for example, through climate change."[1116] We may conceive of "planetary interests", such as the preservation of the ecosystem and biodiversity. Core planetary interests include a reduction in global warming and in activities that contribute to environmental degradation such as deforestation, water pollution and desertification.

Possible Conflicts with Individual, Group, National, Regional, Cultural and Global Interests
In principle, there ought to be no conflict between individual, national, regional and planetary interests. Human life can only prosper if the planet is healthy. Yet, as long as individuals only think short-term, they may not consider the impact of their actions on the well-being of

---
[1116] Al-Rodhan, *Symbiotic Realism, op. cit.*, note 78, p. 12.

the planet and may resist any constraints implied in efforts to protect the biosphere. Rapidly developing countries may not consider environmental protection to be in their immediate national interest. Their primary concern may be economic growth, whether by sustainable means or not. Moreover, some cultural practices may also be in tension with planetary interests, a case in point being the hunting of endangered species such as whales.[1117]

Moral Interests
Universal moral interests are shared by all cultures of the world and are agreed on at least in principle. These are, however, "thin" or "minimalist" moral norms, some of which inform international law and humanitarian law.[1118] Yet, as is outlined in emotional amoral egoism, human nature is emotionally driven, which means that moral concepts that rely on conceptions of humankind as rational beings are unlikely to guide the majority of people while their basic needs go unmet.[1119] There is therefore a moral interest in ensuring that the normative and legal foundations of moral behaviour are robust. In order to encourage the moral behaviour of international actors, conditions need to be created whereby their existence and well-being are ensured.[1120]

Possible Conflicts with Individual, Group, National, Regional, Cultural, Global and Planetary Interests
In some circumstances, the moral interests of different entities can be opposed. A statesman may, for example, have to prioritise the obligation to protect the population of his or her state at the cost of lives elsewhere in the world.

Moral interests in protecting people in situations of conflict and those suffering from the impact of natural disasters may be at odds with the perceived national interests of states which oppose outside intervention or "interference". Protecting the biosphere may be considered a moral obligation to future generations. However, this may also clash with narrowly conceived national interests, and these

---
[1117] Al-Rodhan, Neo-*statecraft and* Meta-*geopolitics, op. cit.*, note 185, pp. 220-221.
[1118] *Ibid.*, p. 221.
[1119] Al-Rodhan, *"emotional amoral egoism," op. cit.*, note 119.
[1120] Al-Rodhan, *op. cit.*, note 185, pp. 222.

same issues may also conflict with regional interests, depending on how they are defined.

Reconciling the Eight Interests

The well-being of humankind depends on reconciling the eight interests set out above. Compromising one of these interests will result in discord and insecurity. For example, allowing the violation of cultural group rights within a particular country is likely to cause societal and perhaps regional instability, particularly if the group is transnational, and potentially global tensions in relation to possible intervention or recognition of a group's claim to self-determination. Disregard for the environmental impact of unsustainable development is against not only the interests of the planet, but also individual, national, regional and global interests.

We might conceive of the reconciliation of the eight interests outlined above as being supported by the application of the multi-sum principle and, thereby, contributing to sustainable security.[1121] Reconciling the eight interests also requires a comprehensive national security architecture. In *The Three Pillars of Sustainable National Security in a Transnational World* (2008), I set out a model for a new NSC that is capable of effectively addressing the issues of today's world. In it, it was argued that the NSC structure needs to be capable of dealing with a broader range of security threats, engaged in long-term threat prevention and concerned with the upholding ethical standards in security policy implementation. This type of NSC is precisely what is required in order to reconcile the eight interests and to ensure that security and stability are sustainable.[1122]

Sustainable national security needs to be informed by the multidimensionality of today's security environment and the connectedness of different dimensions, the advantages offered to states by mutually beneficial security relationships, and a recognition that exchanges and interactions between cultures can have a net effect that serves humanity as a whole. In time, these synergies will generate a global cultural superstructure underpinned by common human values,[1123] even if these are instantiated in different ways within specific cultural and historical contexts.

[1121] Al-Rodhan, *The Five Dimensions of Global Security, op. cit.*, note 512.
[1122] Al-Rodhan, *The Three Pillars of Sustainable National Security, op. cit.*, note 667.
[1123] *Ibid.*, p. 160.

The employment of power has to be driven by concerns of justice. This offers the best way to ensure stability and to promote security in the world. While a state's employment of power should be smart, integrating the use of soft power, a state's foreign and security policy should not simply be intelligent, but also *just*.[1124] The concept of just power should, therefore, form an integral part of the development of security strategies and foreign policies.

6. The Future of Geopolitics in a Transnational World

While geopolitics will retain its importance in the 21st century, points of reference and physical factors influencing the geographic dimensions that shape relations between states will alter as a result of technological advances, shifts in the relative economic importance of different resources, trends in the scarcity of resources and the changing geographic landscapes resulting from global climate change.

The Rise of BRIC Countries

High oil prices and the rise of new financial power centres could initiate a shift in global power relations, infringing on US global hegemony. Several oil-rich states, such as Iran, Russia and Venezuela, have begun to favour the euro over the dollar.[1125] Brazil, Russia, India and China – the so-called BRIC countries – are consolidating their presence on the international stage. The big four emerging energy markets have some of the world's largest populations and mounting economic clout. There are some signs that the BRIC countries will be more active globally and initiate cooperative endeavours. For example, in 2008 Russia hosted a meeting of the BRIC countries' foreign ministers to propose a new international economic order to replace that of the Bretton Woods system. They have also taken a collective stance on issues such as the independence of Kosovo.[1126]

[1124] Al-Rodhan, Neo-*statecraft and* Meta-*geopolitics*, *op. cit.*, note 185, p. 150.
[1125] A. Cohen, "The Shifting Geopolitics of BRIC and Oil," www.ArielCohen.Com, 30 May 2008, http://www.arielcohen.com/articles.php?id=267.
[1126] *Ibid.*; C. Mortished, "Russia Shows Its Political Clout By Hosting BRIC Summit," *The Times* Online, 16 May 2008, http://www.timesonline.co.uk/tol/business/markets/russia/article3941462.ece.

The Quest for Food and Water Security and Its Geopolitical Manifestations

Food and water security in states are affected by a number of factors, including population increases, high oil prices, global warming and the quest for alternative energy sources. The need for sufficient supplies of clean water and for affordable grain is beginning to have geostrategic implications. In some countries, food shortage is precipitating social unrest, which results in state instability.[1127] The Gulf states are beginning to lease land in countries with more fertile soil, creating new potential dependences and interests. Water shortage is also likely to prompt an increasing number of states to invest in nuclear technologies as a means of water desalination, increasing the quantity of states with nuclear know-how and the amount of dual-use materials in circulation.[1128]

Climate Change and Geopolitics

Global climate change is likely to exacerbate water and food shortages, which may lead to significant migration. While climate change will affect every area of the globe, different countries will be affected in different ways. India, for instance, while gaining in geopolitical weight, will be beset by floods, rising sea levels and the resulting environmental refugee flows.[1129] On the African continent, Nigeria and East Africa will be the most severely affected by droughts, desertification and rising sea levels. Many of the states that will be the most affected are likely to be considerably challenged due to a lack of capacities to deal with such issues. Increased migration to Europe from the Middle East and Africa could increase tensions within European societies as well as globally as a result of the degree of interconnectedness today, so long as inclusive national identities and societal structures are not successfully established.[1130] Above all, the consequences

---

[1127] J.S. Morrison and J. Nesseth Tuttle, "A Call for a Strategic U.S. Approach to the Global Food Crisis," Center for Strategic and International Studies, July 2008, http://www.csis.org/component/option.com_csis_pubs/task.view/id.4708/.
[1128] "Saudi Setting Up Fund to Buy Agricultural Land Abroad," *Gulf Times*, 26 August 2008, http://www.gulf-times.com/site/topics/article.asp?cu_no=2&item_no=237858&version=1&template_id=48&parent_id=28.
[1129] J. Podesta and P. Ogden, "The Security Implications of Climate Change," *The Washington Quarterly*, Vol. 31, No. 1, Winter 2007-08, p. 116.
[1130] *Ibid.*, pp. 119-121.

of global climate change will increase the disparity between rich and poor and exacerbate security challenges of various kinds.

The Melting of the Arctic Ice and Its Geopolitical Implications
The melting of the Artic ice is not simply a manifestation of global warming, but actually contributes to it, since the white ice reflects the heat of the Sun while the ocean absorbs it.[1131] As noted earlier, the opening up of new shipping routes would have significant economic implications for a number of countries. It would reduce the shipping distance between Europe and Southeast Asia and between Europe and the west coast of the United States. It would also mean that ships could avoid going through the Panama and Suez canals. In addition, the expected discovery of fossil fuels is already giving rise to territorial rivalries over the Artic.[1132]

The Coming Demographic Revolution
The strategic relationships between major powers are also likely to be affected by significant demographic shifts. The first part of this century is expected to bring about a large scale change. A number of states will experience a slow down in population growth and a change in the age structure of society, marked by a growing proportion of older people. Most of the countries that will experience such a demographic transformation are situated in the developed world. In these countries, the active population will decline, potentially causing economic stagnation. The electorate will also be on average significantly older than in other countries. Moreover, manpower for the military will decline, although this is likely to be offset in these countries by advances in weapons technologies.[1133] Given the cost of such technologies, however, a greater number of strategic coalitions is likely to emerge. The economic and political empowerment of women in traditional societies is also likely to have a significant impact on respective countries' political, economic and geopolitical outlook.[1134]

[1131] "Melting Arctic Shows Need for Climate Pact Group Says," CNN International, http://edtion.cnn.com/2008/TECH/science/09/15/arctic.ice.ap/index.html?eref=time_t ech.
[1132] Al-Rodhan, Neo-*statecraft and* Meta-*geopolitics, op. cit.*, note 185, p. 184.
[1133] R. Jackson and N. Howe, *The Graying of the Great Powers: Demography and Geopolitics in the 21st Century* (Washington, DC: Center for Strategic and International Studies, 2008), pp. 185, 187-188, 191.
[1134] Al-Rodhan, Neo-*statecraft and* Meta-*geopolitics, op. cit.*, note 185, p. 188.

The End of Unipolarity

With China, India and, to some degree, Russia in ascendance, the world seems likely to be less unipolar than it has been since the end of the Cold War. By 2050, China and India are likely to have sufficient technological, administrative and communications capacities to maintain a stable domestic order, a strong military and a more active foreign policy.[1135] In addition, the Arab-Islamic world is not, uniformly, expected to achieve the same political, economic and military weight as China and India. It may also experience greater challenges in a globalising world than China and India, but the Arab-Islamic World, China and India are likely to shade the global system with a greater number of cultural hues, making it less West-centric than it currently is.[1136]

Middle-income countries are also likely to make their presence felt on the world stage. They are increasingly active members of international organisations, and those that have been dependent on the US are gradually reducing that dependency and developing a growing number of ties among themselves.[1137]

The International Impact of Non-State Actors

In addition to the shifting power relations among states, the increasing number of non-state actors on the international scene is also making power more diffuse. Some of the more powerful non-state actors can pose threats to states. Globalisation has helped to empower these actors as a result of the growth of global communications and advances in other technologies, for example.[1138]

Science and Technology: A Geopolitical Force

The technological capacities of states have a tremendous impact on the power relations between states. Modern militaries are increasingly dependent on advanced technology for their communications and

---

[1135] C. Bell, "The End of the Vasco da Gama Era: The Next Landscape of World Politics," Lowy Institute Institute Paper 21, Lowy Institute for International Policy, Australia, 2007, pp. 9, 11-12.

[1136] Al-Rodhan, Neo-*statecraft and* Meta-*geopolitics, op. cit.*, note 185, p. 190.

[1137] P. Khanna, "Here Comes the Second World," *Prospect*, No. 146, May 2008, pp. 60-61.

[1138] R.N. Haass, "The Age of Nonpolarity: What Will Follow U.S. Dominance," *Foreign Affairs*, Vol. 87, No. 3, May/June 2008, http://www.foreignaffairs.org/20080 501faessay87304/richard-n-haass/the-age-of-nonpolarity.html.

weapons systems. Strong science and technological capacities are also critical in economic terms. Currently, the US, Japan and Europe are leaders in terms of science and technology. China and India, however, are making efforts to improve their capacities in this area. Space technology also has a significant impact on a country's power in relation to networked communications and intelligence within the militaries, surveillance and perhaps future space-based nuclear missile interceptor systems.[1139]

7. Conclusion

This chapter set out the analytical and practical basis on which statecraft should be conducted in the 21st century. Statecraft today has to address a number of complex and interconnected issues. In this chapter, I proposed that *neo*-statecraft should be thought of as having four substrates: *meta*-geopolitics, sustainable national security, just power and reconciliation statecraft. In a globally interconnected world, geopolitics needs to consider a variety of unevenly distributed state capacities. The *meta*-geopolitics outlined above considers seven such capacities: social and health issues, domestic politics, economics, environment, science and human potential, military and security issues, and international diplomacy. These facets of state power are interrelated and often mutually reinforcing.

As well as being supported by *meta*-geopolitical analysis, statecraft today needs to address a broad set of issues. Responding effectively to security challenges will depend on the deployment of soft and hard power tools. Moreover, cooperative relations with other states are crucial to effective and timely responses to largely transnational threats. A number of issues are likely to affect the future geopolitical landscape. Demographic trends, changes in economic relationships and technological advances are all likely to have an impact on a state's power in the global system. Attention to international dynamics and new developments are therefore also a critical part of geopolitical analyses.

Far from being redundant, diplomacy remains a critical aspect of statecraft. Public diplomacy is of increasing relevance to the diplomatic task. In a world marked by instant connectivity, where the mass

---

[1139] Al-Rodhan, Neo-*statecraft and* Meta-*geopolitics, op. cit.*, note 185, pp. 199-201.

media is ever present, an important task of statecraft is to sway public opinion both at home and abroad in favour of the state's position. The most effective means of doing so is to respect international law and to promote ends that are generally considered just and fair. Burden-sharing and absolute rather than relative gains will also form a critical part of achieving sustainable national security. The reconciliation of a number of sometimes conflicting interests, ranging from individual to planetary interests, is also a prerequisite of successful diplomacy.

Neo-statecraft also comprises a sustainable approach to national security, consisting of the multi-sum security principle, which captures the multidimensionality of security challenges and appropriate responses, and highlights the need for multilateralism.

Statecraft must also promote transcultural synergies. Innovations and solutions to problems are likely to occur through interaction and exchanges between cultures, since no one culture has a monopoly on ideas and talent. Indeed, history shows that the history of ideas is a history of borrowing and multiple interactions and dependencies. The health of our collective human civilisation will depend on such synergies. Promoting transcultural synergies also serves the aim of advancing intercultural understanding, which is so badly needed today.

The promotion of justice is also central to statecraft today. To this end, statesmen should employ just power as far as possible. Just power is concerned with the protection of human dignity. It reserves the use of force for the prosecution of just wars and the promotion of human rights. In the economic sphere, just power is premised on a fair global economic order in which developing states can function on a more even playing field.

Thus, statecraft today must change to match the changes in the global environment in which statesmen must operate. Statecraft is about much more than ensuring the physical security of the state's population and territory. It involves responding to a multiplicity of interconnected issues and actors through cooperation, reconciliation of interests on a number of levels and transcultural synergies.

CHAPTER 14

HOW SHOULD CULTURES INTERRELATE?
TRANSCULTURAL SYNGERY AND UNIVERSAL
AXIOLOGY

In an increasingly interconnected world, cross-cultural fertilisation and exchanges are likely to take place with increased intensity, reducing social space and bringing people closer together. While contact and exchanges have taken place between people of different cultures for millennia, today is marked by the unprecedented intensity and scope of relations. This offers up great opportunities on a number of levels. Historically, decisive contributions to humanity's collective knowledge have often occurred as a result of borrowing and exchanges. Yet, this more intense contact between people of different cultural backgrounds also has the potential to engender tension and perhaps conflict when combined with economic inequalities and insecurities, and lack of knowledge of the ways and circumstances of others, for example. The factors contributing to misunderstanding and mistrust are many and varied.

How should people from different cultures interrelate? At present, transcultural issues are in their infancy and often take the form of dialogue and alliance building. Efforts include the 2000 UN Millennium summit dialogue among civilisations,[1140] the 2001 UN Year of Dialogue among Civilizations[1141] and the 2008 Muslim World League (MWL) World Conference on Dialogue (IICD), called by King Abdullah Ibn Abdul Aziz Al-Saud of the Kingdom of Saudi Arabia.[1142] These represent positive and proactive steps to ensure peaceful coexis-

---

[1140] K. Gawlikowski, "From False 'Western Universalism' Towards True 'Universal Universalism'," *Dialogue and Universalism*, Nos. 10-12, 2004, p. 37.
[1141] See the UN Dialogue among Civilizations Website: http://www.un.org/Dialogue/sponsor.html.
[1142] See the World Conference on Dialogue Website: http://www.world-dialogue.org/english/english.htm.

tence between members of different cultures and faiths. However, ultimately more than coexistence is required to ensure the future well-being of our collective human civilisation. Transcultural synergy will be needed if we are to deal with the various challenges that we face today. Transcultural synergy refers to the idea that different cultures can have a net effect that is greater than the impact of the efforts of any one culture.[1143] There must also be an effort to identify common fundamental values. The task that lies ahead of us is to identify how various moral languages may express the same core values in different ways. It is important to learn to distinguish between fundamental values that are shared by people across cultures, and the ways in which they have been or are likely to be shaped by specific historical, social and institutional contexts. Dialogue is thus required to gain a better understanding of our common ground. An awareness of one's own cultural identity and a willingness to question the universality of one's own cultural traditions and values are prerequisites for a fruitful dialogue to develop,[1144] and can lead to synergistic processes that may benefit all humanity.

This chapter suggests how we might usefully think about cultures and geo-cultural domains. It discusses the relationship between essentialist notions of civilisations and hegemony, and suggests how this mutually reinforcing relationship may be dislodged. It sets out the concept of transcultural synergy, and discusses how dialogue and the identification of common fundamental values may help bring that synergy. This will be critical to achieving sustainable history.

1. Culture and Geo-cultural Domains

Cultures, as is explained in *A Proposal for* Inclusive *Peace and Security* (2007), may be understood as cognitive structures that shape how people relate to the world and to each other.[1145] Culture is not something fixed, but fluid and continually in the process of being produced and reproduced. Culture may be thought of as depending on its members meaningfully interpreting the world around them in largely simi-

---

[1143] Al-Rodhan and Watanabe, *A Proposal for* Inclusive *Peace and Security, op. cit.*, note 1, p. 91.
[1144] Gawlikowski, *op. cit.*, note 1140, pp. 55-56.
[1145] Al-Rodhan and Watanabe, *A Proposal for* Inclusive *Peace and Security, op. cit.*, note 1, p. 32.

lar ways. This is not to say that culture is uniformly represented. There is in fact a great deal of diversity within cultures. Members of a culture may interpret or represent the same things in slightly different ways. Yet, the images, concepts and ideas must be similar enough that they interpret the world in roughly the same way. In addition, culture is not just about ideas; it is also about emotions and attachment. Indeed, both thinking and feeling form part of systems of representation.[1146] How is culture distinct from "civilisations" or, as I refer to them, geo-cultural domains? The international relations scholar R.W. Cox suggests a useful distinction between culture and civilisation. Culture may be thought of as being synchronic, or concerned with the interaction between norms and practices within a social system that together maintain the coherence of the whole. Civilisation, by contrast, may be conceived of as diachronic, or as a historical cultural form.[1147]

Cox suggests that civilisations may be thought of as continuities in human thought and practices that help to collectivise responses by human groups to current circumstances.[1148] In this view, civilisations are unfinished entities that may be likened to a collective consciousness and, thus, help to inform how we understand and act in the world. A working definition of civilisation, he suggests, might be "a fit or correspondence between material conditions of existence and inter-subjective meanings."[1149] The identification of inter-subjective meanings suggests that there are different ways of seeing the world and different "truths" that are both socially and historically constructed. Material conditions may combine with inter-subjective meanings in different ways, producing different forms.

It is important to attempt to identify the factors that help to determine inter-subjective meanings. If we can answer this question then we may also be better able to understand what factors influence changes within those "realities". Cox identifies four factors: (1) social economy; (2) dominance and subordination; (3) spiritual consciousness; and (4) time and space. The first of these factors refers to the

---

[1146] S. Hall, "Introduction," in S. Hall (ed.) *Representation: Cultural Representations and Signifying Practices* (London: Sage, 1997), pp. 2, 4.
[1147] R.W. Cox, "Conceptual Guidelines for a Plural World," in Cox with Schecter, *op. cit.*, note 4, pp. 161-163.
[1148] *Ibid.*, p. 157.
[1149] *Ibid.*, p. 161.

way in which people organise themselves to meet their material needs. In other words, it refers to modes of social organisation of production and distribution. Cox contends that there is currently a conflict between the dominance of abstract economic laws and efforts to construct economic activities in ways that are perceived as compatible with existing societal norms. Globalisation is being challenged from below by those who are negatively affected by it, and by the affirmation of different modes of capitalism embedded in particular cultural traditions.[1150] This, argues Cox, is at the heart of the tension between globalisation and geo-cultural domains.

Relations between geo-cultural domains are also organised through dominance and subordination, most famously captured by Said's notion of Orientalism.[1151] Orientalism refers to a form of knowledge in which Eastern cultural domains were depicted as subordinate to the West. Power and knowledge were, thus, intertwined and helped to structure relations between West and East along the lines of superiority and inferiority. The imagined characteristics and mindset of the East were set up as the contrary of a rational and progress-oriented West. Moreover, this dichotomy was thought to have existed.[1152]

Spiritual consciousness also helps to shape different realities and ways of acting on them. Acknowledging a spiritual dimension also means recognising that the particular form the spiritual takes is likely to be shaped by particular material conditions and the ways in which people have sought to cope with them. Cox suggests, for example, that monotheism may have emerged from ancient hydraulic empires, where everything seemed to have a single source. It reflects a belief in absolute truth, which may continue in the form of rationalism. Polytheism, by contrast, allows for non-exclusive religions and multiple truths. It is more characteristic of Far Eastern cultural areas than those originating from around the Mediterranean. Pantheism conceives of everything in the cosmos as being related and forming part of a coherent whole. It is most readily associated with Hinduism and indigenous peoples. As Cox points out, cultural domains are not synonymous with a single form of spiritual consciousness. Part of the

---

[1150] *Ibid.*, p. 166.
[1151] Said, *op. cit.*, note 7.
[1152] Hobson, *op. cit.*, note 383, p. 9.

challenge, therefore, is to discern the various hues of spiritual consciousness that help to shape people's thought and behaviour.[1153]

Finally, different cultural groups may place different emphases on time and space. Braudel, as is mentioned in Chapter 6, suggested that different facets of human and social life possess different rhythms. Economic change, for instance, was thought to move at a faster pace than changes in cultural mores. This implies that mentalities move more slowly than changes in material conditions. While changes in aspects of life are related, they do not occur at the same tempo. Braudel identified three "times". The first of these is the time of events. In order to make sense of events, they need to be considered in terms of the second "level", that of conjunctures, which constitutes a medium-term time frame in which economic cycles, social forces, particular paradigms, and so on, may be observed. Conjunctures can be explained only by situating them within the framework of a longue durée (explained in Chapter 1), shaping what comes to be accepted as a common sense order of things. The existence of the state, for example, forms part of this tempo. The longue durée itself has both diachronic and synchronic dimensions.[1154]

Cox suggests that globalisation announces the triumph of space over time, which is most readily perceptible through the economy, particularly the highly mobile nature of finance, as well as the instantaneous connectivity that the media affords.[1155] This captures the sense in which there is instant connectivity in a technologically advanced and globalised era. Yet, it would seem that widespread access to media sources also has the effect of reducing our experience of time.

Contact occurs between people of different cultural backgrounds and collective memories linked to specific geo-cultural domains that, as is noted above, have a historical dimension. Does this mean, however, that these people are on a collision course? Huntington answers in the affirmative but, while realist ways of thinking about geo-cultural domains assume that relations between these entities have always been marked by conflict, history bears testimony to the many and varied exchanges and borrowings that have occurred. We need to

---

[1153] Cox, *op. cit.*, note 1147, pp. 168-171.
[1154] Braudel's different tempos are outlined by Robert W. Cox in Cox, *op. cit.*, note 1147, p. 172.
[1155] *Ibid.*, p. 173

think of geo-culture as forming part of a larger human civilisation, the history of which is a collective one marked by both cooperation and conflict, as is highlighted in Chapter 6.

There are those who argue that the clash is not between cultural domains, but within them. Senghaas, for example, argues that fissures within civilisations are central to their evolution. These fissures are created by tensions between traditional and modernising forces. This may be thought of as a development dynamic. The danger of such a dynamic is that it generates insecurities that may engender the securitization of large collective identities and defensive reactions that risk making the clash of civilisations thesis a reality, even if there is nothing inevitable about it. Avoiding such a scenario will, he argues, depend on fostering social orders that are capable of largely meeting everyone's needs.[1156]

Senghaas' analysis is important in that it encourages one to think about geo-cultural domains as highly complex and continually evolving entities. A greater awareness of the spectrum of views within a cultural region would encourage people to see generalisations about the members of a particular cultural group as oversimplified caricatures of a complex reality. People from the Arab-Islamic world are sometimes portrayed in images and the media as fundamentalists, when there are a wide array of positions, from the traditionalist to representatives of a modern and democratic form of Islam. *Focusing purely on extremism, whether in the Arab-Islamic world or the West, will not alleviate the root causes of tensions between members of different cultures. It will only alienate those who do not recognise themselves in those stereotypes, and generate fear and misunderstanding.* Lack of recognition of the diversity within geo-cultural domains is partly related to essentialising notions of culture and civilisation.

2. Essentialism and Hegemony

Essentialism and hegemony are mutually constitutive. As is mentioned above, the West's representation of the East has been critiqued, most notably by Said, as a colonising form of knowledge bound up with Europe's history of imperialism.[1157] Reason, equality and liberty

---

[1156] Senghaas, *op. cit.*, note 26, pp. 1-8.
[1157] Said, *op. cit.*, note 7.

associated with the spread of scientific knowledge and the Enlightenment are often assumed to be synonymous with the West,[1158] which may be contrasted with an East that lacks these forms of knowledge and modes of thought. This linear conception of European history guided by progress is routine and to be found in most accounts of the Enlightenment. However, as is discussed in Chapter 6, it relies on a highly selective account of the West's genealogy, and of that of the East. Seminal figures of the Enlightenment are assumed to be Western and include such philosophers as Voltaire, Kant, Jean-Jacques Rousseau (1712-1778) and Locke. While the debt to other Western scholars may be acknowledged, such figures are seldom thought to be indebted to Muslims, Hindus or the Chinese.[1159] A reluctance in the West to acknowledge its intellectual debts to the East persists, perhaps partly as a result of what is taught in history books and partly because of the reluctance of scholars of the Enlightenment to acknowledge such influences. The opposition of a West driven by scientific rationalism with a mysterious and occultist East is, therefore, still commonplace.[1160] This, however, obscures the extent to which the Enlightenment was the result of a collective effort.

That said, some European philosophers did swim against the tide of continental chauvinism. Edmund Burke (1729-97), for instance, regarded India as a sophisticated civilisation populated by a highly cultivated people. Voltaire too spoke of the Chinese not as barbarians but as a populace that had made great advances in the areas of morality, political economy and the arts and advised that they may be examples to follow in these areas.[1161] However, the rather more positive vision of the East that Burke and Voltaire held was not representative. The more negative ideas of their peers were far more abundant.[1162]

Mustapha Kamal Pasha stresses that breaking down orientalist essentialism requires that we deconstruct the assumptions of homogeneity and permanence that infuse Occidental discourse. Non-essentialist accounts need to recognise the power implications of es-

---

[1158] W. Pfaff, "Clash of Cultures: Globalization and the March of Western Values," *Commonweal*, 16 June 2006, p. 14.
[1159] Attar, *op. cit.*, note 256, p. 2.
[1160] J.J. Clarke, *Oriental Enlightenment: The Encounter Between Asian and Western Thought* (Routledge, 1997), p. 5.
[1161] Bowden, *op. cit.*, note 334, p. 1365.
[1162] *Ibid.*

sentialism. Essentialist typologies, such as that of Huntington, help to draw rigid political and cultural boundaries that overshadow similarities and borrowing, and help to further the myth of incommensurability between geo-cultural domains and cultures.

According to Kamal Pasha, Eisenstadt's idea of multiple modernities cannot fully escape the sociological and political discourse of Western modernity. While his account wishes to go beyond the West, it still has a Western starting point. We also need to dislodge modern historicism, which privileges rational scientific knowledge and denies the existence of different histories. Kamal Pasha suggests that disrupting the association of modernity and Westernization can help to break down Eurocentrism. Orientalism may be part of the modern political-intellectual lens. According to him, post-orientalist critiques, while acknowledging the connection between power and knowledge, do not take new power constellations seriously enough. Representations of the Arab-Islamic world often fail to appreciate the diversity within this cultural domain. One of the ways that essentialist views of the Arab-Islamic world may be broken down is by highlighting the diversity of cultural groups within this overarching domain. The diversity of cultural groups and also the fissures within this cultural domain should be identified and acknowledged to help resist totalising visions of otherness.[1163]

Essentialism often draws on the familiar dichotomies of modernity/tradition, and the private sphere of religiosity and the secular public sphere of the West versus a lack of separation in the Arab-Islamic world, the pervasiveness of religion in this cultural domain, cultural deficiency, and over emotionality versus the rational characteristics of modernity. Essentialism also represents the Other as something fixed rather than fluid. The life world of the Other almost seems timeless and unchanging, with enduring characteristics. The Other's past, present and future merge into one. The Other is also frequently thought of in exotic or demonic terms. Another familiar strategy of "othering" is "self-enclosure", which emphasises separateness and erases instances of borrowing and mutual influence, and denies the possibility of learning, borrowing and even synthesis. Otherness is also frequently infused with assumptions of deficiency.[1164] Seen from

---

[1163] M. Kamal Pasha, "Civilizations, Postorientalism, and Islam," in Hall and Jackson, *op. cit.*, note 578, pp. 62-63, 65-67.
[1164] *Ibid.*, pp. 67-69.

this point of view, the factors responsible for the rise of the West were endogenous and the Western subject is a dynamic subject.[1165]

Hobson proposes a "relational" approach to civilisational analysis which acknowledges that civilisations are co-constitutive, affiliated and hybrid. He argues that we need to re-imagine the West along "polycivilisational lines". We might, for example, bring to light the extent to which the rise of the West has been related to connections with other cultural domains. As is discussed in Chapter 6, while the East and West have intertwined histories, this connectedness is absent in the West's own historical narrative.[1166]

This lack of historical memory is partly linked to the response to the influence of the Arab-Islamic world on Medieval Europe at a time when the Islamic faith and Arab-Islamic culture had a considerable appeal. Figures such as Jean Germain (1436-1461), a French bishop, disliked those Christians who travelled to the Arab-Islamic world and came back with criticisms of aspects of Christianity, and feared the consequent dialogue. The Medieval European scholar, Bacon, for example, was a vocal agent of the spread of sources of Arab-Islamic culture in Europe and, as a result, spent the last 15 years of his life in prison.

Indeed, concerns about the appeal of Islam in Europe are reflected by the apparent lucidity with which Martin Luther (1483-1546) is believed to have articulated the need for Christian reformation as a means of definitively resolving the "problem" of Islam. Luther's critics accused him of imitating the tenets of Islam through his critique of ecclesiastical authoritarianism and the centrality of the individual's direct relationship with God.[1167]

Cultural essentialism is, thus, intimately tied to power relations. Fixity, homogeneity and separateness are prioritised within an essentialist framework. Therefore, part of any effort to resist essentialism is recognising diversity within difference, contingency, mutability and connectedness.

[1165] Hobson, *op. cit.*, note 19, p. 296.
[1166] Hobson, *op. cit.*, note 384, pp. 150-152.
[1167] El-Diwani, *op. cit.*, note 376, pp. 5-8.

3. The West and the East: Never the Twain Shall Meet?

Representing Western and Eastern thought as widely divergent may also disguise important commonalities related to ideas and fundamental values, which could be instructive in relation to contemporary discussions about values and rights that all too easily succumb to self-righteous universalising or cultural relativism. The West has attributed special importance to democracy and human rights since the Second World War. Many commentators in the West, Fukuyama being the most prominent among them,[1168] assume that the collapse of actually existing socialist regimes signalled the end of ideological battles and the triumph of liberal market democracy with the desire for recognition behind this trajectory. Western politicians have also assumed that others in non-Western areas of the world "deserve the freedoms that they enjoy", and that they would be welcomed as liberators in places such as Iraq.[1169]

Yet, democracy and human rights are associated with a particular conception of the individual and society derived from Christianity, as well as Roman political and legal heritage and, thus, with a specifically European historical experience.[1170] This does not mean, however, that self-government is a European invention. Indeed, democracy is often assumed to originate in the West and is largely conceived of in terms of the types of liberal democracies in Europe, Australasia and North America, its origins being commonly traced back to Ancient Greece. However, it seems that self-governing assemblies may have appeared earlier in what is now modern-day Iran and Iraq. Recent discoveries suggest that democracy is likely to have spread from there eastwards towards the Indian subcontinent and to Phoenician port cities before emerging in Athens.[1171]

One of the reasons why democracy is perceived as a Western concept is that it is often associated with the state, while collective decision making by deliberation has largely been a local phenomena often taking the form of village council systems.[1172] The principles of political freedom and democracy have historically existed outside the

---

[1168] See Fukuyama, *op. cit.*, note 8.
[1169] Gawlikowski, *op. cit.*, note 1140, p. 33.
[1170] *Ibid.*, p. 32.
[1171] Bowden, *op. cit.*, note 334, pp. 1367-1368.
[1172] *Ibid.*, p. 1368.

West. The maqasi al-shari'a (higher objectives of the shari'a), for example, endorse the right to life, religion, intellect, family and wealth, all of which are strikingly similar to the Lockean ideals expounded in the 17th century.[1173]

Indeed, some commentators argue that the philosophical tradition exists within Islam on questions such as universal human rights, minority rights and democracy. The Mutazilite school of Islamic philosophy taught that divine justice implies human freedom. In this view, humankind must be free if God is to justly judge human beings. This is, however, only one position on the issue of human free will. Muslim philosophers who predate the 19th century, such as Al-Farabi, Ibn Sina and Ibn Rushd, thoroughly explored the question of human freedom along with Muslim jurists. Indeed, the common Hellenic philosophical heritage of medieval Muslim, Jewish and Christian philosophy is sometimes believed to be a foundation on which shared ground may be found.[1174]

In relation to rights, the West has approached its "others" with a conception of human nature that it assumed to be universal.[1175] Appeals to human reason, human nature or spirituality have been made in order to provide a basis for universality concerning rights. Today, the effort to ground human rights often takes the form of appeals to natural law.[1176] From this perspective, human rights are viewed as moral rights that people have simply by virtue of their humanity. This is based on the assumption that there is a universal law that is above that of sovereign states.

Natural law was first discussed by Aristotle in relation to the Greek polis. During Alexander the Great's reign it was applied to a wider community as a response to the need for a moral consensus to bring people of diverse cultures together in the context of the empire. Stoic philosophers expanded its application and Roman jurists later developed it further for the same reasons that Alexander the Great did. However, not until the Middle Ages was natural law revived by Aqui-

---

[1173] A. Ibrahim, "Universal Values and Muslim Democracy," *Journal of Democracy*, Vol. 17, No. 3, 2006, pp. 6-7.
[1174] A.H. Al-Rahim, "Islam and Liberty," Review of *The Universal Hunger for Liberty: Why the Clash of Civilisations Is Not Inevitable*, by Michael Novak, Basic Books, 2004, 281 pp., *Journal of Democracy*, Vol. 17, No. 1, 2006, pp. 167-168.
[1175] Gawlikowski, *op. cit.*, note 1140, pp. 31-32.
[1176] F. Dallmayr, "Asian Values and Global Human Rights," *Philosophy East and West*, Vol. 52, No. 2, 2002, p. 175.

nas, and separated from religion and realigned with rationality by Hugo Grotius (1583-1645) and Samuel von Pufendorf (1632-1694).[1177] The idea of natural law led to the development of natural rights encompassing the rights to life, liberty and property outlined by Locke. The social contract ensured the protection of these rights by governments.[1178]

However, it may be the case that references to natural law also existed elsewhere. Whether there is a natural law tradition within Islam is debated. Some argue adamantly that there is none. However, others claim that this may only be the case in relation to pre-modern legal theory, which held that all efforts to determine divine law must be made through scripture. Extra-scriptural determinations derived as a result of reference to rationality or nature are not thought of as legitimate ways to define divine law. However, pre-modern Muslim jurists in both the positivist and the Mutazilite tradition recognised that in instances where scripture failed to provide guidance when making decisions, judges must assert their own discretion. Pre-modern judges seemed to use their discretion in ways based on context-sensitive notions of the individual and social good. Jurists frequently referred to two types of rights: those of God and those of the individual. The rights of God were associated with social issues and distributed rights within society that were thought to embody the public good, whereas the rights of the individual were concerned with personal and individual good which individuals are endowed with by virtue of nature.[1179] Muslim jurists of this period therefore employed a number of foundational claims when distributing rights.

It seems appropriate to recall at this point that the basis of human rights is a normative ideal about how people should be treated. In the most fundamental sense it is about ensuring human dignity. If the Universal Declaration of Human Rights has been able to secure as much support as it has, it is because people of the world's various cultures share the desire to protect and promote human dignity. While we have no innate moral principles, we are all emotionally driven beings who have basic needs, which include the

---

[1177] C. Williams, "International Human Rights and Confucianism," *Asia-Pacific Journal on Human Rights and the Law*, Vol. 1, 2006, pp. 40-41.
[1178] *Ibid.*, p. 42.
[1179] A.M. Emon, "Natural Law and Natural Rights in Islamic Law," *Journal of Islamic Law and Religion*, Vol. 20, 2004, pp. 351-353.

need for a positive sense of self, and some morally relevant emotions which act as a basis for the formation of normative ideals that help to guide our moral compass. We have developed moral codes, because we are self-aware and emotionally self-interested.

4. Asian and Islamic Values

If the West has often been defined against the East, the West is often conceived by non-Westerners as inferior and decadent. In response to the promotion of democracy and the universality of human rights, some promote the notion that there are specifically Asian and Islamic values that are distinct from those associated with Western individualism. Those who espouse the distinctiveness of Asian values stress the importance of the embeddedness of the individual in the collective (i.e. the family and society). According to this argument, the dignity of the individual is realised within the community. Another dimension of the Asian values argument is that order and respect for authority are favoured over individual freedoms.[1180]

Western critics of Confucianism assume that the Self in Confucianism disappears into the social or that Confucianism encourages conformism. However, as Fred Dallmayr points out, this reveals an ethnocentrism premised on the separation between the individual and the state.[1181] There are also those who argue that the Asian values argument is simply the ruse of autocrats who wish to block popular support for democratic reforms. The way in which Confucian values are evoked to support deference to state authority in the Asian values discourse does not acknowledge a central aspect of Confucian ethics, which emphasises the importance of the Self and self-cultivation partly as a means of guarding against abuses of public power.[1182] Indeed, as Brennan and Lo note, the idea of self-cultivation is central to the Confucian understanding of dignity, which is thought to derive from the ability to feel self-esteem and to gain the esteem of others. However, dignity may be lost as well as cultivated through immoral behaviour.[1183]

[1180] Senghaas, *op. cit.*, note 26, p. 92.
[1181] Dallmayr, *op. cit.*, note 1176, pp. 179-180.
[1182] Ibrahim, *op. cit.*, note 1173, p. 6.
[1183] Brennan and Lo, *op. cit.*, note 493, pp. 45-46.

Dallmayr notes that the classical Chinese language used by early Confucians lacked the terms used in modern rights discourse, which suggests that moral theorising by Confucian philosophers is likely to have been different from that in the West. Within Confucian thought, humanness is conceived of as an essential essence that exists prior to social relations in a state of nature, and as a life-long achievement and something that is realised in social relations. Humanness is, thus, not something that is a fixed, pre-social essence, but something that can only be understood in the social contexts connected to the family, the state, society and the global community.[1184] Dignity is something that is cultivated and nourished, but may be neglected as well as lost.

Western liberal rights are challenged not only from the standpoint of Asian values, but also from that of Islamic values. Some Islamic states have adopted a discourse of particularism that implies that their societies are different because of traditions and local beliefs. It rejects concepts of secular law and seeks to replace them with the shari'a, which, it is claimed, provides the foundation of the legal system and the bases for protecting human rights. This discourse is connected to the more general rejection of secular, modernising, and universalistic projects for the Middle East and other Muslim countries.

Another response to universal human rights is the effort to appropriate human rights, in which some Muslim countries claim an Islamic foundation to human rights. The two most influential Islamic statements on human rights are the Universal Islamic Declaration on Human Rights and the Cairo Declaration on Human Rights, both of which argue that human rights form an inherent part of Islam.[1185] However, it is important that the notion of "ijtihad" be employed, given the new realities of the global system regarding gender equality as well as other inequalities. It is imperative that these issues be addressed.

One factor that has been referred to in relation to the caveats identified in these two declarations is the lack of any separation of religion and the state in Islam. As Robert Carle notes, in classical Arabic there are no words that reflect the distinction between the spiri-

---

[1184] Dallmayr, *op. cit.*, note 1176, pp. 179-180.
[1185] R. Carle, "Revealing and Concealing: Islamist Discourse on Human Rights," *Human Rights Review*, April-June 2005, p. 124.

tual and the temporal or the religious and the secular.[1186] The objection to the argument that there are specifically Islamic human rights is that declarations to this effect entail a weakening of international standards.[1187] This has led some to insist that only a secular interpretation of human rights based on natural law can be considered foundational.[1188] Yet, as is discussed above, natural law may in fact have served as a source with which to determine the distribution of some rights for medieval Muslim jurists, and may not, therefore, require secularism. Moreover, as is mentioned in Chapter 9, notions of human rights may also be embedded not just in natural law traditions, but also in ways of thinking derived from monotheism.

Senghaas argues that claims about inherent antagonisms between Asian and Western values are unfounded and do not sufficiently acknowledge the historical and political-economic context. There is thought to be no reason why a democratic constitutional form of government should not emerge in Asia.[1189] From this viewpoint, Asian and Islamic values are, in fact, considered to be similar to traditional European values, since traditional societies are generally structured hierarchically and paternalistically with little opportunity for social mobility within the collective. Senghaas argues, for example, that what we may consider today as distinctly European is the result of secular and conflictual development processes which are by no means distinctly European or Western. From this perspective, individualism and pluralism are the outcomes of a developmental path that is neither linear nor evolutionary.[1190]

Senghaas points out that notions of unity, harmony, order and duty have been employed outside Western modernity and are still deliberately used as development ideologies by the so-called late modernisers. Here, the argument is that the employment of Asian values protects a particular class or elite whose position may be threatened by the impact of modernity as people begin to demand greater participation in public affairs. This is perceived as a repeat of what went before in Europe. Asian values perform an ideological function.

[1186] *Ibid.*, p. 134.
[1187] *Ibid.*, p. 135.
[1188] F. Halliday, *Islam and the Myth of Confrontation: Religion and Politics in the Middle East* (London, New York: I.B. Taurus Publishers), p. 140.
[1189] Senghaas, *op. cit.*, note 26, pp. 97-98.
[1190] *Ibid.*, pp. 92-94.

They are conceived of as a response to a legitimation crisis in economically successful but politically authoritarian regimes.[1191]

The problem that some Islamic countries face, according to Senghaas, is similar to that of some non-Islamic regions – a collapse of post-colonial development.[1192] He concludes, therefore, that it is simply a matter of time, perhaps 10 to 20 years, before democracy and human rights become institutionally embedded as part of East Asian political culture.[1193] He nevertheless argues that the final outcome will reflect local cultural specificities.[1194]

However, the problem with this approach is that it obscures the extent to which there may be historical and philosophical precedents in the East for the European Enlightenment and constitutional government. Common ground may in fact be found by understanding the West's past, and also that of Asia and of the Arab/Islamic world, not as transitions from traditionalism to modernism, or even postmodernism, but as evolutions that were contingent and not universal.

5. Transcultural Synergy

Yet, before transcultural synergy can become a reality, acquaintance, coexistence and cooperation must first take place. In *Symbiotic Realism: A Theory of International Relations in an Instant and an Interdependent World* (2007), I specifically define synergy as "a phenomenon in which two or more separate entities, influences, or agents acting together can create an effect that is greater than that which could have been predicted from the known effects of each individual influence or action."[1195] In relation to geo-cultural domains, synergy was employed to suggest that when members of different cultures work together, the effect is greater than the sum of their individual effects.[1196] Synergistic instances, as is mentioned above, contributed significantly to the high points in human civilisation. Contact need not be a source of conflict and tension, it can also be a stimulus to creativity.

[1191] *Ibid.*, pp. 94-95; 113.
[1192] *Ibid.*, pp. 96, 115.
[1193] Senghaas, *op. cit.*, note 26, pp. 96-97.
[1194] *Ibid.*, p. 97.
[1195] Al-Rodhan, *Symbiotic Realism*, *op. cit.*, note 78, p. 124.
[1196] *Ibid.*, p. 123.

As a result of increased human mobility linked to the economic division of labour in an era of globalisation, societies are increasingly culturally plural and human nature is such that people need to feel that they belong and have a positive identity.[1197] States may respond by seeking assimilation of those minorities within a national identity that is assumed to be already existing and complete. Yet, efforts to suppress differences risk generating tension and conflict. Learning to live together is not unidirectional. It does not simply rely on persuading people to "integrate" into a society; it also relies on mutual recognition and respect, as long as people's beliefs and practices do not harm anyone.[1198] Thus, states face the challenge of fostering social orders in which members of different cultures can flourish. In many countries, demographic trends are likely to mean that immigration will be essential to stability and prosperity. A firm commitment to genuine understanding of the beliefs, values and aspirations of others will form a fundamental dimension of any successful effort to foster cultural synergy.[1199]

A spirit of openness towards the Other and mutual understanding depend in part on knowledge. Significantly, the World Conference on Dialogue recommended the establishment of a culture of tolerance and mutual understanding as a framework for international relations.[1200] Educating against clashes of cultures has a very important role to play in facilitating transcultural synergy, as is noted in *The Role of Education in Global Security* (2007).[1201] While vital, basic educational skills, such as reading, writing and arithmetic, are no longer adequate in an increasingly globalised world. The processes of globalisation bring people into closer contact and, thereby, bring differences, whether real or perceived, into starker relief. There is therefore an amplified need for skills that enable people from different backgrounds to live together. Governments must therefore take a pro-

---

[1197] *Ibid.*, p. 123.
[1198] Al-Rodhan and Watanabe, *A Proposal for* Inclusive *Peace and Security, op. cit.*, note 1, p. 35.
[1199] *Ibid.*, p. 97.
[1200] The Madrid Declaration Issued by the World Conference on Dialogue, Organized by the Muslim World League in Madrid, Spain, Under the Patronage of Custodian of the Two Holy Mosques King Abdullah Bin Abdul Aziz Al-Saud, on 16-18 July 2008, http://www.world-dialogue.org/english/events/final.htm.
[1201] N.R.F. Al-Rodhan, *The Role of Education in Global Security* (Genève: Éditions Slatkine, 2007), p. 51.

active role in developing education programmes with which to increase awareness in society of cultural, ethnic and religious diversity. Awareness of global history and cultures should also form part of people's education, given the importance of understanding how other people "see" the world, their values and beliefs, their sensitivities, grievances, pains and fears.[1202]

Meaning is what constitutes our sense of identity, which determines who we are and with whom we feel we belong. Yet, this meaning is constantly in the process of being produced and, as a result, is subject to change depending on how culture is employed and the meanings produced through exchanges with others.[1203] It is therefore important to promote various types of communication through personal contacts as well as university and scholarly exchanges, and transcultural exchanges for professionals. Collaboration and the development of contacts across borders is, however, hindered to some degree by discrimination against universities in the developing world on the basis of standards and reputation. University exchanges can also be hindered by high fees in some countries. There is thus a need for increased scholarship funds from both public and private sources as a means of encouraging a "brain exchange" rather than a brain drain.[1204]

Along with efforts to overcome these obstacles, language skills are also critical for such communication to take place. National educational curricula must treat foreign languages as key competencies for new generations. Foreign language skills are vital not only in the global setting, but also within states. Languages help to shape how we see the world. Understanding the influence of culture on language can help to facilitate greater cultural understanding.[1205] Learning other people's language can therefore contribute to an understanding of critical aspects of other people's culture as well as facilitating communication in a more narrow sense.

Meanings are also produced by the mass media. The media also therefore have a vital role to play in how people learn about their

---

[1202] *Ibid.*, pp. 13, 43, 51.
[1203] Hall, *op. cit.*, note 1146, p. 3.
[1204] Al-Rodhan, *The Role of Education in Global Security*, *op. cit.*, note 1201, pp. 64, 68.
[1205] *Ibid.*, pp. 69-70.

own and other cultures and faiths.[1206] The Makkah Appeal for Interfaith Dialogue issued by the IICD in June 2008, for example, recommended, among other things, the creation of an international centre for "civilisational dialogue" and the production of multilingual media resources to counter the clash of civilisations thesis.[1207]

The above-mentioned book highlights eight pillars of education that should be employed in the service of global peace and security. These are set out in Octagon 7.

Considerations of justice are also integral to efforts to generate transcultural security in the first instance and, ultimately, transcultural synergy. At the heart of many grievances expressed through the establishment of resistance identities is a lack of justice, often connected to identifiable political problems that are viewed through the lens of justice, understood for the most part as fairness. Foreign and security policies, as is suggested in Chapter 13, must therefore be concerned with promoting a more just world order and employing soft and hard power tools in that service. In other words, state's foreign and security policy should be guided by just power.

One of the key ingredients of coexistence and successful cooperation is trust. Trust between members of different cultural communities and faith-based communities is unfortunately often lacking. This lack of trust is partly due to a lack of exchange and understanding, but it is also the product of denigration and humiliation. Dialogue offers a means through which to increase trust. Yet, it needs to be accompanied by inclusive local and national structures and proactive measures aimed at confidence building. This includes efforts to engage the members of other communities within national contexts. The responsibility for this resides with each community.

Dialogue within such contexts offers a means of developing non-hegemonic understandings of geo-cultural domains, and the identification of areas of agreement as well as impediments to dialogue and mutual understanding.[1208] In addition, dialogue also promises to expose the intertwined nature of our past, present and future.[1209]

[1206] J. Kidner, Director, Coexist Foundation, Draft Speech for the World Conference on Dialogue, http://www.world-dialogue.org/Researches.htm.
[1207] "The Makkah Appeal for Interfaith Dialogue," issued on 6 June 2008, http://www.saudiembassy.net/2008News/ Statements/ StateDetail.asp?cIndex=724.
[1208] Kamal Pasha, *op. cit.*, note 1163, p. 73.
[1209] *Ibid.*, p. 73.

Octagon 7: The Global Education Octagon

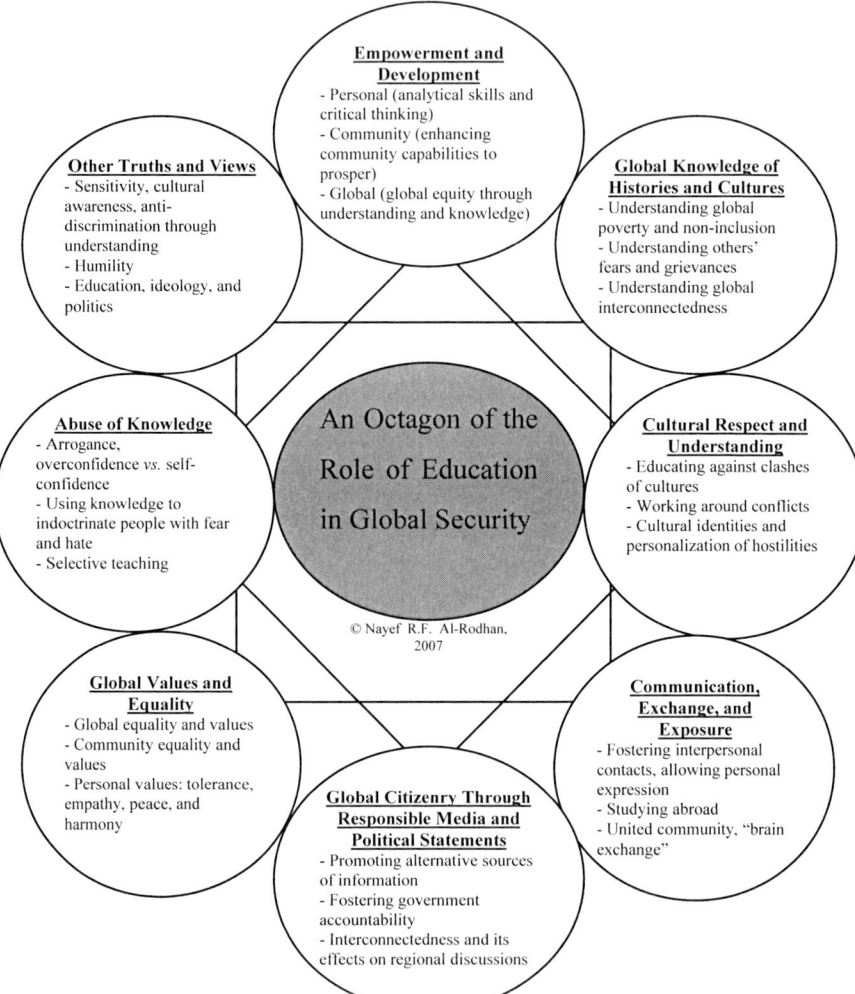

Source: N.R.F Al-Rodhan, *The Role of Education in Global Security* (Genève: Éditions Slatkine, 2007), p. 21, reprinted with permission from Éditions Slatkine.

Common to all endeavours to initiate and further dialogue is the commitment to respect and equality. Karen Armstrong, an expert on Abrahamic faiths, also stresses the importance of listening, understanding the pains of others underlying their discourse, being willing to change our minds, and the inclusion of all positions whether we agree with them or not.[1210] Listening is important, since all too often we have a tendency to concentrate on ripostes.

In *A Proposal for* Inclusive *Peace and Security* (2007), it was emphasised that recognition of people's past and present pains, fears and aspirations is a crucial dimension of awareness. This includes an awareness of what it is like to occupy our interlocutor's position.[1211] This means being aware of the inter-subjectivities of people who belong to cultural domains that are different from our own. Dialogue should also be as inclusive as possible, rather than simply an exchange of like-minded people. All too often we are willing to talk, but only to those who say what we wish to hear. Yet, understanding the diversity and dissonance within cultural groups necessarily means engaging in dialogue with a diverse array of individuals and groups. Cox suggests that the maintenance of world order will greatly depend on mutual comprehension between members of cultures. He suggests that we may think of different cultural domains as having their own inter-subjectivity, interacting in the absence of any overarching theory of history change; in effect, where there is no end to history.[1212]

Dialogic efforts, of course, take place in the context of power asymmetries that shape the world order. Reducing such inequalities would imply, inter alia, making institutional power more representative as well as reducing the technological gap.[1213] As difficult as they may be to achieve, structural changes at the global level will be needed to foster transcultural synergy. Fairer trade is needed and could be promoted by increasing access to markets in the developed world. This would, of course, imply reducing agricultural support and export subsidies, minimising indirect protectionist measures and re-

---

[1210] K. Armstrong, "The Meaning of Dialogue," Box 12, in World Economic Forum, "Islam and the West: Annual Report on the State of Dialogue," Geneva, WEF, January 2008, p. 12.
[1211] Al-Rodhan and Watanabe, *A Proposal for* Inclusive *Peace and Security*, op. cit., note 1, p. 36.
[1212] Cox, op. cit., note 1147, p. 174.
[1213] Al-Rodhan and Watanabe, *A Proposal for* Inclusive *Peace and Security*, op. cit., note 1, p. 100.

ducing developing countries' debt and reducing technology gaps so that people in poorer countries can benefit from the same benefits as those in wealthier countries. The agreement on Trade-Related Aspects of Intellectual Property Rights (TRIPs) should be modified so that developing countries are not denied knowledge or access to medication, and so on.[1214] International institutions also need to be more representative than many currently are. As is mentioned above, the multilateral institutions that make up the backbone of formal global governance mechanisms reflect the fact that they were conceived by the victorious powers of the Second World War. The disproportionate influence that these states have on their functioning compromises their legitimacy in the eyes of those who occupy less privileged positions and feeds sentiments of injustice or a lack of fairness.

6. Universal Axiology and Values

Many efforts to generate a dialogue among civilisations have taken place in recent years, as is mentioned above. Such calls for dialogue are not entirely new. Chinese intellectuals raised the need for dialogue in 1958 with the *Declaration on Behalf of Chinese Culture Respectfully Announced to the Personages of the World*, which was drafted in Hong Kong, Taiwan and the US. It proposed that the Confucian tradition was a useful tool for forging a universal human civilisation, providing insight into the deeper sources of human existence and the common bases of human culture.[1215]

Several approaches to dialogue may be identified. Some argue that dialogue should be guided by a rational search for "truth".[1216] This approach assumes that there is a possibility of reaching consensus on principles that are assumed to be universal and capable of being "discovered" through a search for the true meaning.[1217] This position is underpinned by the conviction that there is a universal human nature. The Makkah Appeal for Interfaith Dialogue, issued just prior to the 2008 interfaith dialogue held by the World Muslim League, for example, affirms the commitment to abiding by rules and ethics of dialogue that emphasise the need for dialogue to be objective and undertaken

---

[1214] *Ibid.*, p. 101.
[1215] Gawlikowski, *op. cit.*, note 1140, p. 41.
[1216] See Mitias, *op. cit.*, note 69.
[1217] See *ibid.*, p. 49.

with wisdom and proof, without ridiculing the beliefs of others, as set out in the Koran.[1218]

However, dialogue based on rational discourse presupposes that a certain degree of common ground already exists between participants. As a result, other commentators have emphasised the need for mutual understanding as a means of forging common ground around which different points of departure may meet. This approach may be identified as the unity in diversity approach. Andrew Targowski, for instance, identifies a "universal civilisation" comprised of autonomous civilisations, such as Western, Japanese, Islamic, Hindu or Chinese. This universal or supra-civilisation is conceived of as fusing autonomous civilisations through the development of a set of universal world values.[1219]

Charles Taylor set out an approach to dialogue in which mutual understanding is a prerequisite for reaching consensus. Consensus would imply a process of mutual learning leading to an eventual "fusion of horizons".[1220] Yet, as Krzysztof Gawlikowski notes, the order may in practice be different, with some degree of consensus preceding mutual understanding, although generally one might assume that some degree of mutual understanding is required in order to achieve some level of agreement. For instance, understanding the different attitudes towards the concept of human rights requires acknowledgement that there are fundamental differences in the interpretation of individual and social relations and human nature.[1221]

Some believe that without embedding the principles of democracy and human rights in local cultural traditions and "incorporating" local authentic values and axioms, principles such as human rights and democracy are unlikely to be able to take hold in non-Western areas.[1222] Tsutsumibayashi, for example, suggests that many Asian people may find the notion of human rights alien because their own moral language, which is no less concerned with respect for life, compassion, poverty, human dignity, freedom and suffering, is less

---

[1218] Kidner, *op. cit.*, note 1206.
[1219] See A. Targowski, "From Global to Universal Civilization," *Dialogue and Universalism*, No. 3-4, 2004.
[1220] See C. Taylor, "The Politics of Recognition," in A. Heble, D. Pennee and J.R.T. Struthers (eds.) *New Contexts of Canadian Criticism* (Peterborough: Broadview, 1997).
[1221] Gawlikowski, *op. cit.*, note 1140, pp. 38-39.
[1222] *Ibid.*, p. 55.

contractual and legalistic than the West's, which has grown out of conceptions of natural law and natural rights traditions. Interestingly, he notes that when the Japanese came to translate the word "right" in the mid-19th century, they had to invent a word for it. The translation that that they chose is *ken-li*, which suggests power and interest. This may have reflected the translators' understanding of the word right as having little association with moral obligations or ethical principles, and being more to do with egoistic acts.[1223] This illustrates that while some of the values underlying principles held dear by various peoples may be very similar, they may be expressed differently and we need to be sensitive to the ways in which common values may be articulated in order to achieve some sort of fusion of horizons. In the context of tensions between human rights and Asian values, this may, Tsutsumibayashi suggests, help people in Asian countries to see that the values they cherish may be expressed by the term human rights, and people in the West to appreciate that human rights may be expressed differently, often without reference to rights at all.[1224]

Similarly, Craig Williams suggests that Confucianism and human rights are not incommensurable as some people claim. The angle from which he approaches the issue is, however, somewhat different. He argues that human rights do not necessarily contain a highly atomised conception of the individual. What is required is a dialogue between Confucianism and human rights.[1225] Williams argues that this kind of dialogue may in the first instance produce a moral minimum. However, over this "thin" moral layer, thicker moral relationships may be constructed. Moreover, he contends that human rights are only a part of moral norms, and that human rights thinking and activity need to engage the facets of moral norms that can help them to be operationalised.[1226] Similarly, it may be the case that Islamic values are not incompatible with universal human rights, even when foundational claims appeal to natural law. This is, indeed, where a universal axiology may need to begin.

Moreover, given that many non-Western conceptions of dignity are not based on a notion of the individual as a radically autono-

---

[1223] Tsutsumibayashi, *op. cit.*, note 73, p. 108.
[1224] *Ibid.*, p. 109
[1225] C. Williams, "International Human Rights and Confucianism," *Asia-Pacific Journal on Human Rights and the Law*, Vol. 1, 2006, p. 39.
[1226] *Ibid.*, p. 46.

mous being, dialogue on the fundamental values that support human rights may also provide the foundations for a "thicker" moral layer that includes some dimension of social justice. Chan points out, for example, that Confucian justice is largely premised on the idea of "gong", which may be understood as "impartiality". A Confucian notion of justice would mean that the government would have a responsibility to ensure equality of life chances for all.[1227]

A universal axiology would need to identify the common normative ideals that we have in our diverse moral languages which underpin fundamental values. This is likely to take place through communication, exploration and increased awareness of cultural and religious diversity, making dialogue as well as research, education and exchanges critical. Given that our moral codes are normative ideals, it ought to be possible to develop a global moral code on the basis of common universal values. The Madrid Declaration affirmed participants' commitment to a number of principles. These include the unity of humankind; equality between people regardless of colour, ethnicity or culture; the centrality of justice to human happiness; respect for the diversity of religions and traditions; and preservation of the environment.[1228]

The Coalition for the Global Commons argues that compassion, justice and cooperation must be at the heart of global ethics if peace and sustainability are to be achieved. Indeed, it argues that we need to be guided by these values not simply because they seem right, but because their adoption is essential to the health of our planet.[1229]

More efforts are needed to identify fundamental common values, as well as to create greater space for dialogue at all levels. The European Council's 2008 White Paper on Intercultural Dialogue "Living Together As Equals in Dignity" is premised on the notion that our collective future depends on the protection of human rights, the rule of law, democracy and mutual understanding. Its release was based on

---

[1227] J. Chan, "Making Sense of Confucian Justice," *Forum for Intercultural Philosophy* 3, 2001, http://them.polylog.org/3/fcj-en.htm.
[1228] "The Madrid Declaration," Statement issued by the World Conference on Dialogue, organized by the Makkah-based Muslim World League in Madrid, Spain under the patronage of the Custodian of the Two Holy Mosques King Abdullah bin Abdulaziz, 16-18 July, 2008, http://www.saudi-us-relations.org/articles/2008/ioi/080719-madrid-declaration.html.
[1229] The Coalition for Global Commons Website: http://www.globalcommons.org/display/CGC2/Values.

the conviction that old approaches to inter-cultural understanding weighted towards assimilation were no longer adequate in culturally plural societies. Inter-cultural dialogue is perceived as a means of better promoting mutual understanding. In fact, it notes that dialogue is in itself a means of protecting and promoting human dignity, increasing participation and awareness, and cooperation. It also highlights the consequences of non-dialogue, which include the perpetuation of cultural stereotypes, tension and anxiety, and a lack of trust, which are likely to feed intolerance and discriminatory practices, and can ultimately only foster a false and short-lived sense of security.

The White Paper suggests that inter-cultural dialogue requires a reflexive disposition in which participants can see themselves as others see them. It also requires respect for individual human worth, mutual recognition, and impartial treatment of all participants. Actions to reduce structural inequalities, and to promote human rights and fundamental freedoms, democratic citizenship and educational practices designed to increase awareness are all measures that are believed to facilitate dialogue.[1230]

Tsutsumibayashi, however, raises some potential difficulties with the notion of intercultural dialogue. He highlights the danger of the emphasis on cultural diversity becoming the victim of political manipulation. Moreover, the question of who gets to partake in the process of cultural delineation has consequences that ought not to be ignored. Cultural categorisation is often intertwined with national identification processes, which may be exclusionary for cultural minorities within states. The oppressive dimension of identity formation may be even more exclusionary when fused with political agendas. Some effort therefore has to be made to separate an intercultural dialogue from politics as conceived in the conventional sense. This suggests the need for a more bottom-up form of communication and exchange coordinated by some form of "neutral hub".[1231] One of the potential challenges that dialogue may face is the potential disparity between the "macro" and "micro" levels. Dialogue and efforts to find commonalities must not simply take place between elites. They must also take place at the sub-state level and be attentive to the contested nature of culture.

[1230] The European Council, "Living Together As Equals in Dignity," *White Paper on Intercultural Dialogue*, June 2008.
[1231] Tsutsumibayashi, *op. cit.*, note 73, pp 110-113.

Moreover, in order to communicate effectively, we need to be aware in any dialogic endeavour of the communication patterns of members of different cultures. Yet, as Muhammad Ayish notes, social science-based communication perspectives are infused with Western universalism. It is important to be attentive to the ways in which different approaches to communication may be embedded in particular cultures, and to develop understandings of different world views and communication patterns.[1232]

Octagon 8 summarises the elements of transcultural synergy and universal axiology.

[1232] Ayish, *op. cit.*, note 491, p. 81.

Octagon 8: Transcultural Synergy and Universal Axiology

- 1 Dialogue
- 2 Agreed upon Rules and Ethics of Dialogue
- 3 Mutual Understanding
- 4 Tolerance and Respect
- 5 Mutual Learning
- 6 Identification of a Moral Minimum
- 7 Reduction of the Technological Gap
- 8 Fair Representation

Transcultural Synergy and Universal Axiology

© Nayef Al-Rodhan (2009)

7. Conclusion

Human civilisation comprises a number of different geo-cultural domains, each formed out of interaction between specific material and intersubjective factors that create different "realities" and shape people's lifeworlds. They are, thus, contingent and fluid. Relations between members of different cultural domains may be cooperative or conflictual, and depend on a number factors.

One means of breaking down essentialist conceptions of geo-cultural domains and highlighting their interconnectedness within a much broader human civilisation is to research and raise awareness of the many and varied instances of exchanges and borrowings that have taken place between different geo-cultural domains. This is important not only for diminishing cultural arrogance, but also for building greater understanding, respect and trust among members of the world's cultures. All relationships of trust and respect are premised, among other things, on reciprocity, and that includes recognition of others achievements and of our debts to them. Dialogue is also a critical and natural means of coexistence. Dialogic initiatives are a positive move in the right direction. They serve as a means of breaking down essentialising discourses that are highly misleading and tend to support the arguments of those who see geo-cultural domains as conflictual and cultural values as incommensurable.

What these apparent differences may express, however, could be connected to differing moral languages in different cultures rather than the result of divergent fundamental values. Dialogue and the development of a universal axiology require people from different cultures to engage in the identification of points of overlap within diverse moral languages. Yet, it is important that they lead to projects and activities aimed at a wider audience. Here, educational, cultural and faith institutions have a critical role to play. This kind of familiarity, coexistence and cooperation is essential for eventual transcultural synergy. However, it is important to remember that dialogue takes place in the context of power inequalities. For transcultural synergy to be realised these inequalities need to be addressed. Efforts to promote the identification of commonalities and fundamental values must also address the question of who gets to be a part of such endeavours and to speak on behalf of cultures.

Part 3

History and the Future of Human and Trans-human Civilisation

CHAPTER 15

WHERE ARE WE GOING?
THE FUTURE OF HUMAN CIVILISATION AND HISTORY

Will human beings continue to exist and, if so, how well will they fare? Will life that has originated on Earth one day become extinct? Will human nature undergo radical transformation as we acquire the capacity to change human biology, leading to the emergence of post-humans? Or will machine intelligence outstrip human intelligence? This chapter explores whether we will make it as a species and, if so, in what form? The future of humanity is not just the topic of science fiction. All major religions have particular perspectives on human destiny. The future of humanity has also been the topic of philosophy. While these may seem like long-term considerations, shorter-term decisions that we have to make today and in the near future will affect the future of human civilisation and the sustainability of history. No matter how human nature changes it will still need to be balanced with human dignity needs through mechanisms of good governance. Climate change, biodiversity, the disposal of nuclear waste, technological advances, scientific research, population growth, and so on, are all current issues that will have an impact on our destiny as a species. While we may be unable to generate accurate forecasts about the future, we are able to make predictions, albeit with varying degrees of certainty. Thinking seriously about the future is required in order to make the right decisions today. There are, as is mentioned in Chapter 5, logically possible truths. Following this line of reasoning, we can identify logically possible future scenarios that are rationally more defensible than others.[1233]

[1233] N. Bostrom, "The Future of Humanity," Anthology Chapter Prepared for J. Berg Olsen, E. Selinger and S. Riis (eds.) *New Waves in Philosophy of Technology* (Basingstoke: Palgrave McMillan, 2008), available at: http://www.nickbostrom.com/papers/future.pdf, pp. 2-3.

With this in mind, we can examine scenarios pertaining to the future of human civilisation and history. Some argue that we have already started on the road to planetary civilisation, reaching previously unknown levels of connectedness, thus reducing social space. This is a phenomenon that we can already perceive as a result of globalising processes. Beyond this, could we imagine a scenario in which technological developments enable colonisation of the solar system or the galaxy? Technological advances raise questions not only about the future of human civilisation, but also about humanness. This chapter explores some of the possibilities for the future of humanity and identifies some of the challenges that humankind is likely to face.

1. The Future of Human Civilisation

The direction in which human civilisation is headed is unclear. Whether the existence of advanced life forms on other planets would be a source for optimism about our own future is a matter that is debated.

Planetary Civilisation and Beyond?
According to some, we are currently undergoing a transition that is equivalent to the transitions engendered by the agricultural and industrial revolutions. The interconnectedness of the global system is believed to be binding people to an extent that has not been known on this scale before. Changes in different realms of life – environmental, cultural, institutional, societal, technological, and so on – are thought to be interacting at an accelerated rate. Time and space are, thus, believed to be undergoing radical modification: social time is reduced and social space increased to a planetary scale. However, while proponents of this position believe that the road to planetary civilisation has already begun, its direction and destination are unknown. We face many dangers, such as global climate change, population growth, environmental degradation and financial market instability, as well as unknown risks related to new technologies.[1234] The question therefore becomes one of whether will we survive as a species.

The Soviet astronomer Nikolai Kardashev argued that there are no inner limitations on the scale of civilisations. He believed that

---
[1234] Great Transition Initiative, Global Scenario Group, "Planetary Civilization," http://www.gtinitiative.org/ perspectives/ global.html.

the self-destruction of or self-inflicted limitations on a civilisation were not based on fact.[1235] Kardashev proposed a scheme for the classification of technologically advanced civilisations comprising four types, based on their energy consumption for interstellar communication. A Type-I Civilisation would be able to master enough energy for planetary-wide communication. This would be equivalent to the current energy consumption here on Earth. A Type-II Civilisation would go beyond this, using the total output of its central star. A Type-III Civilisation would be able to draw on the energy resources of an entire galaxy; and a Type-IV Civilisation would be able to draw on the highest scale of energy and control an entire universe.[1236]

The Kardashev Scale, of course, assumes that more advanced civilisations consume greater energy than less advanced ones.[1237] Carl Sagan, however, argues that these gaps between the different civilisational types were so enormous that a finer gradation was required.[1238] Could it be possible that interstellar communication could be achieved before Type I or Type II Civilisations emerged? According to Zoltan Galantai, it is possible to conceive of a different classification of so-called super civilisations that does not rely on energy consumption. He argues that classifying civilisations on their capacity to harness energy relies on our own experiences and assumptions about advances in technology. Galantai suggests that we might seek a classification based on miniaturisation, using nanotechnology and quantum engineering. In this scenario, more technologically advanced civilisations could exist without drawing attention to themselves by their levels of energy consumption. Furthermore, we may also need to make a distinction between energy consumption and civilisational scale. A civilisation may be able to colonise its own solar system without using energy equivalent to that of its central star.

An alternative typology has been set out: the Torino Scale classifies civilisations on the basis of their capacity to withstand disasters. A first type would be unable to survive a local disaster. A second

---

[1235] N. Kardashev, "On the Inevitability and the Possible Structures of Supercivilizations," The Search for Extraterrestrial Life: Recent Developments, Proceedings of the Symposium, Boston, MA, 18-21 June 1984 (D. Dortrecht Reidel Publishing Co., 1985) p. 498.
[1236] *The Internet Encyclopedia of Science*, http://www.daviddarling.info/encyclopedia/K/Kardashevciv.html, s.v. "Kardashev Civilizations."
[1237] *Ibid.*
[1238] *Ibid.*

type would collapse as a result of a regional catastrophe. A third type would be unable to survive a global disaster. A civilisation capable of colonising a solar system may, for instance, be able to survive the threat of an exploding supernova. A civilisation that succeeded in populating a galaxy could be almost immortal, since no known natural catastrophe could destroy it. The likely distance between colonies could, it is thought, result in speciation.[1239]

In the Panglossian view, based on our evolution to date, there is a good chance that our future evolution will be in a positive direction. Yet, others perceive two immediate problems with such a view. First, our evolution so far may have been highly improbable. Second, past success may not continue indefinitely. Even if our evolution so far was inevitable and not simply a question of luck, there is no reason to believe that this inevitability is permanent. We may even become extinct.[1240]

Cyclical views of history suggest that there may be long periods of stable development in technology and other factors, but that each phase of growth is then followed by decay.[1241] As is mentioned above in the discussion of the individual triumph of geo-cultural domains, a great many approaches to civilisation share a cyclical view of history. Spengler's thesis on the rise, maturation and eventual decline of a number of civilisations adopts such an approach.[1242] The philosophies of history of Toynbee and Ibn Khaldūn were also underpinned by cyclical notions of history.[1243]

Yet, the cyclical view of human history is believed by some to be false for a number of reasons. First, the world had a beginning and human beings have existed long enough (approximately 200,000 years) for there to have been different cycles of human civilisation. Second, and more importantly, the universe itself has existed for a finite period of time. The universe has its own directionality; that of an increase in energy unavailable for mechanical work released as

---

[1239] Z. Galantai, "After Kardashev: A Farewell to Super Civilizations," *Contact in Context*, 2006, http://www.contact incontext.org/cic/v2i2/farewell.pdf, pp. 1-2.
[1240] N. Bostrom, "The Future of Human Evolution," www.nickbostrom.com/fut/evolution.html. Published in C. Tandy (ed.) *Death and Anti-Death: Two Hundred Years After Kant, Fifty Turing* (Palo Alto, CA.: Ria University Press, 2004), pp. 2-3.
[1241] Bostrom, *op. cit.*, note 1233, p. 7.
[1242] O. Spengler, *The Decline of the West: An Abridged Edition* (New York: Oxford University Press, 1991); Cox, *op. cit.*, note 1147, p. 159.
[1243] Issawi, *op. cit.*, note 28; Toynbee, *op. cit.*, note 35.

matter and energy degradation. Nick Bostrom identifies four future scenarios: (1) extinction; (2) recurrent collapse; (3) plateau; and (4) post-humanity.[1244]

Bostrom argues that two possibilities for extinction seem to exist. In the first scenario, the human species may become extinct as a result of evolving into one or more new species. In the second scenario, *Homo sapiens* may simply die out for some reason. These two scenarios may also produce a third in which a transformed human species eventually ceases to exist. Advances in biotechnology and nanotechnology, and the creation of superintelligence could pose problems to humankind's existence, such as the creation of lethal and highly contagious diseases, a new wave of thermonuclear bombs with devastating destructive force or a superintelligence that decides to put an end to the human species. However, advances in such technologies also hold the promise of the future of human civilisation, as Galantai suggests.

Recurrent collapse of human civilisation may, however, threaten the long-term existence of *Homo sapiens*.[1245] Most scholarly studies of collapse have focused on local instances of societal collapse, such as Edward Gibbon's *Decline and Fall of the Roman Empire* (1970).[1246] Others have focused on generic aspects of failure, such as Jared Diamond's *Collapse: How Societies Choose to Fail or Survive* (2005).[1247] The only historical examples of societal collapse have been local. Yet, we might imagine that new types of threat or the characteristics of an increasingly interdependent world might engender a global societal collapse.

Human civilisation might increase in sophistication, reaching a peak, and then level off. Among potential occurrences that may dramatically increase the sophistication of human civilisation is the capacity to transform our biology through technology. Were we to reach a stage where we could master our biochemical processes, we could dramatically extend our life expectancy. Drugs and other neurotechnologies could allow human beings to further alter their personalities. Other cognitive enhancements could augment intellectual abili-

---

[1244] Bostrom, *op. cit.*, note 1233, p. 9.
[1245] *Ibid.*, pp. 8-9, 11.
[1246] E. Gibbon, *The Decline and Fall of the Roman Empire* (London: Phoenix, 1980).
[1247] J. Diamond, *Collapse: How Societies Choose to Fail or Survive* (London: Penguin Books, 2005).

ties. Nanotechnologies will also imply profound changes in manufacturing, medicine and computing. Machine intelligence could be radically enhanced. There might also be institutional innovations that, for example, could allow humankind to predict future occurrences and reach more advanced forms of organisation. There is no reason to believe that these developments are implausible.[1248]

There are no natural laws in the universe that would prevent the development of post-humanity. Post-humanity in his definition would have at least one of the following characteristics: (1) a population greater than one trillion persons; (2) life expectancy greater than 500 years; (3) cognitive capacities at least two deviations higher than the present human maximum; (4) near or complete control over sensory input for most people most of the time; (5) a considerable reduction in human suffering; (6) any alteration of magnitude or profundity comparable to any of the above. Uploading (i.e. transmission of a personality to a computer), for example, could bring about a post-human condition in that it would, for instance, increase life expectancy and enable the control of sensory input.[1249]

In terms of the longer term prospects for humankind, it has been suggested that it is unlikely that the human condition will remain at its present state. Some believe the next few centuries to be critical for humanity. If superintelligence were to become a reality, we might imagine that a new post-human civilisation would increase survival chances and reduce the risk of extinction. However, as the time scale increases, the possibility of recurrent collapse also decreases. The plateau scenario is, thus, thought to be potentially feasible over a longer timeframe. A highly stable form of organisation may emerge at some future point. Thus, the likelihood of post-humanity becomes a distinct possibility over a longer period.[1250]

Are We Alone?
We may not be in the habit of asking questions about extraterrestrial life forms. However, when considering the destiny of humanity, whether we are alone in the universe becomes very pertinent. While most people find the prospect of discovering that we are not alone exciting, others claim that they would be much less enthusiastic. In-

---

[1248] Bostrom, *op. cit.*, note 1233, pp. 15-17.
[1249] *Ibid.*, pp. 19-24.
[1250] *Ibid.*, pp. 24-26.

deed, it has been argued that the discovery of extraterrestrial life would be a bad omen for humankind. In our own galaxy, there are some 100 billion stars and the observable universe houses some 199 billion galaxies. We know that many of these stars are orbited by planets, some of which could be like Earth. Many of these solar systems are older than our own. Yet, to date, we have found no evidence of life on other planets.

This may suggest that a "Great Filter", a term borrowed from Robin Hanson's "The Great Filter: Are We Almost Past It?",[1251] or probability threshold exists in which one or more highly improbable evolutionary steps are needed for intelligent civilisation to emerge on an Earth-like planet that would be observable with our present technology. The important question is where the probability threshold is located, that is, is it behind us or ahead of us? If it were already behind us we could assume that the emergence of intelligent life on Earth was highly improbable. The period between the formation of the Earth and the emergence of the first known life on Earth is several hundreds of millions of years, suggesting that the occurrence of life on our planet was a highly improbable outcome. The Great Filter may therefore be behind us, since it would suggest that the emergence of intelligent life is so improbable that we are rare products of a very particular set of circumstances and that we are likely to be alone in the universe. However, the other, less palatable possibility is that the probability barrier has yet to come. It may be that extraterrestrial life did exist, but became extinct, because it could not master the technological advances required for its continued evolution. This would not be good news for humankind. If other species have failed to master space colonization, then this does not bode well for us.

However, if we were to discover life on Mars, for instance, this would suggest that the emergence of life is not an improbable event. However, if discovered life forms were fairly primitive, it would be heartening, suggesting that we have already passed the Great Filter. However, if we were to discover a very complex life form, it would imply the opposite, raising again the question of whether humankind will make it as a species and, if so, in what form. Some commentators therefore welcome the prospect that ours is the only intelligent civilisation, which exists as a result of a highly improbable

---

[1251] R. Hanson, "The Great Filter: Are We Almost Past It?" 15 September 1998, http://hanson.gmu.edu/greatfilter.html.

set of factors. We might then have already passed a very high probability threshold.[1252]

2. A Post-human Destiny?

One of the great differences that separates us from our ancestors is technology. It has been the main driver of improvements in lifestyle and life expectancy, changing the nature of work, the comfort in which we live, the medical help available and educational levels. It has also been one of the key factors driving developments that may pose problems for the maintenance of the current level of human civilisation, such as population growth, climate change and environmental degradation, although it may also hold the key to maintaining it. This is not to say that technology has determined or will determine our destiny. However, it is recognisable that it has played and will continue to play an important role in shaping human civilisation.[1253]

It may be possible to enhance human capacities through genetic engineering, nanotechnology, psychopharmacology and neuronal interfaces (e.g. brain-computer interfaces). A post-human may be defined as a being that was once human but has been transformed both physically and mimetically to an extent that it ceases to resemble a human genetically, physiologically, neuro-psychologically and neuro-chemically. Control over emotional responses and a remodelling of motivational structures would also be implied.[1254] Diagram 11 depicts the various ways in which a post-human condition may be achieved.

A post-human is likely during its life or that of its ancestors to have gone through a trans-human stage. Trans-humanism is a movement that holds that human beings can and ought to transform what it means to be human. Employing technology, human beings are believed to be capable of evolving into two types of being: trans-human, in which machine and biological bodies are mixed, and post- human, in which humans and technology become one.[1255]

[1252] N. Bostrom, "Where Are They? Why I Hope the Search for Extraterrestrial Life Finds Nothing," published in the MIT Technology Review, May/June Issue, 2008, pp. 2-4, 7-9.
[1253] Bostrom, op. cit., note 1233, p. 4.
[1254] M. More, "On Becoming Posthuman," Free Inquiry, Vol. 14, Fall 1994.
[1255] K.S. Seybold, Explorations in Neuroscience, Psychology and Religion (Aldershot: Asghate, 2007), p. 138.

Diagram 11: The Post-human

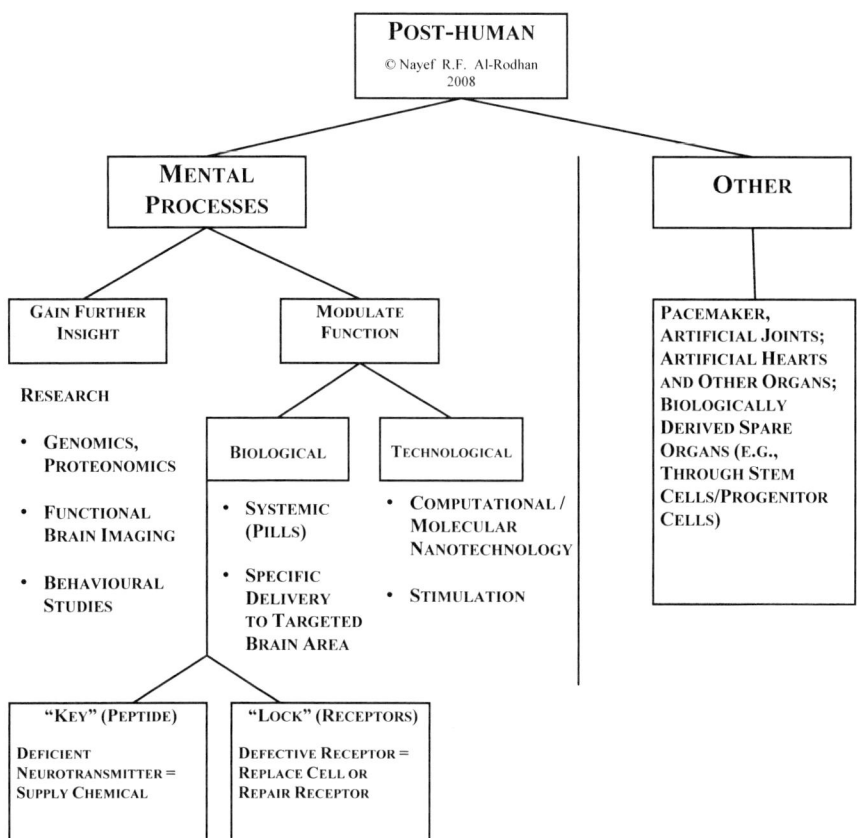

Source: N.R.F. Al-Rodhan, *"emotional amoral egoism": A Neurophilosophical Theory of Human Nature and its Universal Security Implications* (Berlin: LIT, 2008), p. 125, reprinted with permission from LIT.

Kevin Warwick, Professor of Cybernetics at the University of Reading, has a mechanism implanted in his arm that allows his nervous system to communicate with a computer. This kind of experimentation could lead to other types of implants that might, for example, enhance vision or hearing. It is hoped that eventually brain-computer interfaces will improve the quality of life for people with disabilities and neurological diseases.[1256]

Enhancement refers to "[a]n intervention that improves the functioning of some subsystem of an organism beyond its reference state; or that creates an entirely new functioning or subsystem that the organism previously lacked."[1257] Altering our mental processes may be achieved through various means. Systemic methods (i.e. pills) may be, and already are, used to influence self-control, inhibitions, and so on. Drugs may also be administered to targeted areas of the brain through a pump to alter neurochemistry in a desired way, such as to sustain a stable, positive mood.[1258]

Genetic engineering may also be employed to produce new characteristics. Genetic engineering enables specific genes to be isolated and altered. It may be used to create or increase the prevalence of particular traits in the gene pool. At present, its use is restricted to animals and gene therapy for the treatment of disease.[1259] Moreover, the types of cells that have been altered so far have been somatic (most) cells rather than sex cells. The use of sex cells remains extremely controversial, since altering sex cells would pass whatever modification that were made to the next generation. Less controversial uses of gene therapy might include fine-tuning the immune system or preventing dementia.[1260]

Another way in which human physiology and psychology may be transformed is through the use of molecular nanotechnology. Molecular nanotechnology would enable the creation of human organisms

---

[1256] *Ibid.*, p. 141.
[1257] N. Bostrom, "Dignity and Enhancement," in *Human Dignity and Bioethics: Essays Commissioned by the President's Council on Bioethics* (Washington, DC: President's Council on Bioethics, Washington, DC, March 2008), p. 179.
[1258] Al-Rodhan, *"emotional amoral egoism," op. cit.*, note 119, p. 126.
[1259] *Ibid.*, p. 126.
[1260] L. Walters, "Human Genetic Intervention: Past, Present, and Future," in H.W. Baillie and T.K. Casey (eds.) *Is Human Nature Obsolete? Genetics, Bioengineering and the Future of the Human Condition* (Cambridge, Mass.: The MIT Press, 2005), pp. 380-381.

atom by atom. This would mean that we were no longer limited to genetically altering biological matter. If such an eventuality were to become a reality, we could be able to alter our physiology, morphology and perhaps even psychology.[1261]

One reason for advocating trans-humanism is that human beings in their present state age and eventually die. Not only do their physical states decline, but their intellectual and cognitive abilities also suffer with time. The evolution of a human into a trans-human could, for example, take place through modification and enhancement of the present human body, through gene alteration to increase longevity, drugs to improve memory, and so on. Fukuyama points out that the use of biotechnology to prolong life would have significant demographic and social implications that would go far beyond the current problems faced by societies with declining birth rates and increased life expectancies.[1262]

As yet, there is no certainty about the exact causes of aging. A number of theories do, nevertheless, exist. One theory derives from molecular biology and is based on cellular mechanisms that determine when the body's functionality declines and eventually perishes. The human body is comprised of two kinds of cells: germ cells in the female ovum and male sperm and somatic cells. With the latter there is an upper limit to cell division. There are a number of theories as to why this upper limit exists. External factors, such as smoking, radiation and cellular chemical waste may prevent cells from replicating accurately and subsequent errors in copying DNA are what leads to age-related diseases like heart disease and cancer. Another theory argues that telomeres, which are attached to the end of each DNA molecule and assist in the accurate reproduction of cells, get shorter with each new generation of cells.

Yet, it is also known that certain cells – germ cells, cancer cells and particular kinds of stem cells – do not possess this upper limit due to the presence of the enzyme telomerase, which stops telomeres from reducing in length. There is also a gene – the SIR_2 (silent information regulator No. 2) – which represses genes that produce

---

[1261] E. Drexler and C. Peterson, with G. Pergamit, *Unbounding the Future: The Nanotechnology Revolution* (William Morrow and Company, Inc., 1991), ch. 1, http://www.foresight.org/UTF/Unbo und_LBW/index.html; More, *op. cit.,* note 1254.
[1262] F. Fukuyama, *Our Posthuman Future: Consequences of the Biotechnology Revolution* (New York: Farrar, Strauss and Giroux, 2002).

ribosomal waste in yeast cells and leads to their eventual death. Given these discoveries, it is possible that there may be some genetic way to control the process of aging.[1263]

The transition from trans-human to post-human would be completed with the creation of cyborgs or robots endowed with the same human nature, such as an emotional repertoire, the capacity to reason, consciousness and spirituality. Trans-humanists maintain that at some point in the future, we will have the capacity to upload personalities into cyborgs and, thereby, escape many of the constraints imposed by biology. According to advocates of trans-humanism, this is not the stuff of science fiction, but will be achievable within the next three decades or so.[1264] Uploading is a term used for the procedure of transferring the human mind to a computer. This would involve, first, creating a sufficiently detailed scan of the human brain, and, from this, creating a three-dimensional neuronal network and neuro-computational models of the various kinds of neurons in the network. Finally, the entire computational structure would need to be copied on to a supercomputer. Once uploaded, many copies could be produced of the same mind.[1265] Despite the optimism of trans-humanists, neuroscientists express doubt about whether a person's identity could be uploaded from the carbon-based brain in which it currently resides.[1266]

Another approach to artificial intelligence is suggested by some nanotechnology experts. It is thought that one possible way to further our insight into the human brain is to construct nano-machines that deconstruct the human brain, recording the position of neurones, synapses, and so on. With an understanding of the workings of various neurones, this kind of information could be run through a computer to simulate neural networks.[1267]

Artificial intelligence capable of outsmarting human beings and developing a certain degree of autonomy may represent a threat to human well-being and even the continued existence of our species. Those who fear that this may be the case are likely to be assuaged by

---

[1263] *Ibid.*, p. 57-59.
[1264] Seybold, *op. cit.*, note 1255, p. 138.
[1265] Bostrom, *op. cit.*, note 1233, p. 22.
[1266] Seybold, *op. cit.*, note 1255, p. 139.
[1267] N. Bostrom, "When Machines Outsmart Humans," 2000, http://www.nickbostrom.com/2050/outsmart.html, p. 3.

the fact that we do not yet possess sufficient knowledge of brain structure and function to create human-equivalent intelligence, not to mention superintelligence far surpassing the capacities of even the brightest of human beings. This would mean that The Singularity would have been achieved – The Singularity being the creation of smarter-than-human intelligence.[1268] It is likely that advances in this area will be made as a result of endeavours such as the Singularity University, a new visionary institution backed by Google and NASA that will offer courses in artificial intelligence.[1269]

Superintelligence refers to any form of intelligence that surpasses that of any human in almost all fields of knowledge, creativity and social skills. It may take a number of forms. For example, it could be achieved in a digital computer, a combination of computers or cultured cortical tissue. This would not be simply another new technology. Superintelligence is radically different. Its capacities for scientific research and technological advances would far outstrip those of any human, which means that it would lead to technological advancements in all fields. Superintelligence may be expected to lead to: extremely powerful computers; advanced weaponry; space travel and self-reproducing interstellar probes; control of the aging process and the elimination of disease; more sophisticated mastery of human moods, emotions and motivations; uploading of personalities to a computer structure; reanimation of cryonics (frozen patients); and realistic virtual reality. Superintelligence would also result in the further development of superintelligence – the copying of artificial intelligences, which will essentially be software. Artificial intelligence is also potentially autonomous. This prospect is particularly worrying for humans, since artificial intelligence, if capable of independent initiative, may not share the same objectives as human beings. Moreover, the mental processes of artificial intellects may not be exactly the same as those of humans. For all these reasons, superintelligence is not the same as other technological advances and should not be thought of in the same way.

While many of these potential implications of superintelligence appear concerning and potentially dangerous for humans, artifi-

---

[1268] "What Is The Singularity?" The Singularity Institute for Artificial Intelligence, http://singinst.org/overview/whatisthesingularity.
[1269] D. Gelles, "Google and Nasa Back Vision of Computers Smarter Than Humans," *Financial Times*, 3 February 2009.

cial intelligence may also lead to enhanced moral thinking and policy planning superior to that of humans. Although this may mean that we could delegate certain ethical and policy problems to computers, we would need to be extremely careful in terms of establishing the initial conditions under which superintelligence operates. The goals and values that it is endowed with would be of critical importance. A threat to the whole of humanity might present itself if, for instance, the creators of superintelligence set it up to serve only a select few humans. Some argue that the risks associated with superintelligence could be minimised by establishing it as quickly as possible and as safely as possible so that any issues may be addressed now.[1270]

At present, we do not know enough about the brain and individual neurons to replicate brain function artificially. However, in as soon as we have enough knowledge to simulate a standardised neuron and enough insight into the structure of the synapse, and once we can make artificial neurons work together in the way that the brain does, it will be possible to reduce the computational power required to simulate the brain. This would therefore rely on less dramatic increases in processor speeds. However, in order to simulate the brain's functions, computers would also need a great deal of memory. Development of the hardware capacity required for human-equivalent artificial intelligence is believed to be a distinct possibility in the first quarter of this century.

Yet, superintelligence requires software as well as hardware in order to become a reality. The software issue may be approached in a number of ways. At one end of the spectrum, we might envisage a knowledge base and inference engine. This approach would, however, require a considerable amount of human input. Another option would be to enable computers to learn by interacting with humans as a child does. But, learning processes are not yet fully understood. The artificial neural networks currently used in most applications employ a supervised form of learning that is not believed to be biologically realistic and only works on a small scale. In addition, in order to simulate the functioning of the human brain, an adequate foundational

---

[1270] N. Bostrom, "Ethical Issues in Advanced Artificial Intelligence," http://nick bostrom.com/ethics/ai.html, pp. 2-8. Revised Version of a Paper Published in I. Smit, W. Wallach and G.E. Lasker (ed.) *Cognitive, Emotive and Ethical Aspects of Decision Making in Humans and in Artificial Intelligence*, Vol. 2 (Baden-Baden: International Institute of Advanced Studies in Cybernetics, 2003), pp. 12-17.

structure is required. The human brain has an initial structure that is in part genetically coded but, at present, neuroscience is incapable of determining how much of the structure is genetically coded. If the adult human brain depends to a large degree on a genetically derived architecture that has developed over thousands of years, creating human-equivalent artificial intelligence could prove exceedingly difficult. Yet, present neuroscientific research suggests that as the human cortex develops it is quite generic, which suggests that a fairly limited amount of neuroscientific research may be enough to develop human-like artificial intelligence. As soon as we have the capacity to simulate human-equivalent artificial intelligence, superintelligence will become a possibility, at least technologically.[1271]

The creation of superintelligence would imply that The Singularity has been achieved. The implications of this are enormous, although we cannot fully comprehend what they may be, since we are not ourselves endowed with smarter-than-human intelligence. However, The Singularity does suggest that technological advances would be exponential. Superintelligence would, for example, mean that the creation of even smarter minds would be easier.[1272]

3. Ethical Issues

The question of enhancement raises a number of ethical concerns. These range from worries about fairness in relation to the availability of enhancement procedures, to the ends to which these procedures may be put and the degree to which such devices may threaten human nature as we know it.[1273] Shaping and reshaping ourselves seems to defy selection pressure and to bring us potentially to the last technological frontier. The implications of nanotechnology are not yet known. What seems clear is that it will be revolutionary. At the same time that it offers tremendous possibilities, it also poses serious challenges. This means that there will be a need to regulate the use of nanotechnology. Humankind will have to make decisions about what it considers legitimate and illegitimate use. Equally, in relation to gene

---

[1271] N. Bostrom, "How Long Before Superintelligence?" http://www.nickbostrom.com/superintelligence.html, Originally Published in *International Journal of Future Studies*, Vol. 2, 1998, pp. 5-9, 12.
[1272] The Singularity Institute for Artificial Intelligence, *op. cit.*, note 1268.
[1273] Seybold, *op. cit.*, note 1255, p. 141.

therapy, society will be charged with deciding what may be considered a disorder. For example, are disabilities disorders that society ought to correct? Should we allow gene therapy using sex cells?[1274] As explained earlier, the replacement of genes in sex cells and early embryos, involving germline gene therapy, means that modifications will be passed on to the next generation. While it may have a number of less controversial applications, such as the prevention of dementia among the elderly, it may also be employed to pass on particular characteristics to our children, which is highly controversial.[1275] Moreover, as Fukuyama points out, one of the reasons why the US National Bioethics Advisory Commission sought to prohibit human cloning was the ethical issues raised by human experimentation and associated abnormalities. Yet, he also notes that while the questions raised by human experimentation are hindering rapid development of genetic engineering, they are not insurmountable.[1276]

Will people choose to develop this superintelligence? According to some, the answer is yes. Superintelligence will bring with it tremendous economic as well as military and social benefits. Even if resistance is strong, these motivations will override it. Yet, as is pointed out above, human-equivalence and superintelligence may pose a threat to humankind itself and, as long as there is no way of ensuring the subservience of artificial and superintelligence to human beings and their well-being, there will be enormous opposition to continuing research into artificial intelligence.[1277]

Would enhancement affect our dignity? Or might enhancement weigh positively on human dignity? Bostrom suggests that enhancement and dignity interact in complex ways. He focuses on dignity as a quality, which may be conceived of as a virtue or an ideal. Enhanced composure, self-control and concentration, for example, could add to human dignity rather than detract from it. Yet, at the same time, enhancing other facets may reduce our dignity. Increased compassion, if completely unregulated, might reduce our composure and self-control. Would our dignity be enhanced if some of our capacities were greater due to artificial means? There seems to be a connection between the autonomous self and dignity. There is a sense that

---

[1274] Al-Rodhan, *"emotional amoral egoism,"* op. cit., note 119, pp. 128-129.
[1275] *Ibid.*, p. 127.
[1276] Fukuyama, op. cit., note 1262, pp. 78, 80.
[1277] Bostrom, op. cit., note 1271, pp. 12-13.

if we have freely chosen to act in a particular way, it has some a greater authenticity. This implies that if a characteristic given by enhancement were chosen by us rather than given to us before birth, it would somehow be more authentic.[1278]

Fukuyama gives a different answer to the question of dignity. He suggests that if dignity is so hard to define, it must be something linked to human beings as complex wholes. In this case, protecting human dignity in relation to advances in biotechnology implies protecting that complexity, which is formed through the interaction of emotions, reason and a consciousness that we barely understand. Maintaining human dignity against biotechnological advances, therefore, implies maintaining that unity which makes us human.[1279]

4. Conclusion

There is no evidence to suggest that the history of human civilisation as a whole is cyclical, suggesting a continual movement between rise and decline. Similarly, there is no evidence to suggest that we may become extinct. Indeed, we might be justified in hoping that we are alone in the universe, since this would seem to reduce the probability of our extinction. Whether we make it as a species and in what form will undoubtedly be shaped by technology. Will technology alter what it means to be human? The answer to this seems to be yes. The question is how this eventuality will be ethically circumscribed and what it will mean for humanness. Governance in this area is likely to become of paramount importance, and careful, informed decisions need to be made today about enhancement on the basis of maintaining dignity and the well-being of humanity.

[1278] Bostrom, *op. cit.*, note 1257, pp. 3, 8-9, 11.
[1279] Fukuyama, *op. cit.*, note 1262, p. 172.

CHAPTER 16

CONCLUSION: SUSTAINABLE HISTORY AND THE
DIGNITY OF MAN

Has history come to an end and culminated in liberal democracy? Or, are the fault lines cultural and therefore persistent? The error frequently made when discussing relations between geo-cultural domains and the factors that propel history is to conceive of both civilisation and history in narrow terms that hinder our understanding of the forces that drive history and impede the development of mechanisms that may support a sustainable history or durable progressive development. In this volume, I offer broader ways of conceiving of both civilisation and history. I conceive of history as propelled by the tension between human nature, on the one hand, and human dignity needs, on the other. I also understand civilisation as a single human civilisation, which implies that we must examine the whole of human history – a period far longer than the longue durée Braudel understood as geographical time. It is only by considering this longer time frame that we can begin to grasp what drives human beings, and to comprehend history. In *Part 1*, I considered where we are in time and space. This meant going as far back as the creation of the universe and our emergence as a species on Earth. Whichever way we look at it, however, human history is only a fraction of the history of the universe. Our evolutionary history is therefore equally minute when considered in this broader context. This evolutionary history has a profound impact on the present and, as such, is more relevant to today's world than we might like to imagine.

It is important to grasp that human nature has been crafted during this relatively short period of time and owes much to the challenges faced by early humans. They were endowed with a *predisposed tabula rasa* rather than a tabula rasa or clean slate. As a result, human beings are largely driven by emotional self-interest, which equips them with the capabilities required to survive in their environment.

These emotions are neurochemically mediated, and produce patterns of behaviour that are necessary for survival, such as forming community and conjugal bonds. Thus, if we are to conceive of a state of nature it ought to be one in which there are not only fear and insecurity, as realists would have us believe, but also bonds of attachment and other morally relevant emotions. Thus, when we consider the whole of our history, emotions that are not purely negative have been the motor behind the development of humankind. *While humankind is predominantly motivated by emotional self-interest, what also makes us who we are includes the capacity for reason and conscious reflection. It is these latter qualities that have enabled human beings to develop moral codes to help guide us in our relation to others, since humankind is not endowed with innate morality – only with morally relevant emotions. We are therefore emotional amoral egoists.*

Perhaps as part of its emotionally driven needs and consciousness, humankind has also sought to understand the meaning of its existence. Whether theistic or non-theistic, answers to the puzzle of the meaning of life seem to provide a means of reconciling our finite existence with infinitude. We are perhaps the only creatures on Earth that are aware of their certain death and live with this knowledge throughout our lives. The certainty of death seems to prompt humankind to ask how it ought to act. To this end, ironically, it is often death that defines and lends meaning to life. This degree of reflection is, of course, rare, but is something distinct to our species and an important dimension of humanness, whether expressed theistically, non-theistically or as a mixture of both. As outlined in my proposed theory of the meaning of existence, Sustainable Neurochemical Gratification, *a meaningful life is likely to be comprised of those things that provide "sustained neurochemically mediated gratification".* Thus, felicity may be the result of spirituality or love, for example. However, gratification that is unsustainable, such as thrill-seeking, is unlikely to make life meaningful. In many philosophical and spiritual guides to a happy life, some degree of moderation or perhaps sustained gratification is expounded. Theravada Buddhism would suggest that sustained gratification may be attained when we give up desires that can ultimately never be satisfied, while Aristotle argued that a good life could be achieved through moderation.[1280] Epicurius qualified friendship as essential to happiness and eschewed more violent passions and

---

[1280] Pojman, *op. cit.*, note 147, pp. 68-69.

joys.[1281] In my opinion, *a life governed by reason is likely to be more dignified than one shaped by dogma and unbridled emotions.* Might we therefore conclude that sustainable gratification is unlikely to be provided by activities or relationships that involve short-lived and often intense emotions?

As conscious beings, we not only try to comprehend ourselves and our existence; we also seek to understand the world we live in and to gain knowledge about it. How we acquire that knowledge has long been debated, the major point of contention being focused on the extent to which knowledge is dependent on our sense experiences. However, as is suggested in the theory of knowledge – neuro-rational physicalism – proposed in the present volume, we never rely entirely on our sense perceptions, as strict empiricists would suggest. This means that pure empiricism is not an adequate method of acquiring knowledge. Reason is always employed to some extent. This means that most of what we know derives from inference. Yet, at the same time understanding requires the attribution of meaning, which means that interpretation forms part of our acquisition of knowledge. This being the case, knowledge of the social world is culturally, temporally and spatially constrained. In the natural sciences, knowledge may also be indeterminate and based on the best available explanation. This may seem disconcerting. Yet, this lack of certainty also has a positive side. If we can be absolutely certain of very little, we can be dogmatic about very little. Moreover, subjects of knowledge, such as invisible and dark matter, may not be observable with the means we have available today. Recognition of the limits to our knowledge ought therefore to facilitate humility, respect and dialogue. Indeed, collective triumph will also depend both on the application of reason and the recognition that *a great deal of knowledge is indeterminate and may be temporally, spatially and perhaps culturally constrained.* Decisions stemming from what we take to be "true" based on high probability must always be looked at through ethical lenses. Reason alone should not be relied on to guide us in a desirable direction. We are likely, for example, to face a number of choices as a result of advances in biotechnology. These will be ethical choices such as whether to allow the use of genetic engineering to alter hereditary traits.

[1281] D. Konstan, "Epicurus," *Stanford Encylopedia of Philosophy*, First Published 10 January 2005; Substantive Revision 18 February 2009, http://www.science.uva.nl/~seop/entries/epicurus/.

Having examined the foundational issues that provide the basis for understanding the drivers of history, *Part 2* considers what may be required for civilisational triumph and sustainable history, depicted in Octagon 9.

By looking at the example of the Arab-Islamic world, I demonstrate the way in which golden ages of individual geo-cultural domains are the culmination of collective contributions to human civilisation which arise at particular political, economic, social and cultural conjunctures where good governance, learning, an openness to critique, toleration and respect for diversity come together. **The development of human civilisation is built on foundations to which everyone has contributed.** This is the sense in which human civilisation is like an ocean into which rivers representing geo-cultural domains run. The histories and cultures of geo-cultural domains are inseparable, and we would do humanity a great service by recognising this and acknowledging our mutual debts. The key innovations and ideas that propelled the human story forward were joint achievements. There have been conflict and tension, but these are only two possible products of the interaction between members of different cultures. When we view this contact in its entirety, it is dialogue and exchange that have made geo-cultural domains what they are. Once we recognise this, the possibilities in the present era and in the future are far greater and potentially more positive than a "clash of civilisations" thesis would suggest. We must therefore reject the latter.

The future of human civilisation and geo-cultural domains will depend on a *collective civilisational triumph*, facilitated by the creation of conditions under which human needs are met, including broadly defined basic needs, the need for a positive identity and the need to have a sense of purpose and knowledge. This implies conditions under which human dignity and justice are ensured. As is indicated in Octagon 9, minimum criteria for dignity and justice are needed in order to evaluate institutions and practices at both the national and the global levels.

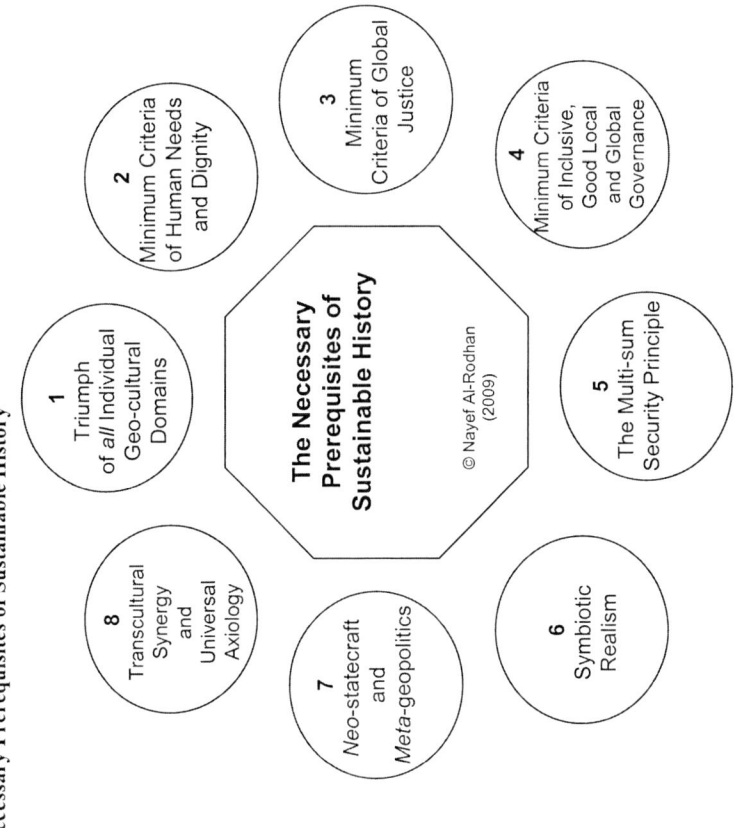

Octagon 9: The Necessary Prerequisites of Sustainable History

Human dignity and justice require good governance, whatever specific form this may take in particular localities. Concerns with good governance should not be associated with the promotion of hegemonic applications of Western-style liberal democracy around the world. While good governance comprises many aspects familiar to Western liberal democracy, its specific instantiation is likely to be different. It is important to recognise that many of the core values of democracy and liberal constitutionalism already exist in many regions of the world. I have suggested what the minimum criteria for good local governance might be. However, ultimately, *we need to explore further which aspects of governance have the widest universal applications by looking at how desirable governance arrangements are conceived around the globe.* Fair representation, transparency, accountability and fairness are likely to be fundamental elements of good and effective governance. Multilateral institutions need to be more representative, and accountable to the citizens of member states and not just to their governments. Civil society needs to be empowered through a universal citizens' charter based above all on a broad conception of human rights that has the protection and promotion of human dignity at its heart.

Sustainable history and civilisational triumph also require security and stability. Yet, they will be attainable only if a comprehensive vision of security is adopted. As is suggested in Octagon 9, a multi-sum security principle that recognises the interconnected nature of human, environmental, national, transnational and transcultural security, and recognition that justice must constitute a central dimension of a more comprehensive framework of security, are urgently needed. The ability to successfully address multidimensional security threats also depends on developing the capacities to respond to such threats in a coherent, coordinated and legitimate manner. Security depends on moving beyond the state-centric paradigm of realism and engaging in burden-sharing, as is outlined by symbiotic realism, which identifies four interlocking dimensions of the global system: the predilections of human nature, global anarchy, interdependence and instant connectivity. Symbiotic realism stresses the importance of absolute rather than relative gains and allows cooperative competition in a non-conflictual symbiotic manner. The global order through which burden-sharing is channelled also has to be politically legitimate. Such a global order would be endowed with mechanisms that allow it to respond to the will of the majority of states.

State power also needs to be thought of as comprising of a number of facets or "capacities" related to social and health issues, domestic politics, economics, the environment, science and human potential, military and security capacities and diplomatic capacities. These aspects of power are, of course, interrelated and often mutually reinforcing. All these capacities determine a state's position in the global system. *Meta*-geopolitics, as I have termed it, needs to consider this broad set of issues. Moreover, an effective national security strategy will deploy both soft and hard power in a just manner, thereby employing just power and focusing on the absolute gains to be made from cooperation.

Increased connectedness and interdependence also make the need for peaceful coexistence and cooperation in addressing common challenges even more vital than they have been before. There is a great deal of scope for relationships that bring mutual gains, even in the context of international anarchy. While the interests of states may not be identical, there are a wide array of issues across which cooperation with partners implies more gains than acting alone. This cooperation, nevertheless, exists alongside unequal power relations. Comprehensive and fair solutions to shared problems depend on ensuring that multilateral institutions and mechanisms are representative of all members. Governance, however, is not simply composed of public global governance institutions; it is also composed of voluntary self-regulation. This is especially the case in relation to corporate actors. While this provides some means of making companies more sensitive to the costs to their reputation of socially irresponsible practices, it reflects a trend in the reduction of formal, legal forms of regulation that may ultimately be needed to ensure just and sustainable growth. The implications of voluntary regulation ought, therefore, to be explored.

In a world marked by instant connectivity, diplomacy remains critical. Yet, diplomacy today has to deal with a wider set of interests that must be reconciled. Moreover, public diplomacy, in particular, is increasing in relevance. The effects of the mass media mean that public opinion can have a far greater impact than in the past. State practices and even events within states are under public scrutiny on a global level. Awareness of the need to influence public opinion is therefore a critical aspect of diplomacy. This does not simply imply sensitivity to the impact of public statements, but is also likely to be served most effectively by respect for international law and the promotion of fair process, as well as cultural understanding. This means, on the one hand, increasing awareness of the intertwined nature of geo-cultural domains and their collective contribution to the development of human civilisation; and, on the other hand, that greater understanding, respect and trust requires active engagement. One of the most central means through which engagement can serve these ends is through dialogue. Dialogue provides a means of identifying the common fundamental values on which various cultures of the world can base cooperation. In order to be effective, dialogic efforts need to take place not just among elites, but at all levels as well as through a variety of means including schools, faith-based institutions, academic research and the mass media, and to be understanding of different cultural communication patterns.

Yet, ultimately transcultural synergy needs to occur, and to do so with the least possible turmoil as we are brought together as a result of globalising processes in more immediate and intense ways. In order for people to experience this as something positive, educational skills should not only include classic educational skills sets, but also those skills required to live alongside people who belong to different cultural, ethnic and religious backgrounds. Dialogue, as well as the reduction of inequalities, will also be critical because justice and fairness play a foundational role in ensuring human dignity and peaceful coexistence. Transcultural synergy will also depend on the emergence of a set of shared human values that may, nevertheless, be articulated in different moral languages. In addition to dialogue, the study of different value systems or a universal axiology and of emergent global values will be increasingly vital in revealing points of commonality rather than essentialising discourses that emphasise incommensurability.

Advances in technology, increased interdependence and instant connectivity will mean that the need to cooperate on questions of governance and on ethical issues will steadily increase. Whether and how we make it as a species will depend on how successfully and how wisely we manage the fundamental issues concerning the future of humanity. Some of these decisions will determine whether what it means to be human will be radically altered, and the meaning of life itself. Since human dignity is so central to well-being, it ought to be the normative ideal that guides us in the collective making of a sustainable history. The requirements of sustainable history are summarised in Box 1.

> **Box 1**
>
> **Sustainable History and the Dignity of Man**
>
> Sustainable history is defined as a durable progressive trajectory in which the quality of life on this planet or other planets is premised on the guarantee of human dignity *for all* at *all times* and under *all circumstances*. It is propelled by the presence of good governance *which balances the attributes of human nature* ("Emotional Amoral Egoism") with *human dignity needs* (reason, security, human rights, accountability, transparency, justice, opportunity, innovation and inclusiveness).
>
> A good governance paradigm that limits excesses of human nature and ensures an atmosphere of happiness and productivity by promoting reason and dignity is critical to sustainable history. A minimum criteria of governance should be met rather than an exact form of governance adopted. Yet, they must be appropriate, acceptable and affordable to each system and cultural domain. These criteria should also meet a certain common global standard to ensure maximum political and moral cooperation.
>
> Humankind is an insignificant part of existence. As "emotional amoral egoists", human beings are driven by emotional self-interest. All thoughts, beliefs and motivations are neurochemically mediated, some pre-determined for survival, others alterable. What makes our existence meaningful is highly subjective and ultimately determined by sustainable neurochemical gratification. All subjects of knowledge have a physical base and, as such, knowledge is acquired primarily through the application of reason.

> **Box 1** *continued*
>
> We should think of human beings as belonging to one collective human civilisation comprised of geo-cultural domains and cultures. The history of human civilisation is a history of mutual borrowings and contemporary events that can be comprehended through an understanding of human time.
>
> As a result of human needs, dignity is central to the sustainability of history. A life governed by reason is more likely to be useful and dignified. Security, stability and prosperity will depend on the application of the multi-sum security principle which captures the multidimensional aspects of security and insists on the centrality of justice to lasting security. Harmonious interstate relations will be guided by the paradigm of symbiotic realism, which stresses the importance of absolute rather than relative gains. In addition, effective statecraft will involve successful reconciliation of all interests and be guided by the concept of just power. Global harmony will also require a synergistic interaction of geo-cultural domains. A set of global values in keeping with human nature and dignity must be identified and developed to ensure moral and political cooperation. Strict ethical guidelines also need to be developed in anticipation of significant technological and biotechnological advances that will have the potential to change what it means to be human and to exist in the world.

These requirements are not only relevant to today's world, but also to the future, since human nature, however it may transform as a result of advances in technology and changes in norms and ideas, will always need to be balanced against the human/trans-human/post-human need for dignity.

GLOSSARY

* Only the author's terms, concepts and theories appear in the glossary.

Collective Civilisational Triumph
The triumph of *all* geo-cultural domains and sub-cultures (see Chapter 16)

Cultural Vigour
Cultural resilience and strength resulting from mixing and exchanges between various cultures (see Chapter 3)

Emotional Amoral Egoism
A theory of human nature that views human nature as largely influenced by neurochemically mediated emotional self-interest (see Chapters 1, 3, 7, 11 and 13)

Emotional Self-interest
Self-interest driven by neurochemically mediated emotions (see Chapters 1, 3-4, 8, 12 and 16)

Fear(survival)-induced Pre-emptive Aggression
Aggression prompted by survival instincts in situations where basic needs are not met (see Chapter 3)

Five Dimensions of Global Security
Human, environmental, national, transnational and transcultural security (see Chapters 8 and 11)

General Theory of Human Nature
A theory of human nature called "Emotional Amoral Egoism" that views human beings as primarily motivated by survival instincts that are emotionally based, pre-disposed through genetic make-up, mediated through neurochemistry and affected by personal, societal, cultural and global states of affairs (see Chapter 3)

Geo-cultural Domains
Geographic areas characterised by cultural similitude (Chapters 1, 6, 8, 12, 14, 15 and 16)

Just Power
The employment of a state's soft and hard power tools in the service of justice (see Chapters 1, 7, 13, 14 and 16)

***Meta*-geopolitics**
A substrate of *neo*-statecraft that takes into account seven interconnected capacities of state power: (1) social and health issues; (2) domestic politics; (3) economics; (4) environment; (5) science and human potential; (6) military and security issues; and (7) international diplomacy (see Chapters 1, 7, 11, 13 and 16)

Minimum Criteria of Inclusive, Effective and Good *Global* Governance
These include: (1) effective multilateralism; (2) effective multilateral institutions; (3) representative multilateral decision-making structures; (4) dialogue; (5) accountability; (6) transparency; (7) burden-sharing; and (8) stronger partnerships between multilateral organisations and civil society (see Chapter 10)

Minimum Criteria of Inclusive, Effective and Good *National* Governance
These include: (1) participation, equity and inclusiveness; (2) rule of law; (3) separation of powers; (4) free, independent and responsible media; (5) government legitimacy; (6) accountability; (7) transparency; and (8) limiting the distorting effect of money in politics (see Chapter 9)

Minimum Criteria of Global Justice
These include: (1) dialogue; (2) effective and representative multilateral institutions; (3) representative decision-making structures; (4) fair treatment; (5) empathy; (6) accountability; (7) transparency; and (8) adherence to international law (see Chapter 8)

Minimum Criteria of Human Needs and Dignity
These include: (1) reason; (2) security; (3) promotion and protection of human rights; (4) accountability; (5) transparency; (6) justice; (7) opportunity and innovation; and (8) inclusiveness (see Chapter 7)

Multi-sum Security Principle
"In a globalized world, security can no longer be thought of as a zero-sum game involving states alone. Global security, instead, has five dimensions that include human, environmental, national, transnational, and transcultural security, and, therefore, global security and the security of any state or culture cannot be achieved without good governance at all levels that guarantees security through justice for all individuals, states, and cultures" (see Chapters 1, 8, 11, 13 and 16)

Neo-statecraft
A new form of statecraft comprising four substrates: (1) *meta*-geopolitics; (2) sustainable national security; (3) just power; and (4) reconciliation statecraft (see Chapters 1 and 13)

Neuro-rational Physicalism (NRP)
A theory of knowledge that recognises the role of interpretation, sense-data and reason in the acquisition of knowledge. Therefore, knowledge is to some extent indeterminate. It may also be temporally, spatially and perhaps culturally constrained. All energy and matter are physical, even if unobservable, making their existence "possible truths subject to proof". Thought processes too are physical and, as such, material. (see Chapters 1, 5 and 16)

Ocean Model of One Human Civilisation
Civilisation conceived as a single human civilisation containing geo-cultural domains that encompass sub-cultures (see Chapters 1 and 8)

Possible Truths Subject to Proof
Ideas that are believed to be logically true even if today we do not have the scientific methodologies to prove them (see Chapters 1 and 5)

Predisposed Tabula Rasa
The human mind is predisposed to certain basic instincts as a result of both our genetic heritage and the totality of our environment (see Chapters 3, 5 and 16)

Prerequisites of Sustainable History
These include: (1) triumph of *all* individual geo-cultural domains; (2) minimum criteria of human needs and dignity; (3) minimum criteria of global justice; (4) minimum criteria of inclusive, good national and global governance; (5) the multi-sum security principle; (6) symbiotic realism; (7) *neo*-statecraft and *meta*-geopolitics; and (8) transcultural synergy and universal axiology (see Chapter 16)

Prerequisites of Transcultural Synergy and Universal Axiology
These include: (1) dialogue; (2) agreed upon rules and ethics of dialogue; (3) mutual understanding; (4) tolerance and respect; (5) mutual learning; (6) identification of a moral minimum; (7) reduction of the technological gap; and (8) fair representation (see Chapter 14)

Pseudo Altruism
Seemingly altruistic behaviour driven by emotional self-interest (see Chapter 3)

Reconciliation Statecraft
A dimension of statecraft devoted to the reconciliation of eight levels of interests: (1) individual; (2) group; (3) national; (4) regional; (5) cultural; (6) global; (7) planetary; and (8) moral (see Chapters 1 and 13)

Specific Theory of Human Motivation
A sub-theory of the General Theory of Human Nature that identifies the major factors that motivate human beings (see Chapter 3)

Sustainable History
A durable progressive trajectory in which the quality of life on this planet is premised on the guarantee of human dignity for *all* at *all* times and under *all* circumstances. This sustainable history is propelled by good governance paradigms that balance the tension between human nature attributes (emotionality, amorality and egoisms),

on the one hand, and human dignity needs (reason, security, human rights, accountability, transparency, justice, opportunity, innovation and inclusiveness), on the other (see Chapters 1-14 and 16)

Sustainable National Security
National security premised on the recognition that mutually advantageous security relationships between states and positive exchanges and interactions between cultures are critical to long-term, sustainable security (see Chapters 8, 11 and 13)

Sustainable Neurochemical Gratification (SNG)
Neurochemical gratification linked to behaviour that is not detrimental to one's own existence or the existence of others. This notion forms the basis of the Theory of Sustainable Neurochemical Gratification that argues what makes our existence meaningful is highly individualistic and ultimately based on durable neurochemically mediated gratification (see Chapters 1, 3-4 and 16)

Symbiotic Realism
A theory of international relations based on four interlocking dimensions of the global system: (1) interdependence; (2) instant connectivity; (3) global anarchy; and (4) the neurobiological substrates of human nature. This theory allows for absolute rather than simply relative gains, based on cooperation and non-conflictual competition (see Chapters 1, 10, 12-13 and 16)

Theory of the Meaning of Existence: Sustainable Neurochemical Gratification (SNG)
A theory of the meaning of existence that argues that whatever meaning we may attribute to existence, life is rendered meaningful by those things, activities, beliefs or relationships – that provide sustained neurochemically mediated gratification (see Chapters 4 and 16)

Transcultural Security
The notion that the security of any culture depends on that of *all* other cultures (see Chapters 8, 11, 14 and 16)

Triumph of Individual Geo-cultural Domains
Success of individual geo-cultural domains through: (1) good governance; (2) cultural borrowing; (3) innovation; (4) more reason; (5) less dogma; (6) respect and tolerance of diversity; (7) inclusiveness; and (8) the success of other individual geo-cultural domains (see Chapter 6)

Universal Axiology
The study of universal values (see Chapters 1, 14 and 16)

INDEX

11 September 2001, 361

A

Abassid Caliphate, 162
Abd Al-Rahman, 166
Abrahamic
  faiths, 403
  religions, 62, 66, 73, 86, 143, 164, 175
Accountability, 13, 15, 27, 99, 172, 174, 180, 197-198, 203, 208, 210-211, 241, 245, 250, 252, 255-257, 259-260, 263, 268-269, 287-289, 294, 329, 342, 348, 351, 404, 440, 443
ACP Group, 284
Additional Protocol to the Council of Europe's Convention on Cybercrime (2003), 353
Adelard of Bath, 158
Adorno, Theodor, 18
Afghanistan, 276
Africa, 174, 232, 247, 291, 301, 340, 380
  Central, 301-302
  East, 380
  North, 33, 60, 152, 163
  Sub-Saharan, 61, 259, 279
  West, 291
African Group, 284
African Union, 274-275, 290
Agenda 21, 278
Agreement on the SAARC Preferential Trading Arrangement (SAPTA), 276
Agreement on the South Asian Free Trade Area (SAFTA), 277
Agreement on Trade-Related Aspects of Intellectual Property Rights (TRIPs), 406
AIDs, 276, 323
  see also HIV
Al-Andalus, 139, 149, 157, 166, 169, 171, 175
Alfonso VI, king of Castile, 157

Al-Ghazali, 155, 158
Al-Idrisi, 158-159
Al-Jahiz, 57, 151
Al-Khazini, 57, 148, 151
Al-Khwarizmi, 143, 146-147, 158
Al-Kindi, 155
Alliance of Civilizations (AoC), 36
Al-Majriti, 156, 158
Al-Mamun, Caliph, 142-143, 146, 149, 163-164
Almohad, dynasty, 164, 171, 175
Al-Nayrizi, 147
Al-Saffar, 156
Al-Razi, 151
  see also Rhazes
Al-Tusi, 48-49
Al-Uqlidisi, 147
America
  Latin, 31, 259, 340
  North, 33, 60, 152, 165
Amygdala, 77
Anarchy, 349
  international, 30, 298, 328, 334, 336, 343, 350, 441
  global, 334, 341, 353, 440
Anatoli, Jacob, 157
Animism, 67
Aquinas, Thomas, 181
Arabian peninsula, 164
Arab-Islamic
  Caliphate, 33
  Empire, 170-171, 174
  golden age, 138-139, 145-146, 154, 171, 174-175, 178, 438
  world, 31, 48, 112, 137-139, 142-144, 146, 149, 151-154, 163-164, 169, 171, 174-176, 178, 183, 230, 257, 382, 390, 392-393, 438
Arab-Israeli conflict, 275
Arctic, 303-304, 381
Argentina, 284
Aristotle, 45, 47, 56, 67, 82, 104, 106, 112, 144, 146, 156, 161, 395, 436
Armengaud son of Blaise, 157
'Asabiya, 21, 25
ASEAN Free Trade Area (AFTA), 276
ASEAN Regional Forum (ARF), 276

Ash'arite, 107, 164
Asia, 30-31, 59, 61-62, 165, 169, 232, 247, 249, 276, 399-400
  Pacific region, 276, 290
  Central, 139, 145, 164, 168, 171, 259, 301
  East, 30-31
  South East, 247, 381
Association of Southeast Asian Nations (ASEAN), 276
Asymmetrical warfare, 368
Atomism, 107, 115, 132-133
  Logical, 107, 116-117, 130, 133
Australasia, 394
Authoritarianism, 393
Averroes, 137, 143
  see also Ibn Rushd
Avian Influenza, 276
Avicenna, 104, 137
  see also Ibn Sina
Ayer, A.J., 105, 110

B
Babylon, 147
  Ancient, 252
Bacillus anthracis, 252
Bacon, Roger, 308
Bahrain, 250
Basel Accord, 207
Basel Committee on Banking Supervision, 277
Baudrillard, Jean, 24
Ben Mahir, Jacob, 157
Bentham, Jeremy, 68, 129
Berkeley, George, 128-129
Bible, Holy, 66, 252
Big Bang Theory, 45-46, 53-54, 62, 95
Biodiversity, 340, 376, 417
Biological
  attacks, 308, 315
  risks, 308-309, 315
  threats, 307, 313-314
Biosafety, 307-308
Biosecurity, 307-308, 314-315, 368
Biosphere, 199, 232, 239, 300, 353, 376-377

Biotechnology, 307-310, 313-314, 316, 421, 427, 433, 437
Blog, 341
Bolivia, 253
Bondi, Hermann, 53
Bosnia, 32
Brahmanas, 174
Braudel, Fernand, 23, 26, 34, 165, 389, 435
Brazil, 282, 284, 286, 379
Brethren of Purity, 57, 151
  see also Ikhwă al-Safă
Bretton Woods System, 379
BRIC (Brazil, Russia, India and China), 379
Britain, 116, 153
  see also United Kingdom and England
British Isles, 157
Buddhism, 55, 63, 67, 88-89, 99, 162, 174, 184
  Theravada, 436
Burden-sharing, 233, 294, 329, 338, 345, 352-353, 440
Burke, Edmund, 391
Byzantine Empire, 141
Byzantium, Christian, 143, 168

C
Cairo Declaration on Human Rights in Islam (1990), 398
Camus, Albert, 91-93
Canada, 284, 299, 303, 340
Candelabra Theory, 61
Carnap, Rudolf, 105, 110
Catholic Church, 49, 181
Chad, 301
Chambers, Robert, 57
Carolus Magnus, "Charlemagne", 154
Chechnya, 32
China, 30-31, 138, 144-145, 153-154, 193, 202, 205, 281, 283, 286, 379, 382-383
  Ancient, 17, 48
Cholera, 303
Chomsky, Noam, 106, 114
Christianity, 55, 66-67, 143, 158, 162, 166, 393-394

INDEX   453

Civil
  liberties, 203, 254, 260, 328
  society, 36, 245-246, 251, 253, 264, 272, 277-278, 286, 289, 291-292, 294-295, 364, 440
Civilisation
  Asian, 30-31
  human, 35, 37, 400
  Islamic, 30-31
  planetary, 41, 418
  post-human, 422
  trans-human, 415
  triumph, 13, 135, 176, 213-214, 218-219, 229, 233-234, 242, 438, 440
Clash of Civilisations Thesis (Huntington), 31, 33, 138, 175, 233, 338, 390
Clean slate, 65, 68, 81, 435
  see also Tabula rasa
Climate change, 195, 199, 232, 285-286, 300-303, 305, 310, 319, 322, 325-326, 329, 340, 376, 379-381, 417-418, 424
Coexistence, 40, 143, 164-167, 173, 176, 196, 218, 240, 311, 386, 400, 403, 413, 441-442
Collective Civilisational Triumph (Al-Rodhan), 348
Comte de Buffon, 57
Confucianism, 55, 174, 184, 397, 408-409
Constructivism, 108, 122-123, 125, 133
Copenhagen School, 233, 311
Copernicus, Nicolaus, 46, 48-49, 147, 157
Corporate social responsibility, 198
Corruption, 169-170, 172, 254-255, 200, 261, 265-267, 329
Cosmology, 40, 45-48, 56, 64
Côte d'Ivoire, 275
Council of Europe (CoE), 274, 353
Creationism, 56, 62, 94-95
  Intelligent Design (IDC), 62
  Old Earth (OEC), 62
Cultural borrowing, 33, 138-139, 142, 144, 156, 158, 177

Cultural Vigour (Al-Rodhan), 79
Culture
  Arab-Norman, 158, 160
  sub-, 34-37
Cybercrime, 232, 236, 306-307, 345

D

Daniel of Morley, 157
Daoism, 55, 88
Darwin, Charles, 56-59, 62-63, 74, 82, 151, 156
Dawkins, Richard, 94
Declaration on the Elimination of Violence Against Women (1993), 202
Declaration on the Rights of Persons Belonging to National or Ethnic, Religious or Linguistic Minorities (1992), 204
Democracy, 124, 172-175, 243, 246, 248-252, 256-257, 274-275, 287, 289, 394-395, 397, 400, 407, 409, 435, 440
  Islamic, 251
  liberal, 13, 19-20, 26, 30, 32
  liberal market, 394
Democratisation, 243, 246, 251, 292
Democritus, 107, 115
Demography, 359
Denmark, 303
Derrida, Jacques, 204
Descartes, René, 106, 113-114, 117, 127, 129, 148, 155
Development, 435-436
  sustainable, 192, 208, 233, 237, 239, 254, 352, 378
Dhimmi, 165-166, 175
Diamond, Jared, 421
Dignity, 27-29, 39-40, 179-186, 189, 191-192, 194-195, 200-201, 209, 211, 213, 218, 229-230, 234-235, 239, 242, 254, 331, 397, 408-409, 432-433, 443-444
  human, 13, 15, 27, 29-30, 39-40, 99, 179-196, 200-201, 203-204, 206, 211, 213, 219, 223, 229, 232, 242-243, 252, 260, 269, 293, 295, 323, 328, 348, 350, 354, 369

Dignity, human *continued*
384, 396, 407-408, 410, 417, 432-433, 435, 438, 440, 442-443
Diplomacy, 237, 305, 313, 336, 356-357, 367, 383-384, 441-442
  public, 305, 313, 341, 357, 383, 441
Discrimination, 167, 170, 179, 188, 191-192
Disease, 21, 129, 187, 192, 195, 199, 232-233, 276, 280, 285, 287, 299, 303, 307-308, 310, 314-315, 325, 363, 365, 368, 421, 426-427
  infectious, 196, 306, 308, 315-316, 325, 327, 335, 363
Diversity, 38, 79, 163-164, 167, 170-173, 175-178, 188, 222, 224, 240, 256, 320, 387, 390, 392-393, 402, 405, 407, 409-410, 438
Dogma, 39, 96, 101, 139, 162, 175, 177, 203, 437

E

Earth-centric universe, 46
  see also Universe
Ecological balance, 191, 195, 199, 208, 211
Economic Community of West African States (ECOWAS), 274-275, 291
Economic Cooperation Organization (ECO), 277
Education, 69, 75, 77, 79, 97-98, 125, 162, 169, 179, 190, 193-194, 201, 203, 252, 254, 257-258, 260, 262, 280, 290, 323, 328-329, 331, 336, 342
Egypt, 33, 139, 147, 151, 153, 171, 202, 234, 302
  Ancient, 147
Einstein, Albert, 50
Eisenstadt, Schmuel, 215
Emotional Amoral Egoism (Al-Rodhan), 27, 65, 74-75, 80, 82-83, 186, 228, 312, 371, 377, 443
Emotional Self-interest (Al-Rodhan), 27, 80, 82-83, 86, 97, 229, 343, 435-436

Empiricism, 69, 101, 103-105, 108, 110-111, 126-132, 134, 148, 437
England, 149, 160-161, 252
  see also Britain and United Kingdom
English Bill of Rights, 252
Enlightenment, 16, 57, 63, 67, 137, 142-143, 181, 391, 400
Environmental
  degradation, 191, 199, 234, 280, 298, 310, 322, 326, 338, 340, 349, 352, 372, 418, 424
  sustainability, 318
Epicurus, 115, 436
Epidemics, 236, 303, 363
Epistemology, 24, 118
  see also Theory of knowledge
  constructivist, 101, 121-122, 130
Equity, 230, 245, 268, 404
Eritrea, 301
Essentialism, 390-393
Ethics, 56, 130, 181, 185, 204, 397, 406, 409, 412
  corporate, 197-198, 206
Europe, 16, 20, 33-34, 57, 59, 61-62, 137-138, 142, 144, 153-154, 157, 160, 165, 169, 175, 207, 214, 247-248, 274, 300, 380-381, 383, 393-394, 399
  Western, 22, 249
European Union (EU), 200
  Western European Union (WEU), 294
European Security and Defence Policy (ESDP), 325
Evolution, 40, 56-63, 66-67, 73, 94, 114, 128, 151, 154, 208, 420, 423, 427
Evolutionary Theory, 56, 58, 63, 66, 151
Existence
  meaning of, 40, 85-86, 90-91, 93, 96-99, 436
Existentialism, 70, 73, 87, 89-91, 95
Extremism, 30, 229, 342, 348, 351-352, 376, 390

F

Fear(survival)-induced Pre-emptive Aggression (Al-Rodhan), 80
Feyerabend, Paul, 121
Financial crisis, 207, 263, 287
Five Dimensions of Global Security (Al-Rodhan), 299, 324
Foreign policy, 276, 334, 345-346, 348-353, 355, 357, 363, 369, 382
Foucault, Michel, 24
France, 16-18, 33, 153, 157, 193, 205, 234, 264, 278, 281, 284
Frederick II, king of Sicily, 161
Frederick of Fribourg, 148
Freud, Sigmund, 71, 82
Fukuyama, Francis, 19, 26, 394, 427, 433

G

Gadamer, Hans-Georg, 18, 125
Gains
  absolute, 383, 336, 346-347, 351, 353-354, 441
  relative, 28, 334, 347, 351, 353, 384, 440, 444
Galilei, Galileo, 146-148
Gamow, George, 53
Ganges Basin, 311
Garden of Eden Theory, 61
Geber, 151
  see also Ibn Hayyan
Gender, 196, 198, 201-202, 295, 343
  equality, 189, 194, 198-199, 202, 398
  inequality, 189, 198, 202
General Theory of Human Nature (Al-Rodhan), 75
Genetic engineering, 75, 309, 424, 426, 432, 437
Geo-cultural Domains (Al-Rodhan), 14, 16, 23, 28-29, 34-36, 39-40, 137-139, 142, 168, 170-173, 177, 213-219, 240, 242, 311, 337-338, 386-390, 392, 400, 403, 413, 420, 438-439, 442, 444
Geopolitics, 305, 320, 355-356, 359-360, 362, 379-380, 383
  classical, 361

Geopolitics *continued*
  critical, 360
Gerard of Cremona, 157-158
Germain, Jean, 393
Germany, 18, 205, 282
Gibbon, Edward, 421
Global
  North, 243
  South, 243, 284, 326, 329
  warming, 232, 301, 303, 335, 340, 365-366, 376, 380-381
Gold, Thomas, 53
Governance
  corporate, 197-198, 206
  democratic, 246, 249
  global, 40, 193, 204, 208, 228, 230, 271-274, 277, 279-281, 285-287, 292-293, 295, 305, 337-338, 406
  good, 13, 15, 27, 99, 139-140, 171-172, 177-178, 231, 243-247, 251-252, 351, 417, 438, 440, 443
  local, 141, 174, 440
  space, 321
Greece
  Ancient, 18, 48, 138, 142, 173, 273, 394
Greenhouse gases, 239-240
Grotius, Hugo, 396
Group of Eight (G8), 197, 277, 281, 284-286
Group of Thirty-Three (G33), 284
Group of Twenty (G20), 277, 284, 287
Gulf Cooperation Council (GCC), 275

H

Habermas, Jürgen, 18
Hadith, 163, 251
Hammurabi Code, 252
Hauser, Marc, 72-73, 80, 106, 114, 128
Hayy Ibn Yaqzan, 144, 155
Healthcare, 187, 189, 190, 193, 201, 211, 254, 280, 290, 292, 310, 314, 321, 329, 339, 371-373
Hegel, Georg Wilhelm Friedrich, 17-19, 25, 106, 112-113, 116, 129

Hegemony, 379, 386, 390
Henry II, king of England, 160
Henry Bate from Flanders, 157
Herman of Dalmatia, 157
Hermeneutics, 24
Herschel, William, 50
High-level Group of Twenty Leaders (L20), 285
Hinduism, 66
History
  cyclical, 20-21, 23, 25-26, 420, 433
  linear, 16, 19, 25-26, 214, 391, 399
  longue durée (Braudel), 23, 26, 34, 389, 435
HIV, 276, 325
  see also AIDs
Hobbes, Thomas, 68
Hong Kong, 284, 406
Hoyle, Fred, 53
Hubble, Edwin Powell, 54
Hugh of Santalla, 157
Hülegü (Khan), 171
Human motivation, 70, 75, 225
Human rights, 13, 15, 27, 39, 79, 99, 179-180, 185-186, 190, 192, 194, 196, 201, 203-204, 210-211, 221-223, 227-228, 232, 235, 246-248, 252, 258, 267, 274-275, 292, 295, 300, 323, 328, 331, 345-346, 350, 357, 369, 371-374, 384, 394-400, 407-410, 440, 443
  Islamic, 399
Humanitarian Assistance, 226-227, 323, 376
Humanitarian Intervention, 235, 276
Humanitarian Law, 206, 377
Hume, David, 104-105
Huntington, Samuel, 29-33, 214-215
Husserl, Edmund, 89

I

Iberia, 33, 166
Iberian Peninsula, 139, 157, 171
Ibn al-Haytham, 48-49, 148, 158
Ibn al-Nafis, 149
Ibn al-Shatir, 48-49
Ibn Hayyan, 151
  see also Geber

Ibn Khaldūn, 20-21, 23, 25, 137, 156, 420
Ibn Nagrila, 166
Ibn Rushd, 137, 143, 155, 162, 164, 395
  see also Averroes
Ibn Shaprut, 166
Ibn Sina, 104-105, 132, 137, 144, 149, 155, 395
  see also Avicenna
Ibn Tibbon, 157
Ibn Tufayl, 104, 132, 137, 144, 155
Inclusiveness, 13, 15, 27, 99, 180, 188-189, 196-197, 210-211, 245, 251-254, 257, 262, 268-269, 292, 328, 443
Identity, 32-33, 38, 79-80, 138, 165, 196, 230
  collective, 185-186, 207-208, 216-217, 230-231, 262, 312, 342, 344, 348, 364, 371, 386, 410
  ethnic, 165
  national, 79, 192, 253, 312, 327-328, 372, 401
  personal, 187-189, 196, 232, 257, 343, 371, 401-402, 428, 438
Ijma, 174, 251
Ijtihad, 139, 163-164, 169-170, 175, 251, 398
Ikhwă al-Safă, 57, 151
  see also Brethren of Purity
India, 174, 394
  Mughal, 139, 145
Indian Ocean, 151-152
Indian Subcontinent, 174, 394
Indonesia, 284
Information and Communications Technologies (ICT), 304-305, 341-343, 345, 349, 353, 357-358
Information Revolution, 358, 368
Intelligence
  artificial-, 428-432
  super-, 421-422, 429-432
Inter-cultural dialogue, 410
Innovation, 13, 15, 27, 99, 139, 146-163, 171, 177-178, 180, 207, 211, 219, 443

Interdependence, 138, 191-192, 195, 199, 211, 291, 293, 305, 311, 328, 330, 333-334, 336, 341, 344, 347, 349-350, 353, 361, 440-442
Interests
  cultural, 370, 374-376
  global, 305, 356, 370, 374-376, 378
  group, 371-373
  individual, 371-375
  moral, 370, 377
  national, 30, 193, 275, 342, 346, 348, 370, 372-375, 377
  planetary, 370, 376-377, 389
  regional, 370, 373-375, 378
International Commission on Intervention and State Sovereignty (ICISS), 299-300
International Committee of the Red Cross (ICRC), 278
International Covenant on Civil and Political Rights (1966), 203, 258, 262
International Covenant on Economic, Social and Cultural Rights (ICESCR) (1966), 374
International Criminal Court, 238, 325
International Criminal Tribunal for the Former Yugoslavia (ICTY), 273
International Federation of Trade Unions, 278
International humanitarian law, 206
International Labour Organization (ILO), 273
International law, 221, 238-239, 241, 271, 273, 324-325, 350, 367, 373, 375, 377, 384, 442
International Monetary Fund (IMF), 193, 205, 236, 244, 273, 281, 283, 288, 291
Iran, 48, 174, 250, 379, 394
Iraq, 124, 139, 174, 302, 394
Islam, 162, 164-169, 174-175, 251, 258, 351, 390, 392-393, 395-396, 398
Islamic law, 140, 160-161, 183
  see also Shari'a
Italy, 158, 161

J
Japan, 205, 207, 282, 308, 383
John of Brescia, 157
John Paul II, Pope, 181
Jordan Basin, 311
Judaism, 55, 66-67, 143, 162, 166
Jumhur, 174
Just Power (Al-Rodhan)
  see Power
Justice
  global, 28, 40, 213, 219-220, 222-230, 234-235, 237-242, 272, 323
  global social, 224-226, 323
  social, 187, 195, 197, 220, 224-227, 229, 292, 323, 409
  socio-economic, 189, 193, 227, 260, 323

K
Kant, Immanuel, 17, 19, 82, 106, 113, 120, 127, 181-182, 391
Kardashev Scale, 419
Kardashev, Nikolai, 418-419
Kayyam, Omar, 148
Kazakhstan, 367
Kenya, 302
Kepler, Johannes, 49, 148
Khan, Genghis, 171
Khun, Thomas, 122
Kierkegaard, Søren, 82, 87-88, 90
King John of England, 252
Knights Templar, The, 161
Knowledge
  innate, 106-107, 114, 119, 127, 130-132
  innate moral, 106, 128
Kojève, Alexandre, 18-19
Koran, 140, 163, 252, 258, 407
Korea, 174, 283
Kyoto Protocol, 326

L
Lacan, Jacques, 18
Lamarck, Jean Baptiste, 57
Landmine Treaty (1997), 278
  see also Ottawa Convention
Latin West, 49, 155-156

Law
  Arab-Islamic, 160
  English common, 160-161
  Norman, 160
League of Arab States (LAS), 275
League of Nations, 281
Least Developed Countries (LDC) Group, 284
Lebanon, 171, 302
Legitimacy, 227, 246, 255, 259, 263, 268-269, 281, 283, 286, 304, 323, 347-348, 363, 406
Leibniz, Gottfried Wilhelm, 146
Lemaître, George, 50, 53
Leucippus, 107, 115
Liberalism, 249
  neo-, 325
Liberia, 275
Locke, John, 68-69, 104-105, 132, 155, 174, 220, 391, 396
Logical Positivism, 105, 110-111, 132
Lorenz, Konrad, 71
Luther, Martin, 49, 393
Lyotard, Jean-François, 24

M

Madrid Declaration (2008), 409
Magna Carta, 20, 252
Maghreb, 20, 156, 164, 169, 175
Maimonides, 162
Majlis al-Shura, 395
Malaria, 303
Maqasi al-shari'a, 395
Marlowe, Christopher, 162
Marx, Karl, 18, 23
Maslow, 82
Mauritania, 301
Media, 36, 38, 123, 201, 246, 253, 256, 259-261, 263-266, 268-269, 304-305, 312-314, 322, 328, 331, 341, 349, 358, 383-384, 389-390, 402-404, 441-442
Mediterranean, 139, 151, 388
Meng-tzu, 174
Mesopotamia, 171
Meta-geopolitics (Al-Rodhan), 355, 362, 383, 439, 441

Mexico, 264, 283, 286, 311
Middle Ages, 48-49, 57, 149, 158, 176, 395
Middle East, 169, 247, 250, 275-276, 380, 398
Migration, 195, 215, 236, 280, 301-303, 311, 338, 344, 368, 380
Military
  force, 229, 300
  power, 298, 334-336, 347, 369
  capabilities, 337
Minimum Criteria of Global Justice (Al-Rodhan), 213, 227, 240-241, 439
Minimum Criteria of Human Needs and Dignity (Al-Rodhan), 179, 209-210, 439
Minimum Criteria of Inclusive, Effective and Good Global Governance (Al-Rodhan), 271, 293-294, 439
Minimum Criteria of Inclusive, Effective and Good National Governance (Al-Rodhan), 243, 268, 439
Minorities, 33, 188-189, 196, 203-204, 222, 245, 253, 257, 262-263, 278, 331, 371, 403, 410
Modernism, 400
Mohammed, the Prophet, 139, 141, 313
Monism, 115, 132-133
Montesquieu, 156
Monotheism, 112, 388, 399
Moral compass, 65, 80, 397
Morality, 17, 65, 69, 72-73, 76, 80, 90, 99, 114, 183, 225, 250, 333, 350, 391
  innate, 66, 69-70, 79, 83, 132-133, 436
Morocco, 139, 157, 162, 164
Multilateral
  arrangements, 200, 347
  institutions, 192, 194, 205, 219, 241, 271, 274-275, 277, 279-280, 283, 289-291, 294-295, 325, 330, 335, 338, 343, 348, 351-352, 406, 440-441

Multilateral *continued*
  trading system,193, 284
Multilateralism, 272-274, 276, 280-281, 283, 290, 292-294, 330, 338, 342, 356, 367-368, 384
Multinational enterprises (MNEs), 277, 287, 289
  see also Transnational Corporations
Multi-sum Security Principle (Al-Rodhan), 28, 40, 229, 231, 298-299, 323-324, 368, 384, 439-440, 444
Mu'tazilah, 163
Mutual understanding, 38, 312, 401, 403, 407, 409-410
Mycenae, 174

N
Nagel, Thomas, 92, 225
NAMA 11, 284
Namibia, 284
Nanotechnology, 316-320, 419, 421, 424-426, 428, 431
  Molecular (MNT), 316-320, 426
Nano-threats, 315-319
National interest, 292, 305, 318, 343, 346, 369, 372-377
National security, 123, 232, 236, 239-240, 299, 301, 304-305, 314, 317-318, 321-322, 324, 326-327, 330, 335, 344, 356, 368, 378, 384, 441
Nationalism, 22, 32
  ultra-, 302
Natural disasters, 195, 232, 299, 303, 310, 339, 377
Natural law, 252, 395-396, 399, 408
Natural resources, 305, 329, 396, 399, 408
Neo-statecraft (Al-Rodhan), 41, 355-384, 439
Neurath, Otto, 105, 110
Neurochemistry, 66, 75, 77-78, 129, 426
Neurochemical Man (Al-Rodhan), 65
Neuro-rational Physicalism (NRP) (Al-Rodhan), 40, 101, 108-109, 125, 131, 133, 437

New Partnership for Africa's Development (NEPAD), 275
Newton, Sir Isaac, 146, 148
Nietzsche, Friedrich, 90
Niger, 301
Nigeria, 301, 380
Nile Basin, 311
Noah's Arc Theory, 61
Non-governmental organisations (NGOs), 198, 205, 208, 260, 263, 265-266, 277-278, 288-289, 293, 338, 343, 352, 358
Non-state actors, 199, 236, 297, 306, 318-319, 335, 340, 353, 357-358, 368, 382
Norms
  cultural, 98, 260, 387
  international, 200, 221, 237-238, 263, 272-273, 298, 324, 327-328, 335, 338, 345, 351, 353, 377
  social, 226, 254, 388, 444
  moral, 79, 228, 377, 408
North Atlantic Treaty Organization (NATO), 200, 274, 358
Norway, 299-300, 303

O
Occidentalism, 250
Ocean Model of One Human Civilisation (Al-Rodhan), 29, 36-37, 39, 214
Oman, 250
Opportunity, 13, 15, 27, 99, 153, 180, 189, 203, 210, 352-353, 358, 363, 367, 382, 443
Optional Protocol to the Convention on the Rights of the Child (2002), 325
Organisation for Economic Co-operation and Development (OECD), 65, 277, 288
Organisation of the Islamic Conference (OIC), 276
Organisations
  international, 205, 208, 236, 285, 288-289, 293, 323, 343, 348
  regional, 275-276, 280, 290-291
  sub-regional, 277

Organization for Security and
  Co-operation in Europe (OSCE),
  274
Organization of American States
  (OAS), 274
Orientalism (Said), 16, 250, 388, 392
Ottawa Convention, 278, 325
  see also Landmine Treaty (1997)
Ottoman
  Empire, 166-169
  Turkey, 139
Ozone depletion, 310-311

P
Pacific Islands Forum Secretariat
  (PIFS), 277
Pacific, 247, 276, 290
  South, 248, 278
Palestine, 139, 160, 171
Pandemics, 274, 276, 298, 362
Pan-sexuality (Freud), 70
Pantheism, 388
Paris Club, 277
Parliament of World Religions, 205
Parmenides, 106, 112-113, 115
Pathogens, 297, 308-310, 314
Peloponnese, 174
Persia, 17, 139, 145, 152, 171
Persian Gulf, 151
Philippines, 284
Philosophy of history, 16-18, 20-26,
  34, 36
Physical nature of the mind, 132-133
Pinker, Steven, 106, 114
Plato, 45, 47, 56, 69, 82, 102, 106,
  114, 120, 127
Plato of Tivoli, 157
Pluralism, 115, 155, 196, 233, 246-
  247, 251, 399
Pogge, Thomas, 220, 223-224
Polytheism, 388
Popper, Karl, 126
"Possible truths subject to proof"
  (Al-Rodhan), 108-109, 127
Post-human, 424-425, 427-428, 444
Post-humanity, 421-422
Postmodernism, 400

Power
  balance of, 30-31, 334, 346-347
  hard, 356-357, 362, 368-369, 383,
    403, 441
  just (Al-Rodhan), 28, 200-201, 355-
    356, 368-369, 379, 383-384, 403,
    441, 444
  smart, 368-369
  soft (Nye), 200, 356-357, 367-369,
    379
Pre-disposed Tabula Rasa
  (Al-Rodhan), 80-81, 127, 130, 133,
    435
Proliferation, 232, 286, 306, 368
Pseudo altruism (Al-Rodhan), 80
Psychoanalysis, 70
Psychopharmacology, 424
Ptolemy, Claudius, 46-47, 146

Q
Qatar, 250

R
Rationalism, 103-104, 106, 111, 127,
  130, 132, 164, 171, 388, 391
Rationality, 69, 73, 95, 122, 155, 171,
  180-182, 186, 396
Rawls, John, 69, 220-224
Realism, 30, 222, 231, 298, 333-335
Reason, 15, 17, 27-28, 31, 39, 65-69,
  72-74, 80, 82-83, 87, 91, 96-97,
  99, 101, 103, 106, 108-109, 111,
  114, 119, 127-128, 130-134, 137,
  139, 155, 162-165, 170, 172, 175,
  177, 180-182, 210-211, 390, 395,
  428, 433, 436-437, 443-444
Reconciliation Statecraft
  (Al-Rodhan), 41, 356, 369-370, 383
Religion, 22, 99, 139, 143
Renaissance, 57, 137-139, 142, 145-
  146, 154-155, 162
Respect, 39, 164, 170-172, 177-178,
  181-186, 188, 192, 204-205, 220-
  222, 240, 252, 331, 345, 353,
  401, 404-405, 409, 412-413, 437-
  438, 442
Rhazes, 151
  see also Al-Razi

Richard I, "The Lionheart", 160
Ricoeur, Paul, 24
Rights
  civil, 246-247, 345
  cultural, 190, 203, 295, 345, 350
  liberal, 398
  political, 203-204, 224, 253, 258, 262, 266, 292
  social, 292, 295
Robert of Chester, 157
Roger I, Count, 158
Roger II, king of Sicily, 48, 139, 421
Roman Empire, 48, 139, 421
Rorty, Richard, 24
Rousseau, Jean-Jacques, 391
Rudolph of Bruges, 157
Rule of Law, 80, 83, 245, 251-252, 254-255, 258-259, 263, 268-269, 304, 409
Russell, Bertrand, 92, 102, 107, 116-121
Russian Federation, 193, 205, 281, 284-285, 303, 367, 379, 382
  see also Soviet Union
Rwanda, 206

S
SAARC Convention on Narcotic Drugs and Psychotropic Substances (1990), 277
SAARC Convention on Preventing and Combating Trafficking in Women and Children for Prostitution (2002), 277
SAARC Convention on Regional Arrangements for the Promotion of Child Welfare in South Asia (2002), 277
SAARC Regional Convention of the Suppression of Terrorism (1993), 277
Said, Edward, 390
Salio of Padua, 157
Salmonella typhimurium, 308
Sartre, Jean-Paul, 18, 90-91, 95
Sassanid Empire, 141, 152
Saudi Arabia, 31, 38, 205, 250, 367, 385

Schlick, Moritz, 105, 110
Science
  Natural, 115, 125-126
  modern, 56, 59
  Neuro-, 74, 82-83, 431
  Scientific Revolution, 142, 144, 146
Scot, Michael, 161-162, 357
Second World War, 193, 205, 338, 394, 426
Secularism, 399
Security dilemma, 231, 298, 334-335
Security Studies, 337, 350
Security
  aerospace, 320-323
  cyber-, 306-307
  energy, 305, 367-368
  environmental, 233, 236, 300-304, 310-311, 314-315, 318-319, 322, 324-326, 329, 368
  food, 277, 292, 314
  human, 201-202, 205, 231-233, 235, 239, 299-300, 313, 317, 320-321, 324-326, 328-329, 350
  military, 305, 366
  national, 123, 232, 234, 236, 239-240, 299, 301, 304-305, 314, 317-319, 321-322, 324, 326-327, 330, 335, 344, 356, 367-368, 378, 383-384, 441
  societal, 233, 311-313
  sustainable, 297, 324, 328, 330, 368, 378
  transnational, 234, 236, 298, 305, 310-311, 315, 319-320, 322, 324, 327, 330-331, 368
  universal, 236-237, 242
  water, 380
Self-help system, 298
Self-interest, 68, 74-75, 223, 235, 323, 333-334, 343, 374
Senegal, 301
Senghaas, Dieter, 233, 390, 399-400
Seven Capacities of States (Al-Rodhan), 305, 390, 399-400
Shanghai Cooperation Organisation (SCO), 276
Shari'a, 55, 143, 160, 183, 398
  see also Islamic law

Shura, 174, 251
Sicily, 154, 157-162
Sierra Leone, 275
Singapore, 247
Singer, Peter, 220
Skinner, B.F., 71
Social contract, 220-221, 396
Socrates, 112, 117, 146
Somalia, 302
South Africa, 284, 286
South Asian Association for Regional Cooperation (SAARC), 276-277
South Korea, 283
Southern Common Market (Mercosur), 274
Sovereignty, 195, 200, 208, 223, 235, 239, 249-250, 273-274, 287, 299-300, 304, 324, 327, 345, 353, 373-374
Soviet Union, 193, 281
see also Russian Federation
Soviet-Afghan War (1979-1989), 31
Space, 50, 52-53, 150, 297, 320-323, 383, 423, 429
technologies, 321-323
Spain, 38
Muslim, 48-49, 143, 153-154, 156, 164, 166, 171
Specific Theory of Human Nature (Al-Rodhan), 74, 76
Spengler, Oswald, 22-23, 25, 214
Spinoza, 106, 113, 129, 155
State failure, 196, 299, 301, 368
Statecraft, 28, 155, 355-384, 444
Sudan, 301-302
Sunnah, 163
Sustainable History (Al-Rodhan), 13, 15, 20, 27-29, 39-40, 45, 83, 85, 130, 138, 178, 187, 211, 214, 244, 271, 295, 297, 331, 333, 355, 386, 435-444
Sustainable National Security (Al-Rodhan), 304, 330, 356, 367-368, 378-379, 383-384
Sustainable Neurochemical Gratification (Al-Rodhan), 28, 83, 85, 96-99, 436, 443

Sustainable Security (Al-Rodhan), 297, 324, 328-331, 368, 378
Switzerland, 299
Symbiotic Realism (Al-Rodhan), 28, 40, 293, 333-354, 356, 368, 439-440, 444
Syria, 139, 151, 171, 302

T
Tabula rasa, 65, 68-69, 80-81, 104, 132-133, 435
see also Clean slate
Taiwan, 406
Tamburlaine the Great, 162
Terrorism, 123-124, 277, 286, 309, 348, 353, 368
Theory of knowledge, 100-134, 437
see also Epistemology
Theory of Natural Selection, 58
Theory of Relativity, 50, 126
Tolerance, 139-141, 160, 164-167, 170-173, 188, 205, 240, 345, 401, 404
Tolstoy, Leo, 86-87, 95
Tonghak, 174
Toxins, 297, 308-309, 314
Toynbee, Arnold J., 22-23, 26, 420
Traditionalism, 164, 247-248, 250, 252
Trafficking
arms, 298, 234, 306
Transcultural exchanges, 33, 137-161, 402
Transcultural Security (Al-Rodhan), 231, 237, 240, 297, 299, 311-313, 320, 322, 324, 327-328, 331, 403-404
Transcultural Synergy (Al-Rodhan), 14, 40-41, 311, 354, 356, 368, 386, 400-403, 405, 411-413, 439, 442
Trans-human, 215, 424, 427-428, 444
Trans-humanism, 424, 427-428
Transnational actors, 338, 346
Transnational corporations (TNCs), 189, 198, 208, 339, 342, 344, 346, 353, 358
see also Multinational Enterprises

INDEX 463

Transnational organised crime, 236, 368
Transparency, 13, 15, 27, 99, 180, 197, 208, 210-211, 241, 245, 252, 254-256, 259-260, 263-265, 268-269, 289, 294, 322, 342, 357, 440, 443
Trilateral Commission, 277
Tripartite Declaration of Principles Concerning Multinational Enterprises and Social Policy (1977), 277
Tunisia, 139, 156, 284
Turkey, 234, 283, 302

U
Umayyad
 Caliphate, 162
 dynasty, 164, 166, 168, 170
Unipolarity, 382
United Kingdom (UK), 193
 see also Britain and England
United Nations (UN), 36, 197, 205, 273, 275, 278, 288-281, 283, 285, 288-289, 329, 338, 367, 371
 Charter, 273
 Commission for Global Governance, 204
 Global Compact, 289
 General Assembly, 204, 238, 300
 Peacebuilding Commission, 273
 Security Council (UNSC), 193, 205-206, 236, 238, 281-282, 284, 299, 309, 330
 Year of Dialogue among Civilizations (2001), 386
United Nations Capital Development Fund (UNCDF), 273
United Nations Children's Fund (UNICEF), 273
United Nations Conference on Trade and Development (UNCTAD), 273
United Nations Convention on the Elimination of All Forms of Discrimination against Women (CEDAW) (1979), 372
United Nations Convention on the Rights of the Child (1989), 372

United Nations Development Programme (UNDP), 244-245, 273, 300
United Nations Economic and Social Commission for Asia and the Pacific (UNESCAP), 245, 253
United Nations Environmental Programme (UNEP), 273
United Nations High Commissioner for Refugees (UNHCR), 273
United Nations Human Settlements Programme (UN-HABITAT), 273
United Nations International Drug Control Programme (UNDCP), 273
United Nations Population Fund (UNFPA), 273
United Nations Relief and Works Agency for Palestinian Refugees in the Near East (UNWRA), 273
United Nations Scientific, Educational and Cultural Organization (UNESCO), 204, 273
United States (US), 32, 193, 205, 207, 230, 249, 264, 281-283, 285, 287, 303, 309, 311, 314, 326, 346-347, 369, 381-383, 406
Universal Declaration of Human Responsibilities (1997), 205
Universal Declaration of Human Rights (1948), 179, 186, 190, 203, 258, 345, 374, 396
Universe
 geocentric, 47-48
  see also Earth-centric Universe
 heliocentric, 46, 48-49
 Heliocentric Theory, 157
Universal axiology, 40-41, 385, 406, 408-409, 411-413, 442, 439

V
Values
 Asian, 39, 190, 247-248, 250, 397-399, 408
 Islamic, 183-184, 243, 397-400, 408
 Confucian, 397
 global, 29, 404, 442, 444
 human, 41, 374, 378, 442
 Western, 399

Vedas, 274
Veil of ignorance (Rawls), 70, 221-222
Venezuela, 284, 379
Vico, Giambattista, 21-22, 25
"Vienna Circle", 105, 110-111
Voltaire, 155, 391

W
Waal, Frans de, 72
Walter de Merton, 161
Waltz, Kenneth, 334
Waqf, 161

Water
  scarcity, 301
  shortage, 303
Weapons of Mass Destruction, 124
West Gothic Empires, 166
Wilson, E.O., 72
Wittgenstein, Ludewig, 107, 121
World Alliance of YMCAs, 278
World Bank, 193, 202, 205, 236, 244, 265, 273, 281, 283, 288
World Economic Forum (WEF), 204
World Food Programme (WFP), 273
World Health Organization (WHO), 273
World Muslim League, 406-407
World Trade Organization (WTO), 273, 278, 283-284, 289, 358

Z
Zambia, 246
Zimbabwe, 246

Nayef R.F. Al-Rodhan (ed.)
Policy Briefs on the *Transcultural* Aspects of Security and Stability

By assessing various aspects of globalization through an analysis of issues currently facing states, decision makers, and individuals within communities, this book provides an essential tool for exploring the future implications of policies and decision-making processes. Topics such as ethics and civil liberties, information technology, the role of the United Nations, migration, and regional security are analyzed by a number of experts in the field, and each brief concludes with sound and concrete recommendations for action at the state level. Each topic is also covered by an editorial that looks at the relationship between challenges and policy recommendations in a new way. The diagrammatic representation of the editorials allows for a comprehensive and effective analysis of the relationship between state policy dilemmas and reactions.
194 pp., 19,90 €, pb., ISBN 978-3-8258-0179-3

LIT Verlag Berlin – Münster – Wien – Zürich – London
Fresnostr. 2 48159 Münster
Tel.: 0251 / 620 32 22 – Fax: 0251 / 922 60 99
e-Mail: vertrieb@lit-verlag.de – http://www.lit-verlag.de

**POLICY BRIEFS ON THE
TRANSNATIONAL ASPECTS OF
SECURITY AND STABILITY**

Edited by
Nayef R.F. Al-Rodhan

LIT

Nayef R.F. Al-Rodhan (ed.)
Policy Briefs on the *Transnational* Aspects of Security and Stability

This book looks specifically at a number of topics that deal with the changing nature of the state in the era of globalization, and the impact of this transformation on global security and stability. Each topic is also represented by a diagram assessing and illustrating the linkages between the challenges currently facing states and recommendations for ways in which the state can move forward. This book may serve as a reference guide for practitioners, students, and academic institutions that work to provide solutions to contemporary conflicts and security threats. Topics addressed include the proliferation of weapons of mass destruction, arms control, energy security, natural disasters, the changing role of the North Atlantic Treaty Organisation (NATO), health paradigms, and US environmental policy.
218 pp., 19,90 €, pb., ISBN 978-3-8258-0180-9

LIT Verlag Berlin – Münster – Wien – Zürich – London
Fresnostr. 2 48159 Münster
Tel.: 0251 / 620 32 22 – Fax: 0251 / 922 60 99
e-Mail: vertrieb@lit-verlag.de – http://www.lit-verlag.de

Nayef R.F. Al-Rodhan
Symbiotic Realism
A Theory of International Relations in An Instant and An Interdependent World

Symbiotic Realism is a theory of relations in a globally-anarchic world of instant connectivity and interdependence. It aims to provide a comprehensive framework for understanding the character of relations generated by four interlocking facets of the global system: the neurobiological substrates of human nature; global anarchy; instant connectivity; and interdependence. It provides a way of understanding how a myriad of actors, including states, transnational corporations, women, the biosphere, and civilizations, help to shape and are shaped by the global system. It also contains a clear normative commitment to moving beyond the present limits of the structure and political organization of the global system towards a more just and peaceful global order.
160 pp., 19,90 €, pb., ISBN 978-3-8258-0477-0

LIT Verlag Berlin – Münster – Wien – Zürich – London
Fresnostr. 2 48159 Münster
Tel.: 0251 / 620 32 22 – Fax: 0251 / 922 60 99
e-Mail: vertrieb@lit-verlag.de – http://www.lit-verlag.de

Nayef R.F. Al-Rodhan
The Five Dimensions of Global Security
Proposal for a Multi-sum Security Principle

This book sets out a new and innovative security principle that is highly pertinent to our times: **THE MULTI-SUM SECURITY PRINCIPLE**. This principle aims not only to promote cooperative interaction between states, but also peaceful coexistence between cultural groups and civilizations. It combines a proposed new classification of global security that comprises five dimensions of security – **human, environmental, national, transnational, and transcultural security** – and the idea that **justice** is a prerequisite for security. Specifically, the multi-sum security principle states that: "**In a globalized world, security can no longer be thought of as a zero-sum game involving states alone. Global security, instead, has five dimensions that include human, environmental, national, transnational, and transcultural security, and, therefore, global security and the security of any state or culture cannot be achieved without good governance at all levels that guarantees security through *justice* for *all* individuals, states, and cultures.**"
156 pp., 19,90 €, pb., ISBN 978-3-8258-0478-7

LIT Verlag Berlin – Münster – Wien – Zürich – London
Fresnostr. 2 48159 Münster
Tel.: 0251 / 620 32 22 – Fax: 0251 / 922 60 99
e-Mail: vertrieb@lit-verlag.de – http://www.lit-verlag.de

Nayef R.F. Al-Rodhan
"emotional amoral egoism"
A Neurophilosophical Theory of Human Nature and its Universal Security Implications

The enduring assumption that human behaviour is governed by innate morality and reason is at odds with the persistence of human deprivation, injustice, brutality, inequality and conflict. This book offers a fresh look at human nature and universal security by proposing a new general theory of human nature, *"emotional amoral egoism"*, and a specific theory of human motivation that draws on a wide range of philosophical, psychological and evolutionary approaches to human nature as well as neuroscientific research. It argues that human behaviour is governed primarily by *emotional self-interest* and that the human mind is a *predisposed tabula rasa*. The author argues that most human beings are innately neither moral nor immoral but rather *amoral*. Circumstances will determine the *survival value of humankind's moral compass*. This insight has profound implications for the re-ordering of governance mechanisms at all levels with a strong emphasis on the *role of society and the global system*. This book is essential reading for anyone interested in the substrates of human nature and its universal security implications in relation to identity, conflict, ethnocentrism, xenophobia, morality and global governance.
240 pp., 19,90 €, pb., ISBN 978-3-8258-0954-6

LIT Verlag Berlin – Münster – Wien – Zürich – London
Fresnostr. 2 48159 Münster
Tel.: 0251 / 620 32 22 – Fax: 0251 / 922 60 99
e-Mail: vertrieb@lit-verlag.de – http://www.lit-verlag.de

Nayef R.F. Al-Rodhan
The Three Pillars of *Sustainable National Security* **in a Transnational World**

In today's transnational world, a sustainable national security policy cannot be achieved through national capabilities alone. Sustainable national security instead rests on three pillars: 1) a multi-sum security principle based on justice at all levels, multilateralism and multidimensionality (including human, environmental, national, transnational and transcultural/transcivilizational security); 2) symbiotic realism in international relations, whereby mutual cooperation among states results in non-conflictual absolute gains; and 3) transcivilizational synergy which results from mutual respect, multiculturalism, cosmopolitanism and cross-fertilization, and will lead to global justice, security and prosperity. This is essential reading for anyone interested in an innovative approach to the complex yet central subject of sustainable national security.
184 pp., 19,90 €, pb., ISBN 978-3-8258-1067-2

LIT Verlag Berlin – Münster – Wien – Zürich – London
Fresnostr. 2 48159 Münster
Tel.: 0251 / 620 32 22 – Fax: 0251 / 922 60 99
e-Mail: vertrieb@lit-verlag.de – http://www.lit-verlag.de

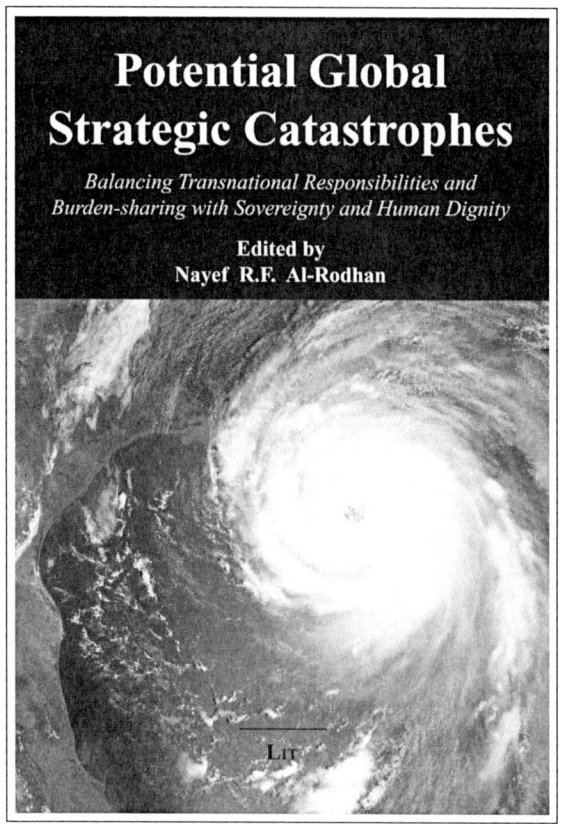

Nayef R.F. Al-Rodhan (ed.)
Potential Global Strategic Catastrophes
Balancing Transnational Responsibilities and Burden-sharing with Sovereignty and Human Dignity

This book is the result of a Symposium on **Potential Global Strategic Catastrophes**, which took place in Geneva, Switzerland in 2008. The catastrophes chosen do not include remote and less immediate events. Only those with the potential to produce multiple cascading strategic dilemmas for states and the international system were selected. These dilemmas include balancing the sovereign rights of states with human rights, transnational responsibilities and burden-sharing under occasional geopolitical uncertainties. The book deals with the theoretical foundations of coping with catastrophes and the relevant inter-state and organisational paradigms. Other sections address specific catastrophes and their potential consequences: pandemics, water crises, global warming, nanosecurity, nuclear catastrophes, financial meltdown, cyber crises, demographic imbalances and forced migrations, state failure and war, massive conventional terrorist attacks and threats to energy supply.
pb., ISBN 978-3-643-80004-6

LIT Verlag Berlin – Münster – Wien – Zürich – London
Fresnostr. 2 48159 Münster
Tel.: 0251 / 620 32 22 – Fax: 0251 / 922 60 99
e-Mail: vertrieb@lit-verlag.de – http://www.lit-verlag.de

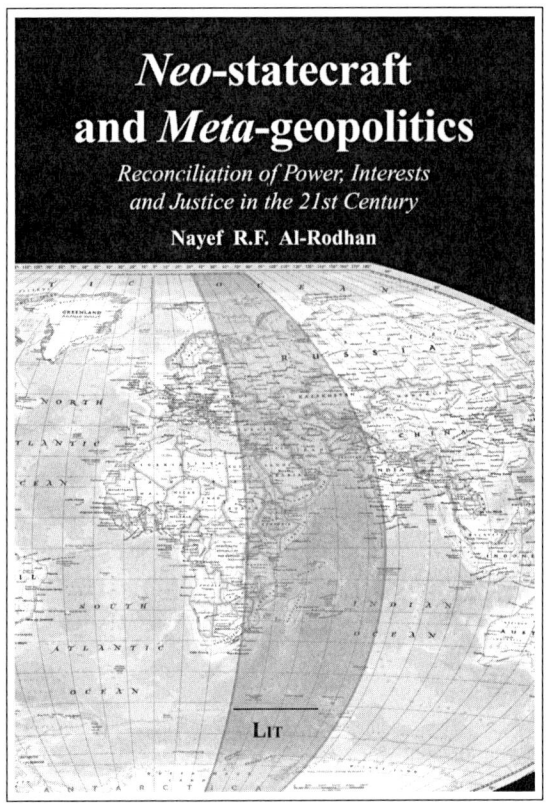

Nayef R.F. Al-Rodhan
Neo-statecraft and Meta-geopolitics
Reconciliation of Power, Interests and Justice in the 21st Century

This book proposes an innovative and comprehensive framework for conducting **statecraft in the 21st century**. Called **neo-statecraft**, this framework is based on the **reconciliation of power, interests and justice**. The author proposes **four substrates of neo-statecraft**: 1) a new structure he calls **meta-geopolitics**, which includes **seven inter-related dimensions of state power** and identifies **a Geostrategic Tripwire Pivotal Corridor (TPC)**; 2) a **sustainable national security paradigm** that stresses the centrality of justice, symbiotic realism and transcultural synergy; 3) a new concept called **just power**, which states that power must be smart as well as just, and that global justice is above all a national interest of all states; and 4) a new concept called **reconciliation statecraft of the eight global interests**.
29,90 €, pb., ISBN 978-3-643-80006-0

LIT Verlag Berlin – Münster – Wien – Zürich – London
Fresnostr. 2 48159 Münster
Tel.: 0251 / 620 32 22 – Fax: 0251 / 922 60 99
e-Mail: vertrieb@lit-verlag.de – http://www.lit-verlag.de